A Mine of Her Own

# A Mine of Her Own

## Women Prospectors
## in the American West,
## 1850–1950

SALLY ZANJANI

University of Nebraska Press

Lincoln and London

Acknowledgments for the use of previously
published material appear on page xii.

⊛ The paper in this book meets the minimum
requirements of American National Standard for
Information Sciences – Permanence of Paper for
Printed Library Materials, ANSI Z39.48-1984.

Library of Congress Cataloging in Publication Data
Zanjani, Sally Springmeyer, 1937–
A mine of her own : women prospectors in the
American West, 1850–1950 / Sally Zanjani.
p.   cm.
Includes bibliographical references and index.
ISBN 0-8032-4914-4 (cloth : alkaline paper)
1. Women miners – West (U.S.) – History.
2. Prospecting – West (U.S.) – History.   I. Title
HD6073.M612U69   1997
331.4'822334'0978–dc20
96-24553 CIP

*To my daughter Mariah,*
*herself a prospector in*
*sociological realms*

# Contents

# Illustrations

# Acknowledgments

I am grateful to the friends and relatives of women prospectors for sharing their time and their memories with me. Material I would otherwise have missed was made available through the generosity of several colleagues, especially Don Chaput, Mary Corkill, Kari Coughlin, James Fell, Jean Ford, Linda Greene, Jane Haigh, Ann Kain, Patricia Klos, William Metscher, Jeremy Mouat, Carrie Porter, Manuel Simpson, Robert Spude, and Louetta Ward. I am greatly indebted to Phillip Earl, who gave me the benefit of his wide knowledge of the subject.

Other colleagues at the libraries, archives, museums, and historical societies where I sought assistance provided much aid and many courtesies. Special mention should be made of Terri Davis, Deadwood Public Library, Deadwood, South Dakota; Eleanor Gehres, Denver Public Library; Todd Guenther, South Pass City State Historic Site, Wyoming; Elisabeth Hakkinen, Sheldon Museum, Haines, Alaska; Joy Horton, Uintah County Library, Vernal, Utah; Jeffrey Kintop, Nevada Archives, Carson City; Marilyn Kwock, India Spartz, and Ellen Fitzgerald, Alaska State Library, Juneau; Pansilee Larson, Humboldt Museum, Winnemucca, Nevada; Georgeanna Main, Mineral County Museum, Hawthorne, Nevada; Bruce Mehlhaff, South Dakota School of Mines, Rapid City; Lee Mortensen and Eric Moody, Nevada Historical Society, Reno; Jerome Munday, San Jose Historical Museum, San Jose, California; Ann Nelson, Wyoming State Museum, Cheyenne; Janet Peterson, Northeastern Nevada Museum, Elko; Orlando Romero, New Mexico History Library, Santa Fe; Susan Searcy and Karen Gash, University of Nevada–Reno Libraries; Marilyn Stark, National Mining Hall of Fame, Leadville, Colorado; and Marcia Stout, Scotty's Castle Museum, Death Valley, California.

Researchers in several states provided valuable assistance: Robert Fisher in Arizona, Lorrayne Kennedy in California, and Ceceile Richter in Alaska. Linda Schlosser assisted in transcribing interview tapes.

## Acknowledgments

Ruth Danner at the Humboldt County Courthouse, Winnemucca, Nevada; Susan Hudson at the Nye County Courthouse, Tonopah, Nevada; Helene Weatherfield at the Mineral County Courthouse, Hawthorne, Nevada; and many other officials went far beyond the call of duty in responding to my requests for old records. The financial support of the Nevada Humanities Committee and a generous foundation that prefers anonymity is acknowledged with appreciation. I wish to thank the editor of the *Nevada Historical Society Quarterly* for permission to reprint material from "The Josephine and George Scott Diaries: A 1914 Desert Journey," which appeared in the spring 1994 issue. Jack and Marge Gibson, with their Jeep, were invaluable guides to the farther reaches of the Santa Fe mining district.

# Introduction: Prospecting

The wilderness envelops the prospector. Under the forest canopy, far from any trail or human habitation, the solitary gold panner kneels beside a stream. In the far North, a small, dark figure moves slowly across ice fields and glaciered mountains. Through the eerie silence of Death Valley, a treasure seeker leads a couple of burros past corrugated tawny hills and undulating dunes toward the sandy plain. Deep inside Apache country, a sourdough makes camp, despite warnings that such a venture will lead to nothing but a tombstone. From the Arctic Circle to the Mexican border, the prospector's world is a remote wilderness, and the prospector an insignificant speck dwarfed by its immensity.

We have a fixed image of how the speck would appear at close range—a lean, bearded, weatherbeaten man in a battered Stetson with burro, pick, and pan. Nothing has prepared us to find instead a lean and weatherbeaten woman under the Stetson. For years the presence of women prospectors has remained a lost piece of history, as thoroughly misplaced as the lost Cashman Mine, which some fortune seekers believe a woman discovered. But unlike many lost mines, the women prospectors unquestionably existed, and they plunged with zest into all aspects of the prospecting life, from the rigors of the ice fields to the dog-eat-dog world of mining promotion.

Women prospectors, no less than their male counterparts, reveled in pioneering through the world beyond the pale. Since explorers first probed the Rockies, the wilderness has meant excitement and discovery. The search for riches gave thrust to the adventure, and prospectors spoke of being possessed by the dream and turning it over in the mind for pleasure—"beautiful fascination," one woman called it. "She was like all prospectors; she got up every morning believing firmly that she was going to hit the Mother Lode" is a recurrent theme in recollections of the women prospectors. If she struck a promising sample the search became intensive, sometimes even continuing at night by lantern light

1

and into winter weather. Josie Earp acknowledged that she "nearly froze to death" when winter closed in on the Palmetto Mountains of southern Nevada and she rejected the pleas of her husband, Wyatt, to desist.[1]

Striking it rich was nonetheless a rarity, and holding onto one's gains rarer still. Even the wildest of dreamers must have realized in saner moments that there were easier and more certain ways to make a living. If this made little difference, prospectors themselves acknowledged that reductive definitions of prospecting as a search for riches did not explain their addiction to the wilderness. Voicing matters that often remained tacit among the less articulate, prospector Idah Strobridge wrote, "If you love the Desert, and live in it, and lie awake at night under its low-hanging stars, you know you are a part of the pulse-beat of the universe, and you feel the swing of the spheres through space, and you hear through the silence the voice of God speaking. Then you will come to know that no better thing is in the world for man than just this—the close-touching of great things; the un-desire of the small, such as the man-crowded places give you; and just enough food and clothing and shelter to support life, and enough work to fill one's days." After Strobridge's husband and all her children died within the span of four years, Idah found the desert a healing place. In this she was not alone. Widows emerged as a particularly strong presence among the women prospectors.[2]

The emptiness of the landscape also suited prospectors because many had turned away from normal society, seeing it as a dull and unpleasant alternative to a life of perpetual challenge and discovery. "Guess I'm different from most women," Fannie Quigley, who lived in the remote solitude of Alaska's Mount Denali, told one of her rare visitors. "I'd be lost in a house on a city lot. I've got to have all outdoors to roam in. That's living. Sure, I work hard, but I love it. . . . There's no monotony on the trail. In all the years I've lived here I can find something different every day." Another woman remembered the noise, dust, odors, and "utter ugliness" of the mining town where she had lived with a distaste that sharpened her appreciation of the clean, uncrowded, open spaces where she prospected. Panamint Annie saw city living, where all services are performed for you by others, as a sorry contrast to the self-sufficiency in which she took pride.[3] Ironically, the better the prospector succeeded in the search for mineral, the more she altered her wilderness refuge to resemble the world she had fled.

One of the problems in defining the prospector stems from the fact that for many it shaded off into a hobby, the sort of Sunday afternoon diversion friends described as "little scratchings around the country." How do we classify Irene True, the ex-madam who drove the truck stage from Winnemucca to the mining camp of Midas, Nevada, and diverted herself with prospecting while waiting for the scheduled hour of return? Probably as a hobbyist, but the answer is less clear for those who earned a living in any way that came to hand in order to position themselves where they could prospect. This was true of Ellie Nay when she and her husband opened a roadhouse where they could sell meals and small necessities to travelers while spending the rest of their time prospecting in nearby Salsbury Wash in central Nevada. Ellie had brought her family to this remote and godforsaken place for the express purpose of finding a mine. Were the Nays roadhouse proprietors or were they prospectors? The definition of an occupation as the principal business of one's life does not necessarily mean that it is the way one earns a livelihood. In doubtful cases the woman prospector can often be distinguished by the depth of her obsession.[4]

Obsession combined with technical knowledge and false science in varying degrees. Known for secretiveness, prospectors generally had little to say about exactly where they went and what they did and indeed seemed to experience genuine difficulties in describing their methods, depending as they did on intuition, subliminally processed clues, and common-sense procedures that appeared simple and obvious to them. Although the American Society of Mining Engineers listed a handful of women members, women prospectors on the mining frontier had little formal training. Nonetheless, many read intensively on geology, no doubt intensively enough to learn the basics: promising terrain in the American West meant mountain chains with deposits dating from Tertiary and Precambrian times; dissolved minerals in water percolating through the cracks in these granite formations created metallic lodes. Experience often took precedence over theory, and prospectors sought features associated with earlier bonanzas. Thus Ellie Nay, having made a rich strike near a sugarloaf mountain, forever after scanned the horizon for a mountain of similar shape.[5]

Once positioned in a promising place, the prospector looked for signs of mineralization. "Listen and the mountains will talk to you," other prospectors told Panamint Annie. "Look for the colors." They meant the white threadlets of quartz; yellows and browns of iron, often associated with gold; greens and blues of copper, silver, and turquoise; black of manganese; lilac of cobalt; pale yellow of molybdenum or lead. The sides of arroyos where the formations were laid open demanded investigation. So did surface irregularities in the terrain, such as outcroppings, a notched ridge, or a change in the character of the rock fragments. Because dense vegetation obscured many signs, the exposed desert lent itself well to prospecting, and the prevailing sunshine of these regions greatly enhanced detection—elements abundantly present in the Death Valley country where Panamint Annie walked the mountains with her pick in hand.[6]

After making camp in a likely area the prospector intensified the search. She panned rivers and streams looking for dull yellow flecks, and she broke chunks from ledges hoping to find signs of mineralization. She roamed the hills hunting for "float," a chunk of mineral-bearing rock broken from a lode and carried away by water. Next she tried to trace the float to its point of origin, a time-consuming process with many wild goose chases and much sampling as she gradually narrowed the area. These efforts could soon fatigue a novice. "We climbed the mountainsides, and clambered among sagebrush, rocks, and snow till we were ready to drop from exhaustion but, found no silver—nor yet any gold," wrote Mark Twain, recalling his prospecting in the environs of Unionville, Nevada. "Day after day we toiled, and climbed and searched, and we younger partners grew sick and still sicker of the promiseless toil."[7]

If satisfied of the value of her find after making crude field tests, the prospector became the owner of the vein, lode, or ledge she had uncovered and proceeded to stake her claim by affixing a notice in the center and marking the four corners of the 300-by-100-foot parcel and the centers of the end lines with posts, blazed trees, or stone cairns. By then she had probably christened her find, often with a name such as

Lillian Malcolm's "Desert Wonder," smacking of exuberant hyperbole. Within the next thirty days she needed to head back to civilization to register the claim with local authorities. When in town she probably took her samples to an assayer for more definitive testing. To retain hold on the claim, by federal law she had to do one hundred dollars' worth of location work in mining the claim within ninety days, and the same amount to retain title to it each year thereafter. At nineteenth-century wage levels this requirement was no mere formality. New Year's Eve in the environs of a booming camp was often a scene of frenetic activity, as claim owners struggled to complete their diggings before the stroke of midnight and rivals lurked in the darkness. Many hired others to perform their location work for them or lost claims because they failed to meet the requirement.[8]

The usual next step—selling the claim—involved labor of a very different kind in saloons and investors' offices. Of course, with a claim of limited value, the prospector might decide not to sell it but instead use it as a kind of bank, mining just enough ore to keep herself in bacon and beans. Happy Days Diminy lived this way for many years, although those who knew her believed she scarcely made enough from her mining to "feed a jackrabbit."[9] Or the prospector might decide to do development work on the claim to demonstrate incontrovertibly its value and sell it for a much larger sum than she was likely to receive on the basis of a few samples. She might be forced to carry out one of these expedients if investors showed no interest in the claim or believed she had pegged its value far beyond its provable worth.

In the search for investors the prospector resorted to every expedient a salesman's ingenuity could devise. She might persuade a shopkeeper to put a rich sample on display in his store window; she endeavored to provoke the interest of the local newspaper editor; she asked the assayer to alert his mining company connections to the opportunity at hand. She called at the offices of wealthy men known to take an interest in mining investment. If local investors showed themselves indifferent to the potential bonanza, she might journey farther afield, venturing out of the mining towns to large commercial cities of the region or even all the way "back East" to New York, Boston, or Philadelphia. Lillian Malcolm, for one, succeeded in raising money to develop her mining claims by talking "common sense" to Pittsburgh businessmen. She could form a corporation and promote stock sales in her mine through an advertising campaign, as did the grandmotherly and unscrupulous Frances Williams. If these efforts set off a rush to the site, that was all the better; with her own claims safely recorded, the interest of others enhanced the value of her holdings. In these promotional activities women prospectors labored under certain disadvantages. Respectable women could not frequent saloons and display ore samples to kindle interest as male prospectors did. Except on ladies' nights, women were also barred from the elegant men's clubs where potential investors abounded. In all their dealings prejudice against women who breached gender barriers hampered them. Colorado mining entrepreneur Delia McCarthy remarked that her hardest task was persuading men that a woman could understand mining.[10]

If the claim sold, the sum realized by the prospector was probably relatively modest and grew still more modest if she owed shares to grubstakers who had financed her quest. Rich at last—or at least much richer than before—many a prospector blew these winnings in the spectacular binges long legendary among the breed. Women prospectors were by no means immune to this practice. Panamint Annie, among others, gambled uncontrollably, and Ferminia Sarras was known for the grand sprees that inevitably followed a lucrative mine sale. Some newly rich prospectors retired to California mansions or changed direction by buying a ranch or entering business—temporarily, that is, because few succeeded in putting prospecting permanently behind them. "Money didn't mean anything to 'em," prospector Carl Wikstrom explained, musing on the inability of prospectors to invest their money wisely and surmount their hand-to-mouth existence. "Money isn't important. What they're doing is. They're painting their name on that mountain out there."[11]

How, we ask, could women have done the things that prospectors must do? Even today, when women's history thrives and popular consciousness of women's capabilities has advanced by quantum leaps, the usual reaction to mention of women prospectors is astonishment. The root of this response seems to be a deep-seated sense that the prospector's life scarcely fitted with anything we believe about

6

women, or women believed about themselves, in the century from 1850 to 1950.

The physical strength required for work in this male-dominated occupation is one source (but probably the least important one) of disbelief in the very idea of women prospectors. All the occupations—maids, laundresses, teachers, telephone operators, and the like—that gained public acceptance as "suitable" for women by the late nineteenth century seem far removed from the woman prospector at work on her claim, pounding her drill into the recalcitrant quartz with an eight-pound sledge, igniting the blasting powder, shoveling away the rock fragments, and sometimes packing out ore samples on her back. Yet women had shared in heavy work since the early days of the Republic, and by 1900 they were represented in all but 8 of 303 occupations listed in the census, albeit sometimes in very small numbers. Some women prospectors had pursued unusual occupations, including a blacksmith, a doctor, a truck driver, and a rodeo champion, even before they entered prospecting. In other ways as well the women prospectors diverged from the mainstream of America's working women. Although domestic service and factory work employed a large percentage of women workers, women prospectors rarely emerged from these fields. Moreover, women prospectors differed in the degree of their commitment. One-fifth of America's 25 million women had entered the work force by 1900, but one factor continued to prevail: the typical working woman was young and single and left work after seven or eight years when she married—unlike the woman prospector, who often considered mining her career and continued her quest for a lifetime. "Mining was her whole life" was the sort of comment frequently voiced by those reminiscing about one of these women.

A stronger reason for astonishment at the existence of women prospectors lies in the "cult of true womanhood" and the doctrine of separate spheres, ideals that constricted the psyche of the nineteenth-century woman as cruelly as the corsets of the period constricted her body. Although most influential among the urban middle class in the East, these doctrines also penetrated the working class and traveled westward with the women pioneers. The two spheres were on the one hand the crass, materialistic, ambitious world of men in the industrializing age and on the other the home, where a pious and submissive "true woman" concentrated her energies on providing a refuge for her husband, nurturing her children, and inculcating them with virtue. Woman, though frail and delicate, was seen as a morally superior being whose central mission was to civilize by guiding her husband, raising virtuous children, and elevating frontier society through churches and insistence on correct behavior. In an effort to preserve these standards, conventional women held their skirts aside to avoid contamination when Lillian Malcolm walked past. They may not have been entirely wrong in perceiving her independent way of life as a threat to true womanhood, laboring as she did in the materialistic world of men, hawking her mines in a milieu of roguery where too much virtue would not have served her well, often setting off for prolonged sojourns in the wilds with men who were not her relatives, and bent not on civilizing her family and her community but on leaving civilization well behind her for the far country.[12]

It may be that the heart of our incredulity at the existence of women prospectors lies in our beliefs on the fundamental nature of womanhood. The doctrine of separate spheres that molded feminine conduct during much of the first century on the mining frontier may have exaggerated woman's civilizing mission and circumscribed her behavior, but it fitted under the rubric of gender-divergent goals, applicable in many cultures and time periods. In her disinterest in matters domestic, living as she often did in a tent or a makeshift shack, and her obsession with her own lonely adventure in the wild, the woman prospector seems to negate much of what a great many people believed then, and believe still, about women. Although some women prospectors combined mining with family life, others brooked no interference with their chosen pursuit. Nellie Cashman made it clear that she was "too busy" following the mining rushes as she pleased to consider a marriage that might tie her down; another woman prospector parted from her husband because he kept her at home cooking and housecleaning when she wanted to be out in the hills hunting El Dorado. Yet the public perception of woman's place lagged behind the reality. Even in a mining town where newspapers regularly reported the exploits of women prospectors, the conception of women encapsulated in domesticity

8

while men did the prospecting continued to hold sway, as a 1908 poem
in the Goldfield (Nevada) *Chronicle* attests:

The hot wind blows from the desert afar,
From the rifted plain and the mountain scaur;
A devel of heat and a spirit of pain
From a sun-baked land that knows no rain;
And it whips up the roadway yellow as rust
And over the cottonwood sprinkles dust,
And scatters the rose leaves down by the wall
Where the woman he strives for waits his call. . . .

Oft weary the limbs that are under him
And many a time his eyes grow dim,
And his soul flies back with the wind on the road
To the flower steeped wall and her abode.
But he is a man and the woman is fair,
And evils are given for men to bear;
And why for the scorch of the sun should he reck
If the struggle be won and the woman to deck?

He follows the trails that are marked with bones
And creep[s] through the sand and the glistening stones;
And the search for the gold goes slowly on
Though the night-laid thirst comes back at dawn;
And the blooms spread over the cactus bed
In Spanish yellow and pink and red;
And the day is long on the glaring waste,
But the woman must wait, for none may haste.

Yes, the woman must wait and the man must seek,
And life is a dream for the strong and the weak.
For time by the garden wall goes by
And out on the desert is room to die.
So she watches the rain beat down on the sod,
And the end of things is left with God;
And the desert wind breathes warm on the rose,
And hot on the waste the sunshine glows.[13]

But what of the women who did not wait by the garden wall while men searched in the "rifted plain and the mountain scaur"?

Sources on these women tend to be brief and fragmentary. Only one dictated her memoirs, two appear in biographies, another set down her reflections on the wilderness, and a few of the more colorful characters crop up in an occasional article. With the exception of two diaries and one collection of papers, women prospectors left few accounts for historians to peruse. Many women prospectors came from the working class and were thus less likely to keep diaries or write letters than middle-class women. Moreover, the character of the prospector ran counter to self-conscious revelation. Not only did prospectors lack that sense of their own importance that moves politicians and the like to preserve themselves for posterity through donations of papers to libraries, but also they tended to be secretive loners, a preference often heightened by the perceived need to conceal their areas of activity from those with nefarious designs and even to mislead. "Never believe a prospector," said prospector Anna Rechel to her friends. "If they tell you to go that way, you go the other way, the exact opposite."[14]

Notwithstanding their general taciturnity, signs of an occasional woman prospector turn up in the West's early mining rushes. The first to emerge in full relief were Nellie Cashman and Ferminia Sarras in the 1870s and 1880s. At the turn of the century the number of women prospectors burgeoned, especially in Alaska and Nevada. Gold rushes in both places had ignited great excitement, and many prospectors believed that other regions had been so thoroughly worked over that Nevada was "the only place left where a prospector had a chance." Samples of mining records often reveal a surprising number of female names, but although records can help determine when and where a woman prospector pursued her activities, this evidence alone does not provide a reliable method of identifying women prospectors, because prospectors often staked claims under the names of friends, relatives, and grubstakers (women prospectors also followed this practice). Although we may suspect, for example, that Sarah M. Grannis, whose name appears on the record books with claims in Colorado's Ten Mile and Sacramento districts in 1860–61, was an early woman prospector, we cannot be entirely certain.[15]

In consequence, the main sources on women prospectors are the old mining camp newspapers. Because the woman prospector was an unusual and exotic figure, newsmen often reported her activities and people remembered her. All too often these news stories are brief. We read that Mrs. McCarthy, "who is famed as a woman prospector," found rich gold ore on her claims at Nevada's Barber Canyon south of Winnemucca, and that is the last we hear of the famous woman prospector.[16] Newsmen wrote more extensive stories when the prospector had a touch of the show woman in her, which tends to skew the sources in the direction of colorful characters. Perhaps the best corrective for this admitted problem is living memory, which unfortunately can take us back no further than eighty years.

Despite these limited sources, a sense of the woman prospector and her role in mining emerges. Even tidbits of information collectively reveal the range and depth of women prospectors in the American West. We are not dealing with a mere handful of anomalies. We are looking at a sizable number of women spread over the geographic breadth of the frontier during the entire first century of its history, seventy-seven who prospected and an additional nineteen physically engaged in mining who probably prospected, in all likelihood the tip of an iceberg perhaps three times larger. The coincidence of a turn-of-the-century mining boom in Nevada with an explosion in the number of women prospectors and the emergence of a widespread belief that Nevada offered more unexplored territory than other western mining areas combined to produce a heavy concentration of prospectors in Nevada, a number further weighted by my own background of research on Nevada mining. Nonetheless, the appearance of women prospectors in locales from Nome to Tombstone establishes their presence throughout the mining frontier.

Documenting the mining activities of women, however, places them in doubtful company that contains a good many madmen, amateurs, and marginal figures who used crude and unscientific methods. All the same, simple methods in the hands of untrained people have often produced remarkable results. The prospectors of the ancient world discovered every important mining site in the Mediterranean area with primitive methods. Many of the most important mines in the American West were found in much the same way, and the consequences were momentous. Mining excitements brought large numbers of Americans west, first in the California gold rush of 1849, later to the Comstock, the Rockies, Deadwood, and a host of other localities. Agriculture thrived and transportation networks developed to support the new mining towns. In time, when the booms slackened, gold rushers fanned out into other enterprises. This great movement of peoples, for good or ill, often began with the probings of the prospectors.[17]

Within the broad picture of western mining, how did the achievements of the women prospectors measure up? Only a tiny fraction of prospectors struck the great bonanzas. Many more made modest discoveries or managed to scrape a living from the wilderness through prospecting much as mountain men lived by trapping. Women prospectors proved no exception to this rule. A handful played a significant part in mining history. Names that immediately spring to mind are Belle Butler, whose discovery of the Mizpah ledge at Tonopah, Nevada, did so much to revive the depressed fortunes of an entire state, and Louise Grantham, whose Death Valley mine produced more commercial talc in its day than any other mine in the West. Others, such as Ellie Nay, the discoverer of Ellendale, and Nellie Cashman, who prospected from Baja California to the Arctic, were successful on a smaller scale. Still others succeeded primarily in surviving during hard times and turning survival into a rewarding way of life.

Measures of financial success, however, are far from the full story of the women prospectors. Their fiercely individual and occasionally flamboyant lives reveal an alternative path. Despite their diversity, certain traits repeatedly crop up. Determination bristles in Ellie Nay's declaration to her husband, "Let's go find a mine of our own," before the two headed out in their wagon to Salsbury Wash and their future fortunes. Courage shows in Lillian Malcolm's intrepid journey across the Alaskan ice. Charity, in Nellie Cashman's nursing of the sick and offering of comfort to the condemned in Tombstone and her fund raising for schools and hospitals. Pride, in the assertion of Nettie Hornbeck, "We are not afraid of man or beast," when she went forth with her mother to mine in the Colorado mountains. Independence, in Mrs. Jennings's rejection of a civilized life as the wife of a big-city newspa-

*Introduction*

per editor for mining in the Wyoming wilderness. Disdain for convention and a taste for much younger men, in Ferminia Sarras's habit of buying the services of young men, along with the most expensive clothes and jewels, on her periodic binges in San Francisco. Addiction to the world beyond the pale, in Idah Strobridge's search for solace in the desert after the death of her husband and all her children. And more than once a touch of madness, as in Happy Days Diminy, long known to be "wild as a March hare" but tolerated in the desert fastnesses of Tule Canyon until she made the mistake of leaving.

These were the women whose lives contradicted the idea that "the woman must wait and the man must seek, / And life is a dream for the strong and the weak." Never did they see themselves as weak. Nor did they wait by the garden wall.

Map 1: Alaska and northwestern Canada

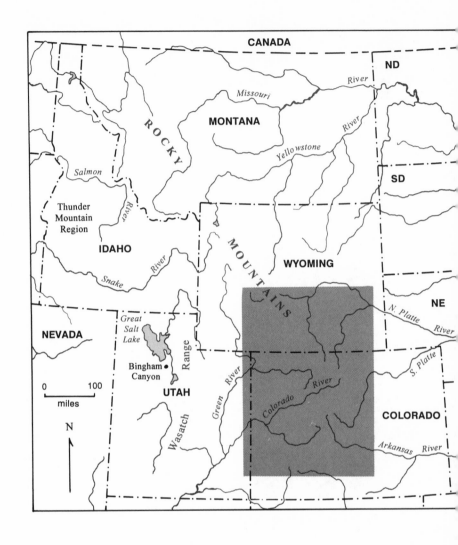

Map 2: The Rocky Mountain West

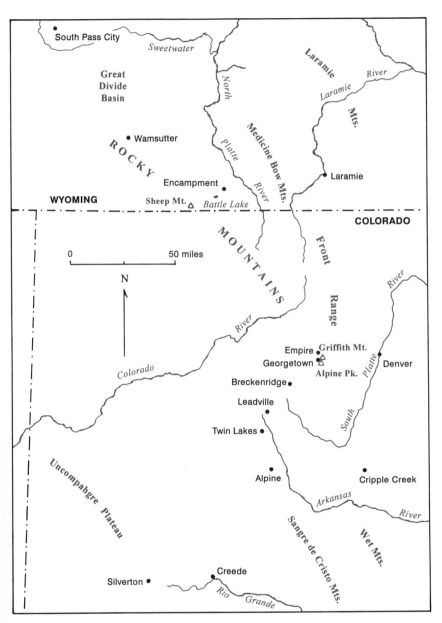

Map 3: Southern Wyoming and northwestern Colorado

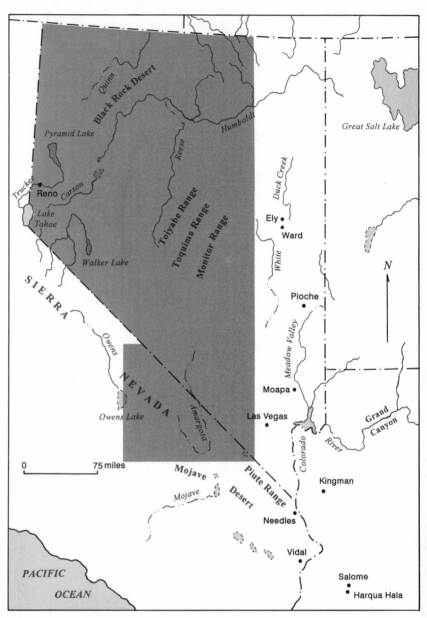

Map 4: Nevada, southern California, and northwestern Arizona

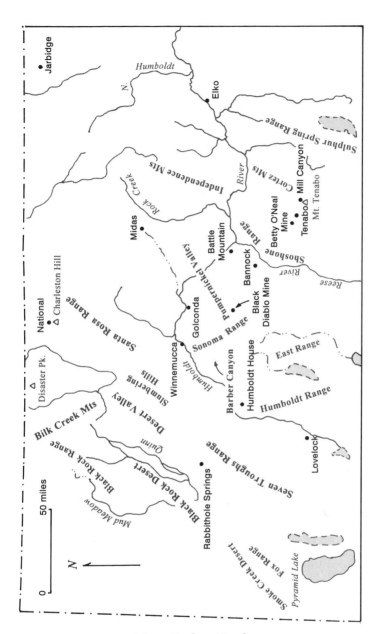

Map 5: Northern Nevada

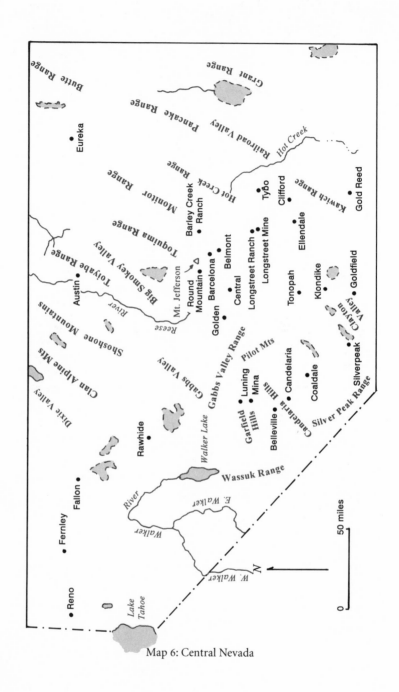

Map 6: Central Nevada

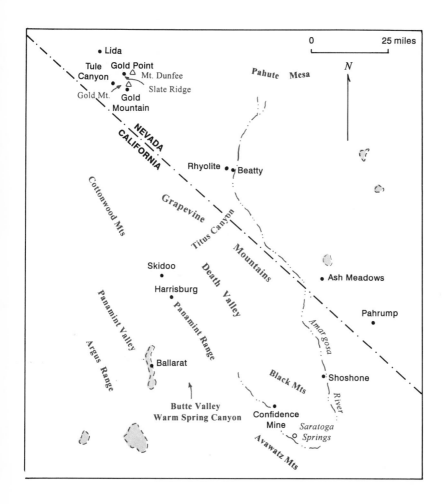

Map 7: The Death Valley region

Part One: 1850–1918

ONE

# Ellen Cashman: Angel
# and Wild Woman

As long as men have prospected in the American West, women have done so as well. Sometimes they have been helpmates sharing the labor of husbands, lovers, fathers, or brothers, but they have also prospected on their own. Historian Janet Lecompte found gold panner among the paid occupations for women listed in the New Mexican censuses of the 1840s and earlier. Wading in the waters of the southwestern rivers, these Hispanic women used wooden platters and goat horns to wash placer gold from sand. A substantial number of Hispanic women gold panners also appeared in the 1850 California census, and local Indian women quickly learned to work the rivers. Although the early populations of many California gold rush camps in 1849–50 were so exclusively masculine that the first Anglo housewives on the scene won praise merely for daring to come, the briefest glance at the census reveals several possible combinations among the gold rush women listed as "miners"—daughters working with a mother or a father and women on their own as friends working together and as lone teenagers. One pair of partners was so well along in years, in contrast to most of the burly young masculine adventurers swarming over the hills and rivers on the western slope of the Sierra, that they received particular mention when they found a pay streak near Marysville: both women were seventy years old.[1]

Another figure scarcely less remarkable among these prospecting women of the California gold rush era was Marie Pantalon, also known as Marie Suise or Suize. An orphan from the mountains of Savoie, where she was born in 1815, she had slept on the streets of Paris, sold newspapers, and come close to dying of starvation. When she read of the discovery of gold in California and the high wages that maids could earn, she embarked for the West Coast, where she arrived in early 1850.

The way French immigrants lived in California horrified her, and she soon felt homesick for Paris, even for the streets where she had slept and gone hungry. But she was not yet ready to turn back. She cut off her hair, donned men's clothes, took the name Marie Pantalon, and went prospecting in the gold country. Although her luck varied, as did that of many prospectors, she managed to purchase a piece of land that contained a valuable placer north of Jackson. Because she feared that armed claim jumpers might wrest her gold away from her, she disguised the land by planting grapes, a very French expedient. A history of early Amador County relates that when she eventually mined her gold in less perilous times, her claim produced one hundred thousand dollars before she finally sold it for twenty thousand. With this fortune in hand the former waif from the streets of Paris bought a large vineyard, embarked on a marriage that ended with the death of her husband, and went on to become a successful wine merchant in Virginia City, Nevada. All her cash sifted through her fingers, however. In the words of Louis de Cotton, a French traveler who met her and recorded her story when she was an old woman more than thirty-five years later, "the unfortunate lady is herself possessed by the demon of gambling and whenever she has some cash on hand, she invests it recklessly in the mines where her money is unavoidably swallowed."[2]

Although this brief outline of Marie Pantalon's story has emerged only in snatches, many authors and newspaper reporters from the nineteenth century to the present day have written about Ellen (Nellie) Cashman, and as a result, she is the first woman prospector whose life in western mining camps from Nevada to the Arctic can be chronicled in considerable detail. These authors depict Nellie Cashman as a heroine of almost saintly dimensions, and the word "angel" recurs in sobriquets and titles: the "Angel of the Cassiar," "Frontier Angel," the "Angel of Tombstone," the "Irish Angel of Mercy." All praise her courage in braving the physical dangers of the wilderness and the human menaces of the warlike Apache and a mining camp mob; her many acts of charity in nursing the sick, providing meals to the destitute, and fund raising for hospitals, churches, and schools; her independence in following the western mining excitements entirely alone without a male relative to protect her; her deep religious faith; and her spotless reputation, which shielded her from any hint of scandal when she went out prospecting with men (not all women prospectors would avoid scandal so successfully). John Clum, an Indian agent and Tombstone newspaper editor who knew her well during the Arizona phase of her career, admiringly called her a "noble woman whose energetic, courageous and self-sacrificing life was an inspiration on a wide frontier during half a century."[3]

This was the general consensus, marred only by an occasional hint of qualities at odds with the saintly persona. For instance, one acquaintance remembered her as "the wildest young woman I ever met," an unusual choice of words for the Angel of the Cassiar.[4] Her portrait shows a white-skinned young Irish woman, with black hair neatly upswept and parted in the center, soft pretty features, full curving lips, and large dark brown eyes. Is there something a little too intent, perhaps even obsessive, in the mesmerizing gaze of those deerlike brown eyes? A close look at her life provides some clues about the wildest young woman on the frontier as well as the angel.

She was born into desperate times. The potato blight had spread famine and death throughout Ireland during the years surrounding her birth near the seaport of Queenstown, County Cork, one of several Irish counties from which a flood of immigrants would stream to America over the ensuing years. Although 1850 has usually been considered her probable birthdate, new research by Cashman biographer Don Chaput has established that she was born in 1845 (Nellie's coyness about her age long disguised the true date). Accounts vary, but it appears that she came to Boston as a small child accompanied by her widowed mother and her younger sister Frances but developed a brogue as thick as if she had spent all her formative years in Ireland. A story later told by Cashman herself that she worked as an elevator operator in Washington DC during the Civil War and contributed to the Union's victory by reporting a conversation she had overheard may well have been one of the embellishments to her early occupation as an elevator operator that she occasionally contributed to her own legend. But two things are clear. The Cashmans remained only about fifteen years in the Boston community where so many of their fellow countrymen had settled permanently. And although in those days domestic service was the leading

27

Nellie Cashman in the Tombstone era (courtesy
of the Arizona Historical Society/Tucson, #1847).

occupation for Irish immigrant working women, as for most American working women, Nellie did not follow that route.[5] She had greater adventures in mind than sweeping another woman's hearth.

Traveling by way of Panama, the Cashmans headed west to San Francisco, where Nellie appears in the 1869 city directory. In 1870 her sister Frances married Thomas Cunningham, possibly an old sweetheart. He had also emigrated from County Cork and spent time in Boston. Over the next decade the Cunninghams raised a large family in San Francisco. Nellie's movements are less easily traced, and unfortunately, little is known of the early years of adventure and experimentation so crucial to her future career. It is likely that Nellie and her mother left San Francisco in the early 1870s for Virginia City, Nevada, then a thriving cosmopolitan mining town of more than eleven thousand people. Here they embarked on the first of the enterprises through which Nellie would support herself in western mining camps over the next thirty-five years, boardinghouses and restaurants.[6]

Since gold rush days, running boardinghouses had been a leading occupation for entrepreneurial mining camp women, both married and single. They provided a service much appreciated by miners and prospectors tired of their own cooking, their own housekeeping, and their own company in a lonely shack. A woman who arrived in a new mining camp was likely to be importuned to open a boardinghouse or at least to cook meals. Like most working women of the period, the boardinghouse keeper labored long and hard—one woman recalled that her day's work began when she prepared breakfast at seven and continued without respite until well into the evening—but it was a means of making ends meet that offered an essential Nellie Cashman could not have found inside the factory gates of the eastern mill towns or in domestic service: independence as the proprietor of her own business.[7] Also, and fatefully, it brought her into close social contact with miners and prospectors. She would have listened, her great dark eyes fixed in rapt attention, to their stories of fabulous mining strikes, fortunes made and lost, and heroic exploits in the world beyond the pale. Not much time would pass before those stories took effect.

Sometime in 1872 Nellie and her mother moved on to Pioche, a remote camp in the eastern Nevada desert reached by an arduous 275-

mile trip by Concord stage southward from the Central Pacific railroad station at Palisade. The move tells us a good deal about the direction Nellie's life was taking. Virginia City in the early seventies was more than a decade old, certainly rougher than San Francisco, but mature and almost sedate in comparison with the raw new mining camp near the Utah border. Although Indians had found silver in the Pioche district in 1863–64, five years had passed before mining development commenced and with it the murderous rivalry of two major mining companies, the Meadow Valley and the Raymond and Ely. The town of perhaps seven thousand that sprang up on the mountain slope studded with piñon and juniper in the early seventies had few rivals in notoriety and riotous living. By the time the Cashmans arrived, Pioche had already blown up and burned once, with considerable loss of life and limb, when Mexican miners celebrating Mexico's independence accidentally ignited three hundred kegs of powder. In its heyday Pioche boasted a livery stable with three hundred horses, a fast freight mule line running day and night with guaranteed five-day deliveries to the Central Pacific, thirty-two steam hoists with a shrieking chorus of whistles, two good theaters, two breweries, seventy-two saloons, and thirty-two bordellos. Silver production that peaked at $5,500,000 in 1872 underlay these flush times. But as mining camp historian Stanley Paher has noted, "the fame of Pioche's rich mines was matched by the disrepute of its crime."[8] Claim jumpers who had erected a rock fort battled with armed counterattackers moving in from a grove of piñon trees on the Raymond and Ely ground. Gunfighters from all over the West gravitated to Pioche, ready to hire on as guards for the mining companies or the wealthy nabobs. Gunplay became so common that more than half of Nevada's killings in 1871–72 took place in Pioche, and the murderers afterward swaggered through the streets unpunished. Legend held that seventy-two graves had been dug at Boot Hill before anyone in Pioche died a natural death. Even so conservative and sober a source as the state mineralogist's report called Pioche "a scene of lawlessness and horrid murders, which have scarcely ever had a parallel in the history of this coast."[9]

At first glance it may seem difficult to imagine what attraction this infamous mecca of harlots and gunfighters held for a deeply religious

Catholic woman of firm moral principles. The reasons appear to have been twofold. First was the sheer excitement that electrified the air in the midst of a mining boom—"life at full tide," as one chronicler of the town has expressed it—and beneath her virtuous and chaste exterior, Nellie Cashman was beginning to show a taste for excitement. Second, it seems clear that she had fallen in love, not with any one man but collectively with the crowd she came to regard affectionately and possessively as her own. Since the days of 1849, this crowd had been perceived as a distinctive breed with many of the same qualities later remembered in Nellie. One gold rusher characterized his comrades as "rough, daring, indefatigable," lavish in their generosity, disinclined to place much value on money, and restless in their perpetual pursuit of new excitements. He called independence and "absolute equality in the world of chance" the chief attractions of the mining life. Temperament already inclined Nellie in these directions, and she quickly learned to be one of the mining crowd. Her old friend John Clum correctly observed that she always preferred the company of men, at least until she ceased to prefer any company at all. By contrast, the miners' acceptance of her may have been less unanimous than most authors assume. For instance, one account of her later exploits in Alaska takes note of some grumbling over this feminine incursion into an exclusively masculine domain.[10] But by and large, the members of the mining crowd showed themselves egalitarian enough to accept a woman so spirited and daring that she would go where they went and do as they did—especially if she agreed to open a boardinghouse.

A September 1872 advertisement for the "Miner's Boarding House" on Panaca Flat near Pioche declared, "Having fitted in good style this old established boarding house, the undersigned would be pleased to meet her friends"; the undersigned was Fanny Cashman. We may speculate that Nellie's earliest forays into the wilds as a prospector occurred in this period and earned her the first and least angelic of her sobriquets, Nellie Pioche. One wonders if Fanny Cashman, the remarkable parent of a remarkable daughter, braved the desert with her on these early probes when Nellie was proving her hardihood as a prospector and chaperoned her until the saintly nimbus that was to envelop her in future years was fully in place.[11]

In 1873 Nellie left the rapidly declining town of Pioche for what was destined to be the greatest exploit of her career, an adventure in which both the angel and the wild woman were much in evidence. After spending a few months in San Francisco she embarked with a party of Nevada miners, while her mother remained behind to make her home in San Jose. For the first time in her life, Nellie was entirely on her own. A flip of the coin decided the party's destination, not the South African gold fields but the Cassiar district where the Stikine River flowed down to the Inside Passage from the Rocky Mountains of British Columbia, nearly a thousand miles south of the region that in little more than twenty years' time would become the scene of the Klondike gold rush. The presence of Nellie, evidently the only woman in the party of prospectors, signaled that she had already succeeded in carving out the place she sought in the masculine world of the gold rushers.

It was a unique place and perhaps also a necessary one if she was to pursue the prospector's life as a single woman in the company of men. She, and she alone, could spend days, weeks, and months in the wilderness with male companions to whom she had no familial relationship without arousing suspicions of sexual involvement with them. Unquestionably, a young woman as pretty, capable, and gifted with Irish wit as Nellie could readily have married on the woman-hungry frontier. Had she shown an interest in men as husbands or lovers, her presence would quickly have disrupted the party of prospectors, because several would have vied for her favors. No doubt Nellie realized that any such possibility would have made her unwelcome on the expedition, as well as subjecting her to unwanted attentions. She must therefore have taken care to establish well in advance of the day when the ship headed north from San Francisco that she was not to be pined for, courted, bedded, or proposed to. Anyone who lingered outside her tent with a bunch of flowers in his hand would be left to linger indefinitely. Newspaper reportage on Nellie always emphasized that she was a "womanly woman just like any other woman," perhaps to convey the message that despite a deep, masculine voice and a laugh like a malfunctioning foghorn she was neither a lesbian nor a tough, hard-drinking roisterer. The sobriquet "angel" so often applied to her probably alluded not only to her virtues but also to the persona she had established for herself as a spiritual being existing on a plane beyond the temptations of the flesh. "I have mushed with men, slept out in the open, siwashed with them, and been with them constantly, and I have never been offered an insult," she later said. "A woman is as safe among the miners as at her own fireside. If a woman complains of her treatment from any of the boys, she has only herself to blame."[12]

Somehow she also convinced the prospectors that a petite and slender lady standing only five feet tall and weighing less than a hundred pounds could hold her own in the rigors of the Stikine River country, with its rugged snow-covered mountains, its conifer forests so dense that sunlight rarely filtered through, its ghostly draperies of pale moss, and its gray drizzling skies. In those days, Nellie later recalled, the Cassiar was "a practically unknown country." Here, in the time to come, gold rushers struggling north toward the Klondike by the Ashcroft Trail would leave the signs of their despair: Poison Mountain, Starvation Camp, and a note saying, "Bury me here, where I failed."[13]

Although her prospecting along the creeks yielded little result, Nellie did not fail. Indeed, to be numbered among the few white women who made the journey to the Cassiar district and survived was no small achievement. The combination boardinghouse and saloon she opened on Dease Lake proved a predictable success. When short days and chilling air warned of the winter soon to come, she decided to relocate to Victoria and return in the spring. She had not been long in Victoria, however, when she received word that her old comrades in the Cassiar were marooned without supplies in the deep snows of the northern winter and sickening from scurvy. She made up her mind to save them.[14]

Like other heroic epics in frontier history, Nellie Cashman's mission to the Cassiar had a strain of madness in it, fully recognized by contemporaries at the time. The *British Colonist* of Victoria called her undertaking an "extraordinary freak"; even sympathetic friends considered it "insanity." How did Nellie suppose that she, an inexperienced young boardinghouse keeper who had not yet weathered a single winter in the far North, could succeed where others had failed? Already the severe cold of an unusually harsh winter had forced three attempts at deliverance led by a hardened officer to turn back to Fort Wrangell. And how did she persuade six men who should have known better to join in her insanity, even for pay? One glimpses here the sheer force of her personality, sweeping aside demurrers with a relentless will. Klondiker Edward Morgan later reflected that this was a woman who had "surmounted all the obstacles with which nature had beset her path and had talked out of existence all those put in her way by men."[15] Both the angel and the wild woman were clearly apparent that winter in the Cassiar. If the angel conceived the mission of mercy, it was the wild woman, unstoppable, reckless, and uncontrolled, who carried it through. Nellie was said to believe she had a protective angel at her shoulder. On the long trek into the Cassiar, Nellie believed in the angel, and those who followed her through the snows of that terrible winter believed in her.

Their journey took seventy-seven days. Plodding forward on snowshoes and hauling fifteen hundred pounds of potatoes, lime juice, and other supplies, they sometimes progressed no more than five miles a day over a trail that often faded into invisibility. Because dogs floundered helplessly in the soft, deep snow, Nellie harnessed herself to pull one of the heavy sleds. The commander at Fort Wrangell, too sane and sensible an officer to believe this mad mission could possibly succeed, sent a party of soldiers out in late January to bring her back before she perished. They found her camped on the frozen Stikine, humming a merry tune as she cooked her supper over the campfire. She invited the soldiers to take tea with her, and over tea the magnetic force of her personality and the hypnotic gaze of her dark eyes once more prevailed. Rather than escort Nellie back where she did not wish to go, the soldiers opted for disobeying their commander. The *British Colonist* noted, "So happy, contented, and comfortable did she appear" on the ice of the frozen river that the soldiers returned to Fort Wrangell without her. The *Colonist* nonetheless entertained little hope that Nellie could survive during "the intense cold that prevailed during the latter part of January along the entire coast."[16] The cold that froze the fingers and numbed the mind into deadly sleep was danger enough, but there were others. One morning Nellie's companions found that an avalanche had swept her tent a quarter mile down the slope and buried it deep under the snow. Digging vigorously, she emerged, undaunted as always. In later years she spoke scornfully of such modern luxuries as sleeping bags. Had she not camped in the snows "in the coldest kind of weather" with only two blankets to warm her for more than two months?

Flying in the face of all logic and probability, her rescue mission to the Cassiar arrived in time to save lives. The condition in which Nellie found her old comrades can readily be inferred from well-documented descriptions of scurvy in the early California gold rush camps and on the overland trails. The cause was the absence of vitamin C supplied by fruits and vegetables in the diet. The first symptom is chronic fatigue at ninety days after the onset of dietary deficiency. Presumably, the miners in the Cassiar quickly became too enfeebled to attempt the trek to Fort Wrangell. At about one hundred thirty days, after the level of vitamin C in the blood sinks to zero, skin sores break out, followed by ominous purplish skin hemorrhages thirty days later. The final stage arrives twenty days afterward when gums swell, teeth loosen, legs become black, swollen, and intensely painful, and death ensues unless the needed fruits or vegetables are soon consumed. Potatoes had long proved a particularly effective remedy, and though the miners on the Stikine evidently had not heard of it, the old California gold rush remedy of tea made from boiled spruce boughs might have been helpful. Since her friends reportedly suffered from symptoms of scurvy before Nellie commenced her seventy-seven day journey, some had died before she could reach them, and she found others in the last extremities, debilitated, with bleeding sores and blackened limbs. The potatoes and lime juice did their work, however, and Nellie took great pride in the survival of all the men she nursed at the camp.[17] This event, the high point of her long and adventurous life, marked the start of the Cashman legend. Until she emerged from the snow at the Cassiar pulling her potato-laden sled, she had been merely an adventurous boardinghouse keeper in the eyes of those around her. Now Nellie Pioche became the frontier angel, credited by some with almost miraculous powers.

Nellie remained nearly two more years in the Cassiar. Before departing she launched the first of the many charitable endeavors for which she would later be renowned, raising five hundred dollars for construction of a hospital by the Catholic Sisters of St. Ann in Victoria. Her reasons for leaving the Cassiar remained unstated, but her subsequent erratic movements suggest that she simply had too many places to go and things to see before she settled down. All the same, the course of her later life shows that she had fallen under the spell of the far North. The poet Robert Service, whom she later knew, as she knew nearly every notable who passed through the mining camps in her day, may have spoken for many of the sourdough crowd that emerged from the Cassiar when he wrote,

> The winter! the brightness that blinds you,
> The white land locked tight as a drum,
> The cold fear that follows and finds you,
> The silence that bludgeons you dumb.
> The snows that are older than history,
> The woods where the weird shadows slant;
> The stillness, the moonlight, the mystery,
> I've bade 'em goodby—but I can't.[18]

One day she would return.

She wandered restlessly over the West for the ensuing year. First she visited her family in the San Francisco Bay area. Then she returned to Virginia City and Pioche, but the excitement she had once found in those towns had long since died away. She may also have tried Bodie, tough swaggering successor to Pioche at its infamous height, but found the new stamping grounds of the western gunmen not to her liking. In 1879 she finally washed up in Tucson and embarked on a more ambitious business enterprise than her earlier boardinghouses, the Delmonico Restaurant. Probably the Delmonico was made possible by the gold dust reaped from her boardinghouse in the Cassiar. Her pioneering spirit greatly impressed John Clum, editor of the *Arizona Citizen*, when she walked into his office to place an advertisement for her new restaurant on the south side of Church Plaza. With typical western hyperbole the ad promised the "best meals in the city," cooked under Nellie's "personal supervision" with every delectable the market could provide.[19]

In his recollections Clum later underlined the pioneering nature of Nellie's enterprise. Women may have been less rare in Tucson than in the Cassiar, but few Anglo women had made their homes in this heav-

*Ellen Cashman*

ily Hispanic city, and the single Anglo woman who launched a business enterprise was rarer still. "Her frank manner, her self-reliant spirit, and her emphatic and fascinating Celtic brogue" much impressed Clum. He felt certain that her strong character would enable her to "achieve along lines that would be regarded as difficult and daring by a majority of the weaker sex."[20]

Nellie did achieve, and the Delmonico prospered as John Clum foresaw. But she soon lost interest. A new mining camp was beckoning 140 miles east of Tucson. Silver discoveries by Ed Schieffelin in 1877 in the hills northeast of Fort Huachuca, where he had been warned that he would find nothing but his tombstone, resulted in a boisterous new mining camp—ironically named Tombstone. By the time the first rich silver shipments reached Tucson in the autumn of 1879, the mining crowd was already converging from all over the West. Nellie could scarcely remain in a sleepy adobe village like Tucson when the excitement lay in Tombstone, "life at full tide" once more, as in the early days at Pioche. "She is as adventurous in pushing forward to a new region as any nomadic miner," wrote an admiring newspaper reporter. "No sooner does she hear of a new camp than she starts for it."[21] Without delay, she packed her bags for Tombstone.

Not only did the move feed the habit of a young woman already addicted to mining excitements but also it brought her greater success in business and a more prominent place in the community than she would have been likely to achieve in Tucson. At first Nellie opened the Nevada Boot and Shoe Store with a woman partner, Kate O'Hara; then she shifted her focus to a store selling groceries and provisions with the assistance of another partner, Jennie Swift. As new arrivals flocked to Tombstone, the stores no doubt flourished, and Nellie added another enterprise, the Arcade Restaurant and Chop House. Then, in February 1881, Nellie's brother-in-law, Thomas Cunningham, died of tuberculosis, leaving Frances and their five surviving children. Although Thomas's condition had no doubt been worsening for some time and his death could scarcely have been unexpected, Nellie, for once, seemed uncertain what action to take. She abruptly sold her Tombstone interests and left for San Francisco. Once there, she reversed course and decided to bring her sister and her nieces and nephews to the Southwest.

37

She briefly tried and abandoned running a hotel in Bisbee, the copper town south of Tombstone near the Mexican border. Now effectively the head of a large family, she could no longer afford to make mistakes.[22]

She decided to concentrate her efforts on Russ House, an elegant restaurant and hotel on the corner of Fifth and Toughnut streets in Tombstone. In that era Tombstone restaurants ran the gamut from the offerings of French chefs to the Can Can Restaurant, so named according to its customers because all the food came out of cans. Knowing the mining crowd as she did, Nellie presented a more tempting menu at Russ House. The miner of that era was a discerning gourmand, always ready to blow his paycheck on a fine meal. Though he might be toiling in the underground tunnels of Tombstone to earn a living, he saw himself as a future nabob on the verge of striking it rich and entitled to the same culinary indulgences as the elite. Catering to the refined and expensive tastes of these miners, Nellie's menu at Russ House offered such a delicacies as lamb with caper sauce, brook trout, beef à l'Espagnol, lobster salad, and New York plum pudding, as well as a good deal of hearty fare. Although the meals at Russ House may sometimes have proved less appetizing than they sounded on the menu, the miners' devotion to Nellie never wavered. The story was told of a traveling salesman who found fault with the beans while dining at Russ House. A tall miner got up from his table, strode over to the drummer, unlimbered his gun, and tersely ordered, "Stranger, eat them beans." No further complaints were heard concerning the quality of the Russ House cuisine.[23]

During her years in Tombstone, Nellie's many good works amplified her reputation as the frontier angel. She raised funds for St. Mary's Hospital in Tucson, which opened in 1880, and brought the Sisters of Mercy to Tombstone to help nurse the sick until a hospital opened its doors in 1885. When the Catholic bishop of Tucson promised to provide a priest if Nellie could generate the funds to build a church, she collected seven hundred dollars through personal subscriptions. To raise more, she organized Tombstone's first amateur theatrical production, "The Irish Diamond," topped off by a grand ball. The new Sacred Heart Church held its first services in 1880.[24]

Nellie also raised money for Tombstone's first school. In view of the conditions in which Tombstone's early schoolchildren attempted to study—a small room with a dirt floor, desks made of boards laid across packing boxes, seats consisting of plank-topped nail kegs, and any book the teacher could succeed in commandeering for a textbook— the situation badly needed the assistance of Tombstone's most effective fund raiser. John Clum left a memorable picture of Nellie's tireless good works: "If she asked for a contribution—we contributed. If she had tickets to sell—we bought tickets. If she needed actors for a play— we volunteered to act. And although Nellie's pleas were frequent, none ever refused her."[25]

Though Tombstone's new church, hospital, and school rose as visible monuments to Nellie's deep involvement with community needs, her private charities, largely unknown except to the recipients, probably exceeded her public works. The dead-broke miner in need of lodging and a meal generally found both at Russ House—and often a grubstake that would enable him to go prospecting as well. Those who knew marveled that Nellie's many charities allowed her to make a living. When epidemic disease swept the city, Russ House became a virtual hospital, and Nellie nursed the sick aided by "Black Jack," one of the queens of the red-light district. As a rule, the prostitutes generously supported the charitable endeavors Nellie embarked on, and she was said to have commented that her "greatest help came from the back street which had no name on the map."[26]

The unlikely image of the virtuous frontier angel and the queen of the tenderloin working side by side illuminates several facets of Nellie's character and good works. The construction of hospitals, churches, and schools has usually been placed under the general rubric of "civilizing the frontier," a mission believed to belong especially to women as morally superior beings under the doctrine of separate spheres. Although it is unlikely that any other woman in the West accomplished more in building community services than Nellie Cashman, the civilizing mission she had carved out for herself had unbreachable boundaries. She would bend her whirlwind energies and her Irish charm to bringing her miners the facilities they needed: a hospital bed when they fell ill, a church where those who shared her devout Catholicism could worship, a school for their children, a meal for the hungry. But she would not lift a finger to change the men themselves, perhaps sensing in her bones that to do so would alter the essence of the adventurous miners and the wild towns she had loved since the early days in Pioche. Accordingly, she absolutely avoided that portion of woman's civilizing mission that entailed opposition to saloons and prostitution and the creation of polite society on the frontier. That effort belonged to Protestant bluenoses anxious to remake the West in the image of the mannerly parlors of the eastern middle class, and Nellie felt little in common with these civilizers. Indeed, in the course of her varied career she even owned saloons. In her old age she spoke cuttingly of "clubs for catty women and false standards of living,"[27] in sharp contrast to her tolerant attitude toward the ladies of the line. Perhaps the frontier angel and Black Jack, both unconventional women who had moved beyond normal social restraints, found a measure of common ground. Again, one catches a glimpse of the wild woman.

Experienced nurse that she was, Nellie must have noticed some worrisome signs in her sister Frances. With Nellie's assistance, Frances had been running a boardinghouse, the Delmonico, to support her family, but she became too ill to continue. Perhaps the loss of weight, the fatigue, and the persistent cough that signaled tuberculosis, the disease that had killed her husband and claimed the lives of more Americans at the turn of the century than any other single cause, had already appeared. For a while Frances seemed to improve, and Nellie made another of her impulsive decisions. Casting aside all that she had accomplished in building the reputation of Russ House as a first-class hostelry, she sold her interest in it to work with Frances in operating a new boardinghouse, which she refurbished as the American Hotel. The name she chose may have suggested her loyalty—intense, like all Nellie's loyalties—to her adopted country. She expressed herself strongly about the "blessings of a free and good government where prosperity reigns and all enjoy the liberty of pursuing the road of wealth and happiness according to the dictates of his own conscience." Later in the Canadian Yukon she would insist on displaying the American flag on a British holiday.[28]

When fire swept through the downtown business district of Tombstone in the spring of 1882, it appeared that the American Hotel might turn out to be the most short-lived of all the enterprises Nellie took up and put down. Though Nellie, Frances, and their friends formed a bucket brigade to wet the hotel's walls, the building repeatedly caught fire. Nellie's arm was badly burned, and flames singed Frances's long hair. After volunteer firemen finally brought the blaze under control, the heart of Tombstone was a charred smoking ruin, but the American Hotel still stood, although the family's clothing had burned and several rooms in the back portion of the establishment were damaged. In later years, as Nellie Cashman's legend grew, some would come to believe that her saintly powers could halt an advancing fire. Evidently, Nellie herself harbored no such illusion. She had prudently taken out plenty of insurance, which fully compensated her for all the losses at the American Hotel.[29]

Just what prompted Nellie to make a prospecting trip into a remote region of Baja California in the spring of 1883 remains a matter of conjecture. Since her departure from the Cassiar, she had operated a dizzying variety of businesses, but mining remained her ruling passion. She invested profitably in numerous mining claims, offered expert advice on others, and continued to tramp over the hills clad in heavy boots, "strong bloomers," and a cloak, making a good copper strike in Graham County, Arizona. Nonetheless, the longing to venture farther afield eventually grew irresistible, perhaps gaining force from the realization that family responsibilities were closing in around her. As Frances's condition worsened, the day when Nellie would effectively become the parent of her five nieces and nephews drew steadily nearer. Perhaps the expedition to Baja was in the nature of a last fling before enforced motherhood pinned down the restless spirit that had flitted over much of the West in the span of the last dozen years. Then, too, there was the matter of the Mexican.

The mythic figure of the Mexican who briefly appears like the magical messenger in a fairy tale recurs again and again in the mining lore of the Southwest (indeed, the resemblance in form between fairy tales and mining lore may well be no mere coincidence). If the Mexican carried a map, it was always ancient, yellowed, faded almost to invisibility, and difficult to decipher. Sometimes the Mexican messenger rewarded the stranger who treated him kindly with one of these maps. Verbal messages were always enigmatic and imprecise, and the conventions of the genre demanded that the Mexican messenger had to die or disappear before he could be questioned in a logical manner.[30] Nellie's Mexican messenger was no exception.

Two slightly differing versions of his elliptical appearance were told. In one he spilled a pile of nuggets on the bar in the Palace Saloon and declared that they came from Mulege in Baja. Then he disappeared, leaving so much excitement in his wake that only "knockers and croakers" would point to the well-known inclination of prospectors to spread disinformation concerning the location of their finds. In another version Nellie assumed the role of the kindly stranger. The Mexican messenger collapsed in the street in front of her establishment. Nellie had him carried inside and cared for him. Necessarily, he died, with the words "Mulege . . . go to Mulege . . . the Valley of the Three Crosses" on his lips. Nellie later found rich gold nuggets in his pockets. Those who think the apocryphal figure of the Mexican messenger hard to credit may turn to the more prosaic explanation that reports of placer discoveries in Baja had created considerable commotion among western miners, and prospecting parties had been at work in the area since autumn.[31]

No matter how these reports on Baja were received, the excitement, combined with Nellie's persuasive powers, was sufficient for her to secure financial backing for a rather expensive undertaking joined by several local notables. The party of twenty-one included mining expert Bill Hogan and future U.S. senator Mark Smith, but a press dispatch made clear that Nellie and Milt E. Joyce, a prominent figure in Tombstone, were the leaders of the expedition. They traveled by train to Guaymas, Mexico, where they hired a ship to ferry them across the bay to Baja. Here they encountered at least two other large prospecting parties also bound for the placers (the Mexican messenger must have covered a good deal of ground and possibly died more than once).[32] The competition of rivals deterred Nellie no more than did the history of mining in Baja, where treasure seekers since the first expedition by Hernán Cortés in 1535 had repeatedly returned from the rugged desert mountains emptyhanded. Like all prospectors, she harbored the conviction that she would be the one to claim the prize that others had missed. This certainty was coupled with a rash confidence in her own toughness, fueled by her exploit against all odds in the Cassiar, that would nearly cost Nellie her life.

The ensuing events in Baja have come down to us in two forms, the legendary and the actual. According to the legend, fostered by Nellie's devoted nephew Michael Cunningham and her ardent admirer John Clum, Nellie's party traveled into the desert on foot, failed to uncover any signs of gold, ran out of water, and came close to dying of thirst. Nellie, the hardiest of them all, struggled on to save her comrades and returned with burros carrying water in goatskin bags that she had obtained from the Santa Gertrudis mission. Since heroines can never fail, the legend held that Nellie alone of all her party had struck gold but the priest at the mission persuaded her to conceal her discovery in order to save the natives of Mulege from the exploitation and ruin that would come from a mining boom. As late as the 1960s the credulous folk who believe in Mexican messengers and other romantic stories continued to search for the lost Cashman Mine.[33]

The truth was otherwise. A contemporary account uncovered by author Carolyn Niethammer and confirmed at the time by Nellie herself discloses that the party reached Guaymas on 24 May, spent four days on the ship that carried them 111 miles across the Bay of California, and traveled on foot packing their supplies on burros for 95 miles over a rough trail through cactus-studded desert mountains, rocky valleys, and sandy plains. A year can pass without a drop of rain in the oppressive heat of central Baja, and water sources are few and far between. Far from saving the men in her party from perishing of thirst, Nellie was saved by them. Eager to reach the rumored treasures of Baja, confident that she could endure the hot, waterless deserts of Mexico as she had weathered the snows of the Cassiar, and once again the unstoppable wild woman, Nellie and an advance party of a few men started out ahead of the main group. When the rest of the expedition eventually overtook them, they found Nellie and two of her companions "near dying of thirst." Her protective angel had not entirely deserted her, however, since succor arrived in time.[34]

The remainder of the expedition proved not only risky but unproductive. On reaching the placers Nellie's party found them completely worked out by Mexican and Indian miners who had left not a trace of gold. Although subsequent dispatches showed that many miners who persisted would succeed in winning modest fortunes not far away in Baja, Nellie's party abandoned the effort almost immediately. During the return trip the captain of their ship went on a drunken binge and began threatening the lives of his passengers. The men in Nellie's party seized control, tied him up, and navigated across the bay themselves. Despite the captain's provocation, Mexican authorities in Guaymas chose to view the passengers as mutineers and clapped the party in jail, the frontier angel along with the rest—an ignominious ending to a thoroughly unsatisfactory undertaking. After they had languished for several days in the foul conditions of a nineteenth-century Mexican prison, the American consul at Guaymas secured their release.[35]

How, in the face of these stark facts, did the legend of Nellie's rescue of her party and the lost Cashman Mine survive and flourish? Perhaps the self-perpetuating nature of fame played a part. Since Nellie was the best-known member of the group, it was assumed that she had to be the heroine of the piece, a belief both shared and fostered by Mike Cunningham and John Clum. But the more fundamental reason probably lay in the need of the West for heroines. People wanted to believe in a woman so brave and strong that she could single-handedly rescue her party and so tenderly concerned for the simple people of Mulege that she would cast aside her long-sought bonanza for their sake. Because they wanted to believe, they did, and the legend of the frontier angel, in ever brighter form, soared above the bars of the Mexican prison.

Meanwhile, Frances was dying. During this period patients with tuberculosis were converging on Colorado, where the pure mountain air was thought to benefit their condition, as indeed it often did. Tombstone's most famous consumptive, Doc Holliday, was to end his life in one of the Colorado resorts that catered to victims of the "white plague." But apparently no similar effort was undertaken to cure Frances. After a period at a Catholic institution in San Diego, she spent the last days before her death in July 1884 with her mother in San Jose.[36]

Thus, at the height of her career as prospector and mining camp businesswoman, Nellie, who had never married or had a family of her own, became the foster mother of a brood of five children ranging in age from eleven-year-old Tom to three-year-old Frances Josephine. Her course of action was clear to her. She must assume the care of these orphaned children, even at the price of her own freedom, and Nellie probably had no illusions about the price. Professional women in her day often did not marry, because the demands of a family and a career were considered incompatible. Although Nellie's pursuits would not have been classified with those of the woman doctor or college professor, her attitude toward her life's work assuredly paralleled theirs. When asked in her old age why she had never married, Nellie told one interviewer that she had "always been too busy to talk about such things"—too busy, that is, with her own career. To another, she lightly replied, "Men are a nuisance anyhow, now aren't they?"[37] Beneath the bantering tone it seems clear that to one who valued her freedom and independence so much, a husband could indeed be a nuisance. When a new mining boom beckoned and she wanted to pull up stakes and move on, he might not agree. When she wanted to go prospecting, he might have other ideas. He might even expect her to stay home and cook his supper and wash his socks. And if a husband posed a potential threat to her freedom of movement, small children needed even more time and attention. They must be not only fed and clothed but also mothered, taught, loved, disciplined, nursed, watched over, provided with a stable home, and given schooling. Here they were on her doorstep, all five of them. It may have been the frontier angel's most severe test.

For the time being, she resigned herself to motherhood. She took over Russ House once more and kept a weather eye on her nephews as they played baseball in the adjoining vacant lots. Though known for snapping out commands "like a master on a wind-jammer,"[38] Nellie used soothing methods for disciplining the children. When fights broke out, she hurried forth from the hotel to make sure the children fought fairly and to pacify the combatants with pieces of pie. Mike Cunningham later recalled staging an occasional affray with his brothers and friends when they grew hungry for pie.

Nellie also rescued the children from serious jams. Mike remembered a time when he and a friend decided to go prospecting like his Aunt Nell and, just like her, ignored the dangers at hand. These were the years when General George Crook was still capturing renegade bands of Apache with many smoldering grievances against the white man, and the lone traveler ventured into Apache country at his peril. Oblivious to the incidents of torture and death at Indian hands that had terrified the people of the border for years, the boys took burros and started northeast across the valley toward the Dragoon Mountains, site of Cochise's stronghold. Fortunately, they did not pass unnoticed by a miner who knew Nellie and came in to tell her where the boys were headed. Apache signal fires flared in the distance as Nellie whipped her team toward the Dragoons in search of the boys. Finally, around ten o'clock at night, she spotted the burros outside an abandoned cabin. More than forty years later Mike, whose adventurous spirits on the occasion had waned with the daylight, remembered the relief that flooded over him when he heard Aunt Nell's voice calling out to him from the darkness. Nellie gathered up the boys and hastened the team toward Tombstone and safety.[39] The fact that she had set off for the mountains entirely alone indicates that the fiasco at Baja had instilled no fearfulness in the wild woman.

Other exploits during these years further amplified the legend of the frontier angel. After five prisoners were condemned to death for murders committed during the robbery of a Bisbee store, a circus atmosphere prevailed, for Tombstone relished the prospect of seeing the killers who had gunned down innocent people in the street receive their just deserts. Nellie, by contrast, feared for the immortal souls of the three Catholics among the prisoners. The *Tombstone Epitaph* reported Nellie "in constant attendance" at the Tombstone jail during the prisoners' final days, along with two Catholic priests. Nellie and the priests succeeded in converting the remaining two prisoners to Catholicism, the only instance of proselytizing on her part that has yet come to light.[40]

If she had won the prisoners' souls, they had won her sympathies. Responding to their fear that after burial their bodies would be exhumed and dissected for medical research, Nellie promised to set a guard over their graves and kept her word. Even the force of her personality could not prevent Tombstone from turning out to enjoy the spectacle of the execution, but she did as much as she could. Interest was so intense that at the trial the *Epitaph*'s reporter found the court-room "literally packed to suffocation." Subsequently, the sheriff issued more than five hundred tickets to those eager to witness the hanging, scheduled for 28 March 1884 in the jail yard. The story goes that a local entrepreneur hatched a scheme to turn a profit from the event by erecting a grandstand that overlooked the yard so that more spectators could be accommodated, a continuation on the frontier of the old and grisly American tradition of the execution as public event. Nellie prevailed on the sheriff to impose a curfew on the last night before the hanging and led a party of miners forth in the darkness to demolish the grandstand with axes. Author Frank Brophy later reflected, "She was one of nature's rare creations, with the form and grace of a woman, the mind of a man, and the spirit of an angel." A careful investigation by Nellie's biographer, Don Chaput, however, uncovered no evidence that Nellie played any part in these events. Chaput suggests that the miners who tore down the extra grandstand may simply have resented the stiff admission prices.[41]

Another cornerstone of the frontier angel legend in Tombstone was the rescue of mine superintendent E. B. Gage when striking miners threatened to lynch him during a prolonged wage dispute. By night Nellie smuggled Gage out of Tombstone in her buggy and took him to the Benson railroad station, where he boarded the train for a discreet leave of absence until tempers had cooled. Nellie may well have been motivated as much by concern for her miners as for Gage's safety. She would have been aware that if the labor unrest deteriorated into crime, the miners would ultimately pay the price. In the Pennsylvania coal fields in the seventies, the Molly Maguires, Irish like Nellie, had turned to violence against the coal operators and ended on the scaffold. Her miners must be saved from such a fate as surely as the large family of an unemployed immigrant must be put up at Russ House until he found work, and money must be raised for the miner injured in an accident until he recovered. Never did Nellie stand aside and wait for someone else to do the things that needed doing.[42]

It would be inconceivable that the heart that overflowed with sympathy for everyone, catty women excepted, could remain untouched by the plight of the Irish in this period. Famine again ravaged Ireland,

and a new generation of Irish nationalist leaders had risen, eloquent in their determination to change the iniquitous land system that enslaved the Irish tenant farmers. Irish immigrants in America played a vital part in this unfolding drama because the funds they channeled to Ireland through the American Land League brought relief to the starving and supported political protest. Nellie, true to form, bent her indefatigable fund-raising efforts to the Irish cause, which she saw as an "unequal contest" by "our less favored kindred" against oppression and want. When factionalism between conservatives and extremists rent the league, Nellie's allegiance went to James Redpath, a fiery old abolitionist with a heart as fanatic as her own. Oppressors outside Ireland also aroused her wrath. Later, on the eve of the Spanish-American War, her feelings against the "treacherous Spaniards" waxed so intense that she spoke wildly to the press about organizing a company of Nevada women who would "be of some effect in a battle," a fantasy that anticipated the participation of American women in combat by nearly a century. In view of the intense involvement of Irish Americans in local politics and Nellie's essential Irishness, an active interest in politics on her part is unsurprising, even in an era when the absence of woman suffrage in Arizona compelled her to work behind the scenes. Though Nellie was said to control the miners' vote, the recollection of an old Tombstone resident that she secured the election of her candidate for police chief is the principal clue on the direction her influence took in local politics.[43]

In 1886 unhappy portents appeared in Tombstone. The price of silver had fallen, water started seeping into the mines, and marginal mining operations closed down. By the end of the year the Grand Central and the Contention mines, the two great mainstays of the district, had gone up in flames and all deep mining ceased. As an exodus from Tombstone began, new booms glimmered beyond the horizon. In the Black Range of southwestern New Mexico a hard-drinking roisterer named Jack Sheddon who had been run out of Lake Valley went to sleep under the tall pines and awoke to find that the rock on which he had pillowed his head was almost pure silver (one of many tales of accidental discovery that abound in prospecting lore). The result was the mining excitement at Kingston. Steadily, the day drew closer when the inevitable clash between Nellie's career and her adopted family would come to a head.[44]

It was a dilemma that none of the women prospectors managed to resolve, perhaps because no completely satisfactory solution existed. As we shall see, women prospectors with families tried every possibility. If she brought the children with her on a prolonged sojourn in the wilderness, as did Dora Wilhelm and Ellie Nay, she maintained a normal family life but sacrificed the children's schooling and isolated them from community friendships and associations. To postpone her prospecting until the children were grown meant the probable sacrifice of her career. By the time the children left home, she would be forty or fifty years old, if not more. Even if she survived so long, in an age when normal life expectancy had not extended beyond the early forties, she had to anticipate diminished strength and vigor in a calling that demanded great physical endurance. Not least, calculated postponement would be thoroughly out of character. Observers of the mining scene invariably commented on the inability of prospectors to stay put when rumors of a new bonanza reached their ears. As Louise Clappe had noted more than thirty years earlier during the California gold rush, "they are always longing for 'big strikes.' If a 'claim' is paying them a steady income, by which, if they pleased, they could lay up more in a month, than they could accumulate in a year at home, still, they are dissatisfied, and, in most cases, will wander off in search of better 'diggings.' There are hundreds now pursuing this foolish course, who, if they had stopped where they first 'camped,' would now have been rich men." Although a hiatus imposed by family obligations was not entirely unknown (Arizona/Nevada prospector Blanche Crabtree gave up prospecting for more than a decade while caring for her small daughter and accompanying her husband as he pursued his career east of the Rockies), tabling the quest for twenty years or more would be a congenital impossibility for most prospectors.[45]

The remaining solution, leaving the children behind, meant abandoning the domestic role of mother and homemaker. All the same, several women prospectors chose this route and sacrificed the joys of raising their young children themselves. For instance, Ferminia Sarras temporarily left her younger children in an orphanage on the Comstock while she went forth to seek her fortune in the Candelaria Hills of southwestern Nevada, and the newly widowed "Mountain Charley" (later Mrs. E. J. Guerin) parked her children with the Sisters of Charity in St. Louis, disguised herself as a man, and embarked on a series of western adventures that included prospecting and working claims in the vicinity of Pike's Peak in 1859–60.[46]

Three years of motherhood and domesticity with a family she had never bargained for proved to be all Nellie could tolerate. She placed the children, now ages six to fourteen, in Catholic institutions and resumed her old restless way of life. The frontier angel's many chroniclers have praised her for assuming financial responsibility for them, and she also smoothed their path in other ways, turning in due time to her friends to secure a position for at least one of her nephews. We do not know how the children reacted to growing up in institutions, although Mike, who rose to become the president of two Arizona banks, remained devoted to Nellie. Nor do we know if she felt a twinge of guilt over her abdication from parenthood. No doubt, like many strong-willed and self-reliant people, she expected equal fortitude from everyone around her, no matter how small. Still, a religious boarding school seems a harsh solution for an orphaned six-year-old child.[47]

Over the next decade Nellie moved through the western mining camps at such a rapid pace that she appeared to be making up for lost time. She hastened to booming Kingston, where the adventurers congregated by the light of candles and burning pine knots in a new set of saloons. She opened another of her boardinghouses there in 1887 and gained praise for the same good works that distinguished her wherever she went. The chronicler of Kingston called her "the Florence Nightingale" of the camp, also taking note of her active role in rounding up the Catholic miners whenever a visiting priest arrived to say mass in one of the dance halls.[48]

The Kingston boardinghouse was only one of many enterprises throughout the West during the years after Tombstone. In January 1889 newspapers reported Nellie on the way to Harqua Hala, Arizona, with a load of goods for sale. Shortly, she would open a restaurant there, as well as the Buffalo Hotel at Globe, Arizona; the Arizona Silver Belt Restaurant in Prescott, Arizona; a boardinghouse in a Mexican gold camp; and perhaps others during sojourns in Idaho's Coeur d'Alene. Sometimes she brought the children along. Mike recalled times in Montana and Wyoming when Auntie Nellie worked at her placering "like a Trojan" and the snow piled nine feet high around the cabin in winter. Not all her nieces and nephews seem to have enjoyed as close a relationship with her as Mike, however. In 1898 she had not seen her oldest nephew, Tom, in so many years that another man nearly succeeded in impersonating him on her expedition to the Klondike.

No doubt betwixt and between her earlier undertakings she embarked on numerous prospecting expeditions, the most spectacular of which was a journey to the South African diamond fields in 1889. Since Nellie afterward had little to say about the episode, it may well have been as great a fiasco as her foray into Baja, and as great a financial loss to her backers, but evidently it whetted her appetite. After her return she attempted to secure financing for another prospecting party. This time, however, even the generous friends who had reached into their pockets on so many occasions shook their heads, and Nellie never succeeded in raising the funds for another trip to South Africa.[49]

In 1895 she made a return trip to Alaska and reminisced with the mining crowd at Juneau about the old days in the Cassiar, now twenty years past: "Many of the boys were just about to go into the interior to prospect, and when I arrived, they seemed glad to see me. They built a huge log fire and made me sit by it and talk of the old Cassiar days. They said it looked natural to see me sitting by a campfire as in days of yore."[50] Service well caught the bittersweet spirit of these occasions:

The battlefield is silent where
    of old you fought it out;
The claims you fiercely won are lost and sold;
But there's a little army
    that they'll never put to rout—
The men who simply live to seek the gold. . . .

For once you've panned the speckled sand
    and seen the bonny dust,
Its peerless brightness binds you like a spell;
It's little else you care about;

you go because you must,
And you feel that you could follow it to Hell.
You'd follow it in hunger,
    and you'd follow it in cold;
You'd follow it in solitude and pain;
And when you're stiff and battened down,
    let someone whisper "Gold,"
You're lief to rise and follow it again.[51]

Nellie herself led a party into an unexplored region where they found paying gravel. Although the signs looked promising enough to buoy the hopes of a prospector, dwindling supplies eventually forced them to abandon their explorations. For the time being Nellie returned to her Arizona enterprises, running a hotel in Yuma. Then, in 1897, came news of the fabulous discoveries in the Klondike. The great gold rush began, and Nellie could hardly stay behind stirring the beans on her stove in Arizona. She attempted to raise five thousand dollars for a prospecting party to the Klondike and again failed to find any backers. In February 1898, unstoppable as ever, she set out all the same with a grubstake raised in Tucson, traveling by steamer from Victoria to Dyea, Alaska.[52]

The route they took was the Dyea Trail through Chilkoot Pass. The aging Nellie had grown far stouter than the slip of a young woman who had harnessed herself to the sled to bring lifesaving supplies into the Cassiar, but she still had grit enough to be numbered among the survivors of the journey that remains one of the great epics of human endurance in frontier history. Through all the hardships, Nellie retained the prospector's unreasoning belief that she, of all the thousands on the trail, would be the one to strike bonanza. The *British Colonist* reported, "She is out now for the big strike, nothing more or less than the Mother Lode of the far-famed Klondike region." She made her way through the boulders and uprooted trees of the narrow Dyea River canyon, arriving at length beneath the peaks of the Chilkoot Pass, where a black chain of human figures with packs on their backs struggled over the snow-sheathed, almost perpendicular surface of the mountain by steps cut in the ice. Horses and dogs could not negotiate the steep ascent; only the human back could serve as transport.[53]

Farther along the way Edward Morgan, a gold rusher whose reminiscences are generally regarded as accurate, had been traveling for several days in temperatures of thirty-two degrees below zero when he
encountered Nellie on the frozen expanse of Lake Laberge. She looked
so small, an "undersized figure, attired in Mackinaw coat and trousers,
with the regulation heavy boots and fur-lined cap." And she was alone.
Noticing that Nellie and her one dog made little progress in pulling her
sled, Morgan allowed her to hook it to his for the next several miles.
Nellie's small sled, though overburdened, contained much less than the
ton of supplies that Canadian North West Mounted Police regulations
required each gold rusher to bring so that starvation in the Klondike
could be forestalled. Nellie explained that she had persuaded the
Mounties at various checkpoints to let her pass, despite their reputation
for permitting no exceptions. Morgan observed that he "could well believe her story of the persuasive power of her tongue, for she had the
gift of palaver and was a most convincing talker."[54] Again, one glimpses
the wild woman.

When they camped at the foot of Lake Laberge, Morgan's partner
forbade Nellie to join them because of her sex, one occasion when the
aura of the frontier angel failed to level all barriers. Nellie moved on
toward the ice-bound Thirtymile River, where Morgan would come to
grief the next day in an avalanche of horse, sleds, and falling rocks.
Sunless days ensued that must have been much the same for the small
figure ahead on the trail, and Morgan recalled "traveling always in an
Arctic dusk" with a sense that "death was just around the next bend,
and that it would be a welcome relief from this terrible cold and the
blind, stumbling march over the ice in the eternal twilight." Many
miles and further obstacles lay ahead. Since Nellie later spoke of the
rapids when other rigors of the trail had faded from memory, it is possible that she camped with many other gold rushers, hacked down
trees to build a boat, and rocketed through when the spring thaw
melted the frozen waters. The ordeal was such that of the one hundred
thousand who attempted the journey at the height of Yukon fever, so
many turned back or died that fewer than half reached their goal, but
at long last, beneath the scar-faced mountain and beyond a roaring
confluence of rivers, the most intrepid of the gold rushers arrived at

the jumble of tents, shacks, cabins, and makeshift buildings that was Dawson.[55]

Pierre Berton, in his definitive chronicle of the Klondike, comments on the "strange lassitude" of the crowd that eddied aimlessly through the streets of Dawson in the summer of '98. Finding the best claims already staked, a third of the population had headed home by August. Lassitude was alien to Nellie, however, and she cast herself into her usual activities with her usual zest. In the midst of the familiar mining camp carnival she opened the familiar restaurant, borrowing a name from one of her old competitors in Tombstone and christening it the Can Can. It was succeeded by the Cassiar Restaurant and several others. She also engaged in the familiar charities, assiduously raising money for good causes. To provide the miner in search of comfort and companionship with an alternative to the saloons, she offered free coffee and cigars in "The Prospectors' Haven of Retreat," a sitting room she established next to the grocery store she ran in the basement of Donovan's Hotel. Although the Haven hinted at her disapproval of the carousing and heavy drinking that went on in the saloons, missionary attempts to change the gold rushers' way of life were never her way. Despite an unsavory incident in which she attempted to influence the mining inspector's decision on one of her claims, Nellie gained the respect and affection of the people around her as always. Mae Field, later known as the "Doll of Dawson," remembered her as "an angel if ever there was one": "One year there was a terrible fire in Dawson, and everyone thought the whole town was doomed to go up in flames. Then Nellie Cashman asked for a bowl of Holy Water, which she threw into the raging inferno. To everyone's utter amazement, the wind changed. Almost instantly the flames were swept in the opposite direction, and the greater part of the town was saved."[56] The legend of the frontier angel shone more radiantly than ever.

As in all the other mining camps through which Nellie passed, her business enterprises served primarily as a means of enabling her to pursue what she really cared about—her prospecting. Author Richard O'Connor saw this lone figure trudging through the wilderness in fur hat, mackinaw, trousers, and boots as one of the rare women in the Klondike who deserved to be called prospectors: "Few women in the

Klondike ventured from the towns and settlements in actual search for gold, the raw gold that had to be wrested from its frozen nesting places in the earth. There were some prospectors' wives who worked by their husbands' side at the diggings, and there were plenty of other women who prospected in the pockets and pokes of the miners. Nellie Cashman, a proud, tough and independent woman, was one of the few who ventured alone into the solitudes." Despite her efforts, she failed to strike the Mother Lode of which she had spoken so optimistically in the beginning. Indeed, all the claims she staked proved to be of little value and primarily served to involve her in that perpetual litigation to which the Klondike was especially prone. Her only real bonanza was a claim purchased with several partners three years after her arrival in Dawson.[57]

Her recollection that she realized one hundred thousand dollars from this claim may well have been overblown, but the assertion that she spent everything she made on charities and worthless mining claims rings true. When her own funds gave out, she turned to Jim McNamee and Big Alex McDonald, the fabulously wealthy and devoutly Catholic "King of the Klondike," who had more properties and partners than he could keep track of and passed out gold nuggets to his visitors like candies. These Klondike nabobs responded generously to Nellie's importunities. "Whatever they gave to Nellie was considered an indirect donation to charity," observed John Clum, "for they were quite sure that sooner or later, their gifts and her winnings would all be disbursed to the needy and afflicted, to churches and hospitals, and, therefore, it was only a matter of time until Nellie would be broke again, and it would be up to them to provide her with another 'stake.'"[58]

Though Nellie's remarkable mother had survived to see her daughter join the Klondike gold rush, she did not live to see Nellie again. In 1899 Frances Cashman died in the Magdalen Asylum in San Francisco, where she had been institutionalized for many years. Her age was variously given as 100 or 103, but her dark brown hair still showed no streak of gray, and nearly until the end she retained the ability to tell marvelous tales of her early days, a gift that lived on in Nellie.[59]

Resisting the dash to Nome, Nellie remained in Dawson until 1904, when a new gold rush in the Tanana district near Fairbanks kindled the hopes of the sourdoughs once more. Then she headed north, declaring that the boys would be needing her to cook their pork and beans. They needed her for that and a good deal more, believing as they did in the frontier angel's almost holy powers. One miner lying on his deathbed said to his friends, "If Nellie Cashman were only here, I'd get well."[60] For years miners had looked on her arrival at a new strike as a good omen, because they were convinced that she had a "supernatural source of information."[61] Toward the end of her life the possibility of making Nellie a deputy U.S. marshal was seriously raised at a time when few women held such positions, and none so far along in years as she. Although nothing came of the idea, the esteem shown by its proponents clearly pleased Nellie. "They look on me as a sort of mother and they wouldn't think of doing anything wrong while I was around," she said. "There isn't a man in Alaska who doesn't take off his hat whenever he meets me—and they always stop swearing when I come round, too. I wouldn't have any trouble in keeping order, because everybody's orderly when I'm round, anyway." Nellie also remarked that she had "never been troubled by bad men" in all her years in the North.[62]

In those days all the men on the Chilkoot Pass looked like devils, haggard, unshaven, and hollow-eyed, with faces blackened by charcoal and eyes shaded by wooden masks to ward off the burning, blinding sun, and some were as bad as they looked. But the night Nellie called "the worst moment I ever knew in the Yukon" came about through no breach in the universal respect that shielded her or any threat from the dangerous men who haunted the trails. She had stopped at the Stony Creek roadhouse in the Kluahane district, eaten a supper of moose and rabbit, and eventually ended up in the middle bunk in a tier of three, with an Indian woman sleeping beneath her and a three-hundred-pound miner snoring like a steamboat whistle in the top bunk. When this human elephant rolled over in the night, the straining canvas beneath him ripped in two, sending him crashing down on Nellie, breaking her bunk and landing them both on the shrieking Indian woman in a human avalanche decidedly more unpleasant than the snow that had swept Nellie away in the Cassiar.[63]

For a while Nellie ran a grocery store in Fairbanks, but she kept prospecting ever farther north in more remote country. First at Coldfoot, sixty miles beyond the Arctic Circle, then farther still to a cabin on Nolan Creek in the Koyukuk region, two hundred miles as the crow flies north of Fairbanks. Robert Marshall, who made an intensive study of the Koyukuk, called it "two hundred miles beyond the edge of the twentieth century." The first rush to the upper Koyukuk occurred in 1900–1903 and died after eight hundred thousand dollars' worth of gold had been taken from the shallow gravels of various creeks. Then, in 1907, three Swedish prospectors struck gold in the bedrock of Nolan Creek. This discovery ignited a new boom, which brought in the influx of gold rushers joined by Nellie. A discovery in the deep channel of the Hammond River in 1911 gave mining in the Koyukuk a fresh boost, yielded more than a million dollars in gold, and renewed the hopes of prospectors. The peak year of this last boom period came in 1915 when three hundred whites and about seventy-five Eskimos lived in the Koyukuk.[64]

After 1916 population and gold production declined steadily, but Nellie stayed on. Nolan Creek was her final gold rush. Here, in the last years of her life, the restless search for excitement that had taken her to mining camps from Pioche to Dawson for more than four decades came to an end. The lesser concerns that had defined Nellie Cashman as the mining world knew her had been stripped away. Out on Nolan Creek, far from the sorrows and needs of humankind, the charities that had busied her for so long ceased to have meaning. Of the gold rush crowd that had been the only love of her life, just a few lingered on, but she felt her place was with them. When friends in Fairbanks tried to dissuade her from returning to the remote Arctic at her advanced age, she stubbornly responded, "Young feller, those prospectors up there need me—and need me badly—and that is the country in which I expect to live the rest of my days." The prospector's dream of untold wealth, just another shovelful deeper in the ground, stayed with her. To the very end, she spoke of making "a million or two before I leave this romantic business of mining" and looked forward to the day when she would uncover a hidden river of gold under the bed of Nolan Creek.[65]

Occasionally, like the mountain men of early days heading in from the wilderness to the annual rendezvous, she journeyed down from her Arctic retreat to visit her family in Arizona, to call on old friends, many of whom now occupied influential positions, and to round up investors to buy stock in the Midnight Sun Mining Company she had formed (even the angel was not too virtuous for the usual promotional activities of a prospector bent on hawking his wares). The interviews she gave on these occasions suggest an increasing distaste for the world she had left behind, especially its catty women, its false standards of living, and its vicious competitiveness "where men cut each other's business to hack," but also the noise of its clanging trolley cars and honking autos. During the terrible influenza pandemic of 1918 she contemptuously dismissed the fears and precautions of her countrymen as "one nose wiping exhibition after another."[66] As we shall see, scorn for those less tough and fearless than themselves and intense pride in their own ability to withstand hardship and danger were recurrent themes among women prospectors.

On her last journey to the outside world, in 1924 when she was eighty, Mike, her favorite nephew, urged her to forsake prospecting in the Arctic and spend her remaining years with her family in Arizona. "It'll be a long time before I reach the cushioned-rocker stage," Nellie told him and also announced her intention to return to the far North in a mail plane. In those early days of aviation her family thought the mail plane a more disturbing idea than her usual mode of transport, mushing over the snowy wasteland alone with a sled and dog team, but she was adamant. "What's wrong with that?" she demanded. "I was the first white woman in there on foot. Why shouldn't I be the first white woman to go in on an airplane?"[67] It appears that the wild woman had outlived the angel.

It was in the Arctic that she became, in the end, her essential self. Her words imply that she loved it less in its softer, gentler seasons, the wildflowered summers, the autumns when mountains turn rosy with low bush blueberry and when golden birches glisten by the creeks, than in the stark mood of winter: "It takes the solitude of frozen nights with the howl of dogs for company, the glistening fairness of days when nature reaches out and loves you, she's so beautiful, to bring out the soul of folks." She saw living in the Arctic as a test of character—"It takes real folks to live by themselves in the lands of the north"—and her urge to prove her own mettle stayed with her to the last.[68] Perhaps the inner meaning of her statement that she had been "alone all my life," which wiped away the years spent with her mother, her sister, and the children as if they had never existed, was simply that she would have liked to be. Alone in this frozen stillness, her spiritual life had grown more visionary and more mad. She became less and less interested in real events and real people but spoke for hours about her mystical experiences with the "poor souls in purgatory." This signified a resurgence of her quintessential Irishness, for the site in Ireland where St. Patrick saw his vision of the damned had been a central feature of Irish Catholicism and the scene of mass pilgrimages since the Middle Ages.[69]

At those moments when reality intruded, Nellie realized that her health was fading and looked to her own death with casual fortitude. On her last trip out of the Arctic she mushed seven hundred fifty miles over the snows in seventeen days, still the same woman once described as "hard as flint, with endurance on the trail equal to that of any man." On her return trip in the spring of 1924 she caught cold, which she humorously remarked was the rule every time she left Alaska. She nonetheless continued on her way, albeit by mail boat on the Koyukuk River rather than the plane that had so alarmed her family. This time she never made it. Suffering from double pneumonia, she was forced to go back to Fairbanks and enter the hospital. Later in the summer, her health somewhat restored, she made a final attempt to return to her Arctic retreat, but eighty miles short of Nolan Creek even Nellie acknowledged that she was too weak to continue. She allowed herself to be settled in a rowboat manned by an Episcopalian deacon and an Indian for what was to be her last trip down the Koyukuk. After another period of hospitalization in Fairbanks, she managed to reach St. Joseph's Hospital in Victoria, where she calmly told the sisters, many among them old friends of hers, "I have come home to die." There, in the hospital she had helped build with the donations of gold dust collected on her first trip into the northern wilderness half a century earlier, she died on 4 January 1925. Newspapermen memorialized her "beauty without ostentation, wisdom without education," and her "flaming, unquenchable spirit,"[70] and the last survivors of the gold rush crowd, scattered now to the four winds, remembered her in their own way.

TWO

# Ferminia Sarras:
# The Copper Queen

Spanish influence played no significant part in the history of northern Nevada. When Spanish nomenclature appears—a street called Rio Poco in Reno or a canyon named Jaime in the Carson Valley—it reflects no more than a real estate developer's disregard for local history or a dude rancher's whim to romanticize a place with a mellifluous Spanish name. Farther south the signs of Spanish presence from a very early date begin to emerge. They are tangible and often mysterious. Arrastras, the large bowl-shaped devices in which Hispanic miners ground ore with the aid of a slow-circling mule, have been found in the mountains near Hot Creek and have not been fully explained. Hispanic miners are believed to have worked the placers in Tule Canyon on the northern edge of the Death Valley country in the 1840s before the California gold rush. A story is told of a party of Mexicans who boated up the Colorado River with a treasure map found in the moldering archives of a cathedral; they were surprised to learn that the site had become a flourishing Nevada mine. The spade of a ditch digger in Rhyolite early in the twentieth century uncovered an old Spanish coin. Buried in the desert sands southeast of Walker Lake was a set of church bells. Theories abound, but no one knows how bells cast in Mexico between 1810 and 1830 came to be abandoned there.[1]

Thus Ferminia Sarras first appeared in the mining camps not far from this place, and like the bells in the sand, she offered no explanations. On just one point did she always make herself clear: she was a Spanish lady of royal blood, not Indian or mestizo, not Mexican or Chilean, the categories in which ignorant Anglos lumped everyone from south of the border. Spanish, *comprende!* So she is described in 1881 in the first Esmeralda County tax records in which her name can be found: "Fermenia Sararis, Spanish Lady, Belleville." So she appears in her portrait, an

oil painting of a handsome woman very much the Spanish lady in a severe high-necked black dress with a rim of lace at the throat, gold ear-
rings, and a gold cross on a heavy gold chain. Her dark hair is swept atop
her head, her brows delicately arched, her lips finely chiseled, her skin
very white. She confronts the world full face, with no coquetry, no
prettifying curls or fancy touches, no attempt to strike a graceful pose.
It is not difficult to imagine the hard, unflinching gaze of those brown
eyes beneath the plumed helmet of a conquistador.[2] Like the old coin
or the bells, the object exists, tangible and real in the handwritten entries in old leather-bound record books and in the portrait. The reason does not. We can only guess why the fine, well-born lady of the
portrait chose a life of hardship and danger in the Nevada desert.

Her story must be reconstructed from scanty and sometimes inconsistent sources. She was born in Nicaragua in July 1840. Genealogical research by a family member indicates that she was a Contreras, a descendant of a conquistador from a noble family of Segovia. Theirs was
a great name in Nicaragua, where descendants of conquistador Jorge
de Alvarado Contreras loom large in the elite and in the annals of the
nation since Roderigo de Contreras governed in the sixteenth century.
Early versions of Ferminia's name in the Nevada records (Sararis, Ser-
raras, Sararez, and so forth) are closer to Contreras; by 1890, no doubt
as a concession to stumbling Anglo tongues, she had simplified her
name to Sarras or Sarrias. Her first husband was a Flores, the surname
of four of her children, though she herself never used the name during
the period within our view. In 1876, when she was thirty-six, she came
to America accompanied by her young daughters: Conchetta, the oldest; Concepción, age twelve; Juanita (soon anglicized to Jennie), eight;
and Emma (possibly also an anglicized version of a Hispanic name),
five. Why she came and whether Flores was with her are among the
many black holes in her history. Probably, they disembarked at San
Francisco, a city she liked to visit when the urge came on her from time
to time to eat a fine meal or put on a gorgeous dress.[3]

By 1880 they were in the Nevada desert. Ferminia temporarily placed
her youngest daughters, Jennie and Emma, in the Nevada Orphans
Asylum in Virginia City. If she thought the rough new mining camps
of Belleville and Candelaria where she meant to go were no place for

61

Ferminia Sarras (courtesy Harlow Kiblinger,
author's collection).

children, she may well have been right. And if she thought little girls could have no part in the life she meant to lead, she was right about that as well. Conchetta seems to have gone with her and around 1881 married Julius Thomasson, a miner who later became a schoolteacher in Bodie, California.

The large role Hispanics had played in the development of the region no doubt had a good deal to do with Ferminia's presence in these mining camps: Belleville, on the western edge of the Candelaria Hills; Candelaria, where Ferminia also kept a cabin, several miles to the southeast; and Pickhandle Gulch (more properly known as Metallic City), a half mile from Candelaria. The first silver mines in the area (then known as Columbus) had been discovered by a party of Hispanic prospectors grubstaked by San Francisco interests in 1864. When the mining district was organized, many claims had Hispanic names—Libertad, Don Lajote, Zaragosa—and Hispanics held a virtual monopoly on the camp. The name of one of the locators on the first recorded claim, Maria Hurtado, suggests that another Hispanic woman prospector may have preceded Ferminia into these barren hills. Another name among these early locators may be linked to Ferminia's story—Parbelo Flores. The most important mining discovery in the district, the Northern Belle, was made by Anglos, however. Over the next sixteen years the Anglo gained control of the district, even going so far as to "rob the claims of their sonorous names and substituting his own ruder nomenclature," according to an early newspaper editor. Many Hispanics nonetheless continued to live and work in the area, including a Pablo Flores, age forty-five, listed in the 1875 Nevada state census but not in the 1880 records. Ferminia might have come to the Candelaria Hills to join a husband. Or perhaps she came to protect the interests of a husband or another relative recently deceased, the route by which many another woman prospector would enter the field. All the same, it is clear that if Parbelo, or Pablo, was her husband, he played no further part in her life after being the hook that drew her from the green, familiar world of Nicaragua into this alien place. Perhaps he had died or she had lost interest in him. When the youngest of her five children was born in Candelaria on 25 January 1881, the year Ferminia turned forty-one, his name was Joseph A. Marshall.[4]

Who was Joe Marshall's father? No doubt many contended for the honor. Women were a rarity in the Candelaria Hills, "a fact which, next to the great American game of draw poker, causes more rustling, contention and petty jealousies than all other causes combined," according to *True Fissure,* the Candelaria newspaper. This rivalry must have intensified when the favors of a fine-looking Spanish lady were the prize. Whoever he was, it seems unlikely that Ferminia formally married him. Certainly she never took his name. Ferminia Sarras she was in her first appearance in the Nevada records, albeit with many variants in the spelling of both her first and last names, and Ferminia Sarras she remained until the last month of her life, all her mining claims and properties owned by herself alone. The Esmeralda County record books do, however, yield several Marshalls, one of whom may have been the man who shared her bed. All are bachelors between twenty-five and thirty-two: Ferminia's taste for much younger men soon became well known. The first possibility is John Marshall, a young man of Portuguese birth who had probably anglicized his name. Though he is listed as a laborer in Aurora, some distance from the camps in the Candelaria Hills, he also prospected. This would have taken him throughout the area and perhaps enhanced his appeal in Ferminia's eyes through mastery of a calling she had begun to pursue. An 1880 discovery of Marshall's, the Big Indian, still offered promise enough to be worked anew a quarter-century later. Another candidate is A. (probably Antone) Marshall, a Candelaria miner born in the "W. Isles" (the Outer Hebrides). His ownership of four mules and a horse suggests that he may later have done freighting or wood chopping. Denuding the surrounding mountains of piñon and juniper to feed the hungry mills at Belleville and Candelaria was a large and lucrative business. In 1881 the steam plants at the Belleville mills consumed twenty-four cords a day, hauled from the mountains by long mule teams and stacked in massive piles that dwarfed men and animals.[5]

The last, and the most lurid, of the possibilities was Charley Marshall, a young man of twenty-five from Louisiana, a wood chopper, and a brutal killer. Charley abandoned wood chopping as winter drew near to work as a hostler in a Belleville stable. In December he embarked on a drunken "jamboree," and the stable owner hired the elderly and presumably more reliable Jack McCann to take his place. When Charley came staggering back from his binge with sickened stomach and aching head, McCann nursed him kindly. Nonetheless, as soon as he recovered, the ungrateful Charley began making threats against McCann for taking his job. These culminated on the night of 7 December in a bout of cursing, after which Charley shot McCann in the stomach. Returning to find McCann fallen across the threshold and still alive, Charley kicked the prostrate man until he ceased to moan. Unaware that the murder had been observed by a witness who had bedded down for the night in one of the stalls, Charley knocked around town until dawn, when a law officer arrested him and, in the absence of a jail, confined him in the baggage room of the Belleville Hotel.

A killing so heinous as this outraged even the none-too-delicate moral sensibilities of Belleville. At three o'clock the folowing morning eight armed and masked men entered the Belleville Hotel and demanded the key to the baggage room from the officer in charge, who yielded it without resistance. They gagged and bound Charley and pulled him into the street, where a silent crowd joined them. Since no tree in Belleville had grown tall enough for a hanging, they strung Charley Marshall up on the crane behind the blacksmith's shop. The coyotes that usually howled on the outskirts of town and the dogs that barked in reply had for once fallen silent. Only the harsh, grating sound of rope scraping over metal broke the stillness of the winter night.

The Vigilantes Make Him Stand on Nothing and Kick at the World

declared *True Fissure's* headline with grisly relish. Assuming that the murder of McCann occurred as *True Fissure* reported it, little could be said in Charley Marshall's defense, but it is well to bear in mind that local newspapers often sought to exonerate lynchers and a different picture sometimes emerges when a variety of sources are available. No effort was made to bring the members of the lynching party to justice.[6]

If the body that swung from the crane was indeed the father of Ferminia's unborn child, it would explain why the family believed him dead and he was never discussed. It would also conform with the tales of violence people told about Ferminia's amours. More than thirty years later a newspaper story alleged that all her husbands had died violently. Nevertheless, the void in her history where Joe's father is concerned might have another explanation. If the man was John, Antone, or an unknown Marshall who has eluded the record books, he could have disappeared from her life simply because, in the words of the Brazilian songwriter, "love is eternal as long as it lasts."[7]

The world where Ferminia loved and Joe was born had its subtle beauties. Spring wildflowers, tall yellow spires, golden daisies, mounds of white bloom, and orange penstemons appeared to float on invisible stems above the sands of the Soda Spring Valley. Mirages of illusory lakes shimmered over the white borax marshes. Greasewood cast a speckled green mantle over the low smooth folds of the nearer mountains, and in the farther distance the jutting crags and eternal snows of the Sierra made so magnificent a panorama that the stage driver would stop to admire it with lordly disdain for the schedules of his passengers.

Yet observers who recorded their impressions uniformly saw the Candelaria Hills as "the most desolate and barren country you can imagine," a hell on earth. Wells Drury, an early newspaper editor, wrote, "The only timber to be seen was the dwarfed greasewood which grows on ground that is too poor to sustain the more aristocratic sagebrush. As for water, there was none to be found in the district—except what was hauled there in barrels and tanks. . . . Baths were a luxury not excessively indulged in, nor was water as a beverage popular." The climate was extreme, as cold as zero or below in winter with occasional heavy snows, sometimes over one hundred degrees in summer, all the hotter in a treeless, shadeless cluster of frame buildings, adobe huts, and tin-roofed dugouts in the hillsides. Nearly every day the wind blew, strongly enough to rip a shack from its foundations, an icy blast in winter, a breath from a fiery furnace in summer, coating everyone and everything in dust. Clouds of it rose from the dry crushers at the mills. Heavy freight wagons rumbling fetlock deep in dust through the streets at every hour of the day and night churned up even more. The mills emitted noise along with the dust. A local engineer likened it to "the sound of breakers on the rocky shore mixed with a galloping horse and a railway train." In these cupped hills, where even the soft chirp of a canyon wren echoes resoundingly, the pounding roar must have gathered to deafening proportions. Amid the noise and the dust swarmed hordes of flies, attracted by the lack of sewers and the residents' habit of leaving offal in the streets. No wonder one early resident concluded, "Candelaria was a great camp. But it wasn't a good place to live."[8]

Roaring mills meant that the mines in the Candelaria Hills were outproducing any others in southwestern Nevada in this period. The Northern Belle alone was to send forth at least ten million dollars' worth in bars of silver bullion before litigation and the exhaustion of the ore body closed the company in 1884. But a "great camp" denotes something beyond mining production figures, in all likelihood the pulsing sense of life at full tide that Nellie Cashman had experienced in Pioche and the mining camp juxtaposition of coarseness and elegance in its most extreme form. In keeping with mining camp traditions of gourmet dining, the people of Candelaria ate fresh strawberries and drank champagne at the same time that hogs wandered through their shacks in search of scraps. So much champagne did they drink that great quantities of empty bottles were later found piled in a canyon. Crates from whiskey, another popular beverage, were a favorite material for home construction in Pickhandle Gulch, so named for the residents' proclivity for battling one another with pick handles, sometimes with fatal results.

Indeed, saloon fights became so common and so lightly regarded that *True Fissure* could comment only half-humorously, "No one killed or half murdered during the past week." With a population as ready to bet on a dogfight in the street as a throw of the dice or a race at the Belleville track, both Candelaria and Belleville strove to live up to their reputations as "good sporting towns" where the revelry went on all night. After midnight "tin can serenaders" paraded from house to house until their racket forced a sometimes reluctant host to invite them inside for liquid refreshment. Candelaria boasted thirteen saloons and not a single church, and Belleville upheld the same unblemished standard. Christmas was celebrated with "tarantula juice," the usual poker and faro, cockfighting, and something special—a dog-and-coyote fight.[9]

We can only imagine how the Spanish lady in the severe black dress and gold cross of the portrait fitted in. The report of Joe's birth by the *Territorial Enterprise* in Virginia City, where Ferminia was neither a local resident nor the wife of a distinguished U.S. senator or mining magnate, suggests that many years before people began to call her the Copper Queen she was a figure of some renown. All the same, neither her aristocratic lineage nor her position as a woman of note would have saved her from being classified by many mining camp denizens as a "greaser." None of the widescale violence against Hispanics that had disgraced San Francisco and the California gold country erupted in the Candelaria Hills, but many shared the prejudices of the day. Wells Drury observed that a local gunfighter who had lost face felt obliged to shoot a "Chilean" to restore his standing, and *True Fissure* published a poem on a Hispanic killed when falsely accused of stealing a horse, ending with the lines, "But a dead Greaser ain't no loss— / Come, all hands take a drink!" The Chinese (generally referred to in the local press as the "heathen Chinee") and the Shoshone also received their share of denigration, perhaps sharpened by an uncomfortable awareness among those of Anglo-Saxon derivation that the foreign-born and other races in the polyglot population of the Hills outnumbered them substantially. When mining production peaked in 1881–83, around eighteen-hundred people lived in Candelaria and Pickhandle Gulch together, with another six hundred or so in Belleville.[10]

Anglos may have attempted to maintain their sense of superiority, but in the Candelaria camps all races and nationalities mingled freely and shared in one another's entertainments. The observation that "we all turn out rag tag and bob tail" for every amusement was literally true. Whites and Chinese joined Indians wearing everything from rabbitskin robes and bright blankets to lace-trimmed gowns, jeans, and button necklaces in ceremonial dances that ended in intensive bouts of poker. When the Chinese teamsters with flying queues who whipped their teams down the grades with high-pitched screams celebrated the New Year, whites wholeheartedly participated in setting off firecrackers and bombs and visited Chinese homes to partake of the delicacies hospitably laid out for callers. The cries of the infant Joe Marshall, whose birth preceded Chinese New Year by only a few days, would have been lost in the sound of these explosions as the large Chinese population of the Hills paraded through the street outside. And nearly everyone, of all races and nationalities, turned out for a Spanish fandango. No doubt Ferminia packed away the severe black dress of a Spanish lady for more festive garb. The names of two of her mining claims, the Whiskey and the Brandy, suggest revelry and good times.[11]

Aside from fandangos, the mining camps probably interested Ferminia less than what lay in the mountains beyond. She soon added a house in Luning, a tiny settlement on the new Carson and Colorado Railway line that linked the Hills with northern Nevada, to those she already possessed in Belleville and Candelaria, but all her dwellings sound minimal, a small stone hut, a "cabine," or a "seller," not always in the better parts of town (one stood beside a Chinese laundry), no more than a convenient pied-à-terre where she could rest for a while when she came in from the mountains. She staked her first claim, appropriately named the Central American, in the Belleville district in April 1883. Joe, then a toddler of two, would surely have been left behind, perhaps in the care of his older sister, Conchetta. Ferminia would not have had an easy time on this first recorded prospecting foray. Gale-force winds, overcast skies, rain, and even three late snowstorms struck the hills that April.[12] But the obsession that was to consume the rest of her life began.

Both Ferminia's properties and her family expanded during the eighties. The camps in the Candelaria Hills had started sliding into decline, and in 1885 Ferminia added to her scattered dwellings a homestead at Sand Springs and a toll road that wound down through the gray mountain walls of Tule Canyon into Death Valley. Whether she operated the toll road herself is not known, nor can we be certain whether she ranched at the homestead. She may have been more inclined to use it as another convenient stopping place. Ferminia was now a grandmother several times over. Conchetta had given birth to the two eldest of her four children; Jennie, reclaimed from the orphanage on the Comstock, had married Edward Enright, an Irish-born miner in the Candelaria Hills, and in 1885 at seventeen had given birth to Bill, the eldest of her four surviving children (four others would not survive). Though scarcely grandmotherly in any but the genealogical sense, Ferminia had reached an age when it would no longer be possible to trace her lovers through the surnames of her children. All the same, when she christened a new mining claim the Amant ("lover"), it may have been a sign that she had a man who pleased her.[13]

Indications are that he was Archie McCormack, Canadian-born and twelve years younger than Ferminia, first appearing in the Esmeralda County records in the mid-eighties. Since he owned no taxable property, he does not seem to have been a man of means, even by the minimal standards of the region. As with the shadowy father of Joe Marshall, the nature of their liaison remains unclear. One source states that McCormack was her husband, but Ferminia did not consider herself married until 1895, and even then her idea of marriage obviously did not entail cozy domesticity around the hearth. McCormack was never in residence with her when the census taker came around. She never adopted his name, and she continued her independent style of life, taking many other lovers. In all likelihood, theirs was a consensual union of the kind common in Latin America for centuries and widespread in the mining camps among both Hispanics and Anglos, an off-and-on affair. Although McCormack evidently prospected, staking the Woodpecker claim in 1886, he failed to pursue it on the same scale as Ferminia. He had another accomplishment that may have enhanced his appeal to her. According to a *Los Angeles Times* story in 1914, she chose him because he was a gunman who could defend her claims.[14]

Ferminia's prospecting was beginning to carry her farther afield. The Amant claim and the New Find, both recorded in 1888, were the first she staked in the Santa Fe district, where she would one day make her fortune. This district is in two parts, one in the Garfield Hills west of Luning, the other in the Pilot Mountains to the east, a bold escarpment of crystalline limestone rising nearly eight thousand feet and taking on the faded purple sheen of ancient silks in a certain light. Before she was done Ferminia had claims in both regions, and she had probably learned every twist in the sinuous canyons, every deer trail that skirted the ridges, and every hidden spring nestled in the rocks. South of the road that leads through a mountain gap to the Gabbs Valley, there is no easy way into the Pilot Range. From Luning one can ascend through New York Canyon by a trail, sometimes only a few feet wide, that winds torturously between nearly vertical canyon walls. Luning is soon invisible—even when in sight, it is barely visible from a distance, a feeble human scratch on the infinitude of mountain and plain.

One emerges from the canyon into another world, a high mountain valley with pale crests sparsely dotted with juniper and sage. It is a world of utter silence, without birdsong, insect hum, or animal scrabble in the brush. Even Nevadans born and raised in the desert remark on its desolation. And yet her family relates that Ferminia delighted in her prospecting journeys. Perhaps she saw beauty here, in the vista, from one of the northerly ridges, of the Gabbs Valley to the north, eroded mountains sliding down to the valley floor, splotches of cloud shadow like inky pools, range on range, rose and cream-colored in the foreground to pale lavender in the far distance. Perhaps she took pleasure in the remoteness of this secret valley from all human worlds. And not least, she believed that riches lay hidden here. She would have taken note of the blue and green shards of malachite and azurite scattered like jewels on the sandy earth. They showed that this was copper country. No doubt the future Copper Queen had learned to test for copper by pouring ammonia into a glass of acid and pulverized ore to see if the contents turned a dramatic blue. Alternatively, she may have dipped an iron wire into the test glass and watched to see if it developed a copper coating. Or she may have devised tests of her own.[15]

She customarily went out alone, on foot, wearing boots and pants and carrying a pack on her back. Few strapping male prospectors carried a pack over forty pounds, and Ferminia was no Amazon, being short and compactly built. But she was known for her remarkable strength, and in this desert country, where game and water were scarce, the prospector had to carry everything he might need. At a minimum, this included water, beans (the prospector's staple), dried fruit, the makings of sourdough bread or tortillas, a piece of canvas that could be used for bedding or a kind of hammock, a pick, an ax for firewood, a knife, and a frying pan. As a journalist had observed of the gold rushers in South Pass, Wyoming, "one can distinguish a thorough mountaineer by nothing more characteristic than his careful attention to trifles. . . . He carries nothing with him on a journey but what he absolutely needs, and the loss of one little trifle may occasion the most serious inconvenience." Other more luxurious items, such as a coffeepot and cup, tin plate, extra clothes, and bedroll, were optional, and Ferminia had to leave plenty of room in her pack for the ore samples she carried out. Probably she also packed a gun, for wolves and

packs of coyotes still roamed these hills, as well as men more dangerous than wolves.[16]

Thirst and exposure posed greater dangers, however. Stories of prospectors who succumbed to these perils abound, including one from
the immediate area that underscores Ferminia's survival skills. In 1909
Helen Rope, a cultured and well-born English girl who kept house for
her brother while he prospected in the vicinity of Luning in an effort
to recoup the family fortunes, thought she would try prospecting herself and set off with a burro and a canteen. Her brother finally found
her in the desert several days later, barely alive from lack of food and
water and violently insane. Screaming and struggling along the way,
she was taken to an insane asylum.[17]

Others before this unfortunate young woman had also imagined
that prospecting was an easy diversion. Louise Clappe, at Rich Bar during the California gold rush, related that the miners often salted the
sand in order to give the ladies who joined "pleasure parties" at the diggings something to show for their visits: "the dear creatures go home
with their treasures, firmly believing that mining is the prettiest pastime in the world." Clappe herself had formerly shared this illusion: "I
myself thought, (now don't laugh,) that one had but to saunter grace-
fully along romantic streamlets, on sunny afternoons, with a parasol
and white kid gloves, perhaps, and to stop now and then to admire the
scenery, and carelessly rinse out a small panful of yellow sand, (without detriment to the white kids, however, so easy did I fancy the whole
process to be), in order to fill one's workbag with the most beautiful
and rare specimens of the precious mineral. Since I have been here, I
have discovered my mistake."[18]

The very idea of a woman as a serious miner remained unthinkable,
even for authors of the day committed to radical change for the working woman. *Our Girls,* written by Dio Lewis in the 1870s, set forth the
jobs suitable for women who had not succeeded in marrying and taking their proper places at home. Their flexible fingers would make them
ideal dentists and watch repairers; their invulnerability to the temptations of gambling and theft suited them to be bank clerks; their high
morals would enable them to cleanse the legal profession. Although the
author also envisaged a female revolution in an array of other fields,

including cooperative farming and carpentry, the broadest imagination could not conceive of the woman who packed out ore on her back in the desert hills through blazing sun and winter snow.[19]

By the mid-nineties Ferminia had shifted her base of operations to Silver Peak, a quiet mining town of adobes on the edge of the white, sparkling Clayton Playa roughly fifty miles south of the Candelaria Hills. As the Candelaria camps declined over the years, pioneers from the area drifted down to Silver Peak. Ferminia acquired an adobe of her own north of Jagel's Saloon and a corral, in addition to her other properties. This may have been a period of financial stringency for her, as it was for many Nevadans caught in the depression that gripped the state. It was said that she had made a fortune in the palmy days at Belleville and Candelaria only to lose it through stocks and bad mining investments, by no means an unusual reversal among the mining camp crowd. A ditty composed in Candelaria went in part:

> I had money in the bank, and friends in every rank
> Of society, wherever I might go.
> On a margin stocks I bought, like other fools was caught
> In trying by that means to make a raise; My broker sold me out,
> I then turned right about
> For buying on a margin seldom pays.
>
> In Candelaria, once again, like many other men,
> Through mining stock I hope to make a raise;
> If the Northern Belle goes up, on wine again I'll sup.
> It's the only stock at present here that pays.[20]

Ferminia's generosity may also have depleted her funds. So long as she had something to give, she never turned away anyone hungry or destitute.

A newspaper article later claimed that during these hard times she worked as a laundress in Silver Peak and other mining camps of the region and became well known as a "picturesque character." Although the source of her livelihood over the quarter-century preceding the era when her mining claims began to sell remains obscure, no other evidence supports this suggestion, and the inaccuracy of the article's portrayal of Ferminia as an ignorant Mexican Indian casts doubts on its reliability. It seems more likely that she derived a small income from her toll road in Tule Canyon, where the sporadic operations of placer miners created some traffic; rented her homestead; and panned a little gold dust from her claims.[21]

If true, another story from the same source illuminates Ferminia's character. Throughout these lean years, when she had not yet sold a single claim, her faith in the value of her mining properties remained boundless. Her starry-eyed stories about her rich gold and copper claims became a joke, and people would ask about her mines just to hear her talk. One mining broker recalled, "The people used to josh her about her mine, but she took their quips good-naturedly and always replied that her property was one of the richest in the country."[22] We may conjecture that a descendant of the conquistadors commonly dismissed as a greaser and a Mexican Indian washerwoman had long ago learned to cultivate a sense of humor.

In 1899, after eleven years of finding no signs of mineral she considered worthy of development, she permanently abandoned Silver Peak and moved north once more to embark on an intensive period of prospecting in the Santa Fe district, staking claims in June, July, and September. Though usually alone, she worked with Joseph Siegel in lining out the Schley claim that fall. The census taker found her at home in 1900. Her daughter Concepción was living with her, but the rest of her family had temporarily scattered. After Conchetta's death around 1893, only one of her children seems to have enjoyed a close relationship with their grandmother. Jennie and her family were living in California. McCormack was off in an ephemeral camp to the south called Siegelton (no doubt after Joseph Siegel), along with Joe Marshall, now nineteen, short and dark-haired. Although Joe had learned prospecting from his mother, he more often worked as a cowboy in the Fish Lake and Gabbs valleys.[23]

Ferminia made her real home in the mountains during those years. In January, March, and even on 26 December 1901 she recorded more claims. Time would show that she had turned herself into one of the best prospectors in the region. Twenty-five additional claims and six mill sites followed in 1902, in the sixty-second year of her life. Ever since she staked the Central American, it was evident that the names of many of Ferminia's claims had meanings, if the riddle could be read. She named the Jennie and the Dolly Emma for her daughters; the Joseph for her son; the Nelly, the Salley, and the Luesa probably for friends; the Archie for her sometime husband, McCormack. But what of the claims she called the Harry, the Bill Thomas, the Johnny Bull, the Frank, the Bill Englis, and the Tom Moro? Were they friends or lovers, past and present? And why did she name one claim the Red Light?[24]

After 1900 the entire landscape of the Nevada mining world altered. The central Nevada mining boom at Tonopah and Goldfield transformed the fortunes of a state sunk in depression and hard times since the decline of the Comstock, and the population exploded. Prospectors set out in force to comb the hills, with claim jumpers not far behind, increasing the need for McCormack's fighting abilities. Investors, long reluctant to sink their money in Nevada mining propositions, began to fantasize about the fortunes lying in wait for those clever enough to snatch the next Tonopah in the making, and Ferminia's mines increased in value accordingly.

Her first sale came in June 1902 when investors bonded twenty-five of her copper claims at eight thousand dollars each. Often these purchases failed to become final, but the initial payments nonetheless enriched the prospector sufficiently for the customary indulgence, a grand spree. Now, whenever the shacks of Luning began to look wretched and godforsaken, instead of an oasis of rest at the gateway to a world of promise, when the mountain canyons felt as forbidding and confining as prison walls, Ferminia could betake herself to San Francisco, and she did. As her great-grandson Albert Bradshaw heard the story:

> She kind of liked the other side of life too, you know, the nice side, the good side, the fancy side. So she'd go to L.A. or San Francisco, preferably San Francisco, and she'd get the finest hotel there was, and go out and buy the finest clothes there was, shoes, hats, dresses—the whole act. And dine and wine and everything, just right up to the first class. . . . She would hire a limousine and a chauffeur, and if she got a little bit lonesome, why she'd go out and get a gigolo, and they'd go out and have a big

75

Mina, Nevada, in 1910 (Central Nevada Historical Society).

party, and have a good time. And pretty soon the money was dwindling pretty fast, so she'd say, "I guess I'd better get back to the desert." She'd come back . . . and she'd get rid of all the clothes, the hats, and the shoes, give them away or whatever, and don her overalls, and take to the hills again and find another mine.[25]

One cannot resist observing that when liberated from the cloistered world of the upper-class Latin American woman in the place rightly known as a "man's country," Ferminia used her freedom much as a man of similar background would have done. In this tradition, wealth was to be enjoyed and generously spread among one's friends, not devoted to the civic purposes of churches and organized charities; individualism was the normal mode, not the galling restraints of teamwork and joint enterprise; and a good deal of blatant philandering was both a pleasurable assertion of the self and a status symbol, not in the least damaging to one's reputation. If Ferminia had been a man, her compatriots would have admiringly called her *muy hombre*.[26]

After her taste of city life it was back to the mountains, much in the style of her aristocratic forebears, who preferred a life of struggle over idleness, but some of the work she long had done with her own strong hands became easier. Now she could afford to hire men to do the annual assessment work on her claims. A cryptic newspaper item on McCormack's arrest on a charge of assault with intent to kill in the summer of 1905 does not reveal whether he had acted in defense of Ferminia's mines. In that same summer came recognition of a kind rarely given a Hispanic woman in Nevada. Railroad construction to serve the central Nevada mining boom necessitated a freight and passenger terminal in the Soda Spring Valley. Although Sodaville was the logical location, a local speculator pegged the land at an exorbitant price, and railroad officials decided to build a new town some distance to the north. The *Walker Lake Bulletin* reported that it would be named after the woman who owned some of the most promising mines in the surrounding mountains—Ferminia. Her family emphatically insists that her name was correctly pronounced "Ferminia," but common usage had long since simplified it to Fermina, much as her surname had been reduced to Sarras, while variable spellings of both proliferated. Moreover, everyone in the area knew her by her first name, ignoring the last. So it was that the town of Mina sprang into existence full blown by the decree of the railroaders in August 1905. At once it became a bustling scene, as passenger cars bursting with gold rushers and freight cars of goods rumbled steadily down the line toward the boom camps to return laden with gold and silver ore.[27]

The next month headlines announced the sale of the "Famous Sarras Group of 40 Claims" to a Boston syndicate for ninety thousand dollars. Those who had formerly mocked Ferminia's faith in the value of her mines were obliged to acknowledge their mistake. The newspaper went on to say that Ferminia had accepted the syndicate's offer after rejecting several previous tenders from other sources, because it entailed the immediate payment of forty thousand dollars in cash. There is no doubt that Ferminia preferred cash, and she liked it in gold. Bradshaw's mother had watched one of Ferminia's mine sales: "They made the deal in the kitchen there, and there was a large sum of gold money for those times—I think she said eight thousand dollars in twenty-dollar gold pieces—there on the kitchen table for this piece of property." Rightly distrusting banks, in view of the numerous Nevada bank failures of the period, Ferminia stashed the gold coins in a safer place—her chicken coop. Well she knew that if anyone disturbed the chickens they would squawk and raise a fuss.[28]

She eluded a newsman anxious to interview her about her deal with the syndicate with smiling good humor: "I no savvy English. Me Spanish woman. Can't talk to you." Joe Marshall served as her spokesman. How much English she really savvied remains an open question. Like many Hispanics, she no doubt had often encountered Anglos who screamed at her in broken English on the theory that high volume and grotesque gestures made them intelligible; at such times it would have been entertaining to bear in mind the saying among her countrymen, "God speaks in Spanish, and the Devil speaks in English." Ferminia declared to the census taker that she spoke English, and if it was true that people used to tease her into telling tales of her fabulous mines for their amusement, she must have told them in the devil's own tongue. Probably, the truth of the matter was that Ferminia spoke English when it suited her.[29]

Just now it did not suit her, because she had decided to extricate herself from the deal with the syndicate. Soon her lawyers were in federal court arguing that "gross advantage" had been taken of Ferminia because her inability to speak English and her lack of business experience had led her to mistake a deal involving a good deal of potentially worthless stock for a cash offer. Accounts of the negotiations, however, make clear that Ferminia's lack of business experience had not prevented her from revoking an earlier agreement when she thought a better one had come along. Evidently, the syndicate caved in before her charges. Over the next two years she received regular payments on a set of claims she had bonded, either from the Boston group or from other investors.[30]

In 1907 newspapers announced the sale of another group of her claims, this time for sixty-five thousand dollars to a San Francisco brokerage firm. No doubt another stash of gold coins went into the chicken coop and the champagne corks popped in San Francisco once again. A newspaper report on this latest sale called Ferminia "one of the most remarkable characters the gold regions ever produced" and added that her advancing years had altered her customary way of life not at all: "Dressed in kahki and leggings, she hikes over the hills all day long, and in spite of her age and effeminancy can outwalk the ordinary prospector."[31]

As Ferminia grew older the configuration of the family that circled around her changed. By 1910, when Ferminia turned seventy, Concepción had died. McCormack had also disappeared. According to a 1914 story in the *Los Angeles Times,* he had been killed around 1906 by a trespasser at one of the mines Ferminia owned, and she eventually claimed a widow's exemption for tax assessment purposes. She told the census taker that she had been twice married, but some believed she had mislaid a few husbands and had actually married four or five times. Perhaps Ferminia's definition of marriage differed from theirs. Jennie, dark, wiry, and wild, without her mother's pride or good looks, had returned from California, leaving her three younger children in an orphanage there, as Ferminia had left her behind in the orphanage on the Comstock thirty years earlier when she went off to the Candelaria Hills; Jennie then broke with her husband of twenty-six years and headed for Goldfield with a new husband, in search of adventure and good times. After a while she brought two of her children to Goldfield, and Ferminia apparently also spent time there, acquiring some properties. When Jennie later came to Luning, she and her family were not invited to live with Ferminia but were installed in a worse shack a certain distance behind hers. Apparently, Ferminia reposed greater trust in Joe Marshall, who was probably closer to her than her other children. He had relinquished the cowboy life of his earlier days for mining and prospecting like his mother and lived nearby during her last years with his wife, her small nephew, and a daughter. When the census taker came around in 1910 before Jennie's return from Goldfield, he found Jennie's little son Tom, then seven, living with Ferminia. Tom may have come to know his grandmother well, but throughout his life he maintained a total silence where she was concerned.[32]

On certain subjects Ferminia made herself very clear to the census taker. In the 1910 manuscript census "Sp." is darkly penned in above Central America as her birthplace and that of her parents. One can almost feel her ordering him to write it there. "Me Spanish woman." Those Anglos who called her a Mexican Indian in their newspapers and made maps on which they designated some of her best claims the

"Mexican Woman's Mine" failed to understand how profoundly they had slighted her. Little did they know how significant a role blood played in heavily Indian Central America. To belong to the small elite of Spanish blood meant to rule on the basis of kinship; not to belong meant loss of status and privilege. And Mexico, though no doubt a fine country, was a very different place from Nicaragua, the land of poets. The responses Ferminia made to the census taker's other questions showed an equally strong sense of who and what she was. Jennie might quite correctly give her occupation as "none"; Ferminia told him firmly that her occupation was "miner" and she was the owner of copper mines.[33]

Copper mining in the Santa Fe district had stagnated from 1909 to 1911. The opening of enormous deposits near Ely in eastern Nevada and in Bingham Canyon, Utah, meant closure for smaller mines unless they could match the low production costs of these large-scale operations. Miners and geologists down to the present day testify to the high copper content of the Santa Fe ore, and Ferminia's claims were second to none, but the deposits did not prove to be extensive, though no one in the early twentieth century could as yet be certain about that. The gross yield for copper, silver, gold, and lead from 1906 through 1921 probably did not exceed $2.5 million, compared with more than $166 million at Ely from 1908 to 1920. Production problems in the Santa Fe district included the absence of water, beyond the trickling of a few meager springs, and a paucity of roads, which compelled some roadless mines to sled their ore down the steep escarpment to loading platforms. In 1912, with the opening of a smelter not far to the northwest, the outlook for the Santa Fe district turned brighter, and Ferminia sold several claims to George Giroux. Leasers began development work at several others along the lines followed by most operations in the district—open cuts and shallow shafts and tunnels but no deep mining. The best of Ferminia's many claims, so far as can be determined today, were those grouped under various names—the Pilot Range group, the Fermina Sarrias Mines, the Mexican Woman's Mine, the Copper Queen, the Emma—in Giroux Canyon.[34]

Another pile of gold coins on the kitchen table meant another handsome young man, even when Ferminia was in her seventies. But the next time her better judgment deserted her. Domingo Velasco, a young Hispanic of thirty, worked as her faithful and attentive servant for several years and eventually became her lover. When Ferminia optioned another group of claims in 1914, she deposited the funds in a Los Angeles bank. As it turned out she would have done better to keep stashing them in the chicken coop. On vacation in Los Angeles, Velasco managed to withdraw the entire sum and ran away to South America with a woman his own age. Ferminia traveled to Los Angeles that June, apparently far more anxious to find Velasco than to recover the money.

Getting wind of this juicy tale, the *Los Angeles Times* regaled readers with lurid headlines:

Life's Lessons Go for Naught
Much-Married Copper Queen Victimized by Lover
Here on Trail of Him and of Vanished Thousands
Bride of Five Gunmen; Past Seventy Years Old.

The newspaper went on to say, "After life-long experience with men, socially and commercially, including five marriages and a successful business career, which won for her the title of the 'Copper Queen of Nevada,' Senora Fermina Sarrias, a descendant of a royal family of the Montezumas, thought that she understood the male sex. But she didn't." Her photograph showed the ruined remnants of beauty, features coarsened in a face still strong and firmly modeled, the white rose-petal complexion of the portrait so browned by the desert sun that the *Times* can hardly be blamed for thinking her a descendant of the Montezumas, and large dark eyes so arresting that their tragic gaze haunts the memory. Not just age but life had shattered the authoritative serenity of the woman in the portrait.[35]

With her legendary strength fast ebbing, Ferminia had less than a year to live. On 1 February 1915, on her deathbed, she made a will. Several, but not all, of her numerous descendants received bequests. Her mines remained much on her mind to the end; she commanded her executors to work them or forfeit their rights in the estate. Then she was dead at seventy-four. Still known throughout Nevada as the Copper Queen, she did not pass unremarked. The local newspaper wrote of her, "She is one of the last of those brave spirits who dared the desert's fierce glare in Nevada's primitive days and blazed the trails that others might follow."[36]

Her descendants believe Ferminia married yet again at the end of her life. As before, this last lover was much younger than she, all of thirty-five years this time. Probate records suggest that he was Fermine Arriaga, an immigrant from Mexico, who is named along with Joe Marshall and Jennie as an administrator of Ferminia's estate. Arriaga, a poor and debt-ridden laborer in the mountain wood camps, probably had great expectations of this marriage. When he learned after her death that Ferminia had left him no money, he swore in his disappointed rage that he would cut the gold teeth from her mouth. Her family, of course, did not allow him near the body. Ferminia was buried in the tiny cemetery at Luning beneath a large and imposing monument worthy of the Copper Queen. At intervals Joe Marshall's wife fashioned paper flowers for it, and the youngest of her children, the one who may have loved her best, took his family to visit her grave.[37]

The monument, stolen by vandals, has vanished now. It is believed to have stood atop the large mound in the cemetery. For years Ferminia's story was lost as well. Members of her family never spoke of their colorful ancestor. Her great-granddaughter, Louisa Enright McDonald, commented, "I think they had a black spot in their background they didn't want anyone to know. . . . They wouldn't tell." Albert Bradshaw concurred that "there was something in the woods" about which they maintained silence. Part of the reason was the desire of Bradshaw's Anglo father to suppress all knowledge of his children's Hispanic heritage. Bradshaw never heard who his great-grandmother was or what an extraordinary life she had lived until an attorney and local historian who had known Ferminia told him about her. Then he began to ask questions and pay attention, but only fragments of the story could be recovered at that late date.

Still, Ferminia's prospecting and mining continued over three generations. Joe Marshall followed these pursuits throughout his life and faithfully maintained the Copper Queen Mine. Her grandson Bill Enright supplemented his usual job as a bartender in Mina with prospecting, which finally killed him. When he failed to return from a prospecting trip, rescuers found him with his feet in a lake perishing from

heat and thirst. More than a century after Ferminia staked the Central
American, Albert Bradshaw still walked the desert prospecting and
mining. Today, long after passing from the hands of her family, Ferminia's mines have at last come into their own. Giroux Canyon is now
the scene of major mining operations, with dumps terraced like Maya
pyramids, rows of trucks with wheels taller than a man, dirt roads the
breadth of highways, and a heap leaching pond larger than early-day
Luning, all for the purpose of extracting the microscopic gold too low-
grade to process in the days of the Copper Queen.[38] The town named
Mina in Ferminia's honor, a tiny hamlet now, survives, although her
place in it faded from view for years.

What became of all the gold coins counted out on the kitchen table
in Ferminia's Luning shack has long been a matter of conjecture. The
main value of the estate, and it was a substantial one by the standards
of the time and place, resided in her remaining mines. Perhaps she had
spent lavishly on her royal sprees as fast as the money had come into
her hands, and Velasco had stolen the last of it. Her obituary tactfully
noted that she had made and lost several "comfortable fortunes" from
her mines.

Yet the image of Ferminia that has come down to her descendants is
that of a secretive woman who became increasingly distrustful toward
the end of her life. Formerly known for her warm heart, her ready
sympathies, and her generosity toward everyone who appealed to her,
she began to believe that people were stealing from her. In short, she
turned into just the kind of woman who might have buried her gold
in a cast-iron pot. A project to visit Luning with a metal detector collapsed after the death of the last family member who could point out
where Ferminia's chicken coop had stood. Bradshaw thought it just as
likely that Ferminia would have buried her gold in the mountains she
knew so well.

Then would she not have hidden a map somewhere? Ferminia's portrait had gone to Joe Marshall. When his end drew near, he gave it to his
foster son, Harlow Kiblinger, with the cryptic injunction, "Never let
this out of your hands." At least one of Ferminia's relatives interpreted
these words to mean that the portrait contained a clue to Ferminia's
lost gold and ripped away the backing in a fruitless search for a trea-

sure map. Kiblinger did not appear to believe in buried treasure. Refusing all offers despite his poverty-stricken circumstances, he kept the portrait of the woman in the severe black dress and the gold cross until the end of his life as an object of talismanic significance and the only beautiful thing he possessed.[39]

When I talked with the ailing Kiblinger in his Hawthorne trailer, I knew I was in the presence of the last living witness, the only one left who had seen Ferminia in the flesh. I told him I had read two different accounts about her: according to one, she was an uneducated Mexican Indian washerwoman; the other maintained that she was a lady of royal Spanish blood. Which did he think was true? Kiblinger, a thin, one-armed, gray ghost of a man with a hacking cough, half raised himself from his couch and answered in a hoarse whisper, "Royal Spanish descent." And there it rests.

But Ferminia is the stuff of which legends are made, and not merely run-of-the-mill legends of buried treasure. She takes on a life of her own in the imagination. One pictures her in an elegant San Francisco restaurant, sipping a glass of port. Across the damask-covered table from her is a young man a little too sleek and fancily dressed. "¿Qué es tu vida?" [How do you live?] he asks, eager to hear about the rich mines belonging to the Copper Queen. She thinks of the far mountains. Soon she will return there to make her way through the canyons with her pack on her back. The hunger for silence and space is already growing within her. "My dear young friend," she murmurs, "you could not possibly imagine." She strokes his smooth young wrist with a work-roughened and jewel-encrusted hand and smiles. In the dark cavern of her mouth a gold tooth gleams like a broken promise.

# THREE

# "Hustlers of No Mean Ability": Women on Their Own

In the distance beyond the sandy plain and the serrated crest of the striped mountain lay the Death Valley country, scene of dark mountain peaks, sand dunes shifted by the whistling winds, cracked and waterless expanses, trails winding through surreal golden canyons devoid of vegetation, and profound silences that magnified the beating of the heart. Myths to quicken the pulse of a prospector swirled there with the sandstorms that dimmed the mountains and the sun. The Lost Breyfogle, the Lost Gunsight, the Lost Pegleg all had appeared and disappeared in these brilliant blue spaces much as the Amargosa River sank from sight to run silently under the sands. Even if the silver ledge optimistically christened the "Wonder of the World" had not been discovered in the Panamint Range in the 1870s, something about this place suggested secrets yet to be plumbed. As historian Richard Lingenfelter has written, "it is a land of illusion, a place in the mind, a shimmering mirage of riches, mystery, and death." More than one prospector had forfeited his life in this eerie landscape, crazed by heat and parched by thirst when he lost his way or murdered by one of the dangerous men who slipped like cloud shadows across Death Valley.[1]

When Lillian Malcolm set off from Rhyolite, Nevada, to prospect in Death Valley in 1905, both the dangers and the possibilities ahead must have loomed large in the minds of many who gathered to witness her departure, but the sole reporter in the crowd seemed preoccupied with Malcolm's clothes. Because women prospectors usually wore pants, their garb attracted a great deal of notice and comment—or worse. In early California a woman in trousers risked arrest and punishment for the visual challenge she posed to traditional sex roles. Marie Pantalon, whose sobriquet referred to her clothes, came to prefer masculine garb and continued to wear it after she ceased prospecting and invested her fortune in a thriving vineyard. Instead of indulging in conventional feminine extravagance on a bonnet feathered with Russian cocks' plumage, a velvet muff decorated with a stuffed owl's head, fifteen-button kid gloves, a ball gown with a long train trimmed with trails of flowers, and other fashions of the day, she disguised herself as a man when she traveled in Europe. When she decided to merchandise her wines herself as a Virginia City liquor dealer, she prudently applied to the city board of aldermen for permission to wear men's clothes, which was granted at the discretion of the chief of police. According to a sarcastic account in the *Territorial Enterprise* of Virginia City, Marie's special dispensation aroused resentment among other women who felt they should enjoy similar license.[2]

San Francisco proved less tolerant of Marie's eccentricities than a mining town such as Virginia City. Visiting there in 1871, Marie was arrested, fined, and forced to "don the proper habiliments of her sex." Although these legal penalties gradually ceased to be invoked, fascination with, and often condemnation of, the woman in unorthodox attire continued. The author of a 1906 article on central Nevada mining related his encounters in the desert with "unexpected objects"— women prospectors—and predictably described their appearance: "She [the woman prospector] scorns high heels and long skirts and all such femininities. Shod with high, stoutly made, thick-soled boots that conceal all the ankle that a short khaki skirt would otherwise disclose, and attired in sombrero and khaki tunic, she tramps over the desert in a most business-like way, and handles a prospector's hammer as skillfully as her Eastern sisters would handle a fan." This fixation on clothes may well have been influenced by the image of the dime novel heroine. Since 1878 Deadwood Dick's female counterparts—Wild Edna, Hurricane Nell, Phantom Moll, and above all, Calamity Jane— had turned into athletic Amazons wearing men's clothes and able to "outrun, out-ride, out-shoot, out-lasso, and out-yell" any man around.[3] When newsmen saw the woman prospector, an athletic Amazon in men's clothes, fully capable of wielding a drill and trekking through the wilderness for weeks, and often quite beautiful, they must have had the same sensation of seeing a familiar tale made flesh that they would have experienced on beholding a young woman in a ball gown and glass slippers alight from a pumpkin coach.

Despite the comment and censure that men's clothes provoked, many women prospectors persisted in wearing trousers, for several reasons. The discomfort and inconvenience of struggling to prospect in long skirts outweighed both their own upbringing on appropriate feminine behavior and the common inclination to defer to community standards. Women independent enough to swim against the tide in their choice of an occupation were unlikely to be conformists in matters of dress. For those unable to command respect on the scale of Nellie Cashman, men's clothes offered a disguise that some women on the frontier used to protect themselves from sexual molestation. In addition to protection, some saw men's clothes as the passport enabling them to enter a world of opportunities that otherwise remained closed to women.

These elements were clearly in the mind of Mountain Charley, as well as Marie Pantalon. Charley later wrote of her decision to "dress myself in male attire, and seek for a living in this disguise among the avenues which are so religiously closed against my sex." She carefully schooled herself to pass as a boy, cutting her hair, trying on the unfamiliar outfit, and "endeavoring by constant practice to accustom myself to its peculiarities and to feel perfectly at home." At first she ventured out only at night, later dared the daylight, and finally felt free to come and go as she pleased: "So rapidly did I progress, that at the end of three weeks I went anywhere and everywhere without the slightest fear of suspicion or detection." In fact, her disguise proved an incomplete success. Many in the Colorado mining camps where she went adventuring seem to have realized that Charley was a woman and tolerated her masculine clothing as a harmless peculiarity. A newspaperman who knew her in those days noted that she always had "a watchful look in her eyes, especially when approaching a strange crowd."[4] Mountain Charley had good reason to be watchful, as her close brush with gang rape would show.

Lillian Malcolm's clothes on the day of her departure for Death Valley were never intended to disguise her gender. Nor were they working clothes (her khaki work pants had been packed inside her saddlebags). Rather, she had dressed to make an impression—and she did. The *Bull-*

Lillian Malcolm, as drawn by Arthur Buel
during her Death Valley days in 1905
(Nevada Historical Society).

*frog (Nevada) Miner*'s commentary on her "Death Valley trousseau" noted that her dress was shorter than the conventional women's riding habit but at least it met the tops of her tan-colored men's boots, thus sparing the crowd the shock of a glimpse of her legs. The *Miner* suspected vanity in her choice of a light felt hat too narrow-brimmed to offer sufficient protection from the desert sun and tentatively concluded, after critical scrutiny, that she might be called pretty, though it is clear that the soft and sweet connotations of that word were lacking. A drawing of her from the period shows her hat worn at a jaunty angle that accords with her resolute, defiant expression and the tension in her erect posture. Hers was a strong and somewhat angular face, firm of jaw, that must have been striking on the stage, for Lillian had been an actress. The way she had braided her long dark hair and knotted it with numerous white ribbons in what the *Miner's* reporter called a "rather fantastic effect" suggested an actress's showmanship. Mounted beside her were the three men in her party, prospectors Tom McCabe and George Peget and newspaperman Anthony McCauley, but they blended into the scenery as mere supporting players.[5] No one recorded what they wore or whether any of them might be called handsome. Lillian Malcolm was, and meant to be, the star.

Unfortunately, we know less about her early life than we do about her Death Valley trousseau. She was born in 1868 in the Northeast, or possibly Scotland, and was said to be of good family. She grew up to become an actress appearing on Broadway with Frederick Warde. Though many a farm girl with arms deep in the suds of a dishpan might have considered the life of a New York actress glamorous and exciting, it offered insufficient adventure for Lillian. When Klondike fever swept the country, she was infected and in 1898, her thirtieth year, headed north for Dawson over the fearsome Chilkoot Trail alone with sled and dog team. One wonders if along the way she encountered and received advice from a veteran musher in the small, select company of women who passed over the Chilkoot that year—Nellie Cashman. The scenario seems psychologically implausible, however, because both these women clearly preferred the company of men. How an actress, with no known experience with the far North, or even with roughing it out of doors, survived an ordeal that defeated half those who set out for the Klondike must have been a tale well worth the telling (and there are signs that Lillian told it well). But the resolute expression in her portrait leaves no doubt that Lillian would be among the survivors.[6]

Although her prospecting in the Klondike yielded only indifferent results and other gold rushers turned back from Dawson in droves, Lillian persisted in her gold fever and turned down opportunities to resume acting, enter the lucrative saloon business, or settle for a safe sinecure as a government clerk. Lacking the saintly aura of the frontier angel, she must also have rejected many suitors. Martha Munger Black, another resident of Dawson in Lillian's day, recalled, "Scarcely a fortnight passed that I did not have a proposal of marriage. If I missed I thought that I was falling off and getting old."[7]

The handsome former actress with skills as a musher that made her an asset on the trails and a way of telling a story that could enliven a long winter evening must have been at least as popular with the manhood of Dawson, but she chose to stay single throughout the period that she remains within our view. At the turn of the century marriage remained the main career for women, and the great majority of American women in Lillian's age bracket were married (79 percent, with another 4 percent widowed or divorced), but a new trend had emerged in the last few decades. Growing numbers of women were deciding to remain single because they saw marriage as a "straitjacket" that would prevent them from realizing their aspirations. Nonetheless, in an age when more conventional women often questioned the morals of the independent single woman, hints appear that Lillian excited the kind of suspicions against which Nellie Cashman had so successfully immunized herself. As the stampede slackened, Dawson so rapidly grew respectable that the Mounties banished prostitutes to the outskirts of town on the pretext of fire danger and the newly arrived matrons formed a "social vigilante" committee to exclude women of "impure background" from social functions. Mrs. Grundy had planted her high-laced shoe firmly in Dan McGrew's territory, and her campaign of ostracism may well have extended beyond the prostitutes and dance-hall girls to the independent single women who had formerly enjoyed freedom from social controls. When Lillian Malcolm passed by in the street, other women contemptuously held their skirts aside.[8]

Despite the scandal that clung to her, Lillian's journey from Kug-garock to Nome sounds less like a debauch in the wilds with two lovers than an exercise in survival. When Lillian and her companions, Charles Lowe and M. J. Conway, set off for the rumored gold in the black sands on the shore of the Bering Sea, it was May, and the ice on the frozen Arctic rivers had started to break up. Lillian leaped from one floating ice cake to another, nearly drowning when she once fell into the frigid waters. At another perilous stage in the course of their 175-mile jour-ney on snowshoes, the three ran out of supplies and came close to starving. Only Conway's skill in hunting ptarmigans saved their lives.[9]

Conditions in Nome proved such as to discourage all but the most optimistic gold rushers. By June people packed the shores so tightly that the newcomers arriving on incoming ships could not find space to pitch their tents. Eleanor Caldwell, a tenderfoot who had traveled to Nome with "brave feelings" intending to prospect, reported that claims had been staked on every square foot of ground from the sandy shores across the muddy tundra to the snow-capped mountains that loomed behind Nome. The realities of Nome soon crushed the brave feelings of the spring day in Washington DC when she had started out. The unappe-tizing and expensive food, the night spent sleeping on a "shake-down" (a skin spread on the floor) in a large room filled with rough-looking men, the popularity of "going gunning" without regard for innocent bystanders, and the threat of a smallpox epidemic that might compel all those in Nome to remain there under quarantine through the win-ter combined to send Caldwell and her daughter back home within two weeks of their arrival, sensibly aware of their own limitations and never to be numbered on the roster of the women prospectors.[10]

Lillian Malcolm was less easily discouraged. Perhaps after surveillance by social vigilantes, submergence in ice-choked rivers, and hunger in the snows, the Nome lodging house where the census taker found her living alone in 1900 (maybe sleeping on a shake-down) seemed a good deal more pleasant than it did to the Caldwells. She apparently suc-ceeded in staking some claims, but claim jumping was rampant in Nome. In the words of Caldwell: "Possession was nine points of the law, the tenth had resolved itself into a question of skill in pistol practice." Though Lillian always wore a pistol in her belt and no doubt knew how to use it, several men forcibly wrested her ground away from her before she had finished recording her claims. She later remarked that most men were chivalrous in all matters except the staking of claims. Lillian fared no better in the courts than she had on the muddy tundra and began to suspect that the claim jumpers had bribed the judge to place her ground in receivership and deprive her of her rights.[11]

Nearly a year of legal entanglements and attorneys' fees with no end in sight finally accomplished what the most extreme hardships and dangers had not, and Lillian left the north country. Besides, word had come of an exciting new discovery, silver at Tonopah in the central Nevada desert. The news from Tonopah seemed to confirm the prospectors' belief that great strikes could still be made in the barren mountain ranges of Nevada, and the siren song sounded anew. Lillian's sourdough friends were heading south, and soon she too was on her way.[12]

At least in the beginning her sojourn in Tonopah was another exercise in survival. Evidently, Lillian had emerged from Alaska penniless but with her boundless faith in a golden future still intact. Struggling to make ends meet until she at last struck pay ore, she put her theatrical talents as a raconteur to work and told stories about her adventures in exchange for room and board. She seems to have missed both the rushes to Goldfield that sent much of the population of Tonopah hastening pell-mell across the desert in clouds of dust in the spring and fall of 1903. As in Tonopah, she arrived the following year, too late to stake claims but eager to secure interests. She later said she considered her Goldfield operations a failure and had not found it easy to return to the scene of her defeat. Perhaps she sought to salve her wounded pride and disappointed hopes farther west, in the bare cream- and buff-colored canyons of the Silver Peak Range. Journeying there alone, as she customarily did on short trips, she had been endeavoring to develop mining properties in Silver Peak since 1902.

Though she was not to be numbered among the nabobs who emerged from the "golden horseshoe" at Goldfield, her hunches had not led her astray. Mining had proceeded by fits and starts in the Silver Peak region since the late 1860s, and in four years' time the Pittsburgh Silver Peak Gold Mining Company would launch a major revival. Moreover, beyond the rusty bald mountain, hidden riches still awaited at Nivloc, Nevada's leading silver producer in the late 1930s. Lillian's instincts do not seem to have pointed her to the exact spot, however. She returned several years later, in 1907–8, to stake claims in the Silver Peak area and organize them in the Scotch Lassie Gold Mining Company, with a Bisbee, Arizona, capitalist as president, but the ground proved to be of little worth.[13]

Lillian next appeared farther south in Rhyolite in September 1905, after the rush earlier that year had abated and men no longer swarmed over the hills like ants. If her tardiness signified another failure, it may not have rankled much because she saw Rhyolite primarily as a base of operations where she could stay when she came in from the desert. Again, her fantasies had vaulted toward the farther horizon. Frank "Shorty" Harris, one of the discoverers of Rhyolite and subsequently a prospecting partner of Lillian's, reflected on the lure of the mountains beyond: "It's a funny thing, and something that I can't explain, but the country that is far away always looks best to a prospector. Somehow he feels that over the big range of mountains are better formations than those around him, and a hundred miles away is a rich outcropping that is just waiting to be staked out." And there was something about Death Valley that intrigued. Poet Rufus Steele understood what drew the prospectors on:

Out there in the land o' sagebrush, in the brown horn-toad's
domain,
Where the clouds float 'round moth-eaten—in the land of
stingy rain:
Where the birds are only sagehens, where the gray coyote
slinks:
Where each little drop o' water is a shinin' pearl that
stinks:
Where the trailless, silent desert like a windin' sheet has
grown—
Alkali made even whiter, redhot sunshine crumbles bone!
Where you swing a pick in anguish, probe the bowels of a hill,
P'raps you'll hear the nuggets callin'—then it's time to
scrawl your will.[14]

That call presently led to Lillian's trip into the region in company with Peget, McCabe, and McCauley in the autumn of 1905, and scrawling their wills might not have been a bad idea, though Peget and McCabe knew Death Valley well. The previous year Peget had gone prospecting with Shorty Harris in the Panamints, where their discovery of a small pocket of gold produced a short-lived rush to the Gold Belt district. Lillian had not yet set foot in Death Valley, but the same intrepid spirit that carried her through the Chilkoot and the ice-choked northern rivers brought her through the desert ordeal ahead. The party encountered bad luck with their animals only three days after setting out. They lost two of their four horses, and some of the pack mules sickened. Comradely feeling did not survive the hardships that ensued. Instead of remaining in the Panamints for two or three months as planned, Lillian and Peget returned to Rhyolite inside three weeks; McCabe and McCauley straggled in later. All four refused to discuss the trip with newsmen, but Lillian's only comment—that the next time she went out with a prospecting party she would "leave the nursing bottle behind"—unmistakably hinted that certain unnamed persons had failed to meet her standards.[15]

Peget retained her esteem, however, and Death Valley continued to draw her. She paused only long enough to buy more mules and supplies for an extended trip and to vent her opinions thoroughly before heading back into Death Valley with Peget. If setting off into the wilderness with a man to whom she was not married had kindled a new scandal, Lillian defiantly held herself up as a role model for other women: "The grandest and healthiest life known is this rough pioneer life. And I don't see why more women are not out in the hills. It ought to be as easy and natural for women to read rocks as it is for astronomers to read the stars. The day will come when they will not sneer at Miss Malcolm. They will not pick up their skirts when I come around. Disgusting conventionality must pay the penalty in any pioneer work."[16]

Like a true queen bee, Lillian did not for a moment imply that other women might hope to rival her exploits in prospecting, but she urged them to enter the mining field in other capacities: "The higher branches of mining offer great inducements to women. I don't mean the kind of work I am doing. But there is surveying and drafting, the study of mineralogy and geology. It is clean, honest money. There is too much hypocrisy in the sexes. Woman can endure as much as a man. Comply with the law and you will have man's responsibilities and man's reward."[17]

Finally, indirectly responding to the unstated question of rape, Lillian offered a testimonial to the sterling character of the prospector and an assurance that the woman prospector in the wilderness need not be afraid: "I love the prospectors. They would die in a pinch for their companions. . . . There are no embarrassing circumstances for me as a prospector. I am as safe in camp as I would be at home. The rough exterior of the prospector usually covers a Chesterfield." Nellie Cashman said much the same thing. But then the frontier angel enjoyed a special status that no other woman on the frontier ever duplicated. Although the greater part of the prospecting fraternity may well have been Chesterfields, the dangers posed by a few were very real, and prospectors were not the only inhabitants of wilderness regions that had long served as havens for desperadoes and reprobates. Journalist John Spears decried the "wretched host" of Death Valley tramps, "more vicious, if possible, than the tramp of civilized districts." Even Leander Lee, a Death Valley resident of many years with an Indian wife well accustomed to coping with all emergencies, never set off on a trip without taking her to stay with relatives. "It would have been unsafe to leave a woman alone there," explained Spears.[18]

Mountain Charley's experience in Colorado in 1859 vividly illustrated the perils Lillian Malcolm and Nellie Cashman declined to acknowledge. Evidently aware that the denizens of the Colorado mining camps knew her for a woman despite her masculine disguise, Charley wore two revolvers in her belt and a sheath knife in her boot for added protection. Yet despite her weapons and the wary look in her eyes, she sometimes behaved incautiously, or she would not have ventured into town on Christmas night, often a time of prolonged drunken revelry in the early mining camps. George West, later publisher of the *Golden Colorado Transcript,* was awakened by pistol shots outside the inn where both Charley and he were stopping. Nothing unusual in that. He was about to roll over and go back to sleep when he heard a woman's scream. As he hurriedly dressed he heard another shot, and Charley's

95

voice rang out in front of the inn: "How do you like that, you damned drunken cowards? You better get back across the bridge, or you'll get another one."[19]

Moments later Charley burst into the inn, bareheaded, flushed, eyes glistening, with a pistol in each hand. She explained that "three or four of those cowardly cusses thought they were going to get away with me" and that she had "winged one of them." Sounds from outside signaled that the brawlers had arrived at the front door to renew their assault. At this point she appeared to lose the steady nerve that had thus far enabled her to defend herself. Her face paled, and the hands that gripped her pistols began to tremble. While others attended to Charley, West went forth to deal with her assailants: "One of them had become partially sobered by Charley's bullet, which had struck him in the shoulder, and with his aid I convinced them of the futility of their dastardly attempt upon the poor girl and they retired with a promise to leave her unmolested." Though this is the only incident described, one gathers that the other dastardly attempts on Charley occurred. West recalled, "They found to their chagrin that she was not 'that kind of a hairpin,' as she was pleased to express it."[20]

The record does not show what kind of a hairpin Lillian Malcolm may have been in Charley's sense of the word, but she was certainly the dauntless kind, whether with companions or alone, in remote country from the Arctic to northern Mexico. "She fears neither man nor wild beast," in the words of the *Humboldt Star* of Winnemucca. It may well be that her second foray into Death Valley with Peget in November 1905, for all its dangers, was one of her safer journeys. Teaming up with Shorty Harris, they made a two-month grand tour of the Death Valley country, prospecting as they went, from the Manse ranch near Pahrump Spring on the eastern edge to Ballarat, the richest mining camp in the region only a few years earlier and now almost moribund. Lillian sang with the motley crew of desert rats assembled for the funeral of the aged Breyfogler, "Old Man" Finley, who had chased the mirage of riches on the desert for forty years. She came on a desert tortoise and marveled at its size ("big as a bonnet"). Perhaps her companions introduced her to roast tortoise. The three of them traveled on to Harrisburg, lately discovered by Harris's partner of the moment, a Basque tenderfoot, shortly after Harris sold his interest in Rhyolite for a song during a drunken binge. By the time of Lillian's arrival, nothing remained of the rush to Harrisburg but a saloon and general store and a handful of miners at work—nor did anything remain of Harris's profits, all merrily squandered on a toot "back East." Whatever Lillian saw in the ephemeral mining camps and heard of Harris's vicissitudes, no doubt related over the campfires at night by a garrulous character who was, in his way, as skilled a storyteller as she, it seems only to have whetted her appetite for mining. Living proof of her assertions on woman's ability to endure as much as any man, she traversed the sandy plains, clambered up cliffs in the Panamints with a will, staked claims, piled up rock monuments, and at length arrived at the camp of the individual known to her and many others as "Mysterious Scott."[21]

Walter Scott, or "Death Valley Scotty," made it his life's work to fool his contemporaries, but he has not deceived historian Richard Lingenfelter. "Death Valley Scotty was a ham actor, a conscienceless con man, an almost pathological liar, and a charismatic bullslinger," wrote Lingenfelter in a definitive exposé of Scotty's machinations. "He was an insatiable attention-seeker, a reckless publicity hound, willing to say or do almost anything for one or more moment in the limelight.... Death Valley Scotty was also the consummate grubstake-eater, the quintessential moocher, who perfected the prospector's homely come-ons and string-alongs to an art form."[22]

When Lillian and Peget arrived to dine with Scotty and his sidekick, the half-Cherokee prospector Bill Key, and Key's pet rattlesnake, Scotty's encampment under a rock ledge in the Black Mountains boasted some amenities unusual in the remoter reaches of the desert, including mattresses, a tin bathtub, a steamer chair, theatrical posters on the rock wall, gourmet foods, and a fine stock of liquors. At that point in his career Mysterious Scott had succeeded in fanning public speculation over the site of his secret Death Valley mine to fever pitch, all to the ultimate end of parting his eastern financial backers from their money. The preceding summer his record-breaking run from Los Angeles to Chicago on a special train, the "Death Valley Coyote," had snatched headlines throughout the nation. Lillian's visit nearly coincided with another of Scotty's publicity stunts: his own faked murder. He may have already begun mulling over the details of a forthcoming caper, the staged ambush at Wingate Pass of a party en route to examine his nonexistent mine.[23]

Lillian and Mysterious Scott do not seem to have liked each other much. Perhaps the former actress, with her experience in show business, immediately saw through the theatrics of the former buckaroo from Buffalo Bill Cody's Wild West Show, and Scotty lost interest in anyone he could not con. Bill Key, the swarthy, long-haired cowboy-prospector from Stinking Water Creek, Nebraska, impressed her much more, and so did his mining claims. In this she showed excellent judgment, for despite the tales Mysterious Scott circulated about his mine, so rich that he could visit it only by the dark of the moon, padding his burros' feet to conceal their tracks and foil the hired desperadoes who pursued him, Key was the only one who had staked claims of genuine value. Lillian took an option on the Key claims and emerged from Death Valley with something to show for her efforts, but once again the big one had eluded her. Shortly after her return to Rhyolite just before New Year's Eve, two prospectors lingered at Emigrant Canyon northwest of Harrisburg because they feared to cross Death Valley without good directions to the next water hole. While they waited, they made the discovery later christened Skidoo that was to produce more than a million dollars in gold. It was enough to make any prospector who had combed the valley in those years turn to the bottle.

Although Lillian ended her desert odyssey convinced that she had persuaded Bill Key to withdraw from Mysterious Scott's shenanigans and devote himself to developing his mining claims, Key soon became more deeply entangled than ever. In the spring of 1906 Scotty had deserted his steamer chair under the rock ledge to star in a play on his favorite subject—himself. Not long after the opening in Seattle a witness charged that Scotty's real intention in staging the ambush at Wingate Pass with Bill Key had been to kill the mining engineer dispatched by eastern investors and to substitute a glowing analysis of his own composition for the engineer's report. Hoping to compel Key to testify against Scotty, the San Bernardino sheriff set off into Death Valley after Key and emerged eleven days later without his quarry. Despite Key's talent for disappearance, Lillian came to believe that her friend was in great danger from Scotty's machinations. It may be that her efforts to help Key were primarily motivated by gratitude toward a man who had once saved her life when she came close to perishing of thirst in Death Valley, but some suspected that her concern betrayed romantic involvement with the handsome Bill Key, with his bronze skin, long hair, black eyes, white teeth, and Vandyke beard. The *San Bernardino (California) Sun* admiringly described him as "a man of striking appearance" who would shine at the most refined social event. One newspaper story openly referred to Key as Lillian's "lover" and "sweetheart." Though her response to these allegations has not been recorded, it was no doubt eloquent and defiant. Lillian hired a lawyer to defend Key and headed into the valley herself to warn him that Scotty planned to frame him for the attempted murder and secure the mining claims for himself. Given the recent history of Mysterious Scott, no plot was too implausible.[24]

We do not know whether Lillian succeeded in reaching Key before his subsequent arrest at Ballarat—or perhaps was allowed to catch up with him—but it is certain that she held a prolonged conference with him in jail as soon as she reached San Bernardino, after hastening her team through Death Valley. Still the former actress and ever aware of the value of appearances, she persuaded Key to cut his long hair, shave his beard, and wear a tailored suit at future court proceedings. As it turned out, shorn locks and more conventional tailoring had little to do with the outcome and probably disappointed the throngs who gathered to stare at this exotic figure during his court appearances. Authorities eventually dismissed the charges against both men when Scotty's lawyer convinced the court that the ambush had occurred over the county line in another jurisdiction. By then, having devoted herself too much to finding and defending Key and too little to hunting up investors, Lillian had lost her option on the Key claims. It appears that Key was not sufficiently smitten with his "brave hearted friend" to allow tender feelings to interfere with his long-standing loyalty to Scotty.[25]

Lillian still held her Silver Peak claims, however, and she soon headed east in search of development capital. She concentrated her efforts on Pittsburgh, where she hoped that news of the promising Pittsburgh Silver Peak mining operation would make local investors particularly attentive. The task ahead required her to summon up all the silver-tongued eloquence at her command, because the reputation of mining investment in southern Nevada and the Death Valley region had nearly reached the nadir. Money was tight in the period of stringency that preceded the October 1907 financial panic, investors had lost millions in the Greenwater copper mining fiasco, millions more would soon slip away when the mines at Rhyolite collapsed, and in Goldfield, despite the solid worth of her mines, overpriced mining stocks spiraled steadily downward toward the October stock crash that would wipe out enormous sums in investor dollars. It was in the deepening gloom of this imminent financial disaster that Lillian was compelled to make her pitch, and her success said a good deal about her persuasive powers. "She is a hustler of no mean ability," the *Tonopah Bonanza* admiringly declared. As usual, Lillian was not too shy to do a little preening after her return to Nevada: "I raised the money in Pittsburgh, and I had no trouble in doing it, which goes to show that there is a great deal of bugaboo about this talk of hard times and stringency of the money market. There is plenty of money to be had for legitimate propositions, if one is sincere in his or her motives. When one goes to businessmen, all that is necessary is to talk common sense. But if one is going to take romantic flights, and go up into the millions on an ordinary proposition, he is going to fall short in his expectations."[26]

Unfortunately for Lillian and the Pittsburgh investors, her Silver Peak mining enterprise proved a failure, and once more her imagination vaulted toward a farther horizon, the Altar mining district in Mexico, south of Nogales. There she journeyed in 1908, and there she remained for the next two years developing a new prospect. When she passed through Reno on a return visit in the summer of 1910, a curious reporter inquired why a woman of such obvious refinement did not abandon prospecting in remote and primitive corners of the world and return to civilization "where you can enjoy the good things of life." Never far beneath the surface, Lillian's resentment toward the women who had ostracized her broke forth anew: "It is due to the criticisms I received from my own sex when I first began to prospect. I would notice, as I passed down the streets of a mining camp, clad in my tallow spattered khaki, the wives of struggling clerks and other low salaried men holding their garments aside as though I might contaminate them. My pride then prevented my turning back." No doubt as a result of her own harsh experiences, Lillian harbored a charitable ideal quite different from Nellie Cashman's churches, hospitals, and collections for the Irish cause. Some years earlier Lillian had announced her intention, if she struck bonanza, to devote her philanthropic largesse to the assistance of women on their own who were endeavoring to become self-supporting.[27]

Despite Lillian's stark exposition on the tension between the woman prospector as the pathbreaking pioneer who had shattered the mold and "disgusting conventionality" in the form of traditional women, the reporter appeared unable to conceive of a woman with no need for female friendship (a need that historians have found caused real emotional pain to lonely pioneer women on the farming frontier). "What companionship of your own sex do you have at Altar?" he inquired. "Absolutely none," Lillian crisply replied, brushing aside the Hispanics and Indians in the region. Nor did she want any, she might have added. Like Nellie Cashman, she preferred the company of men, although her relations with them were on an entirely different footing than Nellie's. The reporter may not have been off the mark when he termed his subject "a most unusual woman." Unusual, that is, in terms of the emotional needs of the general run of womankind. By no means unusual for a woman prospector.[28]

In the course of the following year Lillian evidently sold her Mexican mining interests or failed to uncover values worth pursuing. The summer of 1911 found her in Nevada once more on her way to a new mining district in the Slumbering Hills in the northern part of the state. Here she must have crossed paths (perhaps swords?) with another woman prospector, Mrs. Louise Rupp. It was Rupp who had christened the new strike "Awakening" and staked some of the choicest claims there. The name proved a problem when a poet protested that it had been stolen from his poem, and it later fell into disuse. From the little we know of Louise Rupp, she does not sound much like a representative of "disgusting conventionality." In an era when leading the stampede often made the difference between success and disappointment, she was noted for being among the first at many mining excitements. We can at least be certain that she did not hold her skirts aside from

Lillian Malcolm; Louise Rupp had also broken the taboo and adopted men's clothes.[29]

Although the press wrote enthusiastically of "splendid ore sparkling with free gold" at Awakening and the district developed into a paying proposition, Lillian missed out once again. Even so, she would never stoop so low as Mysterious Scott. Some believed the former Death Valley Croesus was fencing high-grade ore from the mines at National north of Winnemucca while he pretended to work a lease at a northern Nevada mine. Scotty and Lillian evidently encountered each other anew in 1911, for she brought his mascot, the large black cat he liked to say had brought him luck, into Elko to sojourn with her at a hotel. The cat soon demonstrated its talents as a midnight yowler.[30]

In September Lillian moved on to Jarbidge, where prospectors had discovered gold in 1909 at the base of a steep mountain canyon in northern Nevada. Once more she arrived too late to be "first on the ground," as miners say, but her faith in the big strike awaiting her never faltered. She announced plans to spend the next several months prospecting the Jarbidge Mountains in eastern Nevada near the Idaho border, a region where her Alaskan experience would stand her in good stead. The northern Nevada winter would soon be setting in, with snows as deep as eighteen feet in the high country, and the intrepid few who continued to prospect would be obliged to do so on snowshoes.[31]

Thirteen years had passed since Lillian had deserted the New York stage for the Klondike, and she had reached the age of forty-three. Her hard life had taken a toll on her good looks. No longer did newsmen ponder whether she might be called pretty. Instead, they wrote of a "refinement that the desert cannot mar" and a face "carved in intellectual lines." Years of trekking through the wilderness with pick in hand had made her a familiar sight to the mining crowd from Nome to Mexico. In Goldfield, Silver Peak, and Death Valley the will-o'-the-wisp of the big bonanza had brushed close by: "Always in search of fortune, she had it at times almost within her grasp, only to have it fleet away," the *Reno Evening Gazette* observed. Yet although her financial circumstances seemed little improved over the days when she told tales for her supper in Tonopah, she declared herself in "the mining game" to stay.

Over the next several years, her name appeared in the newspapers from time to time; then she drops from our sight. No doubt she retained to the end the buoyant optimism so characteristic of a prospector. Major William Downie had described it in these words after the California gold rush: "He lived for the hour in the sunshine of brilliant hopes." So too did a woman.[32]

Although Lillian Malcolm appeared unaware of other women's activities when she advised them to take to the hills, a growing number of women already participated in all phases of mining save one. The superstition, almost an article of faith to the Cornish miners, that the presence of a woman in a mine brought bad luck continued to bar the employment of women miners in any underground work force until the barrier was at last breached in the 1970s. Nevertheless, no one could prevent a woman from developing her own claim. Who was to stop Mrs. Emma Stith, working alone, from digging trenches, open cuts, and a 175-foot adit tunnel on her claim at the foot of a steep mountain north of National? And when she finally uncovered high values in copper with gold and silver by-products in a district others had long written off, who better deserved to find them?[33]

At the other end of the occupational spectrum from the hard manual labors of Emma Stith, women were emerging as mine owners, operators, and investors, despite the prejudice that often posed obstacles to their activities. As Mary E. Stickney commented in an article on women mining entrepreneurs, "while the advance of woman has been one of the marvels of the age, it must be admitted that in the struggle for economic independence she still finds herself more or less hampered by precedence and conventional considerations, and even more by the timorousness born of conscious ignorance and lack of training. She must have a stout heart who will turn pathfinder in the world of affairs, and especially is this true of the mining field." While noting that many men also approached mining investments as a gamble, Stickney emphasized the internal barrier that woman's conditioning had created against her advancement: "They open their mouths and shut their eyes, as it were, letting themselves be beguiled into the purchase of some vaunted stock, or willing gudgeon in the net of some clever promoter, blindly hoping that they are somehow to win in this mysterious game which they never dream of comprehending, but down in the depths of their frightened little hearts, always expecting to lose." It nonetheless appears that being played for a gudgeon could sometimes provide the introduction to the mining world that eventually resulted in a successful career.[34]

Not one entirely to jettison prevailing ideas on appropriate female behavior, Stickney argued that a capable businesswoman could succeed at mining without compromising her essential femininity and proceeded to give several examples. They included Mrs. E. C. Atwood of Denver, who spoke at the International Mining Congress at Milwaukee in 1900 on how mining could serve as a lucrative business for the woman who pursued it in an "intelligent way." Before her own entry in the mining field Mrs. Atwood had followed a wide range of vocations, some far removed from conventional conceptions of women's work, including blacksmithing, foundry work, carpentry, carriage painting, photography, and printing. After losing heavily in a foolish mining investment, she intensively studied geology, mineralogy, and Colorado mining conditions and salvaged her wounded pride by becoming president and general manager of the Bonaccord Gold Mining and Milling Company at Empire, as well as acquiring mining interests in Cripple Creek and California. She superintended all these mining operations herself, which inevitably led to some discussion of the clothes she wore for repairing machinery underground and overseeing timbering and blasting (suit with box coat and short skirt, knickerbockers, soft cap, and high boots). Other women mine operators covered by Stickney were Mrs. Mary Kent, with mines at Mount Sheridan and other Colorado locales, and Mrs. Mary Murrell, manager of the Highland Mary Mine at Silverton.[35] Marital status is sometimes difficult to determine in such cases, but if no husbands were in evidence, one can assume these women were separated, divorced, or widowed and as much on their own as an unmarried woman in the mining field.

Mrs. Atwood's was not the only instance of a disastrous investment that catapulted a woman into the mining world. When Carrie Everson and her husband, a Chicago doctor, lost their entire savings in an unwise mining investment in the 1870s, Carrie began studying chemistry and mineralogy in an effort to recoup their fortunes. In the course of her experiments she discovered the affinity of oils and other substances for certain minerals. In 1885, with her husband's encouragement and support, she secured a patent. The couple moved to Denver in 1887 and vainly attempted to interest mining operators in Carrie's revolutionary discovery—the flotation process, which mining historian Jeremy Mouat has termed "one of the most significant advances ever made in ore treatment." Dr. Everson died two years later, and Carrie supported herself and her son by nursing. Although she secured backing for a demonstration plant that functioned perfectly and she co-patented another flotation process, by the mid-nineties she lost all hope of convincing mining men that a woman could make an important metallurgical discovery and abandoned the effort. In time, other metallurgists elsewhere independently discovered the flotation process. Its first successful commercial application took place in Broken Hill, Australia, and it spread to America after 1911. When the original patent became a matter of great interest, a search for Carrie Everson began in 1915—too late. She had died a year earlier.[36]

One prominent mining historian has dismissed Carrie's discovery as a "charming tale" and a "romance," because the commercial application of flotation was developed without reference to her work; a good many women and contemporary historians would instead find her fruitless efforts to win attention for a revolutionary discovery both depressing and familiar. Mining engineer Theodore Hoover has written, "All the salient points of the flotation method as it is used today are accurately described in Everson's patent, and with such clearness and distinctness that anyone of ordinary skill in the treatment of ores can, by following the instructions in Miss Everson's patent, easily produce the results being secured at Broken Hill and elsewhere. . . . The real reason for its lack of commercial application was its startling departure from previous known methods." The flotation process made possible the open pit and heap leaching methods widely used in mining today.[37] Given earlier adoption of her pioneering process and a good patent attorney, Carrie Everson's story might have had a very different ending.

Meantime, the women prospectors, along with the rest of the mining world, remained ignorant of the flotation process and continued to mine in the old way. Mary Tracy and her sister Edith, stenographers from Boston, bought a claim from an old miner when vacationing in Colorado, left their jobs, worked the mine themselves with rudimentary equipment, and quickly turned it into a steady producer of low-grade ore. Teams of sisters in mining appear to have been fairly unusual, but the Tracy sisters were preceded by at least one other pair, described in the press as "very attractive" and sweetly named Daffodil and Woodbine Ely. Though they were teenagers of only sixteen and fourteen, the Ely sisters located a claim in the Como district southeast of Dayton, Nevada, in 1882 and developed it with their own hands.[38]

It is not always easy to tell whether women mine owners such as the Tracy sisters also prospected. Yet a woman such as Atwood, with her broad range of activities outside the usual gender barriers, would be unlikely to draw the line at prospecting. Similarly, one wonders if Mrs. M. B. Stewart, a spry lady of seventy who superintended her own mine at Empire and received warm but erroneous praise from the press in 1899 as "the only woman in Colorado who is a practical miner," did not also engage in prospecting.[39]

That was certainly so in the case of Mrs. C. T. Ricketts of Oakland, California. En route to inspect the lease she was operating at Golden, a central Nevada camp, she paused in the midst of a fierce gale to stake several claims high in the Shoshone Mountains and pressed on through the night until she reached a stopping place at three-thirty in the morning. Later, discoursing on her venture and displaying samples, Ricketts impressed the *Goldfield News* as "particularly well informed on mining matters." No doubt it was this faculty that made her a pioneer in the investment field, the only licensed woman broker on the San Francisco stock exchange, according to the *News*. Unfortunately for Ricketts and the investors who joined her, neither Golden nor her mountain claims produced anything of value.[40]

Louise Gilman, another Californian, fared better, indeed so well that the *Reno Evening Gazette* called her "one of the most successful woman mine operators in Nevada." Nye County location records show that she filed several central Nevada mining claims in 1906–7, but her most successful effort proved to be the acquisition and sale of the Daisy group of claims in Round Mountain for sixty thousand dollars. (In the long run, Round Mountain proved more valuable than many of the mining excitements that sent investors into a fever at the Goldfield stock exchange; renewed mining operations in the late twentieth century have so reduced the site that some derisively allude to it as "Round Toadstool.")[41]

Further instances abound. Mrs. John J. Jennings, for example, was as much on her own as Lillian Malcolm, although her husband was alive and well. Mr. Jennings's career as a newspaper editor kept him in New York while Mrs. Jennings resided in the rugged Battle Lake and Encampment districts in southern Wyoming, where she had located copper claims in 1898 and remained to supervise development. The *Mining Age* declared that ten years of study had made her an expert on mining: "Even among the old and experienced miners of that rough Western country, her opinion goes a great way, especially when some new formation of rock is discovered." Mrs. Jennings spoke enthusiastically of her love of mining, took no small pride in her work as a "level-headed miner," and, perhaps anticipating the inevitable question, discussed her clothes (short skirt, knee-high elk-hide boots, and large cowboy hat).[42]

Another notable woman prospector was Anna Mau. She began prospecting around 1893, located a lode at Breckenridge, Colorado, and developed it over the next five years. Because Mau, like Nellie Cashman, was a small, slender woman weighing less than one hundred pounds, the hard labor she accomplished with her own hands when blasting a two-hundred-foot tunnel amazed observers: "She swings the hammer, twists the drill and wields the pick, she fires the dynamite and wheels away the debris."[43]

What brought Mrs. Jennings and the others into the hills has not been disclosed, but certain motives gathered particular force for women on their own, especially widows and divorcees. The first was extreme financial necessity. As we see in more detail when we reach the years of the Great Depression, prospecting could provide a lean but fairly reliable living in hard times. Mrs. P. J. Thomas, who worked a copper mine near Silverton, Colorado, from 1905 through at least 1912 with her thirty-year-old daughter, Nettie Hornbeck, stated this with absolute clarity: "Some women have to go out in the world to make a living. I am one of those women. It was with me and my daughter a

Encampment, Wyoming, site of Mrs. John Jennings's copper mine
(Lorna Nichol Collection, #1005, American Heritage Center,
University of Wyoming).

case of poverty." Perhaps Thomas exaggerated the point, since unlike the frankly unconventional women prospectors, she firmly insisted that woman's place was in the home and that she and her daughter would never have departed from it unless compelled by dire necessity. Hornbeck, echoing her mother, eagerly recounted her feminine accomplishments: "I can sew and cook and do everything a woman can do." Interspersed with the lip service paid to the allure of scrubbing floors, however, was an enthusiasm for mining that Thomas and Hornbeck could scarcely suppress and a swaggering pride in certain accomplishments far removed from the domestic sphere ("We shoot bears").[44]

Another point emerges from the case of Thomas and Hornbeck. It is evident that if they had worked year-round as cooks and seamstresses (their winter occupations), they could have kept the wolf from the door. It was something more than poverty that sent them into their copper mine to wield the drill and sort ore every summer, and Hornbeck stated it vividly: "I can hardly wait for each summer to roll around.

I don't believe I could live without mining now. There is a beautiful fascination about it. Oh, you don't know how it feels to wonder what each shot will reveal. It may tell you that you will remain a pauper or it may tell you that you will become a millionaire." Cooking and sewing offered a living but no beautiful fascination. Mining also gave them a sense of freedom from any restriction and an unconscious pride in their survival abilities: "We live in a cabin and have our ponies. We are not afraid to ride anywhere. We, mother and I, are not afraid of man or beast." For Thomas and Hornbeck, the zest for adventuring in the wilderness so typical of women in the mining field clearly mingles with financial need and the hope of finding a bonanza. Unfortunately, the sources do not reveal whether they eventually opted for the domestic roles they professed to prefer.[45]

Because prospectors rarely discussed the fantasy that sent them into the hills, not much is known about the initial point when the hope of finding a bonanza seized a woman with no previous background in mining and no experienced relatives or mentors. The story of Helen Cottrell, however, provides a rare glimpse of this crucial turning point. According to the press, Helen Cottrell had been "delicately reared" by one of the finest families in Kentucky. By her middle years she had evidently fallen on hard times and joined the rush to Goldfield in 1905, soon departing to run a boardinghouse at the small mining camp of Central. She later frankly admitted that at this time she "did not know quartz from slate." But she listened to the stories of the prospectors and in the spring of 1906 heard a tale about a lost mine that captured her imagination. Years ago a prospector had made a good strike in the wild and distant reaches of the Toiyabe Range. The extraction of silver without smelting facilities proved so laborious that after working the ground for a while, he pulled up stakes and headed for Mexico, where he was killed by the Yaquis—thus entering the realm of the Mexican messenger who can never be questioned concerning particulars. Shortly before his death he had written to his brother in Nevada about the abandoned claim in the Toiyabes. This brother, who told the story to Helen Cottrell, had searched long and fruitlessly for the old stone cabin and the arrastra described in the letter before finally giving up.[46]

Undeterred by her admitted lack of experience in prospecting or in roughing it in rugged mountain terrain, Helen determined that she would find the lost mine. She brought in two men as partners, and the hunt commenced. (Interestingly, in contrast to the rumors that swirled around Lillian Malcolm, no one ever implied that these men were anything but business partners, perhaps because Helen lacked youth and beauty; the *Goldfield Chronicle* described her as one who "looks the part of a hardy woman of the hills.") The search through the mountains was lengthy and rigorous, leaving her clothes in shreds, but Helen was the one who finally found the old stone cabin with chunks of rich silver-lead ore still resting on the forge where the original prospector had left them years ago (no arrastra, however). On her return she immediately deeded her entire interest in the claims to her grown daughter, Orlean R. Seabright.[47]

Despite promising assays and considerable stir, the find did not prove to be a major strike, but the dream remained and Helen became a prospector. She traveled the mountains alone with her pack animals for more than a year and told the press that she had "taken to prospecting with determination and interest" and thoroughly enjoyed it. She eventually discovered and developed claims at the camp that became known as Hornsilver (despite Helen's effort to christen it Orleans in honor of her daughter) in the Gold Mountain Range on the northern rim of the Death Valley country. Last year's boardinghouse keeper now discoursed to the newspapers on well-defined ledges, the sinking of three shafts, assays of considerable richness at the fifty-foot level, the erection of a hoist, and forthcoming ore shipments as confidently and persuasively as any other mine owner. Evidently, she had learned a good deal about mining in a short time, because she directed much of the development work herself, relying primarily on her own judgment. This judgment was clearly sound, for more than a year later ore shipments still rumbled forth from her claims. An attempt by rival claimants to wrest these mines away from her in court obliquely attested to their value. In a decision regarded in Goldfield as a landmark in mining law, Helen won.[48]

Her mine was to prove so valuable in the years to come that Helen Cottrell must be ranked among the most successful women prospectors. In 1912 the Orleans was sold to Le Champ D'Or French Gold Mining Company, and J. William Dunfee, the superintendent, uncovered a new bonanza in it a year later. Although the true figure cannot be determined, the Orleans may have produced more than five-hundred-thousand dollars' worth of ore during the next nine years. Then, after a relatively quiescent period under the aegis of the rascally mine promoter A. I. D'Arcy, production leaped forward once more when Dunfee resumed direction of the mine, now renamed the Ohio Mines Corporation. Nearly three-hundred-thousand dollars' worth of gold came out of the Orleans over the next decade—"reason enough," observes Lingenfelter, "to change the name of the camp from Hornsilver to Gold Point." It was also the presumed reason for naming the seven-thousand-foot peak to the east Mount Dunfee. One wonders if it might not have been more appropriately christened Mount Cottrell after the woman who originally developed the mine.[49]

Another case in which the event that precipitated the woman prospector's obsession stands out clearly was that of an Oklahoman, Gertrude Selma Sober. She was born in Iowa in 1869. After financial reversals, the Sober family, consisting of Gertrude, then almost twenty, her parents, a sister, and two younger brothers, moved to Oklahoma. Gertrude pursued a variety of occupations, teaching school, clerking in stores, working as a secretary, and homesteading—another instance of the pioneering spirit that commonly propelled the future woman prospector across gender barriers. For about two years she lived in a dugout on her homestead and survived during one grim winter on the meager crop of kafir corn she had raised. She abandoned homesteading after 1901 and returned to Oklahoma City. Interested in geology since childhood, she listened with keen attention to accounts of the field trips, in which many women students participated, that University of Oklahoma geology professor Charles N. Gould had been leading into the Arbuckle Mountains. Then she heard the tale that fired her imagination. As mining historian Robert O. Fay tells it, "one day an itinerant peddler painted a picture of fabulous riches in the mountains. She decided this was worth investigating, and she visited the region many times during the next several years, riding back and forth on horseback, with her hammer on the saddle horn. She camped out or lived in a log cabin while prospecting for the 'fabuous riches.'"[50]

For a number of years, her search yielded no results. In 1907 she began prospecting with an aged partner she called "Dad," Dr. R. C. Hope. Two years later, on an August day as she sat resting from the hunt, she began idly hammering on a nearby rock and chipped off a fragment that resembled zinc. The result was the Southwest Davis Zinc Field. The partners formed the Indian Mining and Development Company, capitalized by Dr. Hope, with Gertrude as president. Unfortunately, Gertrude's management skills failed to match the persistence that had kept her in the Arbuckles for some seven years. After initial success the company's poor business practices figured in the decline of mining after 1913. In a pattern far from unusual among the women prospectors Gertrude married a much younger man, miner Chester Field, twenty-two years her junior, in early 1918 when she was forty-eight and lost him within the year to the influenza pandemic.

Although Gertrude turned from mining to boardinghouse keeping and apartment management in later life, she retained her interest in geology. In 1933, the year she turned sixty-four, she received her bachelor's degree in geology from the University of Oklahoma, and the Oklahoma Academy of Science published a paper on enigmatic rocks she wrote when she was nearly seventy. She died in an Oklahoma City nursing home in 1949. Soon after her discovery of the Southwest Davis Zinc Field a zinc monument for Gertrude to be inscribed "Queen of the Arbuckles" was proposed but failed to generate the necessary support (with at least four queens, the women prospectors seem to have produced more than their fair share of royalty). Gertrude is, however, the only woman prospector as yet commemorated in the National Mining Hall of Fame.

The tale of the lost mine, a peddler's story, or "beautiful fascination" with what the next blast of dynamite might reveal struck a particularly resonant chord among women with little resources who worked hard for a meager living, such as Cottrell, Sober, Thomas, and Hornbeck; widowhood sometimes plunged a woman into even more desperate circumstances. Such was the condition of Mrs. Marion Phelps when her husband died, leaving her with two small children and very little money. Too proud to write for help to the relatives she had left back East, Phelps set to work to remedy her situation. With the aid of friends she built a small cabin near Kingman, Arizona, and cultivated a vegetable farm. Phelps and her husband had prospected together, and as soon as she felt that her children had grown old enough to be left with an Indian nurse for several weeks at a time, she continued the search in an area she had thought promising. Eventually, she located two claims, selling one for a sufficient sum to launch her into a successful career in mining. She became known as such an expert in mining matters that her opinion was "sought from Yuma to Albuquerque"—or so said the newspaper. As soon as she could afford it, her solution to the incompatibility of prospecting and raising children was to send her children away to school in Phoenix.[51]

A related aspect of the financial stringencies that often accompanied a death in the family was the need to preserve an inheritance. In a valley north of Juneau, John G. Peterson, foreseeing that death from stomach cancer loomed inevitably before him, schooled his wife, Marie, and his daughters, Irma and Margaret, in following gold veins, mining, and milling. After he died in 1916, they continued to work the family mines themselves until 1923, with sporadic operations thereafter, and the Peterson daughters became known as "the girl gold miners" in the press. Marie Peterson's words, written in 1922, suggest a sense of legacy that transcended financial considerations: "Having decided not to lose the mine to which Mr. Peterson had pinned his faith, risked his fortune and given his life, we have continued developing the mine to the present day."[52]

Probably even more powerful than the financial forces that propelled the widow into prospecting was the need for solace that women of a certain cast found neither in church nor in the companionship of the quilting bee but in the solitude of the desert, a matter in which the woman prospector stands outside the general run of womankind. Historian Glenda Riley has noted that bonding with other women, especially in time of trouble, was an important survival technique for the pioneer woman on the plains.[53] Not so for the woman prospector, who drew her strength from being alone in the wilderness. The story of Idah Meacham Strobridge nicely illustrates this point. Born in 1855, an only child, Idah moved with her parents from California to a homestead west of present Winnemucca, Nevada. After the completion of the Central Pacific Railroad the family operated a popular inn known as

Humboldt House, a two-story white frame structure with a commodious dining room and large shade trees. In 1884, at twenty-nine, the plump and rather plain Idah married Samuel Strobridge, a handsome young man eight years her junior, and the couple began ranching on lands received from Idah's father.

Over the next five years Idah bore three sons and sustained a succession of tragedies that might have devastated a lesser woman. In 1885 her first child died the day after his birth; in 1888–89 her husband and her other children died from pneumonia, and much of the ranch stock froze in the terrible blizzards of that winter. After a brief sojourn in California, Idah returned to Nevada, absorbed herself in the family ranch, and took up prospecting, locating five gold claims in the Humboldt Mountains, organizing the district as "Humboldt," and commencing development work. An 1895 article in *Mining and Scientific Press* held out high hopes for the success of her mines and praised her as a "New Woman" who would "climb a precipitous cliff where the average man would not dare to venture." Despite the energy and acumen Idah brought to every enterprise she undertook, her mining district failed to meet these expectations. Nevertheless, her writings lead us to believe that the "big, still plains that inspire a big, serene life" had assuaged her manifold sorrows.[54]

Perhaps she had even found a kind of joy by herself in the desert: "You only know that it is good—vastly good—to live! Just to feel yourself drawing the breath of life is enough, while taking your outing in this faraway corner, where you seem to have the whole earth and sky to yourself. What more would you?" All this is set forth with an articulateness unusual in a world where prospectors rarely took pen in hand to reveal their thoughts. In 1895, at the age of forty, Idah began to write, becoming "the first woman of Nevada letters," in the opinion of the editors of her collected works.[55] A picture of her from this period shows a woman with hair skinned back, hammer in hand, the plainest of dresses, and no concessions to beautification or adornment. Sadness lingers in her eyes, but her gaze is forthright, and her face shows a strength and even a kind of beauty not yet revealed in the plump and unformed visage of the young wife. New enthusiasms ensued, and in 1901 Idah forsook the desert and moved to Los Angeles.

Idah Meacham Strobridge (Nevada Historical Society).

Although the motives of many women prospectors must remain a matter of conjecture, a desire to be out in the wilderness close to the pulse beat of the universe in the way Idah so memorably described, alone, stripped of distractions, and free to reflect on the meaning of life, may often have played a part. For instance, a taste for solitude may well have been at work when Mrs. Morehouse Mallen, who had emigrated from Germany to America at age fifteen, left her two children (and probably her grandchildren) in Ohio to take up prospecting in Colorado's Twin Lakes country. On beginning her new life in 1880, Mrs. Mallen was fifty-eight, a venerable age in the nineteenth century when normal life expectancy did not exceed the forties. Until her death from apoplexy twenty-two years later, she continued to live in a little log cabin on the crest of a hill, discovering and working some of the richest leads in the Twin Lakes district and selling a few of her properties for a substantial sum.[56]

Mrs. Mallen's preference for being by herself, at several states' remove from her family, epitomizes the taste for solitude so integral to our image of the prospector as lone wolf and sharply contrasts with the stereotype of the woman pioneer who weeps inconsolably for the relatives left behind. Historian John Faragher writes of the "anguish" over the disruption of relationships with other women expressed by women diarists during the "whole hated experience" of emigrating westward. Again, here our conception of the nature of women seems grossly at odds with prospecting. Women are supposed to need and seek out female companionship, but little evidence of sisterhood or networking can be found among the many women who prospected without relatives, male or female, or with male partners like Lillian Malcolm's. Concentrations of women prospectors in the same small camp at the same time may only signify that they, like their male counterparts, flocked independently to the latest rush. In general, the influence of strong female role models offers a more likely explanation than networking for these clusters. Other women, observing at close range the achievements of the spry seventy-year-old Mrs. M. B. Stewart in superintending her mine or perhaps the activities of the articulate and energetic Mrs. E. C. Atwood, may have realized that it was possible for a woman to have a successful career in mining.[57]

Only a handful of women prospected with female partners. No details have emerged on the two elderly women partners in the California gold rush mentioned in chapter 1, but a good deal more information has come to light on the prospecting activities of Mrs. Robert K. Reid, wife of the army surgeon at Camp Douglas in Utah, through the journal of her frequent prospecting partner Mrs. Burlingame. Though Reid has been dismissed by historians as a lady who made her discovery by accident when she picked up a pretty rock at a picnic—a variety of explanation more than once applied to a mining strike by a woman—the Burlingame journal makes it clear that Reid's discovery resulted from sustained and serious effort. Evidently, Reid had previously prospected in California before army volunteers were dispatched to Utah under Patrick E. Connor's command in 1862. Burlingame wrote that she "prospected several Canyons" with Reid in Utah, and General Connor offered them men, supplies, and wagons "whenever we called for them," doubtless to further his policy of encouraging mining in Utah in order to dilute the Mormon influence. Although Dr. Reid's position with the army may have further disposed General Connor to lend assistance, neither Dr. Reid nor Mr. Burlingame apparently accompanied their wives on expeditions, instead assuming supportive roles analogous to wives who kept the home fires burning while husbands prospected. When Mrs. Burlingame learned of an area where minerals appeared promising from George Ogilvie, a Mormon apostate anxious to undercut Brigham Young, she lost no time in organizing a prospecting expedition with Mrs. Reid as her principal partner, as well as a Mrs. McLean, two experienced California miners, and a number of soldiers: "We rode through Salt Lake City, much in the style of the middle ages, with outriders and retainers and all the appliances for camp life."58

Difficulties soon developed when Ogilvie failed to appear at the designated spot to guide them, but the women decided to press on nonetheless on the basis of a map he had drawn for Mrs. Burlingame. During their lengthy passage across a sandy waterless plain the mules began to "show signs of giving out" in the noonday heat. Well aware that "mules will lie down and refuse to rise when very thirsty," the women decided to give the kegs of water they carried to quench their own thirst to the mules. With considerable coaxing the mules consented to keep going, and the party reached the green shady mouth of Bingham Canyon. In short order the miners reported washing color in their pans. That night "visions of wealth floated before our wakeful eyes as we fought musquitoes and bed-bugs," reported Mrs. Burlingame, like many a prospector before and since.[59]

By morning the aged Ogilvie had made his appearance. Fear of Mormon vengeance had overwhelmed him, however, and coaxing him to proceed proved more difficult than coaxing the mules onward on the previous day. At length, Mrs. Reid's persuasive powers and her promises of a share in the mines prevailed. The party proceeded up the canyon for four or five miles, then continued on foot when the terrain became too difficult for the mules. They observed a large copper ledge but unwisely passed it by. Instead they returned to Camp Douglas "in gay spirits" with rich samples of silver, subsequently located as the Vedette and other claims on 17 September 1863, with Mrs. Reid credited as the primary discoverer of one. "Thus were discovered to the 'Gentiles,' the first mines in Utah," declared Mrs. Burlingame with pardonable pride. Historians agree that these were the first claims officially recorded, although the roles played by Mrs. Reid and Mrs. Burlingame faded almost to the point of invisibility and the tale of the casual find on a picnic became the accepted version of events. Next spring came the "Woman's Lode," recorded on 7 May 1864 by nine women, most of them the wives of army officers at Camp Douglas. The filing statement declared, "We the undersigned 'Strong Minded Woman [Women?],' do hereby determine and make manifest our intention and right to take up 'Felt' ore [*sic*] anything else in our names, and to work the same independent of any other man." The name of Johanna Connor, wife of General Connor, appeared first on the list, and historian Brigham M. Madsen finds the statement's bold assertion of independence from male involvement thoroughly in keeping with her character.[60]

The Woman's Lode had no immediate successors, however. More than forty years would pass before another cooperative group of women surfaced in 1907, when some women formed a prospector's association in central Nevada, and few instances of female partnership received mention in the press, one of them under the *Goldfield Review* headline

Ladies Locate Rich Ore Shoot.

Mrs. Robert English and Mrs. James George discovered the richest ore found up to that date on the Yellow Dog claims at Seven Troughs, north of Lovelock, Nevada. Working with mortar and pan they traced a streak of gold to its source and "opened up one of the most beautiful gold-bearing quartz leads in the district." It should be noted that tracing a streak often involved an amount of labor that disheartened the novice prospector. Herman W. Albert watched the prospector known as "Hot Steam" as he pulverized his sample, dumped it into a frying pan, and expertly swirled it until a tiny comet of gold particles appeared. Estimating that Hot Steam had dug roughly a thousand postholes as he panned his way up the hill, Albert declared with dismay, "It seemed like a grim future. I had thought that mines always stuck their noses out boldly on the surface." Mrs. George and Mrs. English must have found the task less grim. Although their husbands prospected and mined in the immediate area, the women evidently preferred to prospect with each other and secured a lease to exploit their find together.[61]

Why were women partners so rare? Because the number of men prospectors was much greater, the chance of finding a congenial partner among them might have been larger, although a sprinkling of other women was at hand. Perhaps when she sought a partner, the woman prospector actually preferred men over other women because of the queen bee syndrome: she tended to perceive other women as rivals who interfered with her image of herself as unique. Not, perhaps, the fairest of them all, but surely the bravest and the most daring, venturing where other women feared to go; the wisest of them all, her opinions sought from Yuma to Albuquerque; and the foremost trailblazer of them all, scornfully breaching the gender barriers behind which more conventional women dithered. One glimpses the queen bee in Nellie Cashman's proud (but doubtful) claim to be the first white woman in the Arctic and in Lillian Malcolm's tendency to carry on as though she were the only woman prospector on the planet, although she surely knew better. Not once, in any of the numerous public interviews, did a woman prospector allude to the achievements of another.

It appears likely that the queen bee syndrome played a part in the women prospectors' seeming ignorance of one another and of their predecessors. Granted that lack of awareness of their own history has obliged women repeatedly to reinvent the wheel. Granted also that long sojourns in the field may have prevented women prospectors from reading many newspaper accounts of other women's exploits and isolated them from contacts. Granted, finally, that the woman prospector stocking up on supplies in town had no hangout where she could rub elbows with other women engaged in the same pursuit, as men prospectors did in the saloons. Still, it is difficult to believe that the women prospectors joining rushes to a new strike could have been unaware of other women in the same movable tribe reassembling in one place after another. Mining entrepreneur David Mackenzie, a veteran of Leadville, the Klondike, Thunder Mountain, and Goldfield, among other rushes, later said, "At all those booms, I've seen the same faces." Some of those faces surely belonged to women such as Nellie Cashman, Lillian Malcolm, and Louise Rupp, who had raced to one boom after another. Moreover, women in mining received a measure of recognition that must have increased their visibility, not only from reporters, who found them more newsworthy than men in the same occupations, but also from professional organizations. Mrs. Atwood presented a paper before the International Mining Congress in Milwaukee; a convocation of mining men at Denver invited Mrs. P. J. Thomas and her daughter, Nettie Hornbeck, to address them in 1912.[62] It was women who denied them recognition, both conventional women and the other individualistic and sometimes egotistical women prospectors.

# FOUR

# The Steam Engine and the Lost Breyfogle: Dubious Enterprises

An occasional sign suggests obliquely that by the early twentieth century the woman prospector was a recognized feature of the western mining camp scene, expected to appear along with the rickety wooden saloon and the white tents sprinkled on the hillside. That, at least, may be the most relevant point to be drawn from the downfall of the notorious Bina Finnegan Verrault. In 1907 Verrault renamed herself Mrs. Hamilton, abandoned her New York "Love Syndicate" (details of which the press unfortunately left to the imagination of their readers), and arrived in Tonopah posing as a woman prospector. Although Tonopahans knew nothing of her real identity, her glamorous gowns soon convinced them that the dazzling Mrs. Hamilton was not what she purported to be, for clothes on the order of Mrs. Jennings's cowboy hat, short skirt, and high elk-hide boots ever remained the hallmark of the woman prospector. It soon became evident that the object of Verrault's prospecting was not mineral but a rich husband. Despite several rumored engagements, each quarry eluded her wiles. Sinking into alcoholism with ever more disreputable lovers, she died in a delirium within a year of her arrival. Her decision to present herself as a woman prospector is nonetheless suggestive. If the woman prospector had not been a well-known prototype, likely to pique the interest and perhaps evoke the admiration of the mining men she hoped to attract to the altar, this clever gold digger would no doubt have chosen a different persona for her mining camp debut.[1]

Mining camps abounded with characters as dubious as Verrault engaged in a variety of swindles that ran the gamut from the paltry deceptions of the "single-blanket jackass prospector" to the large-scale, gilt-edged promotions of the mining stockbroker in his luxurious mahogany-trimmed office. Thus it would be most unusual if none of the women prospectors had taken part in doubtful enterprises. In the main the roster of the women prospectors seems to include fewer rogues and scalawags than that of their male counterparts, but a few question marks emerge, one of them involving placer mining. In 1906 the *Goldfield Sun* called placer mining "notably a woman's field." This seemed to signify no more than the reporter's casual observation that Bessie Miller and the prospecting partners Jennie Enright and Mrs. George Lewis had all been prospecting in the same placer area, but in fact, the mining records justify a broad generalization, because Helen Cottrell and several other women prospectors had also filed placer claims. This predilection for placers may tell us something about the woman prospector. According to a treatise written in the 1930s on placer mining, finding rich deposits in "unsuspected places" with little relationship to existing topography was the forte of the placer miner. Moreover, placer deposits could be sampled at reasonable cost. The placer prospector began by panning samples from gullies or stream-beds, perhaps sinking an occasional shaft to uncover the formation just above bedrock where gold tends to accumulate. Further investigation through open cuts, pits, or drilling would give an accurate picture of the amount of pay gravel and the likely percentage of gold recovery. This being so, women prospectors may have been especially drawn to placer mining because they were innovative enough to hunt for gold in unsuspected places where the normal rules on promising geological formations did not apply. Furthermore, many had limited financial resources but remarkable strength and endurance. Women who could excavate a 175-foot tunnel like Emma Stith or wield the drill as handily as Anna Mau could readily sample a placer prospect for themselves. It may be parenthetically noted that many of Nevada's most diligent placer miners were Chinese, but rather than prospect, they generally worked deposits that earlier miners had abandoned.[2]

Bessie Miller was undoubtedly the preeminent figure among the women placer miners. Hardy even by the standards of the central Nevada pioneers, she hiked fifteen miles from Goldfield in the perilous desert heat of July in 1906 to locate a host of placer claims at the dry lake that was thenceforth to bear her name and hiked back again within a twenty-four-hour period. It was a time of year that one visitor to

Goldfield compared to Dante's inferno with the lid off, a season when the desert traveler can easily dehydrate. As blood thickens, the heart labors, the head spins, the foot stumbles, the tongue blackens and swells, delirium begins, and death ensues. By 1905 death and dementia among the desert prospectors had so markedly increased that public authorities grew alarmed. Bessie Miller was too wise in the ways of the desert to be numbered among these unfortunates, however. Despite her marathon journey, her only sign of impending delirium was the fanciful name she gave one of her claims, the "Star of the Sea." Evidently a hustler of no mean ability like Lillian Malcolm, she succeeded in interesting a syndicate of English investors in her placer ground and received a fifty-thousand-dollar offer within a month. The stampede that ensued to the Miller's Lake placers included several other women prospectors, Mrs. Anna Miller (apparently no relation to Bessie), Mrs. George Lewis, and Jennie Enright (not the same person as Ferminia Sarras's daughter, Jennie Flores, who during her years in Goldfield had abandoned her first husband, Enright, for Lemon Williamson).

Even amid the variegated tapestry of Goldfield's many adventurers, Jennie Enright made a considerable splash, with the result that more is known about her background and her doings than Bessie Miller's, although Bessie was probably the more skilled prospector. By the time she emerged in the news in connection with the Miller's Lake placers in 1906, Jennie Enright, a childless widow of forty-one, had run through a range of occupations. Born on a Minnesota farm, she started a cattle ranch on her own in Montana, where she broke broncos, roped cattle, and branded them herself. Later she made her living as a craftswoman weaving wire in Arkansas but found her life there uneventful. She escaped the boredom by joining the rush to Goldfield in 1904 when the camp was still no more than a scattering of white tents. There, and in the smaller camps scattered over the desert to the south, she made her living in a variety of ways, working as a cashier and operating a bakery in Palmetto, a restaurant in Lida, and a boardinghouse in Tokop, where for six months she was the only woman in camp.

She also took up prospecting in time to participate in the stampede to Miller's Lake. In August, Enright and her partner, Mrs. George Lewis, bonded their claims for the same price Bessie Miller had received and then closed a transaction with a San Francisco purchaser, who got a taste of the rigors of the desert as an unanticipated bonus. Enright and Lewis took him out in a horse-drawn rig to examine the site. When darkness fell, they were still collecting samples. Then a thunderstorm broke, the kind of gully washer that lifted whole mining camps from canyons and floated them into valleys. In the darkness and the torrential rain Enright, who was driving the team, lost her way on the featureless playa. It was ten o'clock before she found a landmark to guide her and three o'clock in the morning when she finally reached Goldfield. The investor alit chilled, soaked, and tired but still bullish on the placers and filled with admiration for Enright's courage and her prowess with horses. After these successes at Miller's Lake, Enright and an unnamed woman partner embarked on a prospecting trip of several months' duration. They emerged from the desert in December in the midst of a heavy snowstorm, having staked twenty-eight claims.

The matter that more often catapulted Enright into the news, however, was lot jumping. When the Goldfield boom escalated the value of town lots, property disputes became rampant, and Enright was in the thick of it. Anne Ellis, a miner's wife who later wrote her recollections, leaves this picture of the Enright method: "One day I heard a big racket, and in these times a commotion meant there was something doing, so I ran to the door, and just below me saw a woman throwing the foundation off a lot. The moment the last stick was off, a mule team was driven in on the run, drawing a tent house on skids—smoke coming out of the stovepipe. So Mrs. Enright jumped and held her lot, a gun in her hand in case of trouble." When a party of men attempted to retake the lot, she drove them off with two six-shooters, then invited them to come inside the fence one at a time for a fistfight. Sometimes called the "Desert Amazon," Enright was described as a fine-looking, well-dressed woman with blue-gray eyes (in a man similarly handy with guns, the press would probably have called them "steely blue eyes").[3]

The lot jumping developed into a group affair, with two more lots taken and several women joining Enright. When their opponents next attempted to retake the properties, the *Goldfield Tribune* described the comedy that ensued: "The three men formed a reconnoitering party and set out for the seat of war loaded with shotguns, muskets, blunderbusses, Colt's, Smith & Wesson's, and all the unused armament which was lying around within six blocks. Approaching the place by a secret route, they surrounded the houses which had been set upon their lots and called upon the inhabitants to surrender." The women emerged, with sarcastic remarks, to laugh at them. Again, the enemy retreated. Enright single-handedly routed the next onslaught. When six men dared her to shoot, she fired two rounds into the ground, which sent them racing pell-mell down the street. They were wise to flee, because Enright's superb marksmanship had won her several trophies in Arkansas. This time an officer arrested Enright.[4]

With this ringleader out of the way, the men expressed the hope that they might "talk business" with the husbands of the other women, but Enright was soon free again, proclaiming her rights, holding her ground, and loading her revolvers, which she used to eject several thieves who attempted to steal lumber from her lot. The only one who succeeded in temporarily ousting her was not a rival claimant to her property. According to Ellis, "her gentleman friend (today we call them 'Sweet Papas') moved in with her. . . . Comes a day when they fight; he fires her out, she pounds on the door, screaming and swearing. Finally he opens it a crack, sticks a gun out, and shoots a few times, just to show her he means business. We are glad, as she is a tough citizen, having killed her man before this."[5] Three years later Enright was still deeply embroiled in property disputes. Her indictment for stealing two houses won her the dubious distinction of becoming the second woman to be criminally charged in Goldfield over several years' time. Her defense was so convincing that prosecutor George Springmeyer (the author's father) requested dismissal of the case. When the census taker asked Enright her occupation, choosing among her many activities may have given her pause, but her answer suggests a sense of humor. She called herself a real estate agent.

By that time disillusionment had replaced the earlier excitement over the Miller's Lake placers. Sampling under the auspices of the Guggenheim interests over a long period had produced disappointing results, and some who had paid handsomely for placer claims later learned that the black sands had been treated with chloride of gold. No names were named, but since fancy prices had been reported for the claims of Enright and Lewis, as well as Bessie Miller, their involvement in the scam remains an open possibility. Anna Miller retained faith in her own claims, however. In 1907, when new samples from her ground showed substantial values in platinum, she hastened to relocate her claims. And none too soon, for news of the platinum presently ignited a second short-lived stampede from Goldfield to the dry lakes. Meanwhile, Bessie Miller continued to prospect and mine in the region. The press reported that she possessed "immense holdings," and mining records certainly confirm that she had staked a large number of claims. When the *Goldfield Chronicle* published the annual statements of mining companies in the Goldfield district in 1908, Bessie's Goldfield Etawanda Mining and Leasing Company was the only one headed by a woman.[6]

Although the identity of those prospectors who performed nefarious deeds with chloride of gold at Miller's Lake has never been disclosed, the scheme appears petty beside the grandiloquent con artistry of Dr. Frances E. Williams, probably the most unscrupulous among the women prospectors. Almost all that is known of her life before 1903 comes from two brief and not entirely consistent newspaper articles. According to these accounts, Frances was born around 1844 and became the sole support of her invalid mother when still very young. At an early age, in New York, she married a navy surgeon named Dr. Peck, who apparently died. She next married Williams, a wealthy St. Louis businessman twenty years her senior. In the course of her life she bore an incredible sixteen children, only one of whom survived. Shortly after her marriage to Williams his business failed, leaving the couple with only two assets, entrepreneurial energies still untapped and a legacy from Frances's first husband: his family recipe for a varnish used on silk hats. The family moved to New York, where Frances and her son, James, concocted the varnish while Williams sold it to hatmakers and peddled it on the streets. In time Frances and her husband developed a new process for bleaching shellac and built it into a highly successful company, which they eventually sold. The Williamses then retired to Florida with a million dollars in assets, much of which they used to purchase orange groves. Retirement lasted only until disaster struck in the form of a hard freeze that blackened and destroyed the crop. Their other investments proved equally calamitous, and the fortune built on silk-hat varnish evaporated into thin air.

This latest reversal left Frances's husband shattered in spirit, but not the indomitable lady one contemporary called the "steam engine." At the age of forty she moved to Boston, with her ailing husband in tow, and embarked on a new career as a physician specializing in electric medicine. Although she reportedly had received medical training, she had never practiced. Her career as an "electro-therapeutist" and her invention of several devices used in this bogus science may have done much to prepare her for a future as a mine promoter. Sometime in the nineties she moved to California seeking a more benign climate for her husband and commenced what she later called a "lucrative practice" in San Francisco. Her first known mining venture was the purchase of the profitable Alpha Mine at Angel's Camp, California. By 1903 she had arrived in Tonopah, alone, since her sick and elderly husband could scarcely have stood the rigors ahead. Now fifty-nine (almost the same age at which Mrs. Morehouse Mallen left her family in Ohio for a new life in the Rockies), she was a stern-looking, tightly corseted figure, with hair skinned firmly back in a bun, a thin fringe of bangs, and large, fierce, dark eyes. The last of her several remarkable careers was about to begin.[7]

Much as we would like to know what led Frances to switch from endangering patients' lives with electric medicine to raiding investors' pocketbooks with mining promotions, this phase of her development is closed to us. In her own time the newspapers hailed Frances as the first woman in Goldfield, present but not signing with the others when the founding fathers organized the new district on 20 October 1903 and the future boomtown consisted of a few white tents scattered among the Joshua trees. Whoever rightly deserves these laurels, none denied that Frances was among the pioneer women in the district. The Valley View placer claim she recorded in the Goldfield district nine days after the organizational meeting testifies to her early presence, and her personality left a strong impression, not only as an unstoppable force but also, in the words of Goldfield pioneer Richard L. Colburn, as "one of the most lovable woman that it has ever been my pleasure to meet." Colburn also noted that Frances engaged others to stake several

Dr. Frances Williams
(Nevada Historical Society).

groups of Goldfield claims on her behalf, but so far as we know, she staked the Valley View, the Oro de Playa at Lone Mountain, the Omega group at the short-lived camp of Ray two years later, and several others with her own hands. At this point Frances did not hesitate to beatify herself: she organized the St. Frances Gold Mining Company to exploit her Goldfield interests.[8]

Her name was soon to appear in the news in connection with an even grander promotional scheme, of which the St. Frances formed a mere subsidiary. Forty miles west of Tonopah a boldly colored treeless escarpment jutted abruptly from the southern edge of the flat desert plain: bare rose-mauve mountains, sculpted and quilled by erosion, and chalk-white peaks, sharply contrasting with the humps and gullies of an area black as coal. Black as coal? Was it possible that the deposits staked in the 1880s near the Coaldale stage station and never taken very seriously might actually be coal? Within three hours of receiving word that they were, Frances Williams set out for the site to acquire these lands, leaving other mine promoters panting in her wake with visions of lucrative contracts to supply the new Tonopah Railroad with coal for its engines and the fast-growing central Nevada mining camps with coal for their heating needs. Frances's success in sewing up the best of the coal lands before anyone else demonstrated her decisiveness and her winning personality; the *Tonopah Miner* called the coup a "sensational feat." William "Uncle Billy" Groezenger, the German prospector who originally staked the coal lands and retained the major share, had refused to deal with anyone but "the doctor."[9]

These coal lands, twelve hundred acres in all, financed by New York, Boston, and California capitalists, provided the centerpiece for a utopian community that Frances offered to investors as "Affiliated Corporations" in a handsome prospectus with green cover and gilt lettering. Unfortunately, our knowledge of its contents depends on newspaper invective, because no copies have come to light—perhaps disillusioned investors hurled their prospectuses into the fire, ripped them up page by page, or crumpled them into the trash instead of preserving them for posterity. The stock offering was widely advertised in the Midwest and elsewhere, and Frances was scathingly excoriated in the pages of the *Tonopah Bonanza* for her "charlatan methods." These included the assurance that investors in the coal company, an electric power company, and the St. Frances Mining and Milling Company would receive dividends within six months. She promised every investor a full quarter-acre of land at Coaldale, "where he can grow all the fruits and vegetables" he needs, and assistance with building a permanent home in the new community. She had platted an elaborate forty-acre townsite around a large central park and christened it Coaldale. As an added inducement, Frances offered "life employment to skilled artisans in any department." Cleverly conveying the suggestion that the lady doth protest too much, William Booth, editor of the *Tonopah Bonanza,* quoted passages from the prospectus in which Frances held forth on the "honesty in my heart": "So you can see, my friends, what my reward will be for being just and honest with you. By being simply careful, energetic, and honest and protecting your interest, my reward is sure to be in the end hundreds of times the amount of money I could possibly take away from you by being dishonest."[10] Frances may have consciously used the doctrine of separate spheres to her advantage, trading on the image of woman as the virtuous bulwark of civilization, too truthful, surely, to involve herself in anything on the order of a dishonest mining promotion.

If the black slopes south of Coaldale had turned out to be coal, perhaps Frances would be remembered today as a beneficent capitalist of extraordinary vision instead of the queen of the charlatans. Actually, it was a species of coal, but one that geologists do not expect will reach fuel grade until it sets for a few million more years. When Goldfield stockbroker Louis K. Koontz later mined coal from the area and sold it to Goldfielders as heating fuel, it melted their grates and ruined their stoves. "They damn near run him out of town," Koontz's son John recalled. The agricultural potential of the Coaldale area proved to be as great an exaggeration as the coal. Here in the deep sands and harsh gravels of the desert, where nothing but scrubby sage and greasewood could gain a foothold, no fruit or vegetable had ever grown or ever would.[11]

Frances was not the only central Nevada mining entrepreneur to give credence to the value of the coal lands, of course. Her severest critic, William Booth, believed in the coal as fervently as she, and his thundering polemic against the "'Frenzied Finance' of Dr. Frances E. Williams" may have been motivated less by disapproval of her promotional activities than by jealousy over her success in acquiring the area before he and his associates could do so. Nor were her methods unusual in a milieu where scoundrels and their promotional schemes abounded. Even financiers generally considered legitimate, such as George Wingfield, the principal owner of the Goldfield Consolidated Mines Company, cost investors millions through overcapitalization and other sharp practices. Among the prospecting fraternity, many practiced petty scams to secure a grubstake or finance a binge (not women prospectors, however, as far as we know). The great Shoshone prospector Tom Fisherman, discoverer of Goldfield and other sites, spent much of his later years cadging grubstakes. He would approach a stranger and display a rich piece of ore with the innocent question, "What you t'ink 'bout this piece rock?" Cannily avoiding specifics on the location of his ore, Fisherman often secured his grubstake and spent it as fast as he could in the nearest saloon. Newsman Elmer J. "Stroller" White described another variation on the prospector's scam as he observed it in Alaska and the Klondike. The prospector walks into camp looking bedraggled and mysterious, "and any prospector who cannot look mysterious when the occasion requires has not learned the rudiments of his trade." Asked if he has found anything worth staking, he displays a rich sample but refuses to say where he got it. Excitement builds in the camp. Just as he intends, the prospector is treated to many rounds of free drinks by those hoping to loosen his tongue. After a while his silent partner, generally a bartender, informs ten carefully selected suckers, in the strictest confidence, that if they will chip in fifty dollars apiece, the prospector will draw them a map and give them directions to his strike. Before they return, with nothing but blisters to show for the trip, the prospector has collected his percentage from the bartender, bought supplies with the grubstake thus acquired, and departed in an entirely different direction.[12]

Viewed in this context, the honesty of Frances Williams probably differed little from that of numerous other prospectors. What set her apart was the scale of her scheme. Most pick-and-shovel prospectors never progressed beyond petty con games for small stakes, and many of the huge swindles were concocted by mining promoters with a close knowledge of advertising but scant acquaintance with actual mining. Promoters of this ilk would garb themselves in the miner's khakis and high boots, with candles stuck in the boot tops and candle grease artistically spattered about to suggest intimacy with the underground workings of mines; prime themselves with a few carefully memorized mining terms like "gangue" and "winze"; and sally forth to one of the elegant mining camp men's clubs where wealthy visiting investors congregated (barred from these clubs unless invited on a "ladies night," the women prospectors could not avail themselves of this opportunity any more than they could verbally advertise their properties through networking in saloons as their male counterparts did). Frances differed from these, and from highly successful and notoriously unscrupulous promoters such as Goldfield's George Graham Rice, in that she combined actual field knowledge of prospecting with promotion on a grand scale. As the lives of Lillian Malcolm and Mrs. C. T. Ricketts have demonstrated, women in prospecting showed no lack of the promotional skills needed to convince investors and used those skills in a legitimate way. What lends a certain ring of truth to the *Bonanza*'s charges of charlatanism was the fact that, unlike Lillian Malcolm or Nellie Cashman, Frances aimed her pitch not at the wealthy and sophisticated investors who could afford to gamble on mining stocks but at the small farmers to whom she promised land that would grow every fruit and vegetable and at the craftsmen to whom she guaranteed lifetime employment. "We send this invitation [to buy stock] as a voice from the wilderness, to the afflicted and oppressed and distressed workmen of mankind."[13] One pictures a midwestern farm family standing on the Coaldale townsite that was never developed, sand blowing around them, the empty sagebrush plain stretching away toward the gaudy rose, white, and black peaks of the escarpment, and remembering the fertile fields they sold to attain this prize.

Frances sued the *Bonanza* for libel and published a withering counterattack against the "malignity and mendacity of this man [Booth]" in the pages of the *Tonopah Miner.* While airily acknowledging certain "trifling errors" in the Affiliated Corporations prospectus, she defended the financial solidity of her enterprises, professing a listing in

Dun and Bradstreet and an income of three million dollars a year. Booth, she suggested, had been paid to defame her in his "blackmailing newspaper." She closed with a blast against the offending editor: "I submit to a discriminating public opinion the character, or rather the infamy, of a man who, knowing that my male relatives are absent from the State, cowardly seizes upon the opportunity to brutally attack the veracity and business honor of one whom he sees fit to sneeringly designate in print as 'this woman'"—a variant on what historian Antonia Fraser has called the "Only-a-Weak-Woman Syndrome." Coming from the "steam engine," it must have evoked hearty guffaws in Tonopah, which grew louder a few months later when local authorities placed Frances under bonds to keep the peace after she pursued Goldfield attorney Henry Lind with a gun. Lind hastily departed for California on a well-timed business trip. The offense that provoked Frances to the brink of violence has not come to light.[14]

Nothing further was heard of Frances's libel suit, suggesting that the *Bonanza*'s charges contained more than a grain of truth. Nonetheless, Frances continued to live and work in Goldfield, where she enjoyed a large measure of respect as a Goldfield pioneer and businesswoman known as "a shrewd judge of a good mine." Clearly, the Affiliated Corporations promotion, fraudulent though it was, had in no way offended the mores of the business community. Until the death of her invalid husband in January 1908 she devoted some of her time to him and to her medical practice in San Francisco, but she remained actively involved in prospecting and mining. Her erect figure, clad in a khaki suit, was a familiar sight as she supervised the work on her Goldfield claims until she sold them in June 1906 to a company formed by several of the most prominent mining men in Goldfield. The sale brought her a large sum in cash, but the most lucrative of her endeavors was probably the deal she had closed less than two weeks earlier, the famous Frances-Mohawk lease.[15]

After leasers George Hayes and M. B. Monnette struck an Aladdin's chamber of ore in the spring of 1906 in their lease on the Mohawk Mine, they could scarcely believe the bonanza would last, and they realized that even if it did, all the gold in their allotted territory could never be exploited before their time ran out. When they offered to sell the lease to George Graham Rice, he delayed because his partner, "Shanghai Larry" Sullivan, insisted that their mining engineer first make a two-week examination of the mine. Frances, by contrast, had lost none of the decisive boldness that characterized her lightning journey to Coaldale, or any of her scorn for those with projects that "failed to incubate." When the opportunity came to join with Goldfield's most successful mine promoter, David Mackenzie, in purchasing a four-thousand-dollar sublease on a small subsection of the Hayes-Monnette ground, she seized it at once while Rice and Sullivan still lingered at the starting gate. The name of the sublease, the Frances-Mohawk, reflected Frances's heavy involvement. From his luxurious offices trimmed with mahogany, furnished with overstuffed leather chairs in which investors could take their ease, and manned by forty clerks, Mackenzie launched his promotion of the Frances-Mohawk Mining and Leasing Company with a barrage of telegrams. One messenger boy alone remembered carrying out five thousand of them and returning with thousands of orders.

Nonetheless, success did not immediately follow. Although Frances and Mackenzie vigorously pressed development with the most modern and expensive equipment of the day, including a heavy electric hoist and Goldfield's first air compressor with machine drills, shipped by express at great cost from distant cities, more than a month passed before they struck ore that looked even remotely promising. Fortunately, they had the capital to keep going, and soon the work force broke into a "veritable jeweler's shop" underground. The first shipment of high-grade ore went forth two months after they broke ground, and others rolled steadily down the tracks thereafter. So rich did the strike prove to be that by the time the lease ended in January, the company had mined $2,275,000 worth of ore from a section of ground 200 by 375 feet. Frances reportedly made a "comfortable fortune" in the heady days when the Frances-Mohawk was the envy of the western mining world. But when a feud between mining titans destroyed the company less than three years later, she had already lost every tithe.[16]

Frances expended her last fortune and the energies of her final years prospecting and developing mines south of Goldfield on the northern rim of the Death Valley country. A newspaper of the period described

ON THE 300 FOOT LEVEL, FRANCES M. HAWK MINE
WHERE MILLIONS OF DOLLARS WORTH OF GOLD ORE HAS BEEN MINED.
GOLDFIELD NEVADA

Underground in the workings of the Frances-Mohawk lease, Goldfield,
Nevada (Larson Collection, Nevada State Museum, Carson City NV).

the region vividly. Leaving the fledgling camp of Hornsilver and heading south toward Death Valley, one climbs the Slate Ridge, then descends toward the valley that separates this spur from the Gold Mountain Range. Here a mysterious blue haze hovers on the horizon about
six miles away, giving the traveler the strange sensation that beyond
this curtain lies the edge of the earth, the margin where it drops away
into nothingness. Winter covers the mountains with snow; summer
brings furnace blasts of heat from Death Valley, penetrating every ar-
royo, so that work can be carried on only "between gasps." These were
deserts harsh enough to tax the energies of the young and hardy, let
alone those of a woman now in her sixties, but Frances journeyed into
them unfazed.[17]

Her new ventures commenced with the promotional ballyhoo at
which she excelled. In mid-May 1908 she secured a lease at Hornsilver
and organized the Frances Lime Point Mining Company, capitalized at
one million dollars, with a "small block" of stock offered to lucky investors at ten cents a share. Development proceeded rapidly, and the

first wagonload of ore attracted considerable attention when Frances paraded it through the streets of Goldfield. Announcements of promising assays in gold received the usual fanfare. Again, as at Empire and Miller's Lake, the paths of the women prospectors intersected without joining. Mrs. C. A. Wright, described in the press as "one of Nevada's foremost feminine prospectors," had located promising claims and organized the Nevada Goldfield Extension Mining Company with herself as president and general manager in 1905 at nearby Gold Mountain, where Frances also had holdings. Not far from the Frances Lime Point, the petite figure of Helen Cottrell could daily be seen supervising her work force at the Orleans, Hornsilver's banner producer in that period. But Frances, like most women prospectors, seemed to prefer male partners. She chose men for all the officers other than herself on the Frances Lime Point, and when two women sought involvement in her next enterprise, she appears to have given them short shrift. David Mackenzie, a tall, rawboned, Canadian-born boomer in his middle thirties, was her most important partner.[18]

Scarcely two months after Frances launched the Lime Point a much more promising plum dropped into her lap. Several years earlier she had secured the Royal Flush group of claims in the Gold Mountain district and afterward ignored them, being caught up in other ventures. Then, in the early summer of 1908, the young man she had hired to do the annual assessment work on her Gold Mountain claims came to her with a sample "literally alive with gold" in his hands and a story to quicken the blood of any mining entrepreneur. He said that as he worked on the Royal Flush something shiny in a ledge about eighteen inches wide caught his eye. He had gouged out a chunk of ore with his pick, and he would tell Frances where he found it—for a price. (Bear in mind that although Frances owned the claims, the Royal Flush group encompassed a large territory, and many a mine owner had wasted all his capital digging in the wrong places.) The steam engine had lost none of her old decisiveness. She set off for Gold Mountain faster than word of the new strike could leak out—and that was very fast. In the words of the *Goldfield Chronicle,* "She came, she saw, and she paid." She also took samples from the ledge. The subsequent assayer's report almost surpassed belief: $4,305 per ton![19]

By the time the resulting stampedes from Hornsilver and Goldfield reached Gold Mountain, Frances and her associates had long since set to work repairing the monuments and boundary markers on her claims. She next set a small force of miners to work on the ledge, and the first wagonload of ore went off to Goldfield. After the Downer Brothers, a well-known and reputable assaying firm, and the Goldfield Reduction Works had finished processing the ore, the returns again strained credulity. Ore from the fabulous Frances-Mohawk had averaged $120 per ton. The ore from the Royal Flush averaged $739 a ton, and picked samples showed values of $329,000, reportedly the highest assay ever recorded in Goldfield, a district known for its unusually rich ores. Frances lost no time in organizing the Frances Gold Mountain Mining Company. Goldfield investors, aware of the extraordinary assays, snapped up all available stock immediately.[20]

Another element that buoyed stock sales was the popular theory that the Royal Flush was in truth the legendary Lost Breyfogle ledge, an idea that Frances made every effort to encourage. Whether it was the charlatan's trick of someone who had planted artifacts in an old abandoned tunnel on the Royal Flush or whether she believed it herself is difficult to say. Perhaps when camping out in that hallucinatory country, as she often did, even the hard-headed and practical Frances fell under the spell of the grandfather of all mining legends. The story of Charles Breyfogle, the prospector who traveled into the desert in the 1860s, picked up rich samples of gold, and later emerged too crazed by his wanderings to find the spot again, has been told in many forms and placed in many locales, but the weight of opinion held that his lost ledge lay on the northern fringe of the Death Valley region (just the right location for the Royal Flush). One variant holds that Breyfogle shammed madness to conceal his strike and secretly mined the ledge for several years before the Indians killed him. It was some such version, evidently, that caused Jeanne E. Weir, history professor at the University of Nevada and founder of the Nevada Historical Society, to journey south from Reno in the autumn of 1908 to examine the Royal Flush, no doubt at Frances's invitation. Weir felt rather proud of herself for roughing it on the "hurricane deck of a Nevada cayuse" on her trip into the desert. It is likely that along the way the most lovable woman Richard Colburn had ever met beguiled Weir with the full force of her charm and regaled the historian with tales of her own experiences in the wilds. At the Royal Flush, Weir observed and removed several artifacts from the abandoned tunnel: an old drill and spoon, an old-fashioned British-made hammer, and a Sheffield steel tamping rod of the kind used to load holes with black powder in the era that predated dynamite. These relics convinced Weir that the site had been mined during the Civil War when Breyfogle roamed the desert.[21]

The press trumpeted the story when Weir announced her conclusion: "One of the mysteries of the desert for over fifty years was a mystery no longer. . . . The cause of many a daring prospector leaving his bones to bleach on the desert, was none other than the present day Royal Flush mine." The stir that followed can readily be imagined. Subsequently, a letter written to Frances by Weir elicited a brief and crisp response that the doctor intended to close her San Francisco practice and devote all her time to her mining claims instead of the juicy reminiscences of a pioneer woman prospector that Weir no doubt had hoped to elicit. Perhaps Professor Weir had served her purpose.[22]

Despite this authoritative certification of its status as the Lost Breyfogle and the extraordinary initial assays, the Royal Flush failed to produce pay ore during the winter of 1908–9. Frances pressed development work forward, driving several tunnels and sinking a shaft, at the same time continuing operations that had as yet yielded no significant returns at the Lime Point. All this activity cost money, and some believed Frances had lost heavily in the bank failures that wracked Goldfield in 1907–8 and reduced many a mining nabob to penury. She had deposited funds from the Royal Flush promotion at a viable bank, but many of her earlier gains may have been wiped away in the failure of the State Bank and Trust. Then in late March 1909 a trial commenced in which the Goldfield Consolidated Mines Company, owners of the Mohawk Mine, sought damages from the Frances-Mohawk. The ostensible reason was alleged improper timbering during lease operations; the real reason lay in the determination of George Wingfield, known for his ruthlessness toward enemies and rivals, to destroy David Mackenzie. Incidentally, that also meant Mackenzie's principal partner in the Frances-Mohawk, Frances Williams. Perhaps Frances foresaw that Wingfield, who usually accomplished his purposes, would succeed in destroying the business of the most successful broker in Goldfield. Perhaps she also knew that, at sixty-five, she no longer possessed the resilience of Mackenzie, who would rise from disaster and go on to follow one mining boom after another into the 1920s.[23]

Two days after the trial began Frances suffered a massive heart attack. She had gone to a restaurant for her supper as usual, chatting pleasantly with friends and remarking that she "felt finely." On her return to the Grimshaw Hotel, her usual residence in Goldfield, an agonizing pain seized her, and she asked the proprietress to help her to her room. Within hours she was dead.

Her mines failed to live up to their initial promise. James Williams, a Chicago businessman and the only survivor among her many children, quickly relinquished the presidency of the mining companies in which he had inherited his mother's controlling interest but nourished sufficient faith in the Royal Flush to retain a large block of stock for some time. Despite promising reports from mining engineers over the decades, the mine never produced well, however. Unless Frances had somehow conjured those amazing assays into existence, the Royal Flush must have been no more than a rich and isolated pocket of gold—which is by no means inconsistent with the theory of the Lost Breyfogle. According to Weir, sticky-fingered politicians with a fondness for curios stole all the Royal Flush artifacts from the Nevada Historical Society's museum except the old drill.[24]

In retrospect, Frances Williams's own story seems far stranger than the familiar mining legend of Breyfogle. How commonplace the image of a crazed giant of a man stumbling barefoot out of the desert with chunks of gold in his hands compared with the life she had led. Over the course of her long career she had buried two husbands and all but one of her many children, made a fortune on silk-hat varnish and lost it in orange groves, and built a new career in electric medicine and abandoned it to join the last gold rush on the western mining frontier, where she created another life for herself as a prospector and mine promoter at an age when many were content to knit by the fireside. She had inveigled poor investors to their doom with her promises and her nonexistent coal lands. Then she had made and lost another fortune from the Frances-Mohawk only to be herself ruined by a bigger shark than she. Was the Royal Flush only the last and cleverest of her promotional schemes? We will never know whether, in her heart of hearts, she believed she had at last found the Lost Breyfogle in the place where the blue mist gathers at the edge of the world.

FIVE

# Ellen Nay: Native Daughter

It was late in the afternoon of 31 March 1909 when Ellen Clifford Nay made the discovery that caused her to cast off her sunbonnet and race through the sagebrush toward her husband. As she told the story afterward:

> When we got back to my claims it was about 4 o'clock in the afternoon. I strayed up the wash a ways and found a boulder half hidden in the sand. I knocked off a little piece, examined it, and found a pretty speck of gold. I knocked off a larger piece, and my gracious, it was half covered with yellow stuff that looked like gold, but I couldn't believe my eyes. I threw off my bonnet and away I flew to Joe. I told him I couldn't believe it was gold—there was too much of it. I never saw so much gold on a single piece of rock before. But Joe insisted it was gold and he, too, began to get excited. He wanted to know if there was any more of it and I told him the rock was too big for me to carry. Joe forgot all about being lame, and away we went. I wrapped the boulder up in my apron and Joe carried it. It weighed 75 pounds and was just full of gold.[1]

In later years it was sometimes said that Ellen stumbled on the gold-studded boulder by accident while she was hunting her father's stray cattle, a typical explanation. The folklore of prospecting abounds with tales of the lucky accident that led to the discovery of a rich mine—the rock picked up to throw at a bird, a cow, or a wandering burro; the nugget welling into view from the ripples of the stream where the prospector was washing his overalls; the mineral-laden chunk dislodged while killing a rattlesnake, hunting an antelope, or burying a dead partner. Perhaps the enduring popularity of such tales lay in the hopeful message they bore: any fool, no matter how ignorant of mining, had a chance to strike it rich. Other versions of Ellen's discovery presumed that her prospecting must have been a casual Sunday diversion, as common among ranch wives in mining country as the city woman's

Ellen Nay holds her pick and a sample of gold ore while her husband Joe
stands beside her (Lottie Nay Collection, Central Nevada Historical Society).

afternoon game of whist and no more serious. Even Ellen's own relatives told these stories. According to her nephew, Joe Clifford, "Ellen's
discovery was just an accidental freak of luck. She knew how to
prospect, and her husband prospected a lot. They were up there fool-
ing around, and she found that float. Hell, anybody couldn't miss that
float. . . . It was pure gold. . . . It was on the side of the hill, scattered
down the mountain there, and she just had to pick up some of it."[2] But
those who mistook the shining boulder wrapped in her apron for a
freak of luck failed to understand the consuming ambition that had
brought Ellen Nay to Salsbury Wash.

A few months later newspapers would be calling Ellen the "brave,
honest true and intrepid woman, whom all Nevada delights to honor,"

and a "native of the desert upon whom the hardships of a rigorous frontier life . . . had left but gentle traces," and there was more truth in these remarks than in much else that was said about her.[3] The fourth of Edward and Esther Clifford's eleven children, nine of whom survived, Ellen was born on 29 August 1879 at Tybo, a central Nevada mining camp in the Hot Creek Range, some thirty miles northeast of Salsbury Wash. Among the women prospectors whose backgrounds are known, she is one of the first to be born on the mining frontier. Her father, a short, stocky Scotch-Irish immigrant, at first worked in the Maryland coal mines, where he married the English-born Esther, and later in Pennsylvania, Colorado, and Wyoming coal mines before bundling his family into a wagon and heading for Nevada. There he became construction foreman at the Spanish Belt Mines in Barcelona when silver discoveries by Mexican prospectors belatedly resulted in a brief spurt of development in the mid-seventies. Somewhere along the way he learned prospecting from an old Scot who advised him to "look in the bug holes, lad," that is, in the indentations in quartz where iron has leached out leaving gold behind.

The grand schemes of investors at Barcelona soon collapsed, and the Cliffords moved on to Tybo, where Ed found work in the lead-silver mines. But the Tybo boom was faltering. In 1879 the principal mining company failed, and a year later the camp had practically expired. In 1882–83 Ellen's father apparently decided he would no longer toil underground in the dark tunnels where he had spent the last decade of his life, nor would he tie the fortunes of his growing family to mining booms that repeatedly turned to quicksand under their feet. Once more he bundled Esther and the little ones into the wagon, this time to homestead a sheep ranch on Willow Creek in the remote Stone Cabin Valley, where Ellen grew up. Nye County records for 1883 listing the Cliffords' taxable property as the homestead and one milk cow suggest a period of considerable hardship. No doubt, before Ed built the new frame house, the family lived near the creek in the rectangular building of gray stone blocks that gave the valley its name.[4]

Never one to reminisce, Ellen seems to have had little to say of her early years. She spent them in a remote desert world as isolated as any on the frontier. No railroad, or even a major trail route, passed anywhere near the Stone Cabin Valley. Aside from the handful of miners working on at Tybo, the nearest settlement was the Nye County seat, then the little town of Belmont, more than thirty miles northwest, as the crow flies, across the desert and the Monitor Mountains. Even neighbors were few and far between in an era when one could still drive a team for a hundred miles without seeing a human habitation. The valleys of the Kawich Mountains, far to the southeast, harbored an occasional rancher, as did the mountain meadows where the rough wagon road ascended toward Belmont. But excepting these scattered pioneers, the Stone Cabin Valley, with its occasional springs creating sudden surprising patches of green grass amid the vast plain of gray sage, its galloping bands of mustangs, and its rims of ruddy mountains on the east and the west, remained the private domain of the Cliffords for nearly twenty years. "You're sort of isolated," said Joe Clifford more than a century later. "There's a damn lot of hard work. But it's our life, and we like it."[5]

Ellie, as her family called her, would have learned the hard work very young, with so many little brothers and sisters to help care for and the unending tasks of cooking, laundry, and cleaning that were the lot of ranch women. Her schooling was minimal, not beyond the fourth- or fifth-grade level, probably in a one-room schoolhouse where most of the pupils were her own brothers and sisters, but she learned her ranch tasks well. According to her daughter "Leafy" (christened Olephia), she became "one of the best cooks who ever lived." She must have learned the men's work too, wearing knicker pants beneath her long skirts and riding the range. Tiny as she was, a "little bit of a thing" scarcely over five feet tall and weighing only ninety pounds as a full-grown woman, she must also have stood at her father's side when he worked iron at the forge and learned to use a hammer and saw when carpentry needed to be done.[6]

But of all the things she learned during those early years in the Stone Cabin Valley, the one that took root deep within where dreams are nurtured was prospecting. She learned it first as a small child, tagging along behind her father and brothers, hurrying to match her short steps to theirs, watching, her dark head cocked birdlike to one side, to see how they chipped at the rocks with their picks and what they were hunting.

144

As she grew older and began to pin her long, straight brunette hair on her head in the puffy upswept style of the period, she continued to go out with them, the only woman in the family who did so. Although her father still called her "little girl" in reference to her tiny stature, he apparently encouraged her. Perhaps he knew it made no sense to tell a daughter who could bend irons at the forge and handle lumber as well as any man that she should confine herself to more feminine pursuits. Or perhaps he enjoyed sharing his own enthusiasm with her. Prospecting was no mere game to Ellen. In time the dream of the rich strike would flower into a fierce ambition, later it would soften into a private passion, but never would it leave her.[7]

In the mid-nineties two young Mormon cowboys, the brothers John and Joseph Brigham Nay, decided to leave their home in Pine Valley, Utah, and go adventuring. John, accompanied by two cousins, left first. They meant to join relatives at Belmont, but instead of going there by the most direct route, they planned to make a long sweep south to Ash Meadows on the fringe of the Death Valley country, ride on to Bishop and eventually north to the Reese River Valley and Belmont. Had they realized the dangers lurking amid the bright sunshine and turquoise springs in Ash Meadows, then a nest of killers and desperadoes far beyond the reach of the law, the Nays might well have changed their plans. But luckily nothing worse befell them than an encounter with the formidable desert frontiersman Jack Longstreet. When the Nays rode up, the big, long-haired Longstreet appeared in the doorway of his white stone cabin, no doubt with his gun at the ready, as was his habit, and inquired suspiciously, "You boys Mormons?" The Nays, guessing that Mormons were distinctly less welcome than outlaws in Ash Meadows society, hastily protested that they were no such thing. Longstreet may or may not have believed them, but he accepted their explanations and offered them the warm southern hospitality with which he treated those travelers who were fortunate enough not to encounter him behind the barrel of a gun.[8] One day Joe Nay would also meet Longstreet, under very different circumstances.

The young men continued their odyssey, joining up with Joe in the Reese River Valley and finally arriving at Belmont in 1896. There, perhaps at a dance in the old Cosmopolitan Saloon, Joe noticed a petite, dark-haired seventeen-year-old at the organ while the assembled pioneers swung heartily around the floor in a Virginia reel. He might have shared a dance with Ellie Clifford, as the singing notes of Henry Stimler's fiddle filled the room and John led the old fiddler's own daughter, Lottie, out onto the floor. When the Nay cousins returned to Utah, Joe and John stayed behind. They found work as cowboys and began "riding the line," an imaginary line beginning in the Kawich Mountains and extending ninety miles west across the desert to Silver Peak. Their task was to guard the wandering cattle herds belonging to ranchers in the Monitor and Smoky valleys from the depredations of rustlers ranging north from hideaways in the Death Valley region—just the kind of adventure laced with danger they had sought when they left Utah.

All the same, riding the line across the Clayton Playa, past the long rosy mesa east of Montezuma, and along the low piñon- and juniper-studded hills for so many miles with scarcely a glimpse of other human faces along the way was lonely work. At the most westerly point even Silver Peak, with its handful of miners, must have beckoned like Dodge City at the end of a Texas trail drive. On the eastern end of the line they had a choice. They could stop for the night with the old bachelor Irishman Richard Breen at his ranch in one of the valleys of the Kawich. Or they could ride thirty miles farther north to the Stone Cabin Ranch, where there would be the laughter and lively talk of nine young Cliffords, and probably music as well, for Ellie played the piano and Joe Nay was fond of strumming the guitar and singing cowboy songs in his deep bass voice—if he had someone to sing to. When the Nay brothers came right down to it, the choice between a night spent in the company of the taciturn old Breen and riding another thirty miles to the Cliffords to linger for two or three days was no contest. Besides, as Lottie Stimler put it, "Joe had a case on Ellie."9

In late autumn 1899 Edward Clifford issued an open invitation in the pages of the *Belmont Courier* to all of Nye County to attend the wedding of his daughter Ellen and Joseph Nay. On the night of 7 December in the old redbrick Belmont Courthouse, a Catholic priest married the young couple, Joe wearing his best suit, his luxuriant mustache neatly combed, his blunt-featured, kindly face beaming down on the bride in her white cashmere dress trimmed with chiffon, lace, and satin ribbons, the veil over her dark hair fastened with natural flowers. She was twenty; the bridegroom, eight years older. A wedding party with wine, cake, and ice cream followed at the Cliffords' town home in Belmont. The assembled population of Nye County then repaired to the Cosmopolitan for a wedding dance that lasted until four in the morning, almost time for the roosters the Nays had received as wedding presents to begin crowing.[10]

During the following year Ellie and Joe divided their time between the Stone Cabin Ranch and Belmont, where their first child, Emma Nevada, named for the well-known nineteenth-century opera star, was born in December 1900. In the course of that year an event occurred that was to alter forever the lives of everyone in Nye County and, indeed, the entire state of Nevada: in the spring of 1900 Jim Butler discovered silver ore at the site that was to become Tonopah. By early winter Nye County's pioneers had begun to converge on the new mining district, their hopes sharpened by a generation of hardship and poverty. Ellie's father came early, one of the first to be apprised by his old friend Jim Butler of the opportunities at the new strike. Clifford, however, gained little profit from being among the first arrivals and came to believe he had been done out of his fair share. John Nay and his future wife, Lottie Stimler, also arrived early; John was one of the first men Butler hired to work his claims, and Lottie ran the first boardinghouse in Tonopah. Ellie and Joe followed in the spring of 1901, soon enough that baby Emma Nevada was said to be the first infant in Tonopah. With no ranch or business of their own and no means of support other than Joe's occasional jobs as a cowboy, they had little to lose by taking a chance on a new mining boom. Still, leaving the ranch work that was all he had ever known for the mines marked a major shift for Joe Nay, one that may well have been influenced by his relatives' presence at the camp and his young wife's intense interest in mining.[11]

Life in early Tonopah generated great expectations, as boomers from all over the West rushed to the new site, white tents sprouted on the hillside, and the days when the Cliffords could invite the entire county to their daughter's wedding began to look humorously antique, but it also entailed a good deal of hardship. Joe worked in the mines and hauled water with teams to the thirsty camp. The family lived in a tent with dirt banked up on the sides through the snows and icy winds of winter. A raging blizzard in the winter of 1901–2 severed Tonopah from the outside world for two weeks. Provisions ran so low that the camp's forty or so residents decided to pool everything they possessed and eat together in the boardinghouse. Fuel dwindled rapidly to a few logs of green cedar, which they saved for cooking in the boardinghouse stove. "It was practically impossible for anyone to keep warm," observed Jay Carpenter in his history of Tonopah. "They merely attempted to avoid freezing." When the "black plague" (influenza and pneumonia) struck, Tonopahans gathered for the camp's first funeral, and Joe Nay, with others chiming in, sang hymns learned long ago to provide the dead man with some semblance of a ceremonial departure.[12]

In March 1902 Joe came close to joining the unfortunates he had sung to their final rest in the Tonopah cemetery. During a visit with Ellie's family at the Stone Cabin Ranch, Joe agreed to go out riding with her older brothers, Jim and Ed. Because 11 March was a cold day, with new snow on the mountains, and Joe had brought no warm clothes, he borrowed them from his father-in-law. He also borrowed old Ed's usual saddlehorse. No one seems entirely sure why the Cliffords decided to ride so far south toward the ranch in the Kawich where Jack Longstreet now lived, having moved north from the Ash Meadows spread where John and his cousins had once met him—or those who know do not care to say. For some time, the Cliffords had been embroiled in a worsening dispute with Longstreet. Before the day was done that dispute erupted into a shootout that removed a chunk of Longstreet's beard, scraped a blood blister under Jim Clifford's nose, and left the unarmed Joe Nay bleeding on the ground, shot just below the left knee as he tried to scramble from his horse and take cover. One of the Cliffords spurred his horse back to the ranch for a wagon, since Joe was unable to ride. When they finally brought her wounded husband home late that night, Ellie found his boot filled with frozen blood.[13]

According to his daughter Leafy, Joe spent much of the following year in the hospital. Because the Nays had little money, his mounting medical bills were largely paid for by the warmhearted and open-handed Butlers, already so rich from the Tonopah mines that they could afford to be generous. Three months after the shooting, when Joe was carried into the Belmont Courthouse to testify in Longstreet's trial for assault, the sickening odor from his wound suggested that he might yet lose his leg. Fortunately, this did not happen, though a part of the bone had been blown away and none of the operations he underwent in subsequent years succeeded in removing the last scraps of lead from his leg. Joe emerged from the ordeal forever lamed and in pain, with his vigorous wife compensating for him in more ways than most people realized, but with no bitterness in his heart. Longstreet's acquittal on the assault charge galled him not at all because he evidently believed, as did many others, that Longstreet had mistaken him, garbed as he was in another man's clothes and riding another man's horse, for old Ed Clifford. "He didn't mean to hit me," Joe would say. "He didn't do it on purpose." Ellie, by contrast, found little reason for absolution in Longstreet's probable intention to shoot her father instead of her husband. She was endowed with no small measure of what was known in Nye County as the "Clifford temper," and her anger at Longstreet for the harm he had done her husband would burn brightly as long as she lived.[14]

During the period Joe remained in bed and Ellie worried that he might die or lose his leg, a little-noticed event occurred some thirty miles south of Tonopah, not far from the spot where the Nay brothers had made their winter camp at Alkali Springs in the days when they rode the line. Harry Stimler, Lottie's brother, and his boyhood friend William Marsh located claims at a new site discovered by the shadowy Shoshone, Tom Fisherman. They named the spot Grandpa, quipping that their piece of the desert would turn out to be the grandfather of all new Nevada mining strikes, and events would prove them more right than they ever dreamed.[15]

None of the Nays participated in the rushes to Goldfield during 1903, but old Ed Clifford once more hastened to the scene at an early date. His name appears among the thirty-six original organizers of the district when it was rechristened Goldfield in October 1903. In a reprise of his Tonopah experience the elder Clifford failed to profit from the advantages of early arrival by staking or buying a good claim. As a well-to-do rancher with savings to invest, he could easily have purchased some of the future premier mines of Goldfield when penniless prospectors offered to sell them for next to nothing during the summer of 1903. Instead, he invariably backed the wrong horse, ignoring the treasure troves hidden in the area one day to be known throughout the nation as the "golden horseshoe." When others grew rich and strutted the board sidewalks like Spanish grandees, Ed Clifford emerged embittered from his experiences in Tonopah and Goldfield. Still, even though he had twice failed to secure a valuable mine for himself, he had learned a thing or two: how town lot sales at the height of a boom could bring nearly as much money as mines and how mines could be successfully promoted.[16]

Although the Nays were slower to join the rush to Goldfield than Ellie's father, John and Lottie had arrived by the spring of 1904, and Joe and Ellie followed soon afterward. Goldfield was "drunk with money" in the palmy days of the last great boom on the mining frontier, but little of it filtered down to Ellie and Joe. He worked in the mines, as much as his lame leg allowed, and she took in laundry. When he came home he would take her place at the galvanized iron tub and washboard, while she hung rough work clothes out on the line and ironed. Interestingly, the Nays' willingness to ignore the customary differentiation of tasks into "men's work" and "women's work" went in both directions: Joe proved as willing to take Ellie's place at the washtub as she was to take a man's place at the forge. Their descendants remember their opposite temperaments: Joe, kindly, soft-spoken, and good-natured, a man of quiet strength; the strong-willed Ellie, warm, quick, volatile, and hot-tempered. But these opposites had melded into the tightest of bonds. They are remembered above all for being together in everything they undertook, one never far from the other. So they were when they eked out a living together at the laundry tub in their Goldfield days.[17]

In late April 1905 Ellie joined the rush to Gold Reed, where she located her first claim, the Red Bird. Gold Reed, at the southern edge of the Kawich Range some fifty-three miles east of Goldfield as the crow flies, was situated in desert terrain so harsh that the editor of the *Tonopah Bonanza* thought it necessary to issue an unusual warning to prospectors contemplating the trip. They would need plenty of provisions, including feed for their animals and water for themselves. The nearest small desert spring was a fifteen-mile ride from Gold Reed. These hardships failed to deter Ellie, even though she was more than five months pregnant with her second child. Her claim proved worthless, however, and she returned to Goldfield. In a humble shack in Columbia, a suburb of Goldfield, Ellie gave birth to her second daughter, Olephia, on 13 August 1905.

In December 1905, when the baby was just a few months old, the Nays joined the stampede to Clifford (later renamed Helena), the new camp that Ellie's father and brothers were promoting on the basis of a discovery by Indian prospectors. Although the newspapers reported that Mrs. Nay did a "rushing business" with her boardinghouse at Stone Cabin during the excitement, the Nays appear to have reaped only marginal advantages from the highly successful promotion conducted by the Clifford family. The claims the Nays staked in this district in January 1906, two by Ellie and one by Joe, did nothing to improve their impoverished condition, and they were soon back in Goldfield.[18]

Ellie would have had a good deal to think about as she stood at the washtub day after day with her arms in the soapsuds. All around her women prospectors were making news staking, developing, and promoting claims. According to the *Goldfield Sun,* the "petticoat brigade" was "taking a prominent place in the rejuvenation of old Nevada."[19] Ellie may have read of the exploits of Bessie Miller, Lillian Malcolm, Frances Williams, and many others in the local newspapers. If all these and many more women were making headlines, could Ellie Nay, who knew the terrain where she had spent her entire life, as an Alaska sourdough or a Boston doctor would never know it, be far behind?

So it was that Ellie turned to her husband and said, "Dad, let's go find a mine of our own!" She did not plan to join the stampedes that still sent the more volatile elements of Goldfield and Tonopah dashing toward the livery stables at the news of each new mining excitement. Ellie had already tried hastening out with the crowd to Gold Reed and

Clifford. Moreover, she had the experiences of her embittered father to guide her. Perhaps she also thought of the children, for Ellie was no Mountain Charley, dumping her little ones in an orphanage while she pursued her fortunes. She might well have concluded that racing all over the map of Nevada after each mirage that flickered on the horizon would be no life for her little girls. It would be better to station her family at a kind of base camp where they could scrape a living while searching for a mine, although this solution would necessarily entail taking eight-year-old Emma Nevada out of school. Ellie and Joe settled on Salsbury Wash, a crease beside a sugarloaf mountain in the arid sagebrush country about twelve miles southwest of Stone Cabin Ranch.[20]

Salsbury Wash had already been through a cycle of discovery, abandonment, and renewed interest. According to a newspaper report, prospectors staked claims in the area in 1900 before the strikes at Tonopah and Goldfield galvanized the mining world. Finding no further indications of pay ore, the prospectors neglected their assessment work and allowed the claims to lapse. In the winter of 1908–9, when Ellie and Joe packed their meager belongings and their little daughters into the wagon and headed out, a few prospectors had started working the Salsbury Wash area again, but none struck the gold that Ellie's disparagers later declared too obvious for anyone to miss.

Chary as prospectors tend to be of any competitors on the scene, the presence of these others was important to the Nays. Tonopah was a day's ride away, and prospectors would need supplies and an occasional good meal. So would travelers on the road from Tonopah to Tybo, Clifford, and other points east. They would be sure to patronize a roadhouse where they could buy matches, kerosene, and other small necessities. Ellie would serve meals and Joe would help with the dishes and attend to the travelers' horses. In between, and first and foremost, the Nays would go prospecting.[21]

Little Leafy well remembered those prospecting expeditions, which commenced in Salsbury Wash and continued throughout her girlhood. Her parents would hitch up their horses, Kit and Deck, and load in their little daughters, a keg of water, eggs wrapped in newspapers and packed in cans, and other foodstuffs, along with Ellie's prospecting paraphernalia, the mortar and pan, magnifying glasses, and so forth. By night they camped out, enjoying Ellie's delicious fried potatoes, fried beef, and Dutch oven biscuits, cooked over a fire of sagebrush coals.[22]

Sometimes the Nays left the children with grandmother Clifford while they went prospecting. As it happened, the big discovery took place on one of these trips about four miles from the Salsbury Wash roadhouse when Ellie admitted she had grown tired and discouraged. She later related the circumstances: "I had found some float before that looked good but couldn't find where it came from. So we went back to prospect the claims which I had located on the twelfth of March. You see, Joe was rather lame and couldn't get around very well, so when we located the claims, I built the monuments and Joe wrote out the location notices. I located the claims in the name of myself, my brother Ed, and my mother. I had found some black rock that looked like some rich stuff found by my husband once, and I had carried that rock in my eye."[23]

Her discovery of the gold-covered boulder half-hidden in the sand ensued, but with darkness falling fast, it was too late to trace the ledge whence it came. "I told Joe to do the panning, and I would go out and bring in some more float." (It was quite clear who was in charge and also more than probable that, unlike many husband-and-wife teams in which a woman novice learned from a prospector husband, the former Utah cowboy had learned how to use the mortar and pan from his wife.) Around this time one of the Salsbury Wash prospectors stopped by. Although the Nays refrained from showing him the golden boulder until they had traced the ledge, they could scarcely conceal their excitement. "We didn't sleep much that night, and we were up at four o'clock to look for the ledge."[24]

Sometime that night Ellie's brothers Ed and John trailed in after unsuccessful prospecting at another site. With characteristic generosity their sister welcomed them to share in her good fortune. After the four of them drove their wagon to the site of Ellie's discovery in the early morning light, they split into teams and started working their way slowly up the gulch to trace the ledge, Ed with Ellie in the lead and John with Joe some distance behind. After some two hours of hunting and about a half-mile from the original find, John raised his hammer to strike a quartz boulder and realized it much resembled the specimen wrapped in Ellie's apron. "We've got it!" John and Joe called out in chorus. Almost simultaneously, Ellie and Ed were chipping into the ledge. Her voice came ringing back, "We have too!" At that moment, her pick poised for the strike she had sought since girlhood, Ellen Nay was twenty-nine years old and had been eking out an impoverished existence on the fringes of the mining world for nearly all her married life. "Oh, Lord," she later sighed, "I never supposed there was so much gold in the world."[25]

From this point onward Ellie receded into the background, eclipsed by her male relatives: her brothers, her husband, and her father. Old Ed immediately appropriated control of the strike from a daughter long accustomed to obeying him, and Ellie acquiesced. In the words of a friend of Ed's, newspaperman Lindley Branson of the *Tonopah Sun,* "Mr. Clifford, the father, who with a mind born to command like unto that of Napoleon, enjoined absolute secrecy and planned out a campaign of procedure." Another observer saw him as a Moses leading his children into the promised land: "Memnon-like his silence is maintained; stoical is his visage and determined is his bearing when the resting place of the Golden Fleece of 'Salisbury Wash' is sought by this one or that one who foolishly thinks he can . . . acquire some 'inside' information."[26] Invariably, the images evoked were patriarchal and authoritative.

The head of the house of Clifford's management of the golden fleece proved so unusual that a good deal of criticism ensued. First, the discovery was kept a tightly guarded secret for nearly two months. The family did not begin recording its first claims in the Ellendale district until 19 May, more than six weeks after Ellie's discovery. Next old Ed leaked the story to Branson, but even after the pages of the *Tonopah Sun* began to foam with hyperbole on "America's greatest surface showing" and the rediscovery of the legendary Lost Breyfogle, the Cliffords allowed no one other than Branson to see the strike and undertook no development work. None dared transgress edicts backed by the guns of old Ed's formidable sons. This prolonged concealment of Ellie's find contrasted sharply with the usual evolution of mining strikes. Jim Butler had called Clifford and others to join him at Tonopah. When Stimler and Marsh made the first locations at the future Goldfield district, they welcomed other prospectors in the hope of stimulating interest in the new site and even gave away claims that later proved to be valuable. In these and many other instances mining to produce returns or demonstrate the value of a claim in order to attract development capital or sell an interest for a fancy price was the prospector's normal modus operandi.[27]

Several reasons have been suggested for the Cliffords' policy of secrecy. Newspapers other than the *Tonopah Sun* (purportedly mortgaged to the Cliffords and recognized as a Clifford mouthpiece) obviously hoped for a new mining strike to invigorate the region, now that Tonopah and Goldfield were fading from boomtowns flush with money and adventurers into ordinary mining towns. At the same time, their hopes were tempered by dark suspicions that the new discovery would turn out to be another worthless Clifford promotion. As the *Goldfield News* put it, "until the public has seen these fabled riches, we say, 'it bears the earmarks of a fake.'"[28]

On balance, it seems likely that at this point Ellie and her family could have had no idea whether the mineral indications would continue at greater depths or peter out, as do most gold strikes, and they had determined to profit regardless. Moreover, since Ellie's original golden boulder and the second one found by Tom lay on the surface, the families may have genuinely feared that a swarm of highgraders helping themselves to samples might strip the site. When visitors were eventually permitted to view the site under carefully controlled conditions, Ellie sat on the ledge with her skirts spread out watching the rich streaks "with jealous eye, that no one used a pick." The Cliffords also hired gunmen to prevent the curious from picking up specimens. While not discounting the likelihood of highgrading, Leafy ascribed the long period of secrecy to the families' need to "get their claims lined out" before other prospectors crowded in. It has also been suggested that they were waiting for the legal time period to elapse in order to relocate the claims of other prospectors in the district.[29]

A lesser enigma also stirred newspaper speculation. Why had Ellie located her claims in her own name, together with her mother and her brother Ed, without including her husband? Her family offers no an-

Buyers vie for choice town lots at Ellendale, Nevada, June 1909
(Melvin "Buster" Filippini Collection, Central Nevada Historical Society).

swers. One newspaper suggested that it was done to sidestep an agreement Joe had made with a grubstaker; if so, his backer must have heartily cursed himself for ignoring Ellie. It seems more likely that Joe, who actually wrote the location notices while Ellie built the monuments, took pride in her accomplishments and thought it unnecessary to add his name to hers—or hers to his on the equal number of claims recorded in his name. If such was his line of thinking, he harbored none of the casual sexism of the newspapermen who faulted Ellie for omitting the name of the husband who worked with her but found nothing amiss when a man left out the name of the wife who prospected at his side. Nor did Ellie's name remain buried in the location notices. The new town, Ellendale, was named for her, as were the mining district (Ellen) and neighboring Mount Ellen.[30]

At last, on 11 June 1909, the rush to Ellendale, likened in the press to the dash of Sooners into Oklahoma Territory, was unleashed. Argonauts in a motley assortment of rigs, including wagons hauled by six-horse teams and autos bursting with passengers, bolted and jolted forth from Tonopah along the rough and dusty road. A brisk sale in town lots for as much as $550 apiece yielded substantial profits to the Nay and Clifford families, who had acquired the land. This was also the occasion of the long-awaited public viewing of the main ledge on Ellie's claims. Even experienced mining men and skeptical reporters were impressed, while newspaperman Branson spun off into rhapsodies over the "mother lode of southern Nevada," gold scattered "like wheat on newly plowed ground," the "most remarkable occurrence in the history of mining," "giant ledges," "blocks of rock laced with pure gold," "pieces of leaf gold as large as a dime," and the like.[31]

For a brief time, Ellendale boomed. Supply wagons rolled forth from Tonopah, one of them a block-long caravan of five wagons piled so high with freight that Tonopah's electric wires had to be raised to permit their passage (the ascent of these heavily laden wagons along the "snake-like windings" of the infamous Ellendale Road must have evoked some interesting language from the teamsters). The requisite saloons appeared, beginning with the Northern and the North Star, along with the Royal, the Montana, and the Breyfogle restaurants. One of these reportedly based the price of a meal on how deeply the legs of a customer's chair sank into the sand. The Nays built a stout frame house, and other family members erected homes close by. Affluent arrivals in camp rented a "rooming cottage," a fancy tent advertising a door, a window, rugs, and "elegant beds" with "silk floss mattresses." Others lived less elegantly in garden-variety tents, as had Ellie and Joe in the early days at Tonopah. A barber set up shop, promising not to charge extra for beards that required "an axe or a mowing machine before the Sheffield steel is applied." Two newspapers commenced publication, the *Ellendale Star*, a Branson publication, and the *Ellendale Lode*, published by Kenneth Booth and W. J. Fording, but the camp proved so peaceful that news was sometimes hard to come by. Branson claimed that at its peak the population of Ellendale reached five hundred, but he probably included all the mustangs and monstrous rattlers, some thick as a man's arm, that abounded in the region. The path to Ellie's ledge, once so secret that members of the families had not dared to walk there lest their footprints betray the spot, became so deeply churned by the feet of constant visitors that it began to resemble a railway track bed.[32]

During these heady times Ellie's happiness overflowed. She held court at the ledge for visiting reporters and mining men, pointing out rich showings of gold for their inspection. A reporter from the *Goldfield News* found her the "chief and most interesting figure in the play" and a "cheery, sunny little woman." Inside her clean and brightly decorated house, which he pronounced "as comfortable as any townhouse," he provided this portrait of Ellie with her small daughters:

> Two little tots played at her feet, and her watchful eye and her kindly admonitions showed that she was the tender and loving mother as well as the intrepid plainswoman. She was still in an exhilarated and excited frame of mind and was thoroughly and refulgently happy over the important event that had come into her life. She had but recently made a gold discovery that had excited the mining world and had attracted the sight seers from every direction; a town had been founded and given her name, and a flag waved over a mountain which thereafter was to bear the name of Mount Ellen. Perhaps that was enough to exhilarate anyone.[33]

The odd mix of sexism and admiration in the press over Ellie's discovery mirrored a contradictory swirl of attitudes. An occasional misogynist saw the woman prospector as an unwelcome intruder in a world reserved for men. "It's hard telling just where a man is safe in these days of advanced thinking," a reporter had observed apropos of the new women prospectors' association. More often reporters saw the woman prospector as a curiosity, and often a curiosity of remarkable achievements. A whiff of sarcasm sometimes intruded, as in a South Dakota newspaper's allusion to a woman prospector's "God given rights." Perhaps the most schizophrenic feature of press coverage on women prospectors in mining camps was its failure to alter the image of women by a whit. The same central Nevada newspapers that reported the exploits of Ellie Nay, Frances Williams, Lillian Malcolm, Bessie Miller, and many others could publish the poem on the woman who waits by the garden wall and print such platitudinous maxims as

We Love Woman for the Very Weaknesses of Her Nature
above the day's headline. Historian Sandra Myres correctly points out that the "*reality* of women's lives changed dramatically as a result of adaption to frontier conditions while the public *image* remained relatively static."[34]

Ellie's exhilaration must have peaked at the camp's first (and only)

Fourth of July celebration. Joe, with some assistance, started the day with a thirteen-gun salute fired from the mountains. At ceremonies later that morning Ellie and her father were the guests of honor. When the speaker introduced Ellie as the "uncrowned queen" of Nevada's banner mining camp, men threw their hats in the air and the canyons resounded with cheers. Fittingly, the orator of the day declared that "Ellendale pays homage to a woman" and gave unusual emphasis to the role of women in building the American nation and the West: "We must give to our mothers, sisters, wives, and sweethearts the honor that of right belongs to them in the upbuilding of the mighty empire of this westerly world." The crowd then turned to the spirited contests of a customary mining camp Fourth of July—a women's egg race, fat men's race, old men's race, three-legged race, sack race, wheelbarrow race, boys' burro race, tug of war, and baseball game. Youngsters set off a fireworks display as soon as darkness fell. Then willing hands carried the beds out of the Ellendale Hotel to make way for a "grand ball" that lasted far into the night.[35]

Within ten days of the celebration the first wagonload of ore rolled forth from Ellie's claims, protected by old Ed with a Winchester on his knee and another gunman with "no fear in his heart for man or devil." Although the returns on carefully selected ore fell far below Branson's improbable predictions, the skeptical *Tonopah Miner* called the shipment "rich enough to satisfy anyone." All the same, the Ellendale boom began to evaporate. The families had signed leasing agreements on their claims soon after the Fourth, but Fred Seybolt, a special correspondent for the *Tonopah Miner,* wryly noted that those who expected the "heavens would be obscured by flying rocks" from the operations of energetic leasers proved mistaken. Seybolt's "tramp over the hills" revealed many leases "being worked in a desultory fashion that does not inspire any confidence, or not being worked at all." Leasers had been the making of Tonopah and Goldfield, but evidently many who signed for blocks of ground at Ellendale had expected to sell their leases or to secure development capital that never came. On 24 July, Seybolt noted that "an air of dullness" pervaded the camp. Businesses were closing and people were leaving. Soon Ellie's father and brothers followed suit. After 31 July the *Ellendale Star* ceased publication (no issues of the *Lode* have as yet come to light).[36] From the first rumor that sent Ellendale fever raging through Tonopah to the day when mention of the new camp evoked only shrugs, little more than two months had elapsed.

For a while that winter Ellie and Joe decamped, leaving mining operations in the hands of subordinates. They bought a winter home in southern California, following the tradition of Nevada's new mining rich. Ellie's brother Jim had bought a California home with the proceeds from Helena; Al Myers, the "father of Goldfield," built a mansion with golden doorknobs in Long Beach; the Butlers bought a San Jose home with their Tonopah fortune, as well as a ranch and a hotel near Bishop. But Ellie and Joe soon realized that idleness in the warm California sunshine suited them not at all. They sold the California place, and in May 1910, a time made memorable by the visitation of Halley's comet, they were back in Ellendale, then nearly a year old.[37]

A study by the Nevada State Bureau of Mines indicates production of $52,000 through 1910 in Ellendale, a respectable showing in comparison with Helena (for which the same study lists no production at all) and other small camps but clearly no mother lode in a class with the great central Nevada strikes, even when allowances are made for the practice of not reporting returns by small leasing operations. Tonopah was to produce $146 million by 1940, and Goldfield at least $87 million in the same period. Both those who condemned Ellendale as another worthless Clifford promotion and the author who later claimed it produced a million dollars' worth of ore fell wide of the mark.[38] Despite Branson's overheated predictions, no sign of mineralization at depth had been found. Ellie's gold appeared to be shallow surface deposits that early mining operations had nearly exhausted.

The year 1912 marked a turning point in the lives of the Nays. For more than ten years, they had followed Nevada's mining booms. Prospecting had been Ellie's consuming interest since girlhood. It still was. In Leafy's words, "she loved that prospecting. She never got it out of her mind." Now Ellie had success to spur her on. She had made a valuable gold strike, better than anything her father or brothers had found in all their years of prospecting. Who was to say she could not repeat her triumph in other ventures, if she hunted new bonanzas? Or she could search her own ground, for despite all indications, she herself stoutly believed that more gold lay hidden in the silent hills of Ellendale. Many in the mining world stayed chained to hopes like these for a lifetime: John Lemoigne, who journeyed back and forth from his Death Valley claim for forty years; Baby Doe, who grew old and mad beside the Matchless Mine.[39]

But there was risk in hunting new bonanzas, even for a prospector of proven ability like Ellie. How many mining nabobs had seen their money drain "back into the ground," as the saying went, squandered in fruitless new ventures? How many had spent their lives "like chaff blowing around the country," as one prospector phrased it? And Ellie had children to raise. Now, with the profits of Ellendale in hand, it lay in her power to give them the life she considered ideal. That did not mean the city life of the new mining rich the Nays had sampled in southern California, where they had decided, "No more stuffy cities, where you have to pay to breathe, / Where the helpless human creatures move and throng and strive and seethe," like the unknown pioneer poet who scrawled on the door of a shack not far from Stone Cabin. Ellie's concept of the ideal was grounded in a sensible awareness of her own limitations and a complete lack of the social ambitions that fired such newly rich women in the mining world as Eilley Bowers and the "unsinkable" Molly Brown. It meant being where you belonged, with your own people in your own kind of country. That is, it meant growing up on a remote desert ranch as she had. Joe agreed with her, as always.[40]

Together they decided to buy paradise, or so it seemed more than half a century later when Leafy looked back on her girlhood. The Barley Creek ranch nestled between the sheltering arms of low hills northeast of Belmont on the western edge of the Monitor Range where Barley Creek winds from a narrow canyon into the broad, gray, sage-covered expanse of the Monitor Valley. Occasional floods, when Barley Creek raged down from the heights, carving its channel ever deeper and welling out from its banks into a wide pond, washed silt into the fields. Across the Monitor Valley from the ranch house, above the buff-colored rocky parapets at the base of the Toquima Range, loomed the peaks of Mount Jefferson, nearly twelve thousand feet high, shining white in winter, blue-veined as the snows melted, glowing rose at

dawn. Barley Creek ranch cost the Nays ten thousand dollars (about two hundred thousand in today's dollars), plus an added outlay for the cattle herd of Hereford-Durhams that would roam the high country around Table Mountain. These purchases nearly exhausted the Nays' share of the Ellendale profits.

At that time Barley Creek ranch consisted of little more than a log house, shaded by big willow trees, and a good deal of uncultivated land. The Nays set to work with a will to turn the rundown homestead into a ranch on a par with the best in the Monitor Valley. Along with her many other activities at the ranch Ellie often hammered away at the anvil, making branding irons and iron hinges for the big gates and welding broken machinery. In this she unwittingly carried on the tradition of America's colonial women, who had crossed gender lines when necessary to operate sawmills and shoe horses. "Handy Betsy the Blacksmith" had made cannon during the Revolution, and the 1900 U.S. census still listed 190 women blacksmiths. Nonetheless, in Ellie's time and place, a woman working at the anvil was considered distinctly unusual. "I never heard of a woman before doing all those things," said Leafy, "and she loved to do it."[41]

The log house was of a kind that would not have been unfamiliar to Daniel Boone. It had scrubbed wood floors and hewn log walls hung with guns, knives, chaps, and pictures. The cabinet containing Ellie's prize ore samples occupied a prominent place. Ellie's preoccupation with prospecting had faded not at all. Leafy said she "never stopped talking about prospecting and mining" in suitable company. "It seemed like she was always studying rock, and she had little boxes of specimens that she bought somewhere, and that was all different kinds of ore in there. . . . When the men would bring in ore, she'd go to that little box and she'd tell them just what kind of rock they had found, whether it was porphyry or cinnebar or silver or gold quartz. She could tell right off what it was."[42]

Through all the years at the ranch the Nays held on to Ellendale. The various leasers who mined the Nay claims off and on struck several small bonanzas, one in 1913 and two more in the late 1930s, validating Ellie's unflagging faith. In later years, after their daughters had married and moved away, Ellie and Joe spent the winter months at a home they had purchased in Tonopah, leaving a hired hand in charge of the ranch. Sometimes they worked the Ellendale claims, shipping an occasional small truckload of ore. Even in the leanest times traces of gold sparkled now and then to keep hope alive. Leafy, as a young married woman, panned enough gold at Ellendale to purchase a great luxury, her first washing machine. Emma Nevada's husband, a big Spanish miner named Bonifisal Ornelas, uncovered another golden boulder that glittered like the original strike.

One of the family gatherings that loomed largest on the calendar was the annual assessment work outing. In late spring or early summer the Nays and their daughters' families would journey to the shack that was all that remained of the town so optimistically laid out in the spring of 1909. There they remained for a week or so to complete the assessment work required by law to retain title to unpatented mining claims. Ellie gained weight in later life until finally the slim, quick sprite who had weighed less than one hundred pounds on her wedding day turned into a heavy, ponderous old woman—never too old and immobile, however, to work at Ellendale. Selling Ellendale or allowing her claims to lapse remained unthinkable.

Although her obsession with prospecting never faded, it turned into a private fantasy over time. On a family outing to Virginia City, Ellie brought her prospector's pick, ever hopeful that she might discover something that thousands of prospectors who swarmed over the Comstock before her had missed. When riding anywhere in the family car, she constantly scanned the landscape looking for another sugarloaf mountain, the distinguishing feature of Ellendale. She often made Leafy's husband stop the car so she could get out with her pick and take a sample of rock. Still, none of the prospecting trips that began in the days when Ellie and Joe bundled their children into the wagon and continued whenever Ellie's cry brought the car to a screeching halt resulted in staking a claim or developing a mine after Ellendale.[43]

The pattern of their lives abruptly changed when Joe suffered a massive heart attack while washing the windows for their return to the ranch in the spring of 1939. After his death nothing would do for Ellie but to sell the ranch where they had worked together, side by side, for nearly thirty years. Despite her ceaseless activity, her own health began to deteriorate when she reached her sixties. On 2 April 1947 Ellie died in a Fallon hospital from pulmonary congestion at the age of sixty-seven. She received a Catholic funeral; Joe had died a Mormon, the only respect in which they were not together. After her death the family at last sold Ellendale, for four hundred dollars.[44]

Without Ellie's unquenchable hopes to keep it alive, Ellendale reverted to nature. The last shack no longer marks the spot, and among the myriad sage-covered hills it is now difficult to tell where the camp once stood. All that remains of Ellendale is in scattered mineral collections, where a few incredible samples glisten with gold like the boulder the Nays wrapped up in Ellie's apron on that long-ago afternoon.

# "Hers Were the Only Hands to Assist Me": Daughters, Sisters, Wives, and Lovers

At first glance, the woman prospecting with her husband appeared to be doing what American women had done on farms in colonial times and continued to do on the frontier, contributing to the family economy by sharing tasks outside the domestic sphere. In this view, the store-keeper's wife occasionally worked behind the counter and the rancher's wife helped round up the cattle, while never relinquishing her primary domestic responsibility. Like the westering women on the overland trails, she participated in masculine tasks only as a temporary necessity, eagerly anticipating a return to her proper feminine sphere. She modestly stood aside while her husband took credit for their mineral discoveries, well knowing that his was the world of public achievement and hers the private role of wife and mother. Indeed, one frequently encounters the belief among women in mining country today that the prospecting wives of an earlier time rarely received the credit they deserved. "Women prospectors are figures in the shadows," wrote Agnes Reddenbaugh, who was raised in central Nevada, "since there would be the temptation to give the credit to the husband (and/or sons)."[1]

Yet when history divulges the particulars, it becomes clear that these verities about the modest helpmate, regretfully torn from her sewing circle and her calico curtains to stand by her man, were not invariably correct. Ellen Nay, as we have seen, did not prospect to assist her husband in his occupation; rather, the initiative was hers, and her husband agreed to join in her obsession. Ellie was not the only prospecting wife to exert strong, even dominant, influence on the family's occupational choice, and in two instances in which relationships weakened or broke down, the women saw themselves as full partners and demanded the financial rewards due them as such. All this suggests that when sufficient detail is lacking, it would be unwise to make any assumptions on which spouse's preferences sent a prospecting couple into the wilderness. Nor would we be well advised to draw any conclusions, in the absence of clear evidence, on which one possessed the superior abilities. Along with the helpmates the spectrum of women who prospected with male relatives includes several figures with strength, competence, and independence comparable to that of Lillian Malcolm or Helen Cottrell.

A few women went into the field with male relatives other than husbands. Though we may not always catch a glimpse of the father and brothers who schooled a girl in prospecting, as did those of Ellie Nay, an occasional father-daughter team has come to light, including a pair of Texans who gravitated to the oil boom at Beaumont after the Galveston flood ruined them financially. M. A. Rice, the daughter, must have been an enterprising young woman. At twenty-one she founded a newspaper, the *Beaumont Oil Review,* and continued to edit it until she and her father decided to go prospecting in Idaho's Thunder Mountain district in May 1902. With a party of nine others they made a difficult and dangerous journey through the melting snows of the Idaho high country. As usual, we learn more about Rice's clothes than we do about the prospecting activities that earned her the sobriquet "Queen of Thunder Mountain." Nevertheless, she was the one the other prospectors thought had the entrepreneurial savvy to market their mining claims, notwithstanding the clichés of the period about woman's proper sphere of refinement and seclusion from the crass, materialistic world of men. In November the Queen of Thunder Mountain emerged in Chicago with sacks of sparkling gold samples to exhibit, powers of attorney from all concerned, and an impressive command of practical mining.[2]

Blanche Johnson Cascaden was another young woman who prospected with her father. Charles Johnson had searched the hills around Tucson from 1890 until he joined the rush to the Klondike. Soon afterward his daughter Blanche, then seventeen, left college to join him, along with the rest of the family. A "great lover of the outdoors," Blanche readily took up prospecting and continued her father's gold mining after his

Thunder Mountain, Idaho.
The arrow indicates the mining district (Idaho
State Historical Society, #63-35.2).

death. For many "hard and lean years," she mined like a man and gained little reward. So painful and difficult was this period of her life that she preferred not to discuss it, turning instead to the year when she at last "struck it lucky." She stayed with the mining game, as well as marrying twice and raising two children. More pain and difficulty lay ahead after Blanche buried her husband in 1923 and both her grown children within a decade. The time arrived when she no longer felt able to mine her claims at Livengood near Fairbanks or work eighteen- and twenty-hour days. She retired to Fairbanks, but she never lost the prospector's unquenchable conviction that "the best ground is still there."[3]

Blanche Cascaden had learned to share her father's occupation, but Jennie Hilton's obsession was entirely her own—indeed, she may have spread the contagion to her brother. Born in Ohio, Jennie moved to California with her family and became a teacher after her parents died when she was sixteen. She also began to study minerals and geology intensively, with the inevitable result that the dream of prospecting began to take hold. In the summer of 1890 she visited an older brother in Phoenix and persuaded him and an uncle of theirs to go on a prospecting trip in the mountains around the Gila Valley. The Hiltons found nothing of value, but the die was cast. Jennie returned from this initial sortie convinced that she could prospect "on her own hook" as well as any man. She withdrew her savings from the bank and resigned her teaching position. More fruitless prospecting alone in the Santa Rita Mountains of southern Arizona the following year failed to dampen her eagerness. In the winter of 1892, with her savings rapidly diminishing, she opened an assaying office in Prescott in central Arizona. So popular did it become with the local mining fraternity that there was general disappointment when she closed her business the following spring after the arrival of an exciting letter.

Her brother wrote that he had found the "best looking auriferous rock in the territory" at Harqua Hala, Arizona. Jennie needed to hear no more before she was on her way to join him in the bare, treeless mountains southeast of Salome. Following discoveries of gold in 1888, prospectors had flocked to the district, women among them. Nellie Cashman hauled a load of merchandise there in 1889 and ran a restaurant in the new camp for a while, no doubt prospecting on the side. Rose

Long Johnson stayed some sixty years longer. She had sold her hotel and boardinghouse in Phoenix to head for Harqua Hala, where she acquired the Harqua Hala Extension Mine. In 1953 she lingered there yet, the last living resident of the district, still hoping for a bonanza in the mine where she had sunk every cent she possessed.

Jennie Hilton fared better at Harqua Hala than Nellie Cashman or Rose Johnson. She spent the summer of 1892 prospecting the district and located seven claims, the best of which she christened the Kansas. Needing money for development, she journeyed to Los Angeles in search of investors and, after repeated failures, finally sold a half-interest in the Kansas to a railroad engineer for one thousand dollars. (Without the promotional talents of Lillian Malcolm or Frances Williams, Jennie seems to have found the salesmanship side of the prospector's task a good deal harder than tramping over the hills.) Several weeks of digging and blasting proved the value of her mine, but investors refused to listen to her pitch or tried to put her off with empty promises.

Jennie Hilton was not destined to grow old beside her mine like Rose Johnson, however. In 1896, four years after her discovery, she finally succeeded in selling her remaining half-interest in the Kansas to a Salt Lake firm for twenty-five thousand dollars. Uninterested in the seaside home, the European tour, and other characteristic indulgences that followed a big sale for many of the newly rich in the mining field, she immediately put the funds to work to develop her other claims, declaring with redoubled enthusiasm that she was "in mining for life."[4]

Besides the woman who prospected with a father or a brother, a few went into the field with lovers. Indeed, because the press and the historians of the day preferred to pass over such women in silence, there may have been more of them than we know. In the early 1900s, for example, Louis Carara proposed to Carrie Torelli, a Colorado woman, that for a half-share in any mining claims they found, she should come prospecting with him in Nevada and maintain a comfortable home for him, after which they would marry (it will be noted that Carrie was expected to combine both prospecting and domestic duties). During a year's work in the hills the couple located a number of marketable claims in the Rawhide area, which Carara sold for high prices. He then abandoned Carrie. Too angry to mind about publicizing what in 1908 was likely to be regarded as her disgrace, Carrie sued to enjoin him from disposing of the claims, insisting that a half-share rightfully belonged to her under the terms of their partnership agreement.[5]

At the Chisana (formerly Shushana) River in Alaska, deep inside the present Wrangell–St. Elias Park Preserve in an area remote and difficult of access even by the rigorous standards of Alaska, a woman prospector named Matilda Wales made her way in 1913. Possibly with Indian assistance, three men had made initial discoveries of placers and a gold quartz lode the preceding year. One of them was William James, a California miner who had joined the rush to the Klondike and remained to prospect, supporting himself by hunting and trapping. When James returned to Chisana, Mrs. Matilda Wales accompanied him. Although she is rumored to have been a dance-hall queen, she had evidently gained a considerable reputation in Dawson for her prospecting, since an Edward Erickson had engaged her to locate claims for him in the new district. She accomplished this mission by the end of June, though she faced considerable difficulty in protecting the properties in the face of claim jumping and violence until the local recorder arrived three weeks later. Lillian Malcolm was not the only woman prospector who had occasion to observe that male chivalry did not extend to the staking of mining claims in Alaska. During the stampede to Chisana that emptied the mining camps of the region that summer, the marital status of Matilda Wales remained ambiguous. She has been described as the wife of William James, but probably she did not become so until a year of cohabitation with him made her his common-law wife, at least by the accelerated customs prevailing in Alaska. It has been suggested that the supposed immorality of Matilda Wales resulted in a disposition to ignore her achievements in mining during Alaska's last major gold rush. Had she been a more respectable woman, she might have received some of the adulatory coverage accorded Nellie Cashman.[6]

Being abandoned or ignored is hardly the kindest of fates. Still, Carrie Torelli and Matilda Wales fared better than Mary E. "Mollie" Sawyer, also known as Mollie Monroe: she was institutionalized. Mollie came to Arizona in the mid-1860s with a party of prospectors when she was about twenty. She lived for a time as the common-law wife of George Monroe in Wickenburg and prospected with him and his friends, but her liaisons were not confined to Monroe. The "wild and reckless manner of her life" must have made her a dashing figure, dressed in buckskin pants, fringed and beaded jacket, and a broad-brimmed hat, riding into Prescott at a gallop, packing guns, smoking cigars, and ordering her whiskey straight. Apparently, Prescott officers arrested her several times for wearing men's clothes. The *Arizona Journal-Miner* observed that "her beauty and fascinating manner brought men to her feet, and also later on to their ruin or death." Although her many acts of charity toward ailing and needy miners and prospectors sound worthy of the frontier angel herself, her "dissolute" morals drew the censure of newsmen, who made it clear that Mollie was no angel. She was credited with the discovery of two rich gold mines. After selling one she immediately gambled the proceeds away, being as addicted to gambling as her Virginia City counterpart, Marie Pantalon. Besides prospecting with her lover of the moment, she also ran a saloon for a time and worked as a cowboy.[7]

In 1877 authorities committed her as insane. She briefly escaped from a Phoenix asylum in 1895 and made her way, barefoot, into the desert for more miles than anyone believed she could cover without perishing before Indian trackers retrieved her four days later. "If I'd a' only had my breeches and my gun I'd a' been all right," she declared. In 1902, a quarter-century after she was committed, she died in the Phoenix institution. Despite a good deal of newspaper commentary on her dramatic escape and the possible cause of her madness, the most interesting question remains unanswered. We learn nothing definite about the deranged behavior that led Arizona authorities to judge her insane: historian Susan L. Johnson has pointed out that Mollie's "appropriation of the trappings of male privilege—masculine clothing, multiple sexual partners, men's work"—may have contributed to that conclusion.[8]

Beside the flamboyant Mollie, "who is known to all old timers as the girl cowboy, who in her day could ride anything with four feet, chew more tobacco and swear harder than any man in Arizona," in the words of the *Phoenix Herald,* the men around her faded into the scenery, and even in less exotic cases, the tendency of observers to concentrate on the figure they perceived as the unusual one in a prospecting couple—the woman—sometimes countermanded the disposition to regard women as unimportant adjuncts to their male companions. For instance, after Mr. and Mrs. James Miller left their New York home to prospect in Nevada in 1906, newsmen passed over Mr. Miller as unremarkable and titled the story "A Lady Prospector," not omitting the customary discussion of her clothes. "A woman with nerve enough to suffer the privations of a year among the mountains and deserts of Nevada certainly deserves to discover a Brown Palace," the story concluded, with an admiring tone predicated on assumptions about the weaker sex.[9]

If James Miller appears a cipher, Lena M. Stebbins's companion vaporizes into near invisibility. The sources do not reveal if the John F. Stebbins whose name sometimes appears along with hers in the mining records was her husband or brother, but there is no doubt that Lena's claim was the prime discovery. As with so many women prospectors, it was success hard earned. Round Mountain, a hump-backed mass of rock, stands disconnected from the western edge of the Toquima Range of central Nevada almost sixty miles north of Tonopah in the midst of difficult and forbidding terrain. An early visitor described it thus: "There is nothing to be seen but sage, rock and sand, sage, rock and sand, in endless, dreary alternation. . . . The gray, lowering sky, the smoking alkali hot springs in the farther distance and the frowning, jagged peaks of the Toiyabe mountains, which seem to start out of the plain almost at right angles, make up a tout ensemble reminiscent of Dante's weird pictures of hades." He marveled that the "few wild cattle and wilder horses" he saw could survive in such a desolate place. Lena and her indistinct companion survived as well. John had searched the area in the autumn of 1905, probably with Lena. Although her name does not yet appear in the Nye County mining records, she is known to have prospected for several years before making her big strike. When a rich gold discovery ignited a stampede to Round Mountain in late March 1906, both Lena and John had been locating claims in the vicinity for some time. Not until May, however, did she record her best claim, the Antelope, which she sold to a group of Goldfield capitalists for a large sum.[10]

Those least likely to enjoy much result from their labors, and most likely to disappear with scarcely a trace from the historical records, were the Indian prospectors of both sexes. Often one reads that an Indian revealed the site of an important strike to white prospectors and received as recompense a handful of silver coins, a pair of overalls, or even a bullet in the back, but rarely do these sources mention the name of the original Indian discoverer. It is known that Indian women joined in mining from an early date. One California forty-niner recalled seeing them pan the rivers of the gold country with wicker baskets coated with pitch. Others must have considered them competent, or the disreputable white prospector Jim Richardson would not have bought Indian girls from their tribes and compelled them to prospect for him as he journeyed around Nevada (Richardson sold his slaves back to their tribes when legal authorities evicted him from the state in 1907). In Death Valley an Indian woman named Mary Scott discovered the future Confidence gold mine. After revealing the site to her cousin, Bob Black, she received twelve bottles of desert wine in recompense. Author William Caruthers also tells of Anna (no last name given), another Death Valley Indian woman, who discovered and worked a gold claim that enriched her indolent white husband, who later abandoned her.[11] What happened to Minnie and Johnnie Peavine was another sorry tale of exploitation, but these two did something almost unheard-of among the ill-treated Indian prospectors. They sued.

If the account that appeared in a Goldfield newspaper is correct, the Peavines, a prospecting couple from the Shoshone tribe, entered into a grubstake agreement with James and Ed Clifford, brothers of Ellie Nay, under which the Cliffords provided the usual supplies and a horse, together with a promise that the Peavines would each receive an undivided quarter-interest in any claims they discovered. On 6 October 1905 the Peavines struck promising silver ore about eight miles from the Stone Cabin ranch in the hills on the eastern edge of the valley and notified the Cliffords. Together the four of them staked eighteen claims at the site the Cliffords christened after themselves (later Helena). The Cliffords wrote out the location notices, explaining to the Peavines that their names did not appear there because government regulations forbade so many names on location notices (a falsehood). Unfamiliar with government regulations, the Peavines accepted this explanation, but they understood enough about the complicated legalities of mining repeatedly to request a deed of conveyance for their interest.

The Cliffords put them off for over a month. Then they produced a paper that they told the Peavines was the deed of conveyance. The Cliffords made them promise to keep the paper a secret, however, and especially cautioned the Shoshone couple never to show it to a lawyer. In this document the Cliffords agreed to pay $6,666 "to be equally divided between said Johnnie and squaw" when the mining claims were sold. Understanding little English, reading none, and believing the document to be as represented, the Peavines made their marks.[12]

Although the ore at Clifford proved disappointing and the district made no significant shipments, the Cliffords succeeded in selling their claims to Pittsburgh capitalists for a reported $250,000 in an early display of the promotional skills they would later perfect at Ellendale. News of this deal produced a rush to the site in December and more profits for the Cliffords from the sale of town lots. The Peavines, meanwhile, did what the Cliffords had tried to prevent them from doing. They showed the paper with their marks on it to a lawyer, W. F. Ford. The result was a lawsuit for the Peavines' promised share and also a demand for their fair portion of the property sales in the new camp. The death of Minnie in early January 1906 may have caused her husband to lose heart, however. After the lawsuit briefly complicated the Clifford sale in early February, Johnnie Peavine apparently agreed to accept a small settlement instead of holding out for the much larger sum owed him and his dead wife, and Minnie's legal administrator abandoned the claim made on her behalf.

The aftermath of the Peavines' story was less than inspirational. Despite the lack of pay ore, the town of Clifford continued to prosper through 1908, when it boasted saloons, dance halls, and more than a hundred dwellings—and the Cliffords prospered with it. James bought a fine home in California, while his father's benevolent donations built the Knights of Columbus hall in Tonopah and made him an important patron of the Catholic church. It is doubtful that Johnnie Peavine saw anything from the sacks of twenty-dollar gold pieces brought to Tonopah in an express wagon guarded by riflemen and paid to the Cliffords by the new owners. Several years later a Tonopah grand jury indicted his attorney for embezzling his settlement.[13]

In the usual poorly defined way the Indians' intimate knowledge of the land also figured in a discovery by one of the most successful women prospectors of all time, Belle Butler. Isabella (Belle) McCormick was born at Prince Edward Island, Nova Scotia, probably in 1860. Her parents migrated with Belle and their two other children to the Fish Lake Valley in the remotest regions of southern Nevada in 1865. Later they moved to run a boardinghouse in Tybo, a mining camp in the Hot Creek Mountains. Here Belle met Maurice Donohue, a vaquero who also prospected and mined. Fond of horse racing and fine steeds, Donohue must have had a vaquero's reckless charm, though he was nearly as old as her father. In 1876, when she was sixteen to his thirty-nine, Belle married Maurice.[14]

Over the next dozen years the aging vaquero lost his charm. Donohue seems to have been unemployed for long periods, which must have brought hardship to Belle and their three surviving children. He was also prone to long absences, perhaps prospecting and seeking a livelihood, perhaps spying on Belle, for he had grown increasingly distrustful of his young wife. A vicious circle developed. The more jealous Donohue became, the more he drank and mistreated Belle, further alienating her and fueling the causes of his jealousy. Increasingly, Donohue's suspicions centered on Jim Butler, a ne'er-do-well rancher from the Little Antelope Valley who spent a great deal of time in the Shoshone camps and bore the reputation of a squaw man. No woman would have seen Butler as a great catch, nor, if the tendency to obesity evident in his later photos had already set in, did he cut a dashing figure. But he was a kindly young man of warm sympathies, and Belle had probably learned that dashing figures did not wear well. In September 1888 she filed for divorce from Donohue.[15]

The result was explosive, Butler in flames and Donohue expiring in a pool of blood. Tybo residents would tell the tale for the rest of their days. Mary McCann Sharp, one of them, called it "the eternal triangle, two men and a woman dissatisfied with her husband . . . and seeking romance abroad, an idler who might well have found a more innocent pastime, a jealous husband who drank deeply seeking revenge . . . all the way to the inevitable, the death of one or both of the men." The inevitable arrived on a September evening in 1888 in a Tybo street where Donohue waited with a pistol in his hand for Butler. They grappled,

Belle Butler around the time of her great discovery
(Virginia Butler Brewer Collection, Central
Nevada Historical Society).

and Donohue fired several ineffectual shots, one of which struck an innocent bystander in the arm, the others of which set Butler's hat and coat on fire and inflicted an injury that left him infertile. Butler shot with deadlier effect. According to Sharp, when Donohue lay wounded in the street, Butler grasped him by the shoulder and raised him up. Donohue pleaded for mercy, but Butler responded with a fatal bullet through the head. Although the coroner's jury may have heard this, they gave more weight to Donohue's many previous threats and returned a verdict of "justifiable homicide." Butler went free, except that years later he told a friend that he never again enjoyed an untroubled sleep. "You see it all over and over again in the dark."[16]

The following spring, after a decent interval had passed, Belle married Jim Butler and moved out to the ranch in the Little Antelope Valley, though one of the children refused for some years to live with her father's murderer. There they raised a little hay, ran a few head of stock, and managed to eke out a meager living for the next eleven years, supplemented for a while by Butler's salary as district attorney. Then came the event that was to transform the fortunes of the Butlers—and indeed of all the hard-scrabble pioneers who hung on in central Nevada during the lean years. The folklore of the discovery, as Butler told it, was in the realm of lucky accidents. En route to the small mining camp optimistically christened Klondike, he picked up a rock to throw at his burro and realized that he had something in his hand worth assaying. Few historians find this explanation convincing. It has long been suspected that Butler's perfect command of the Shoshone language and his intimacy with the Indians had led him to a discovery far removed from the normal route to Klondike. He may have learned of the site through an Indian mistress named Mary, a story still told among the local Shoshone, or he may have been informed of it by the great Shoshone prospector Tom Fisherman, but his presence was no quirk of fate.[17]

It was May 1900, the year Belle turned forty and Jim forty-five. Returning to his ranch, Butler agreed to allow a friend, Tasker Oddie, to assay the sample in return for shares in the future claim for himself and the assayer. When the test showed high values, Oddie and the assayer became so excited that they dispatched an Indian runner to the Butler ranch with the news and urged Jim to stake his claims forthwith. The indolent, easygoing Butler failed to share their sense of urgency, however. He temporized. He made excuses. He had hay to put up at the ranch and other chores to do. At length, as the pioneer newspaper editor Carl Glasscock told it, the "efficient" Belle decided that the claims could be "more satisfactorily located under her direction." In late August she finally got Jim wound up to make the effort, and the two of them set off together in a spring wagon drawn by two burros to stake their claims.[18]

At the site Jim presently would christen with a Shoshone name, Tonopah, they spent many hours in the prospector's signature pastime, chasing runaway burros, and Belle spent many more hauling water from the wells several miles away. Although Belle might have learned how prospecting was done from her first husband, who prospected and mined extensively, there is no definitive evidence that she had done earlier prospecting, and mining records show no claims staked in her own name before this fateful trip. Evidently, she had some standing as a prospector, however. Reddenbaugh recalled, "Many 'old timers' thought that Mrs. Butler found Tonopah—and that she let Jim Butler take the credit. She was always prospecting." Jim, lacking prior experience, enjoyed a lesser reputation among the prospecting fraternity. On hearing that Jim had a good eye for ore, one of these contemporaries responded, "Ha! Jim Butler didn't know any more about ore than his burros."[19]

In between trips to the wells and chases after the burros, Belle carefully prospected the area with Jim for about a week and eventually struck out on her own, somewhat patronizingly encouraged by Jim. That day Belle staked the Mizpah, recorded in her own name and christened in honor of a friend of hers. The Mizpah, richest of all the Butler claims, was to bring fortunes to the Butlers and many others. The newly wealthy Butlers sold their Tonopah holdings and left the beggarly little ranch in the Antelope Valley far behind them for luxurious retirement in California. When Belle died in 1922, newspapers eulogized her as the "Mother of Nevada," renowned for her charities to the destitute and even to animals (those charities had included assistance to the struggling Nays for Joe's prolonged hospitalization and surgery

Top: Belle Butler (*the only woman*), Jim Butler (*second from left*), and others observe early development work at the Mizpah Mine, Tonopah, Nevada, one of the most successful mines discovered by a woman (Nevada Historical Society).

Bottom: By 1912 the Mizpah looked much more impressive (Erma Ramsey Collection, Central Nevada Historical Society).

after the gunshot wound in 1902; Ellie Nay was an old friend, known to Belle since birth when both lived in Tybo).[20]

Jim Butler always acknowledged Belle's role as his codiscoverer: hers "were the only hands to assist me in locating this notable group of mines—now Tonopah—she locating the now world famous Mizpah, gives her first place of all among miners' wives." At the time of her death he went even further and declared in an interview that the initial discovery at Tonopah had been hers, not his. Without evidence confirming Belle's presence on the first trip to Tonopah, historians have uniformly discounted this version as the unreliable outburst of a grief-stricken man, and in general, the newspapers and textbooks that shaped public conceptions of the momentous discovery have slighted Belle's role. This 1906 account provides an instructive example: "The day that Jim Butler sampled the Mizpah vein was the greatest day in Nevada's history. That one act meant much for the man and state, in that it made the lucky prospector immensely rich; paved a golden way for a great army of others; built up modern cities where there were only . . . deserts; threw open a rich field for many railroads, and greatly increased our population. What a great outcome from such a simple act of sampling."[21] All true enough, except that it was not Jim who did the sampling. Down to the present time the principal annual celebration in Tonopah is known as "Jim Butler Days."

When so little can be unearthed about the previous prospecting activities of the woman who struck the fabulous Mizpah, it can scarcely surprise us that the available sources on other prospecting wives are often little more than oblique hints. So it had been for years before Belle's time, and so it would long continue. Back in the 1868 gold rush to Wyoming's South Pass district, journalist James Chisholm wrote of seeing Mrs. Fannie Gallagher: "This morning I visited the gulch diggings, and saw the gallant Major working like a Trojan shovelling in the dirt. Even Mrs. Gallagher was doing a little amateur work with a pan, exhibiting with great glee to her lord the tiny results of her prospecting." Unlike other women in mining, Fannie succumbed to homesickness: "She sometimes pines for home so pinefully that I get quite sympathetic on the subject." Though virtually everyone in South Pass panned, from the children who scooped their candy money from the stream gravels to the wives who endeavored to augment the family income, Fannie's prospecting may have been less amateurish than the visiting journalist realized, but history remembers her in a quite different capacity—as the adoptive mother of Calamity Jane. The most serious mining woman in South Pass, the only one known to make her sole living from the streams and one of the oldest who has come to light anywhere in the West, was the eighty-four-year-old Mrs. Brennan. Using a crude rocker (a riffle box in which energetic agitation and flowing water caused sands from the hopper to pass through, leaving golden specks caught in the canvas apron and the riffle bars), she managed to wrest about $1.50 a day from the frigid waters in 1907, winning a well-earned reputation for her toughness and persistence.[22]

No fame by association with Calamity Jane brushed Mrs. William Aldred, one of several women mine owners in the Georgetown, Colorado, area. Her husband had located the Geneva Mine on Alpine Mountain in 1891 and excavated a three-hundred-foot tunnel at great expense without striking pay ore. At this point Mrs. Aldred took over, much as Belle Butler decided that the claims in the San Antonio Mountains could be more efficiently located under her charge. Mrs. Aldred changed the direction of the adit and struck good ore in short order. Her husband wanted her to halt there and mine, but Mrs. Aldred, acting on a hunch, insisted that the tunnel be pressed farther into the mountain. There she struck an even better vein that enriched both the Aldreds and the town. In addition to her joint role in the Geneva Mine, Mrs. Aldred owned the Plato on Griffith Mountain some forty years later, which suggests that she mined independently of her husband and continued to do so over a long career.[23]

In 1896, when Mrs. Aldred was developing the Geneva, the California Miners' Association accepted Mrs. Amelin Lichau, a San Francisco doctor's wife, and Mrs. Mattie Cramer as their first card-carrying woman members. Together with Amelin's husband and another man, the two women owned several claims in Angels Camp, where Amelin declared that they "roughed it with the rest—frequently taking a hand in the actual work of development." They also studied the subject with the woman prospector's characteristic enthusiasm. "I have always taken a deep interest in mining and read all the literature available on the subject. Beyond the mining news I read scarcely anything else in the papers," said Amelin. In the course of justifying to a reporter the "radical departure" of admitting women to membership, the secretary of the association spoke of frequent encounters with "experienced lady miners," especially in Colorado.[24]

Fannie Quigley's radical departures from woman's traditional place took a different form. During one fall's hunting when game was scarce in Alaska, Fannie killed and dressed two caribou, a bear, and a moose, while her husband returned empty-handed. The next day she threw her skirt at him with the mocking remark, "Here, you do the housework. I'm the hunter in the family. Gimme the pants."[25] Since she evidently saw her relationship with her husband as a competitive one, she may have regaled her visitors with similar tales of her superiority in mining.

Fannie's sharp features, in a face with high cheekbones and dark frown, along with her petite stature, harsh tongue, and sulphurous cursing, developed over a lifetime of screeching at sled dogs, no doubt gave rise to her sobriquet, the "Little Witch of Denali." She had fled a humdrum life in a Bohemian settlement in rural Nebraska for the excitement of the Klondike, where she became a dance-hall girl in Dawson. She soon abandoned the dance halls, however, to follow new mining rushes as a cook (a way of life for the woman prospector since the time of the frontier angel). Her first marriage, to Angus McKenzie, swiftly came and went in the course of these adventurous forays. During the 1905 stampede to Kantishna, northwest of Mount McKinley (present Denali), where she was the only woman in camp, she became the common-law wife of prospector Joe Quigley. In 1918 the Quigleys finally exchanged marital vows before a U.S. commissioner using a Montgomery Ward catalog in place of a Bible. Visitors who had enjoyed the comforts of her hospitality afterward wrote of her remarkable pioneering abilities, climbing mountains "as easy as any man" on a sheep hunt, catching grayling for dinner in the creek, frying doughnuts in bear grease. Ernest N. Patty, who stayed at the Quigley cabin, observed, "I had never known a more indomitable soul than Fannie Quigley. She had enough energy, courage, and intelligence to supply a dozen women."[26]

Even in this remote area far removed from social conventions Fannie Quigley had not entirely rejected traditional conceptions of appropriate female behavior. She might have shot, butchered, and packed in the caribou herself for one of the dinners that guests compared to Roman feasts in the wilderness, but she always put on a clean dress for the evening meal. When Patty attempted to cut some stove wood for her, she sharply reprimanded him, "Put that saw down. I cut the wood around here. Your job is [mining] up on the mountain. My job is running the camp." Yet her domestic duties never prevented her from staking numerous claims. Virgil Burford, who mined on the creek where she held several claims, has noted that she was known as a prospector, as well as a dog musher, trapper, hunter, and gourmet cook. Mary Lee Davis, a 1928 visitor, concurred, calling her "a prospector, and a good one."[27]

After Joe suffered serious injuries in a mining accident, the Quigleys optioned some of their mining claims, and Fannie was treated as an equal partner, receiving the same share as her husband. The Quigley claim that proved to be the most valuable was the Banjo, the largest hard-rock producer of gold and silver in the Kantishna region and one of the best in the entire Yukon basin. The affluence at last gained from their mining properties, as well as Fannie's increasingly sharp tongue, may have hastened the breakdown of their marriage. Joe divorced Fannie, married a young nurse, and settled in Seattle, where he hunted seashells on the beaches. Fannie remained in the Kantishna cabin, drinking grain alcohol ever more heavily. She had predicted that she would die in Kantishna, and in 1944 she did. One night she froze to death, too far lost in an alcoholic stupor to keep the fire burning.[28]

Had Mrs. Frank Riggs received a partner's fair share as Fannie Quigley did, there would have been no story to tell about her, and her existence might have been virtually unknown to us. The pioneer newspaper editor Carl Glasscock thought the only feature that distinguished Riggs from other bearded desert nomads was the presence of his wife, who traveled and prospected with him in the stampedes to Alder City, Virginia City, Leadville, and Deadwood. They ended up at last in the Death Valley area, where they located a silver mine around 1880. If Glasscock's dates are correct, Mrs. Riggs would then have been about thirty and Frank some ten years older. From time to time the Riggses would drive to Daggett, a station on the Santa Fe Railroad, sell about five hundred dollars' worth of ore they had loaded into their buckboard, and purchase supplies before starting back on the hundred-mile drive to their mine.[29]

This way of life changed with the completion of the Tonopah and Tidewater Railroad to booming Goldfield in 1907 and the opening of Riggs Station only twelve miles from their mine. Now that reasonably priced transportation was at hand the Riggs properties, which had produced some remarkable specimens of almost pure silver, suddenly became more attractive to investors. Riggs journeyed east to complete a deal for some of his claims with New York investors. On receiving seventy thousand dollars from them in cash, he proceeded to blow it all in a royal bender that occupied two years and took him around the world. Glasscock expressed a sympathetic view of the delirious effect of sudden wealth on "a prospector who had been limited to beans, bacon, whiskey and hard work for half a century"—never mind that Mrs. Riggs received nothing for her years of hard work.[30]

During his prolonged bender Mrs. Riggs continued to work the mine and make ore shipments with the aid of a single helper. When Riggs finally showed up at the cabin "broke and penitent," Mrs. Riggs at once made it clear that henceforth their financial relationship would be established on a new basis: "Riggs," she said, "you been a damn old fool. You ain't going to be it again. Hereafter this ain't the Riggs mine. It's the Riggs and Riggs mine. No business goes on without my name on the papers."[31]

Riggs readily agreed, doubtless thinking himself lucky to have gotten off so lightly. Henceforth all mining business was conducted in the name of Riggs and Riggs, and the ideas of Mrs. Riggs prevailed. It was said that she insisted on setting the price for their claims so unrealistically high that no one would buy. Actually, her rationale was a prudent one. She believed that unless they received a price high enough to provide them with security, they might as well keep making a living from their mine as they had done for years—and if Frank Riggs had a great deal of assessment work to do on a large number of unsold claims, that may have been part of his penance. The couple finally sold the mine to Los Angeles capitalists shortly before Mrs. Riggs died. Although her words sound uneducated and folksy in the tale of her ultimatum, Mrs.

Riggs may have had a serious and contemplative side not unlike that of Idah Strobridge, as well as a preference for living in the desert. A Goldfield friend later described the Riggses as "saturated with the philosophy of the silent places" and expressed regret that their reflections had never been written down. Glasscock, however, thought "print is a feeble thing with which to record a philosophy that is lived and felt rather than voiced."[32]

One of the few women who prospected and wrote of her experiences was Josephine "Josie" Marcus Earp. The dark and beautiful Josie was many things—actress, tale teller, reputed pinup girl, turbulent spirit, inveterate gambler, and tireless fanner of the sacred flame that burned before the legend of her adored husband, Wyatt—but never a philosopher. Apparently, the prospecting bug first bit Josie when she was in Nome, where she sometimes panned gold on the beaches while Wyatt ran a saloon. She was nearly forty in 1900, common-law wife for almost twenty years to the veteran of the gunfight at the O.K. Corral, who was then past fifty, and she was childless, much to their mutual regret, because every infant she conceived had miscarried. When the Earps sold the Nome saloon and headed down to Tonopah in the winter of 1901–2, along with Lillian Malcolm and many others in the mining crowd, the urge to prospect grew even stronger. For a while Wyatt occupied himself in a variety of ways, opening a saloon, freighting, serving as a deputy U.S. marshal, and acting as the "persuader" who repelled claim jumpers from Belle Butler's great discovery, the Mizpah, and inwardly he had for many years harbored the dream of owning a cattle ranch. The prospecting he had done earlier in Arizona, Colorado, and Idaho had yielded no results. But the locus of occupational decision making had evidently shifted since the time just before the Klondike gold rush when Josie declared herself "willing to follow wherever Wyatt should lead," and her wishes prevailed. Josie recalled many years later, "The plan of action I wanted to undertake could lead to a big strike. It had happened to others and could just as well happen to us. Our final compromise was prospecting while we scouted for a suitable ranch site. . . . At this time we started what became our habitual manner of choosing which way we should go: in the event of a disagreement we drew straws."[33]

In short order Wyatt dropped his Tonopah occupations, and the couple began prospecting in earnest, with the general idea of spending the hot summers in Los Angeles and the rest of the year wandering the deserts of Nevada, California, and Arizona. Their camping outfit consisted of a team and heavy wagon, outfitted with a tent, mattress and springs, folding chairs and table, iron camp stove, and utensils. "Our prospecting days were well planned, and we worked systematically. After all, it had become our business, and we treated it with the respect due a profession."[34]

Their early efforts in the vicinity of Tonopah met with little success, however. "We wandered many miles and worked on our prospecting most days, till the days became weeks that finally stretched into many months, without finding anything worth developing." Time and again they hastened to camp with a likely-looking sample, pounded the ore in a mortar, and panned it with a horn spoon, and time and again the report from the assay office proved disappointing. The autumn of 1902 found them in Silver Peak camping in the shelter of a broken-down adobe, perhaps the one that a few years earlier had been home to Ferminia Sarras. The nights turned colder, and the idea of wintering in Los Angeles looked increasingly attractive to Wyatt. Josie agreed to sell their camping outfit to the local assayer. Then, at the eleventh hour, "I found a likely looking piece of gold ore that assayed so rich we turned back and bought our outfit back. As it was, we spent a couple of weeks fruitlessly prospecting for the source of the sample. We never found it and nearly froze to death trying." Their experience increases one's respect for the unrecorded hardships that Ferminia must have endured alone in those mountains. Despite snow and storms, Josie pressed on with the search until Wyatt threatened to carry her bodily to the railroad station. Later that winter they did stake three claims in the nearby Palmetto Mountains.[35]

Over the next three years Josie remembered "winter wanderings up and down across the Mojave, sometimes in California, sometimes in Nevada or Arizona." Domestic duties seem to have been predominantly done by Wyatt. He made camp, fixed the bed when it was set up in the wagon, and also shared the cooking, since he liked to cook and Josie often felt tired at the end of the day. Wyatt's dream of a ranch had been abandoned after a half-hearted attempt. At last, in 1906 on the edge of the mountains south of Needles in California, Wyatt made the strike the Earps had been hoping for, gold with a small percentage of copper. "Not as rich as my float near Silver Peak, but good enough for a living," noted Josie, and this time they had located the ledge. The Earps christened the mine the "Happy Days." Although it held no fabulous bonanza, they gained some return from its development. They built a cottage nearby in Vidal and spent part of every year there until shortly before Wyatt's death in 1929. "Best of all, the dream came true! We still traveled a little on the desert, prospected for the fun of it. . . . Those were the happy years!" Glenn Boyer, editor of Josie Earp's memoirs, notes that the Earps filed more than one hundred claims in the area.[36] It is likely that the trajectory of the Earps' lives during this period—several years of prospecting, followed by settling in at a claim that appeared worth developing, with occasional forays into further prospecting—was a common one. In those instances in which a woman appears working a mine, it is often the result of a long quest, but the process that preceded settled development remains hidden.

Josie Earp may have been no philosopher, but she was certainly enamored of the desert. She rhapsodized over the desert sunsets, "each one different, every one subtly beautiful." The Earps often walked to a hillock and silently watched sunset and moonrise together. She enjoyed the awakening life of the desert after dark, the "wild, chilling, yet half-friendly cry of the coyote," the swooping nighthawks, the mournful hoot of the gliding owl, and the rustling of small creatures in the sand. She felt the peace. In the course of these desert journeyings her taciturn husband paid her two compliments she was to treasure for the rest of her days. He once said, "There aren't many women that keep as well as you do. You never need a doctor. For my money, you suit me pretty well." On another occasion, as they bedded down in their wagon inside a shed in the midst of a cold rain and Josie assured Wyatt that she preferred the sound of rain on the roof and the smell of fresh damp air to a room in the Palace Hotel, he grew even more effusive and called her "a dead game sport right down to the ground."[37]

Although Josie Earp dictated her memoirs, she did so many years after the fact, and a diary of a woman's prospecting trip written as it happened remains a great rarity. The Josephine and George Scott diary, "A Thousand Miles of Desert and Mountains: A Prospecting Trip across Nevada and over the Sierras," therefore holds a good deal of interest. Unlike most diaries, this one was a mutual endeavor, dictated by George and typed from notes taken down in shorthand by Josephine, difficult as it is to imagine her sitting with her typewriter on a box between her knees in the shade of a greasewood bush in the remoter reaches of the desert. The diary is actually a scrapbook that contains not only the typed journal but also clippings, photos, bills, letters, and labels from canned foods (probably Josephine's domestic touch). While written in the first person in George's voice, the diary may have incorporated Josephine's observations along with the cannery labels.

The prospecting trip the Scotts undertook, beginning on 4 March 1914 and ending in the fall, brought them from the Moapa Valley northeast of Las Vegas, Nevada, to the Amargosa, to Goldfield, and across the Sierra by Sonora Pass to California—not the thousand miles of desert of the title. By George's calculations, it was fewer than six hundred. Their outfit consisted of a wagon equipped similarly to the Earps', a team of burros to draw it, and an additional pair of burros loaded with pack saddles. The Scotts were apparently childless and previously lived in Orangevale, a suburb of Sacramento. George was unemployed, and their financial circumstances appeared modest but not desperate. Although they could afford their basic supplies, they rummaged through a scrap heap for usable items, and Josephine made hairpins from bent wire. George had done a little writing on mining and construction subjects and may have hoped to do more based on the experiences to be recorded in the diary. As we have seen, middle age was by no means an unusual stage of life at which to embark on prospecting, and when Josephine and George were about to turn fifty-two and fifty-six respectively, they may have felt that if a long-cherished fantasy was not soon realized, it never would be. One thing is absolutely clear, because the Scotts state it in unequivocal terms: the prospecting trip was Josephine's idea.[38]

The Scotts found Las Vegas well stocked with novice prospectors like themselves and also with advice for novice prospectors, all of which they gratefully accepted. It is fortunate, however, that they had no oc-

casion to act on that portion of it that related to swallowing black gun-
powder as a remedy for rattlesnake bite. Their most respected adviser
was John Paxton, a lifelong prospector who sagely told them, "The average prospector never finds anything until he has to climb over it."
This no doubt encouraged the Scotts to believe that even novices like
themselves had as good a chance of stumbling across a ledge of pay ore
as anyone else.[39]

Much of the advice concerned handling the burros, a consuming
preoccupation for the desert prospector, who depended on the "jack"
because it could survive in the back country on less feed and water
than a horse at the same time that he cursed it for its intractability. The
Scotts feelingly wrote of the prospector who said that three-quarters of
his twenty-eight years on the desert had been spent looking for his burros and recounted their own difficulties in rich detail. At Tule Springs,
Josephine put on her boots and led the burros around in the water, giving them "practice" so they might consent to cross. Elsewhere the burros had to be blindfolded before they could be pulled across a bridge,
or Josephine had to lead them through heavy sand while George urged
them on from the side. The Scotts made recurrent reference to the burros' "ugly moods": Jack lay down and refused to go farther twelve times
in an afternoon; "the burros were not anxious to resume work and Jack
showed his views about it by kicking at me twice."[40]

Although wild jacks sometimes hung around the camp sounding
the call of the wild and the Scotts spent a good deal of time chasing
runaways, their major problem lay in keeping their burros in motion.
North of Goldfield in July they noted, "Nothing we could do would
force the grays into more than just the slowest kind of a gait—a mile an
hour. And Chino limped. . . . I led Tucson while Chino was tied to the
rear axle. Tucson dropped on the trail twice and refused to get up, although a small stick applied to her ears soon brought her to her feet.
And how she pulled back and sagged and showed every sign of distress.
But when we reached camp and she knew that the day's work was done,
she walked nimbly around the neighborhood browsing and feeding."
Yet even as Josephine "baked bread for us and the burros" and the
Scotts gradually schooled themselves in the intricacies of burro management, a harbinger of a new way of life for the desert prospector

came roaring over the horizon in a cloud of dust. On a road near Yerington, Josephine "unloaded the shotgun" to ward off a speeding automobile that had earlier forced their wagon off the road.[41]

The Scotts' difficulties with their burros and the hardships the couple encountered give a sense of other women prospectors' experiences in the desert. Like all Nevadans outdoors, they had to contend with the wind, sometimes so strong that it ripped the tent pegs from the ground, and with the heat; worst of all was the combination of the two: "The wind comes off the desert and the skin fairly shrunk under its heat"; "the hot wind burned our eyeballs again so that they were all aflame"; "a man does not decay on the desert, he dries up. Josephine's lips were swollen and caked with alkali when we came in." "We have been sitting in a furnace," they observed after the trip from Ash Meadows to Rosewell. Once Josephine nearly succumbed to heat stroke. On another occasion, as George returned from a long, hot tramp, he saw a mirage of Josephine coming to meet him, an image that perhaps contained the inner truth that he thought of his wife as his savior, rather than the desert traveler's customary image of a pool fringed with greenery. Sometimes, to avoid the heat, they traveled in the night and early morning and laid up for the rest of the day: "We turned in and just as soon as I shut my eyes Josephine told me it was time to get up. I consulted my stem-winder—Ansonia, $1.25—and noticed that both the hands pointed straight up. . . . I hung on to the ties till 2:40, then we turned out and made our coffee and fed the burros by the light of the stars. . . . We broke camp at 4:40 and reached running water, near Carrara, in five hours." At best the Scotts could cover about twenty-eight miles in a day and a half, and usually a good deal less. As a rule Josephine drove the team while George walked; occasionally, they changed places. The Earps had shunned the desert during the hot summers; the Scotts had probably opted for summer because their plan entailed crossing the Sierra before the snows fell.[42]

Recalcitrant burros and scorching heat were not the only troubles encountered by the Scotts. They also had to deal with pests: "In Ash Meadows the air is fairly alive with horseflies and deer flies. We killed some 700 horse flies in our camp, at Fairbanks, and they attacked us so fiercely that we could not have staid there if we had not destroyed them." Elsewhere they noted "tarantulas in everything." By that time they had learned a lesson: "We sleep in the wagon, as it gets us entirely away from such things as rattlesnakes, tarantulas, scorpions, centipedes and hydrophobia skunks."[43]

Varmints aside, they compounded the difficulties of the journey by making their share of mistakes. At one point Josephine remarked that their record for taking the wrong road was practically flawless, with the result that they sometimes landed in a deserted mining camp with no water. "Mistakes are fatal on the desert," George darkly observed. Other novice prospectors were arriving at the same conclusion. The Scotts told of one man who, after getting himself similarly lost, declared that he was "going back to the city where he belonged and knew enough to keep alive." A poem pasted into the diary hints that the Scotts may have entertained the same thought at times:

> I've got to get back to the city,
> My room where the trolley line curves;
> With "L" trains o'erhead every minute
> That act like a dope on my nerves.
> I want to hear fire bells ringing,
> The rattle ty-bang of the street,
> Where hawkers of fish and of berries
> Their cries for more business repeat.

They noticed that they had developed a habit of grumbling.[44]

Yet they persisted, even though the lucky strike they had hoped for failed to materialize. They prospected occasionally, but the diary conveys none of the true prospector's obsessional excitement. Perhaps they found the search less absorbing than they had anticipated. George did the greater part of the prospecting, while Josephine performed the lion's share of roasting and panning ore samples, as well as most of the domestic responsibilities and some of the hunting. It is likely that the Scotts had hoped to live off the land to a larger extent than the Nevada desert afforded. Although they sometimes ate doves for breakfast or shot a jackrabbit and shared it with the dog, several days could pass without seeing so much as a rabbit, and when George once came on a duck and a snipe at a Tule Springs water hole while hunting, they

Josephine Scott shoots a rabbit (Special Collections, University of
Nevada–Reno Library).

seemed like such ornaments on the empty landscape that he could not
bring himself to shoot them.[45]

No information has yet emerged on the lives of the Scotts after they
completed their trip. Possibly, the seed of prospecting, once planted,
brought them into the field again on future occasions. Despite the
hardships they endured, they found much to interest them on their
journey. They seemed to derive less pleasure from the scenery than the
Earps did, though Josephine admired the spring wildflowers in the
Amargosa. What most excited their attention was the odd characters
they met, individuals who, in Wallace Stegner's memorable phrase,
took on "the dignity of rareness" in their remote surroundings.[46] The
Scotts recounted the stories of these desert rats with the rapt appreciation of tourists encountering an exotic tribe. Prospecting undoubtedly
contains a large element of tourism, albeit of a more strenuous variety
than vacationing on a cruise ship. For the Scotts, who did not depend
on prospecting for a living or pursue it with much determination,
prospecting provided the pretext that enabled them to "come into the

country." Tourists they were but of a rather special kind—tourists less intent on the scenery or the ruins than on meeting the natives.

Another prospecting couple, Dora and Sherman Wilhelm, differed from the Scotts in that they made their entire living from prospecting and mining and remained in the field for fourteen years, with only occasional sojourns in town. They resembled the Scotts in that at the outset they too were what journalist James Chisholm had termed "inexperienced incapables" during the South Pass, Wyoming, gold rush. Both Dora and Sherman had grown up on Iowa farms. Sherman, a railroad detective, had mined and long wished to prospect, although he had never had the opportunity to pursue it. Miraculously, in view of his greenhorn credentials, he secured a grubstake from a well-heeled friend interested in mining investment, and Dora and he, with their three-year-old son and infant daughter, set off from Missouri in 1896 for an odyssey in a covered wagon that was to take them through thousands of miles of wilderness in Colorado, Idaho, California, and Nevada. Early in this journey Sherman learned to prospect from an experienced hand in Colorado.[47]

Whether Dora, in turn, learned from Sherman is not clear, but how well she learned is described in *Last Rig to Battle Mountain*, the recollections of her oldest son, Walt. As early as the winter of 1896–97 she had already turned into an expert gold panner working hundreds of ore samples: "While Sherman prospected, Dora would pan the gold he brought in. She was a natural born gold panner. She loved to do it. If there was the tiniest speck of gold in a sample, she'd find it. She was so good at the craft, before they left Colorado other miners brought samples for her to test. She got so expert she could give a fair estimate on what rock that panned would run per ton," the assayer's essential skill. She devised her own test for copper, sprinkling a few drops of vinegar on the blue-green streaks that could mean copper or silver and rubbing them with a knife blade to see if copper coloring would show on the steel.[48]

Some, however, found it difficult to believe that a woman could develop expertise on mining matters. Dora knew how to put such doubters in their places: "As Mom's fame as a gold panner spread, one wise guy tried to fool her. He brought a mortar full of muck for her to pan. She thought it queer the man had ground it. But like a good sport she panned it down. Then she told the guy, 'Your muck is worthless. You'd have to fertilize it if you wanted to start a brick yard. Did you name the claim the *Humbug*?'"⁴⁹

Although Dora gave birth to five more children in the course of their travels, she continued to hunt mineral. Walt remembered a period in the Mother Lode country: "Mom did a lot of panning on her own. She never had any spare time, but when she felt like panning she took the time. I used to help her. She'd shake roots, clean out crevices with wire hooks and I'd carry the muck to water. While we were in Columbia she panned several ounces and kept it in a buckskin bag." One can well understand why Dora had little spare time, caring for a family of nine in a covered wagon in country so remote that she sometimes did not see another white woman for eighteen months at a time. All the Wilhelms shared the domestic responsibilities. The older children helped with cooking, laundry, and care of the younger ones, and Walt hunted game for dinner, but Dora still had a great deal to do. Like Ellie Nay and Fannie Quigley, she excelled at producing delicious meals under primitive conditions. Sixty years later her children still waxed lyrical when remembering the pies, cobblers, and shortcakes she made in a Dutch oven, the fried wild chicken with cream gravy, the thick antelope steaks, and the wild chickens and quarters of venison barbecued in a pit.⁵⁰

Despite the hardships, Dora loved their gypsy life, and the children reveled in it. When they sometimes passed through a settlement the townsfolk pitied the covered-wagon brood because they had no permanent home, and Walt pitied them right back for the confined lives they led, with "nothing new to see or do": "We kids romped in different meadows, climbed mountains and went swimming in all the rivers of the West. We were free, and tough as wild horses." Although their nomadic life taught the children the practical skills of outdoorsmen, they had little opportunity to attend school, unless Sherman happened to be developing a mine in the vicinity of a schoolhouse.⁵¹

Dora was one of the few women prospectors who attempted to take her children into the field with her for anything longer than a short jaunt, but even she found it necessary to leave them behind in the end. In 1909 in the hills south of Battle Mountain, Nevada, Sherman at last made a rich strike at the site later christened Bannock. At first he couldn't believe it and thought he might have gone crazy. After an associate had confirmed the value of the gold samples in his hands and started back to town with the location notice, Sherman simply sat on the hillside in a daze reflecting on how easily he could have missed this bonanza: why had he left the trail to sit down at a lower spot on the hill? Why had he noticed and kicked the little chunk of reddish quartz nestled under the sagebrush that he could not have seen from a standing position? The sheer unlikelihood of the find led him to the verge of Carl Wikstrom's belief that nothing is really random and the prospector is guided to the rock by forces beyond human understanding.[52]

After taking out a few more samples "Dad never touched the diggings again until Mom got out there." He knew he needed Dora, not to take care of the family but to mine by his side. Not only did he value her skill but also he felt that no one else could be trusted not to highgrade specimens from the rich streak. Accordingly, Dora left the children with a Finnish woman in Battle Mountain and came out to Bannock to mine. Sherman excavated the shaft, and she dug out and sorted the highgrade.[53]

Soon a camp sprang up, and the Wilhelms allocated leases and set a force of miners to work on the less rich but still valuable quartz veins that radiated from the center. Traffic became so heavy that the Wilhelms had to build a shack over the diggings and post guards, and Dora had to do her sorting and sacking down inside the mine. Eventually, the sheer size of the task compelled Sherman to bring miners into the central area to do the blasting and mucking (shoveling and wheeling away the rock fragments following a blast), while Dora sacked the highgrade and Sherman smelted it in a furnace he had set up on the spot. The two of them continued their mining until the rich streak pinched out at a depth of about thirty feet. In 1910 the Wilhelms sold their share of Bannock and bought their first home, in Long Beach, California, where the girls enjoyed civilized living and the boys mourned the loss of the old freedom.

Their retirement in the reputedly idyllic spot where wealthy people of the day congregated to enjoy life lasted no longer than that of the Nays. Soon Dora was riding astride a burro through the Piute Hills in the Mojave Desert west of the Colorado River to investigate a silver strike (Walt does not explain what became of his father). In the summer of 1911 she returned with a mule team and one of her young sons to develop the silver mine that became commonly known as "Dora's Diggin's," though more formally identified as Wilhelm. Her mine shipped ore for four years. Even in her seventies Dora continued to spend a good deal of her time with two sons living in Mojave Desert towns and to head out into the hills for another prospecting trip at every opportunity.[54]

The lives of the women who prospected with male relatives in the era from the California gold rush to World War I present some suggestive contrasts and similarities to the lives of women who prospected on their own. One circumstance stands out clearly: the incompatibility of prospecting and raising children. Those who had young children left them behind: Mountain Charley, with the Sisters of Charity; Ellie Nay, with her mother; Marion Phelps, with an Indian nursemaid, after she judged the children old enough for her to leave. "For the first few months these absences were keen tortures. My children would haunt my dreams and play about me in my waking hours—the separation seemed intolerable, and for the first month an eternity": thus Mountain Charley recalled the pain of prolonged separation from her children.[55] The Wilhelms brought their children with them only until the strike they had sought for years demanded the full-time attention of both parents.

The unavoidable mismatch between child rearing and prospecting—career conflict in an extreme form—undoubtedly influenced the kinds of women who entered the field. Women of mature age, childless or with grown children, were a strong presence. Helen Cottrell, Belle Butler, Mrs. P. J. Thomas, Mrs. Morehouse Mallen, and Frances Williams all had grown or teenaged children. In the main it does not appear in these cases that prospecting was a fantasy long deferred; rather, it seems an opportunity seized by women no longer occupied by rearing children. Even Frances Williams, the indomitable steam engine, might have had some difficulties in juggling the quest in the wilderness along with giving birth to sixteen children. Among younger women it is unclear whether the absence of children in numerous instances represents chance, miscarriages brought on by physical hardships, or a deliberate decision to forgo motherhood in order to prospect more freely. Josie Earp regretted her miscarriages, although children would inevitably have decreased her opportunities for "wanderings with Wyatt." But what of Mollie Sawyer, as well as Mrs. Riggs and Fannie Quigley in their younger days? Did Sawyer decide that motherhood would curtail her adventures in the Arizona mining excitements? Did Quigley and Riggs, both evidently well endowed with the prospector's taste for living in remote places where few other human beings ventured, feel that a brood in the cabin would interfere with the solitude they cherished? They would have been mothers then, no longer as free to reflect in the stillness or to prove their mettle by pitting themselves against the elements. They may have rejected motherhood much as Nellie Cashman rejected marriage as an assumption of domestic burdens at the price of freedom. Their lives are the only answers they give.

One historian has suggested that women who came to the Klondike gold rush as wives "tended to be more rigid and less adventurous than their single counterparts." Incidentally, a similar observation has been made concerning married men during the California gold rush. William Downie explained why he avoided including married men in a prospecting party: "They would whine about their wives; wonder how their children were getting along; speculate upon the possibilities of a speedy return; and at night, when we bachelors rolled ourselves in our blankets and slept the sleep of the just, they would grunt and groan, and pray and weep, and gaze at the stars, and make themselves unfit for the work at hand."[56] Downie's complaint of course dealt with married men who had left their families behind for prolonged periods. Only two married women did this: Frances Williams, who could not bring her invalid husband, and Mrs. Jennings, who could not bring her New York newspaper editor husband. The clearcut gender difference between the number of men, long presumed by historians to be large, who left spouses behind to prospect and the small number of women who did so may have a twofold explanation. Women, if they agreed to marry at all, accepted the traditional conception of a wifely role and did not go forth on their own. Moreover, husbands such as Joe Nay and Wyatt Earp may have been more willing to join in the prospecting trip proposed by a wife than were the wives left behind by prospecting husbands of the sort who whined, groaned, and gazed at the stars in Major Downie's expeditions.

The theory that wives were less adventurous rests on the view that their domestic responsibilities precluded other endeavors and extends beyond the Klondike. Analysis of the overland trail diaries of westering women has led scholars to conclude that most had been reluctantly uprooted from homes where they would have much preferred to remain, in a familiar cocoon of friends and relatives. The child care issue suggests that the conflict between domestic life and wilderness ventures was very real, but the annals of the women prospectors otherwise lend little support to these assumptions. Aside from those women raised on the mining frontier (Belle Butler and Ellie Nay), most of the married women whose backgrounds are known had followed the mining excitements as single women and taken up with men of like inclinations whom they met there. Matilda Wales, Fannie Quigley, Mollie Sawyer, and Josie Earp (who ran away from home as a teenager to join a theatrical troupe and proceeded to booming Tombstone) all belonged in this category. Thus, all four had already chosen a way of life that continued after they became common-law wives, and none sought self-worth through what Carl Degler has described as the "sense of identification with other women" to be attained by confining their activities to the domestic sphere in accordance with traditional separation of sex roles, unless Fannie Quigley's mutant sense of woman's place can be so described. Such women readily combined daring enterprises with marital relationships, but it should also be noted that Dora Wilhelm, one of the few known to have traveled west as a wife, showed no lack of adventurous spirit, and mutual enthusiasm set the couple on the trail.

In many cases, however, we do not know who initiated the idea of prospecting. When clear evidence exists, the idea was more often hers than his. This finding starkly contrasts with Faragher's study of women on the overland trail, not one of whom had initiated the decision to move west. Faragher also relates that when a woman who believed she had found gold in a stream was ridiculed by a man in her emigrant party because "women were not permitted to play that role," she meekly dropped the matter. Fannie Quigley or Mollie Sawyer, by contrast, would surely have reduced the ridiculer to rubble, a scenario that signals why strong female personalities and a certain configuration of family dynamics seem to have been the general rule among women who became prospectors. Women who lacked these qualities or accepted submissive roles did not persist at prospecting. In its broad outlines the female frontier in the mining West, which magnetized adventurous spirits of both sexes, may well have differed from the female cultural world of the agrarian West.[57]

The possibility arises that married women appear less adventurous only because we know less about their adventures. The journey of the Riggses into the Death Valley country at a time when much of it remained far beyond the pale may have been more fraught with perils than Lillian Malcolm's, but no one interviewed Mrs. Riggs on her experiences. The diary of the Scotts' trip through the fiery furnace with recalcitrant burros has never been published. Josie Earp's recollections appeared in print after her death, but the chapters on prospecting have received little attention from a public fascinated by the events at Tombstone that culminated in the gunfight at the O.K. Corral. Matilda Wales's adventures with William James on the way to Chisana may, for all we know, have exceeded Nellie Cashman's epic journey to the Cassiar. The remote wilderness beyond the towering jagged heights of the Wrangell and St. Elias ranges had long barred all but the most intrepid from the Chisana region. One trail led over the Nizina and Chisana glaciers, where travelers encountered constant storms, snow blindness, and "difficulties of traversing glacial ice." And that was the easy way. More often travelers rafted down the rivers and in winter traversed the frozen streams with dog sleds.[58] But Mabel Wales's passage remains untold. No one ever asked.

As this suggests, the sources on married and single women differ substantially. Most of the detail we have on married women comes to us through memoirs, occasionally from the women themselves (Josie Earp and the Scott diary), but more often from visitors who found them performing remarkable feats in distant areas and were much impressed (the recollections on Fannie Quigley are especially rich). Thus we see these women primarily through the eyes of others, rather than hearing what they might have chosen to say about themselves. With the exception of the single interview with Ellie Nay, no reporter interviewed a married woman with a husband on the scene, and sources comparable to the newspaper interviews with Nellie Cashman, Lillian Malcolm, and Helen Cottrell (all women on their own) are lacking.[59]

Both recollections and newspaper reportage were strongly shaped by the writer's own image of what women ought to be. Accordingly, the unseen doppelgänger who wafts behind their words is woman as the weaker sex, incapable of the dangerous physical feats undertaken by men; woman in the domestic sphere, nurturer and moral guide to husband and children; woman the civilizer, with her churches, her teas, and her quilting bees, eager to re-create small-town America in the wilds. What therefore interested the writers most about the women prospectors was their deviations from the observer's image of womanhood—Fannie Quigley shooting grizzlies and keeping her feet warm in their innards while she butchered them; swaggering, hard-drinking Mollie Sawyer; Mrs. Riggs setting forth into the Death Valley region when it was roamed by desperadoes on the lam and there was no possibility of town society in the company of other women. Married women, whose marriages were presumed to signal acceptance of their proper place in the scheme of things, may have been especially singled out in this regard. In the few instances in which women prospectors speak to us at length in their own voices, reactions to the image doppelgänger dwindle into unimportance beside the issues that interested them more. Both Idah Strobridge and Josie Earp have little to say about their physical exploits, beyond making clear that their passages through the wilderness were scarcely to be compared with rolling past in a Pullman railroad car. Nor do any signs appear of a need to socialize with other women, to civilize the wilds, or to explain their lack of interest in these matters. Both women valued the desert as they found it, empty and untouched, and the primary thrust of their accounts seems to be to convey their joy in the wilderness experience and the fascination of prospecting.

Although the reaction to perceived deviations from the image of proper womanhood has influenced much of the writing on women prospectors, a certain class bias has also been at work. Male reporters tended to concentrate on clothes and physical exploits—the ever-fascinating masculine garb, the adit a woman blasted through hard rock with her own hands, the trek through the wilderness. The rare woman writer, by contrast, focused on intellectual accomplishments (while not neglecting to satisfy the public's insatiable curiosity about clothes). One guesses that the woman mucking out ore, working a rocker, and hacking out samples was something of an embarrassment because she was a working-class figure who despite her physical feats had demonstrated nothing that redounded to woman's credit as defined by middle-class standards of achievement. For instance, in Mary Stickney's article on early Colorado women in mining, a valuable source, the emphasis is on their role as capable owners and managers "relegating all the rude work of shaft and tunnel to hired labor" and as the mistresses of lovely homes who have not sacrificed their femininity by entering the mining business. The ghost of true womanhood lurks in the background, and the only deviation from it that Stickney wishes to acknowledge is in the intellectual realm: "This knowledge and skill is by no means beyond the grasp of the feminine brain, while moreover it does not of necessity impose assumption of coarse masculinity nor inevitable encounter with pick and shovel."[60]

It is doubtful that all women prospectors viewed their own careers in such restricted terms. They took great pride in the entire range of their accomplishments, the mucking and blasting along with the mine ownership (Mrs. P. J. Thomas and Nettie Hornbeck, for example). The standards by which they measured themselves did not include the ideal of true womanhood. Rather, they relished equaling or exceeding male achievements and, possibly, those of the rivals whose existence they never openly acknowledged: one another. In some areas, however, traditional divisions of labor lingered on. Most of the wives whose activities on prospecting trips are detailed did the cooking and laundry while spouses tended the animals, set up the tent, dug the privy, and so forth. The major exception, in surprising contradistinction to his macho image as gun-toting lawman, was Wyatt Earp, who assumed a large share of the customarily female tasks.

Another arena of activity in which wives reverted to a traditional role was the mine sales and promotion phase of prospecting. We cannot, of course, know how large an influence Dora Wilhelm, Ellie Nay, and Belle

Butler exerted when discussing a pending mine sale with their husbands, and on the basis of what is known about the last two, it is not unlikely that their wishes carried great weight. But this occurred behind closed doors. No matter how large the role they had played in the discovery and development of the mines, they deferred to their husbands and withdrew to the private sphere in keeping with the dichotomy that allocates the world of public achievement to men. They nonetheless expected to receive the entire measure of financial rewards due them as full partners. Fannie Quigley and Minnie Peavine were treated as such, and when Carrie Torelli and Mrs. Riggs were not, ruckuses ensued, following which Mrs. Riggs had the final say on mine sales.

Women with a different relationship to the men with whom they prospected showed less disposition than wives to step modestly aside. Jennie Hilton, who prospected with her brother, sought investors for her mines herself, and M. A. Rice, the Queen of Thunder Mountain, was empowered by her father and the other men in their prospecting party to promote their mines along with her own. Evidently, being a daughter or a sister was a less restrictive role than being a wife. Moreover, Hilton and Rice had been independent professionals before they took up prospecting, a teacher and a newspaper editor, respectively, and this background may have given them a confidence in the business world that wives who had known only homemaking and prospecting did not possess.

Provided they received the financial share rightly due them, prospecting wives generally accepted their role as women in the shadows. No accounts by Belle Butler on the discovery of the Mizpah have appeared, and presumably none was requested by reporters, who assumed as a matter of course that the key role on that day so heavy-laden with consequences for Nevada's future must have been played by Jim Butler. Nor, after Belle finally got her procrastinating husband into motion, did she ever publicly suggest that his were the only hands to assist her.

Part Two: 1919–1950

# SEVEN

# Queen Mary and the Tugboat Annie of the Desert: The Postwar Era

By the end of World War I the world of the prospector had changed forever. No longer was it possible to envisage him as the explorer in the vanguard, climbing "like a huge fly upon the bald skull of some lofty mountain," in the hyperbolic words of a nineteenth-century orator, with "the power and glory of the Republic" marching in his wake.[1] The age of exploration had passed, and the West had turned from a frontier to a settled region, although large islands of wilderness remained. Prospecting continued to draw women of strength and courage—and surviving in remote country still demanded a great deal of both—but the epic sagas, such as Nellie Cashman's mercy mission to the Cassiar and Lillian Malcolm's starvation journey to Nome, lay in the past. None of the latter-day women prospectors ranged so widely as they had in their travels from the Arctic to Tombstone and beyond, and in a world of diminished opportunities for grand adventure, none would again experience "life at full tide" as they did in the seething streets of the frontier boomtowns. Now wind whistled through the broken windows of deserted houses in Goldfield, site of the last of the great gold rushes. Small excitements over a new strike still gathered a handful of hopefuls, but these were mere feeble tremors in the public psyche compared with the mighty earthquakes that had caused thousands to embark on long and perilous journeys during the first sixty years of mining on the western frontier. No longer was it possible to be the first woman on the scene of a new mining rush; one could only be the last among the crumbling shacks and blowing tumbleweeds of a dying camp.

As the West changed, so did the swirl of attitudes that had long surrounded the women prospectors. No longer perceived as rebel adventuresses, they gained greater acceptance and aroused less interest. No longer, in the more civilized West, would a reporter grouse that they trespassed on man's exclusive territory, although the difficulties of convincing men that women could know anything about mining had not yet been laid to rest. Wearing men's clothes was not the burning issue that had landed Marie Pantalon in jail; although the woman executive in a pantsuit still lay ahead, widespread use of men's clothes by young women on western ranches had evidently made the woman prospector's garb less shocking. Not least, the woman prospector had gained acceptance from other women. The doctrines of true womanhood and the sense of woman's mission to civilize the frontier had weakened, and the need to validate one's worth by forcing others to conform had lost its virulence. No longer would more conventional women hold their skirts contemptuously aside from someone like Lillian Malcolm or sharpen their tongues on a Nellie Cashman. With few exceptions the latter-day women prospectors seem to have been well liked by other women.

Along with the new attitudes toward the women prospectors came an important technological change in prospecting: widespread use of autos. Because far more distance could now be covered in much less time, the car facilitated the emergence of the weekend prospector and even the one-day sojourner and made living in remote locales much more comfortable and less hazardous than in the past. When auto prospecting started in the first decade of the twentieth century, it was confined to the wealthy few who could afford one of the expensive new machines. After the war, autos increasingly gained ground and the burro became an anachronism, along with the rig drawn by horses or mules. Only a few prospectors still struggled with recalcitrant and ill-tempered burros as had the Scotts or faced disaster at a dry water hole as had the Earps. At the same time, they lost the burro prospector's backhanded advantage: "Don't get sore at the burros when you have to hunt them a long ways," an experienced prospector had advised Herman Albert; "that's how you find mines." No one ever struck a bonanza while changing a flat tire. The rise of the auto also brought an end to some of the more dramatic episodes in the annals of the women prospectors. In January 1907 one could read in the *Elko Independent* of Mrs. H. A. Dyer, a woman prospector compelled to abandon her wagon after the loss of one of her mules; she then walked forty-five miles through a heavy snowstorm into Ely, "every step of the way being an ordeal that would have tested the grit of many a man to the straining point." By the twenties such stories of dangers surmounted had disappeared from the news. As life grew easier, however, the women prospectors lost a measure of the admiration that had rightly surrounded the likes of Mrs. H. A. Dyer.[2]

In any technological revolution a few inevitably resist. Shorty Harris, one of Lillian Malcolm's old prospecting partners, declared, "I never had much use for a flivver," and gleefully related how he had gotten even with an Indian who had cheated him by selling his car to the miscreant for next to nothing; Harris claimed that the ensuing struggle to buy tires and spare parts had kept the Indian's tribe broke for years. "Klondike Helen" (Helen Seifert) held much the same view of autos as Harris. Like Lillian Malcolm, she had started prospecting on the Klondike and later headed south to Death Valley and Silver Peak. In 1938, when her story cropped up in a newspaper, the knob of hair beneath her battered cap had turned gray, but she was still strong enough to earn a comfortable living by doing the assessment work on other people's mines while pursuing her own prospecting. Her claims were scattered all over the Silver Peak region. She had abandoned her coupe in Death Valley when she became disgusted with the constant need to repair it and thenceforth relied on her own two feet, carrying her grub and bedroll on her back. "A fifteen mile hike is a short jaunt to her," remarked the *Reno Evening Gazette*. At one time she camped seven miles from the nearest water source, making a weekly trip to fill her bucket and canteens. The reporter asked her a question that would not have been unfamiliar to Lillian Malcolm or even Mountain Charley: Wasn't mining a "difficult occupation" for her? Klondike Helen crisply responded that a sound knowledge of minerals had eliminated the difficulties and added that she found as much excitement in a new specimen of ore as other women did in a new bonnet. (Clearly, the old scorn for feminine frivolities had persisted.) Along the desert roads her energetic figure could sometimes be seen striding past, wearing a man's old khaki army coat and pants, her pack on her back and her prospector's pick dangling from her belt.[3]

The eternal optimism that kept Klondike Helen in the field for so many years remained the prospector's most obvious characteristic, and the postwar women prospectors appeared as bounteously endowed with it as their predecessors. But their numbers—and those of their male counterparts—were much diminished. "Why has the once great prospecting army been cut down to a mere handful?" rhetorically inquired Jack Bell, former prospector and all-purpose adventurer, and proceeded to offer two of the reasons. First, the readily accessible sites that could be spotted through surface indications had already been discovered. Second, the prospector had fallen victim to the higher cost of living. "Gone are the days when he could take a fourteen burro string and live on a small grubstake," lamented Bell and estimated that by 1930 it cost four or five times as much as before to keep a prospector in the field.[4]

Others linked the shrinkage in the once great prospecting army to the disappearance of the boomtowns and to Prohibition. Boomtown entrepreneurs, professionals, and especially saloonkeepers, now driven underground or out of business by the Eighteenth Amendment, had been an important source of grubstakes. Though the women prospectors had rarely received grubstakes, they had relied on the investors and promoters who abounded in the boomtowns. The departure of the mining promoters who formerly clustered in these towns and the continued rise of the trained mining engineer at the expense of the amateur curtailed this source of funds. In 1907 one could read of the experience of Mrs. John Vance, a prospector in northern Nevada, who took two investors from Boise on a two-day trip through the snow to show them her claims on aptly named Disaster Peak. "We were forced to dig through snowbanks in many places on the trail and we linked ourselves together with ropes when taking narrow passes," she recalled. In the postwar era, if Vance had succeeded in beating any investors out of the bushes, they would no doubt have remained comfortably at home in Boise while their mining engineer scrutinized the claims. Unless she could impress this skeptical professional, the latter-day woman prospector had little chance of receiving the fifty-thousand-dollar option. Vance had won after she dug through the snow for several hours to open up her tunnel for the investors' inspection.[5]

Of course, old ways of life die hard, and even in an age of diminished rewards some careers that began before the war continued: Nellie Cashman, the frontier angel, supplied reporters with colorful copy until her death in 1925; Mrs. Aldred forged forward with her mining operations in Colorado, as did Blanche Cascaden in Livengood; Josie and Wyatt Earp still prospected and ran their mine until his failing health obliged them to remain in Los Angeles; Dora Wilhelm's adventures in the desert had not yet ended; Fannie Quigley continued to amaze all beholders with her wilderness capabilities; and reporters wrote of the activities of the Alaskan "girl gold miners," Irma and Margaret Peterson, with something of the old zest. Nonetheless, most of those whose doings enlivened the news during the golden age of the women prospectors from 1898 to 1910 had disappeared from view. Increasingly, news on the women prospectors came to light not through tales of their exploits and discoveries but through their obituaries.

It is from this source that we learn of Maggie Johnson, called "Black Mag," the only black woman known to have been actively involved in mining, although at least one other had some connection with it. Aunt Sally Campbell, the first non-Indian woman in the Black Hills of South Dakota, had ridden in as a cook with George Armstrong Custer's exploratory expedition in 1874. After Indians annihilated Custer's force at the Little Big Horn, Sally returned to the Black Hills with an early party of gold seekers. She either staked a claim on French Creek or was presented with one by her companions. She did not, however, work her ground or prospect further but immediately moved on to Crook City, where her skills as cook, housekeeper, and nurse were much in demand.[6]

By contrast, there could be no doubt that Maggie Johnson was personally involved in mining. She was born in Louisiana in 1855, probably a slave but one who claimed the ability to read and write. Her father had been born in Africa. Why she became one of the small number of black women to go west remains unclear, but around 1885, the thirtieth year of her life, after a short period in Austin and Eureka, she made her home on the northwesterly slope of Mount Tenabo in northern Nevada. Long before Maggie began mining on the mountain, mules heavily laden with silver ore had traversed the trail from Cortez one

209

canyon to the south to the mill that gave Mill Canyon its name. In 1886 mining operations shifted to a newly constructed plant at Cortez. Mill Canyon, which prospectors had combed without success, had been dismissed as barren, but Maggie took a different view.

Soon she had a number of claims, and she refused to grant leases on any of them, because she preferred to work them herself. In 1900 she was doing just that, assisted by a young Irish male partner and her sister, Annie Numrice (or Nunnice), fourteen years older than she. Mill Canyon saw a minor boomlet in 1909, possibly the juncture at which Maggie sold one of her claims for seven thousand dollars, before reverting to its previous state of neglect. In her last years rheumatism crippled her so badly that she could no longer work her claims or even perform her annual assessment work, but she stayed on with faith undiminished, convinced that her claims would one day bring her a fortune. Despite her preference for a lonely life, she was no embittered and twisted hermit uncomfortable in the company of others. According to the *Eureka Sentinel*, she had a "genial and open hearted nature" and "many warm friends throughout the county."[7] Probably, like many women prospectors, she enjoyed occasional socializing provided it was interlaced with large spaces of solitude. Also, over the span of more than thirty years she no doubt had grown attached to the austere beauty of Mount Tenabo ("Lookout Mountain" in the Shoshone language), where the lingering spring snow in the narrow canyons made white hieroglyphs on the high purple slopes.

Her life as a woman miner ended in 1920 when she was brought to the Eureka County hospital too seriously crippled to continue living at Tenabo and aged beyond her years. Recognizing that her mining days had ended, Maggie sold her remaining interest in the Lost Treasure and Cumberland Extension mines to Benjamin Goodhue, a white miner in his middle fifties who had been her boarder, and probably her partner, for ten years. In the summer of 1924, at sixty-nine, she died. Although she had ended as a charity case, time would prove her right on the value of her mining claims. Today the huge machines of modern mining have wrested from the innards of Mount Tenabo the fortune that Maggie Johnson never lived to see.[8]

As some mining careers that had begun in the nineteenth century were ending, new ones were beginning. When they first began driving to the Death Valley region for short visits in the late 1920s, Louise Grantham and Dorothy Ketchum seemed to typify the new weekend prospectors, but in time Louise came to appreciate to the old-fashioned virtues of the burro. Moreover, mining in Death Valley began to occupy a larger and larger part of her life. As journalist John Spears had observed of this region more than thirty years earlier, "it is said that the desert quickly turns the brains of some men—makes them monomaniacs, so that once they have made a journey across it they become fascinated and return to it again and again, as an opium eater to his drug." On some women it had much the same effect. Since the days of Mrs. Riggs and Lillian Malcolm, mining women had shown an affinity for Death Valley that continued during the era between the wars.[9]

Louise Grantham's success in mining was to surpass by far the work of these women, as well as that of a good many of the men who had watched her early efforts with patronizing indulgence. When Frank Brock, a mine promoter and real estate developer, started bringing Grantham and Ketchum from the Los Angeles area to Shoshone, a California hamlet east of Death Valley, both were fine-looking young women. Grantham, a nurse, had short sandy hair and a boyish look and always wore jodhpurs; Ketchum, a doctor's wife with dark hair and olive skin that gave her a Hispanic look, was the prettier one, so pretty that children liked to sit beside her just to look at her. The two women are still remembered for their kindness. They would bring presents for the children, take them riding in Dorothy's expensive black Studebaker just for fun, and drive Indian children in need of medical help to distant towns where they could receive treatment. The denizens of Shoshone may have called the two strangers from Los Angeles "grab 'em and ketch 'em" behind their backs, but they made room on the long slab bench where everyone waited for the dinner bell to ring at the boardinghouse. Even the women residents of Shoshone (admittedly few in number) liked the pair and enjoyed Louise's sense of humor, although they looked askance at her hairstyle (Louise was probably the first woman prospector to cut her hair).

At first glance what Louise Grantham and Dorothy Ketchum saw in Shoshone is less easy to guess. Author William Caruthers has described the place as a mesquite thicket, a weatherbeaten ramshackle store, "a few listing shacks on a naked flat," and "whirlwinds spiraling along dry washes to vanish in hummocks of sand." A number of prospectors lived in dugouts and rude shelters along the gulch that trailed behind Shoshone up the smooth rounded hill said to be an old Indian burial ground. But the country around this rudimentary settlement had been painted with a fine palette, blue water and green reeds in white salt-encrusted marshes, white and gold and rose shadings on the hills, lavender mountains in the farther distance. Probably what kept the two young women driving north from Los Angeles was not Shoshone but the promise that beckoned from the hills beyond and the high hopes that spun among the listing shacks along with the whirlwinds. Among those who gathered on the slab bench the talk was all of mining, with the reiterated refrain, "Looks like he's got 'er made." Louise and Dorothy listened intently and said little, and not much time passed before the litany of "got 'er made" took effect.[10]

Soon they began prospecting, at first with their initial mentor, Frank Brock, and usually together, but sometimes Louise went forth without Dorothy. On one of these occasions Louise and Brock were searching the area near Saratoga Springs. Night fell bitterly cold, with an icy, cutting north wind, and they agreed to combine their bedrolls and sleep together for warmth. Brock later told people that after they nestled in and began to feel warmer, he attempted to fondle Louise. She responded with a firm push and reminded him, "We agreed to sleep together for warmth and nothing else. Also, I don't like men." Thus was born the rumor that Louise and Dorothy were lesbians, the only women prospectors about whom this allegation was made. It is well to bear in mind, however, that the source was Brock, a rejected lover who might have wanted to get even with the woman who spurned his advances by slinging a mudball at her. Even if he quoted Louise correctly, she may have merely intended to stop him as effectively as possible, or she may have meant that she didn't like men who attempted to grab her in the desert in the middle of the night. Not improbably, Louise's short hair, which had inherited the shock value formerly attached to masculine clothes, gave force to the rumor.[11]

Without the supervision of Brock, who seems to have been a poor prospector as well as an individual who aroused general antipathy in Shoshone, the hunt for mineral proceeded much better. The two women started prospecting in Butte Valley, so named for the sandstone peak, boldly striped with browns, yellows, oranges, blues, and grays, that juts forth in the midst of a secluded valley in the southern Panamints. This region was also the favored stomping ground of prospector Ernest Huhn, known as "Siberian Red." A big, husky, red-haired German said to have escaped from Russia at the time of the revolution by way of Alaska, Siberian Red had seen a good deal of the world and was nearly thirty years older than Dorothy and Louise. He was known for his high-stakes gambling, at which he would readily wager his last dollar with reckless panache, and his superb poker playing. Whenever he joined the boys for a game in the "Mesquite Club" at the back of the Shoshone boardinghouse, he regularly cleaned them out. Yet he was always broke. He did road work in the winters and occasionally hired on in other people's mines to keep himself in bacon and beans. Soon the three of them—Louise, Dorothy, and Siberian Red—were inseparable.[12]

This arrangement did not occur without initial resistance on the part of Siberian Red. As Deke Lowe, a long-time resident of the Shoshone area, has put it, Siberian Red saw the women as "useless ladies pretending to be miners," and he could be very rough on novices. Asa Russell, who learned his prospecting under Siberian Red's tutelage in the mid-twenties, has related that each time he picked up a piece of float, Siberian Red would knock it out of his hand and sharply admonish him that idly picking up float when he did not intend to trace it to the point of origin was a bad habit. He also provided Russell with cloths of different colors and instructions: whenever Russell found a worthwhile vein, he was to wrap a sample in a piece of cloth and tie strips of the same color on top of the nearest tree and at ground level to prevent him from missing the site when he returned. (To the chagrin and fury of Siberian Red, he lost the spot where he had picked up an unusually rich sample on this trip with Russell because he thought himself too experienced to bother with the colored cloths.) Siberian Red may well have been harder on the "useless ladies" than he was on Russell, even if he saw them as a potential source of grubstakes and development funds. As a confirmed bachelor, his unease must have increased as he realized that one of them was romantically interested in him. Probably it was Louise who found this aging wanderer, with all his rough edges, a good deal more appealing than a slick promoter such as Frank Brock.[13]

In time the threesome became a twosome—Louise and Siberian Red. Dorothy ceased coming to Shoshone and turned into a silent partner; Louise spent so much of her time there that she became known as the "girl prospector." While Louise and Siberian Red never became lovers, so far as is known, they did become good friends and partners in one of the most important talc mines in twentieth-century America. Although old-timers in Shoshone believe that Louise bought into Siberian Red's talc claim, Linda Greene, author of a history of mining in Death Valley, has concluded that Louise and Siberian Red located eleven claims between 1931 and 1935 on the Warm Spring Canyon talc deposits lying easterly from Butte Valley in the Panamints. The talc was of high quality and readily accessible, but initial development proceeded slowly. Transportation over the rough road by truck was so difficult that Louise and Siberian Red decided that they needed pack animals to carry the talc down to the main road and hatched a plot to get hold of the string of five burros that prospector Ben Brandt stubbornly refused to trade for Louise's pickup truck. According to author Caruthers, they were all sitting on the slab bench in Shoshone when Louise remarked to Siberian Red in a voice loud enough for Ben to overhear, "If Ben didn't waste so much time hunting those jacks, he might find a mine." She went on to describe to Siberian Red the many advantages of her truck, Ben weakened, Louise got her burros, and "one of the best prospectors on the desert was ruined forever" by his enslavement to the truck.[14]

By 1942 the Warm Spring Canyon Mine was no longer a five-burro affair. Louise had succeeded in raising development funds, grading a truck road, and turning the mine into a thriving operation that ultimately produced at least 830,000 tons of talc. If they said "looks like she's got 'er made" back on the slab bench in Shoshone, they would, for once, have had it right. In the 1950s Louise further expanded operations, purchasing all the Warm Spring Canyon talc claims not already in her possession. Talc has many uses, from insecticide carrier to rice-polishing medium, with the largest proportion absorbed by paints and ceramics, but Siberian Red, who continued to regard gold as the aristocrat of minerals and to smolder over the ledge he had lost, used to speak of it disparagingly as "plain baby talcum powder." Nonetheless, the mine's success made his last years in his small cabin in Shoshone comfortable and kept him in gambling money, even if he never bought the small yacht he had once fantasized about. When he died, he left his share in the mine to Dorothy.[15]

In addition to her widely acknowledged capabilities as a mine manager, Louise became the kind of benevolent capitalist that Frances Williams had falsely claimed to be. She turned the Gold Hill mill site she had acquired in Warm Spring Canyon in the early thirties into what one superintendent of Death Valley National Monument called "the finest mining camp of any in the Monument." It included her home, a mess hall, shop, generator building, dormitory, and several additional houses, all noted for plumbing and solid construction. She built a swimming pool with a plastic dome for her miners and later brought in television and other amenities. All this existed in a desert oasis of wild grape, reeds, oleanders, and fig trees. Beneath the surface lay what Greene terms the "most extensive underground talc-mining operation" in California. Until 1959 the Grantham Mine continued to produce more commercial talc than any other mine in the West. Louise eventually sold her interest and retired, after many years of prospecting and mining in Death Valley. Although the site is no longer being worked today, a recent report estimated the recoverable value of the Warm Spring and Galena Canyon talc mines at $246 million. The location and development of the most important mining operation in the canyons had been no small achievement for a useless lady pretending to be a miner.[16]

In the 1920s, as middle-aged women, Mary Grantz and Josie Pearl reached the northern Nevada region where both would prospect and mine for the rest of their lives. Their presence in the same place at the same time offers a glimpse of something suspected in the camps where women prospectors appeared simultaneously without socializing or cooperating: overt rivalry. The different paths of their careers also illustrate the large role luck plays in mining. One would develop an important mine and die virtually unknown. The other would attain scant success in mining and yet become one of the most publicized and fondly remembered among the women prospectors.

Josie Pearl lived most of her life on the mining frontier. She was born Josephine Reed, one of twelve children, in Evening Shade, Arkansas, on 19 December 1873. After a brief sojourn in Tennessee the family moved to an adobe on a ranch in Colorado's San Luis Valley. The Reeds were poor and times were hard. Josie wore homespun dresses; often ate wild rabbit for dinner, when she ate at all; carded, spun, weeded, and cooked at the ranch; and worked while still a child as a hired girl for other families, grubbing out sagebrush with a mattock or doing housework. When her father decided to seek work in the Tres Piedras coal mines in 1885 when she was twelve, Josie begged to go along to cook and keep house for him and escape the drudgery at the ranch. In Tres Piedras she began prospecting, wandering the hills alone and bringing rocks home for her father and his friends to identify. Although she soon contracted tick fever and went back to the ranch to recover, she was hooked. According to Alma Schulmerich, who wrote a biography of Josie as she told it herself, "mining seldom left her thoughts for any length of time."[17]

Josie staked her first claim at age thirteen while staying at her pregnant sister's ranch on Rat Creek to help with the housework. When she accompanied her brother-in-law into the hills to help him find conveniently located stands of timber for the mines, she came across a piece of rock flecked with gold. The Reeds readily succeeded in selling her claim for five thousand dollars, all of which was immediately spent to pay their debts and purchase long-postponed necessities. At fourteen Josie permanently left the ranch to attend cooking school in Denver and went on to work as a mining camp cook—far from the only woman prospector to follow this route—first in Leadville and later in Creede. By the time she turned twenty she had grown into a fine-looking young woman, blonde, tall, strong, generously proportioned, and as they put it in northern Nevada, "raw cut." At a dance in Creede when she had bedecked herself in her most fashionable finery, a black beaded dress and a hat swirling with plumes, Josie met a tall, well-educated young mining engineer from California with black hair and hazel eyes, and she began to feel a "tickling around the heart you can't scratch." In 1903 Josie and Lane Pearl were married.[18]

Mary Grantz, by contrast, came to the mining world much later in life. She was born Mary Louise Grenz on 4 December 1879 to a family of German extraction considerably more prosperous than the struggling Reeds. They lived on a farm near Tigerton, Wisconsin, and Mary Grantz resembled Josie Pearl in one important respect—her determination to leave the farm. Her first job away from the farm, so far as her family recalls, was in a doctor's office when she was very young. It ended abruptly when the doctor's wife cast the girl out for having an affair with her husband and created a scandal that is still remembered nearly a century later. That may have had something to do with Mary's departure for Florida with her younger sister, Emma. At twenty Mary was as short as Josie was tall, only five feet one or two, like all the Grenzes. Her photograph shows a pretty girl with soft features and a slightly long nose. There is no mistaking the eager sparkle in her blue-green eyes. Clearly, she could hardly wait for the adventures that lay ahead.[19]

After their marriage Josie and Lane Pearl followed the shifting currents of western mining. He found jobs in various Colorado mines. Quickly bored with housekeeping, she worked in hospitals and boardinghouses and continued to prospect, imagining how much better their lives would be if she made a discovery that they could develop together. Lane, who never came along, called her tireless searching through the hills and canyons "mining fever." Later they joined the rush to Goldfield, where Josie may have operated the Pearl Restaurant and worked as a cashier in the elegant Palm Grill, an establishment offering such fare as quail on toast served on fine china laid on white linen for up to two hundred patrons nightly. "Elegant," as newspaper columnist Ernie Pyle later noted, was one of Josie's favorite words, but the solitude of the world beyond the pale had started drawing the young woman more strongly than the posh side of life in the last great boomtown. She continued to prospect, riding her horse out into the desert and staying overnight until time to report back to work the following morning.

Mary Grantz
(courtesy of June Anderson).

She also combed the region farther to the south around Rhyolite. And she continued to have no luck.[20]

As Goldfield slid into deepening decline, the Pearls moved on to the Ward Mine near Ely around 1910. Major copper discoveries in the region had brought quiet, steady, and long-lasting production without the boisterous spirits of wild towns such as Creede and Goldfield. Lane worked as a mine foreman, and Josie returned to running a boarding-house and later a hotel. She also continued to prospect in every spare moment, concentrating on gold in the belief that silver prices had fallen so low that it was no longer worth the effort. She located three claims, but another discovery as promising as the one made on Rat Creek when she was thirteen continued to elude her.[21]

When the influenza pandemic swept the world in 1918, Lane fell ill. Josie had twice saved his life. The first time a fire had broken out in the shaft house of the Colorado mine where he was working and seriously injured the hoist operator. Although Josie had never run a hoist before and the flames licked around her, she sounded the alarm and, following the operator's instructions, succeeded in bringing the cage up with Lane and his men inside before the fire could destroy the hoist and trap them below. The second time, again in Colorado, a fire started in the powder house while Lane and his men were in the mine tunnel. Expecting an explosion that would seal the tunnel's mouth at any moment, no one would go inside—except Josie. With a light in each hand she raced along the tunnel, her calls lost in the clatter of machinery. Fortunately, she was close enough to a shallow niche to squeeze against the wall when the horse-drawn ore car came rumbling through. She reached Lane in time, and everyone safely escaped the mine. Against the influenza, however, her courage, her love, and her Amazonian strength were of no avail. She could only nurse Lane and watch him die.[22]

His death, after some fifteen years of marriage, left her widowed, childless, and alone at the age of forty-five. At first she drifted, roaming southern California, returning briefly to Colorado, attempting new beginnings that she soon abandoned in Tonopah and Searchlight. Later she opened the Pearl Inn in Bodie, a California mining camp known forty years earlier for its bad men and high murder rates. Between serving lunch and beginning supper preparations she panned the old tailings for gold dust. An assayer friend melted her dust into gold buttons, which she called her "safety deposit box."

By 1929 Bodie began to decline, and Josie headed for northern Nevada. She ran the boardinghouse at the Betty O'Neal Mine, recently reopened by mining magnate Noble Getchell following nearly forty years of dormancy. After the Betty O'Neal she cooked for the cowboys in northern Humboldt County at the "Upper Clover" and "Lower Clover" portions of the Taylor ranch, an enormous livestock empire that at its apogee counted more than ten thousand head of cattle, sixty thousand sheep, and large herds of horses. She took up prospecting once more, recording her first claims in 1934. She also acquired another husband, a miner from the Betty O'Neal whose existence seems to have been concealed from her biographer but not from the shrewd Ernie Pyle. (There is also an indication that before Lane Pearl, Josie had misplaced another husband she did not care to discuss.) One of the other ranch cooks remembers Josie's last husband as a dark, good-looking man twenty or thirty years younger than Josie. He used to spend the weekends with her at the Taylor ranch and eventually disappeared without explanation, possibly on realizing that her buoyant tales of the millions she was about to make in mining were the product of what one old friend called her "creative imagination." Josie strewed her fantasy fortunes liberally around her in those lean depression years. She promised to take Ernie Pyle where he could pick up gold nuggets from the ground that would make him rich and vowed to leave the other ranch cook a small fortune, but like a typical prospector, she deluded no one else so much as herself. As an old miner had warned the Wilhelms when Sherman protested that he would never exaggerate his finds, "That's what you think now. . . . You won't aim to, none of us do. It's one of them things a feller can't help."[23]

Josie gave Schulmerich a detailed description of the prospecting trips she made during the thirties and forties. At this point the "mining fever" that had been a pastime throughout her life became her primary occupation. "Gold is devilish stuff," she told Schulmerich. "It gets into your blood and then you can't leave it alone." She bought a burro, christening him Trampo; put on overalls, heavy shoes, and a sunbonnet;

and set off as the early prospectors had done. Her pack included sow-belly, dried beans, prunes, coffee, and the makings of sourdough bread, but she also counted on shooting wild game during the period of a week to ten days that she would spend alone in the field. Trampo predictably gave her problems of the same kind the Scotts, as well as Mrs. Reid and Mrs. Burlingame, had experienced with their animals: when tired, he lay down wherever he was, "pack and all." Like many other prospectors, she took deep pleasure in the peace and solitude of the desert and in the creatures she encountered there, from the antelope to the spotted skunk. She thought camping at a small green oasis beside a hidden spring far preferable to the noise, odors, and bustle of a boomtown such as Creede. As Carl Wikstrom has said, the true prospector, who is in large measure a philosopher, needs this space to think about who we are and why we're here.[24]

By day she scoured the ledges, canyons, streambeds, and mountain crests hunting the blackness of iron and manganese, the green of copper, and above all, the flecks of gold that sometimes formed a curl after the final slosh of her pan. The Juanita gold claim that she at length decided to develop, however, was not one she had staked in the course of her wanderings but a gift from two other prospectors in gratitude for the meals she had cooked for them—so said Josie. Judging from the recollections of those who sampled her cooking at the Taylor ranch and found it unappetizing and unsanitary enough to offend even the none-too-finicky standards of cowboys, these must have been two very hungry prospectors. Josie did much of the work at the Juanita herself, and hard work it was for a woman in her sixties, mucking ore at the base of the shaft, clambering out to haul it up on the windlass, then heading down the ladder again for another load.

Her boast that mining had made her worth one hundred thousand dollars one day and broke the next was almost certainly just another of her tall tales. Nonetheless, Josie managed to scratch a lean living from her mines during the last thirty years of her life. Her survival through hard times augmented her reputation. Said Robert Stitser, who knew her well, "People in that era had come through a depression where a vast percentage of the population, at least in that neck of the woods, had hit bottom or pretty close to it. They really had a lot of admiration for a person like Josie Pearl who could make a living like Jeremiah Johnson off the ground."[25]

The trajectory Mary Grantz followed to northern Nevada has been less well documented than that of Josie Pearl. In Florida, Mary and her sister Emma became hairdressers, styling hairpieces to be used by the wealthy in the bouffant, upswept styles of the period. Judging from a picture in which Mary has done her reddish-brown hair in a puffy, off-centered coil that must have been the height of fashion, they were their own best advertisements. In view of Mary's fondness for men in later life, she probably had no dearth of romances when she was young and very pretty. But evidently, no relationship was serious enough to result in marriage and sever her close companionship with Emma. In fact, it was Emma who became the first to break away. When the two sisters decided to go adventuring in Montana, Emma taught school in Missoula and Butte and in 1915 married a shoemaker from Wisconsin who had been logging with her brother in Oregon. The couple returned to Wisconsin. At first Mary, an extremely possessive woman, was furious over this defection. Nonetheless, she stayed on in Montana and joined her brother Walter and his new wife on the homestead they had taken up near Butte. The rattlesnakes, wind, and dust soon discouraged Walter and his wife, however. They too returned to Wisconsin, never to venture forth again from the farm.[26]

Mary did not go back to Wisconsin, causing her mother to say again and again, "I don't know what she's crawling around all over the world for." Her reasons for suddenly heading for northern Nevada and taking up prospecting pose a question for which family recollections regrettably provide no answer. The only clues are the establishment of the northern Nevada Charleston Hill Mining Corporation in Montana in 1916 by Joseph P. "Perry" Clough and the Butte address he gave in a Nevada mining transaction the following year. Walter and his wife had found only dust and rattlesnakes in Montana, but Mary may have found Clough, a mining and real estate promoter based in Arizona. When Mary staked her first claims in northern Nevada in the autumn of 1919, Clough's name appears in the record books of the same period. At forty Mary still had the good looks to turn a man's head, even a married man with two grown children. This time the wife lost to the other woman, and it was not long before Clough and his wife were divorced and he married Mary Grantz.[27]

During the twenties and thirties the Cloughs intensively promoted their mining interests, as well as far-flung real estate in Florida, Arizona, Seattle, and Oakland. Mary was "very, very aggressive," a family member has said—no doubt a useful quality for pressing sales. An indistinct family story that survives from this period suggests that the Cloughs were run out of a desert town for living together without benefit of clergy. If this contains a kernel of truth, it is improbable that the absence of a marriage license had anything to do with the episode, because living together was widely practiced and tolerated in the Nevada mining towns. More likely, the cause lay in financial misdeeds, which could and did get people hustled out of town. Even the kindhearted Josie Pearl had lied to herself and everyone around her about the value of her claims. The difference was that Mary, in the dubious tradition of Frances Williams, sold stock and collected money for her promises. Nor did she make an exception for her own relatives, many of whom invested and lost money in the Clough mines. In 1922 Emma brought her husband, Ernest Miller, and her two little daughters from Wisconsin to work the Charleston Hill gold mine north of Winnemucca for the Cloughs. Although the Millers worked with a will and endured a good deal of hardship at this remote cluster of cabins in the mountains, the Charleston Hill never paid. The Cloughs managed all the same to live "high on the hog" on their promotional tours; the Millers received worthless promissory notes in lieu of wages and also lost all their savings, which they had invested in the Clough mines. Even so, the old closeness between Mary and Emma endured. The Millers next moved to Washington state to manage an apartment house for the Cloughs. There Emma died of cancer and the Millers entered a period of serious privation. June Miller and her younger sister were raised by a relative in Milwaukee and worked in a restaurant to put themselves through school. Their father wanted nothing further to do with Mary, an attitude heartily shared by other relatives in Wisconsin who had lost money in her mines. When Emma's body was brought home to Wisconsin for burial, curses rained on Mary during the funeral.[28]

Despite this estrangement from her family, Mary gained a relative who almost became the child she never had. When the wife of one of Mary's older brothers died and he remarried, he gave up two of the sons of his first marriage for adoption and sent the third, a teenager named Leon, to Winnemucca to live with Mary. She raised him, worked him almost as hard as she worked herself, and came to rely on him when lean times struck her down with the rest. As they used to quip in Winnemucca when the two of them went past in the car with Leon Grantz at the wheel, "She drove him and he drove her."[29]

By the late thirties Mary was no longer living high on the hog; indeed, getting by took all her considerable ingenuity. Clough is believed to have died during one of their promotional efforts in Florida. The northern Nevada mines now belonged entirely to her, but none was paying. All the same, she hung on to them. "Queen Mary" found work as a housekeeper in San Francisco, returning periodically to Winnemucca to keep up her assessment work, with which Leon greatly assisted her. Mining was "her whole life," her niece June later observed, and even when all the mines in her possession appeared worthless, she refused to abandon them.[30]

On the eve of World War II these two northern Nevada mining women presented an odd mixture of differences and similarities. They were nearly the same age, Mary being only six years younger than Josie, who was nearly seventy. Both came from farm backgrounds. Both were widowed and childless. Both had arrived in northern Nevada in middle age within a few years of each other and remained for the rest of their lives. And both became totally committed to mining. Yet their appearances and personalities could hardly have been more different. Josie was a tall Amazon who could lug a fifty-five-gallon gasoline drum from the pickup truck at her remote camp and carry a hundred-pound sack of sugar on each arm; Mary was a tiny whirlwind of energy who went all over the hills "just like a man." Josie was known for her bizarre clothes: flowered housedresses, jodhpurs, large gaudy hats or funny little ones "like a rag woman," a man's overcoat, several skirts and blouses worn at once, and a sweeping trail of scarves and sweaters. Ernie Pyle noticed the incongruities: "Her dress was calico, with an apron over it; on her head was a farmer's straw hat, on her feet a mismated pair of men's shoes, and on her left hand and wrist—six thousand dollars worth of diamonds! That was Josie—contradiction all over, and a sort of Tugboat Annie of the desert." Mary, by contrast, was always well dressed and never wore overalls, even when prospecting, but she too enjoyed flashing her jewelry. Her niece June recalled seeing her "dressed to the nines," wearing a mink stole and glittering with diamonds. These sparkling displays may have had something to do with her sobriquet, "Queen Mary."[31]

Their personalities contrasted even more sharply than their appearances. Josie was warm, colorful, generous, noisy, and gregarious, and everyone who met her had a story to tell about her. Those who knew her saw her as a "performer" and a "genuine character." When she came out of the desert for a visit to Winnemucca or Lovelock, she would stay with friends, who were always happy to have her company for as long as she cared to remain, and would go forth with a jovial crowd for a night on the town. Robert Stitser, son of one of Josie's closest friends, remembers, "She always exemplified a happy mood, and her glass was always half-full. It was never half-empty. She was going to hit a bonanza over the next hill. It was great to be around her because she never seemed to be unhappy or whining or complaining." Mary enjoyed considerable respect among the local citizenry, but her personality was another matter entirely. Although she lived in Winnemucca during the winters instead of 115 miles away on the edge of the Black Rock Desert like Josie, the usual response to a question about her is, "I knew who she was but I didn't know her" instead of a good story. She read a great deal and kept to herself. "She didn't mix with people at all," observed one of her nieces. This slightly aloof attitude may have been another element in the "Queen Mary" label. Royalty, after all, does not mix.[32]

The presence of two prominent women prospectors in a sparsely populated place at the same time raises an inevitable question concerning their relationship. Duane Devine, who worked with Mary over a long period, supplied the answer: "There for a while one was trying to outdo the other on the mining. One was trying to be the big chief, and the other one was trying to keep up with her. . . . We used to laugh about it." Clearly, gender was the engine that drove this competition. Neither Josie nor Mary measured herself against the male prospectors and mining entrepreneurs in the area. It was the other woman who

Josie Pearl (Nevada Historical Society).

threatened the position of the queen bee of northern Nevada mining to which each aspired.[33]

Then came the stroke of luck that boosted Mary far ahead. South of Golconda, above the deep white dust and whirlwinds of the lower Pumpernickle Valley, rises the Sonoma Range, low grassy mountains, scantily sprinkled with trees and brush, where springtime brings the look of worn, green plush. Occasional dark outcroppings, signaling manganese to the prospector, punctuate the slopes. Here Clough had staked a manganese claim, the Black Diablo, and Mary had maintained it, despite the fact that imports from the Soviet Union made manganese mining unprofitable. Then American manganese suddenly escalated in value. The outbreak of World War II cut off the Russian supplies, and the role of manganese in steelmaking made it vital to the war effort. Depots were established in Nevada in 1943 to collect the output of manganese mines, the U.S. government began stockpiling manganese in Utah, and suddenly the Black Diablo became a valuable property. The open pit mine, which never employed more than nine men, was smaller than the large-scale operations, but Duane Devine, who worked the mine for Mary for most of the period from the onset of the war until the ore bodies had been exhausted in 1953, estimates that the Black Diablo produced at least ninety thousand tons of manganese, for which Mary may have made as much as $150,000. And that, he observes, was in the days when a dollar "went a little wheres." Through some strange alchemy of bookkeeping the stockholders reportedly received no returns. During this period Mary also profitably mined tungsten, another material critical to the war effort.[34] When success at last was hers, she had been in the mining game more than twenty years.

At this point, in her middle sixties, Mary might have retired with her diamonds and one of the younger men of whom she was becoming enamored. Instead, she prospected intensively. Her many letters to her sister-in-law and former companion on the Montana homestead, Claire Grenz, in which she described her mining activities in detail, were discarded by the family after Claire's death on the assumption that they held no interest for anyone. It is fortunate that Duane Devine remembered some of these prospecting trips. Mary and he would head out in a pickup truck and spend the day hunting manganese in the Sonomas or the next range across the valley to the east. Mary would work her way up a gulch or a hillside, looking for float, trying to trace any float she found to a ledge, doubling back when the disappearance of specimens suggested that the ledge might be somewhere behind her, and searching for a "contact," the spot where different metals come together and ore is often found: "She was pretty wise on that line. She done pretty good on that for a lady. And she wasn't scared—she was a working little scamp. . . . No grass growed under her." Mary staked five more claims, one of them tungsten, in 1945. None proved valuable, however, and the new manganese claims she tried to develop, one across the gulch from the Black Diablo and another beyond the valley, turned out to be too low-grade to bring a profit. In the years to come, attempts to repeat her success with the Black Diablo would dissipate a large part of her gains.[35]

Meanwhile, the extensive prospecting Josie Pearl did during the forties suggests both the persistence of her dream of striking bonanza and a competitive awareness of Mary's current ascendancy. From 1945 through 1951 Josie staked a large number of claims but sold no mines to investors and extracted little ore. Despite the scant value of her mining interests, she claimed to be continually entangled in lawsuits and crowed over having once chewed up and spit out a fraudulent legal document when it was presented to her. Being a shrewd judge of character saved her from many of the pitfalls that abounded in the mining world. Catherine Rueckl, a friend from Winnemucca, recalled, "She saw through everyone that crossed her path. They didn't fool her for a minute, and some of the so-called outstanding engineers and geologists who came into her part of the world were very impressed with themselves, but they didn't impress Josie." Although gold remained her primary thrust, she located a site from which she sold a few opals to local jewelers and to tourists on the streets in Winnemucca. At most she had two miners working with her and shipped a little ore. More often she had only her own hands and the assistance of various teenaged boys sent out to her cabin by their families in the summers for a few weeks of hunting, fishing, and desert living with Josie in exchange for lending a hand with her mining. Stitser, one of these young visitors, remembers going to a high plateau with Josie to dig out tourmalines with pick and shovel and sledding the ore down the steep hillside. He admired her ability to do such heavy work at an advanced age.[36]

The Cove Creek cabin in the hills near the Black Rock Desert where they stayed was almost as well known a personality as Josie herself; Pyle called it "the wildest hodgepodge of riches and rubbish I'd ever seen." Even the road leading to it was an experience: "There really wasn't any road to Josie Pearl's cabin—merely a trail across space. Your creeping car was the center of an appalling cloud of dust, and the sage scratched long streaks on the fenders," he wrote. When the visitor alighted, thickly coated with white dust, the gobbling tom turkey by Josie's door attacked, unless Josie emerged from her tarpaper shack to bash him in the head with a shovel. Her yard was typical for a prospector, being littered not only with samples of geologic interest but also with all manner of oddities found in the desert. Author Nell Murbarger observed, "Tables were crammed with ore samples, rocks, petrified wood, geodes, rusty relics, purple glass, miners' picks and candlesticks, prospectors' pans, parts for cars, and miscellaneous trivia." Ignoring the hodgepodge, Stitser remembered the place as a "garden of Eden" nestled among the poplar trees, with a large, fenced vegetable garden irrigated by springs and a shack farther up the canyon near a wonderful orchard of cherry trees. Deer, sagehen, and jackrabbits abounded, and Josie and her guests could cut a willow pole beside the creek and catch plenty of trout for dinner whenever they chose.[37]

Women, unlike Stitser, tended to notice Josie's housekeeping. According to Murbarger, "the walls of her cabin were pinned with assay reports, newspaper clippings, letters, picture postcards, tax receipts and cash register slips. Boxes, clothing, pots and pans were strewn about the room which had the general atmosphere of utter chaos." Rueckl remembered that one room of the two-room shack was so full of furniture, including an organ, that no one could sit down and the other room was stuffed to the ceiling with packages of newspapers that Josie burned in the roaring black iron stove, since the desert provided little fuel: "Why the thing never blew up I don't understand." Rueckl stepped outside with "great relief," and it is not difficult to see why Josie and her visitors generally slept out of doors in good weather.[38]

It may be that many women prospectors gave housekeeping an equally low priority. There are indications that rather low housekeeping standards prevailed in nineteenth-century America. Bad evidently turned to worse in the mining camps, where Mary McNair Mathews found Virginia City women incompetent housekeepers more concerned with entertainment and self-adornment. This general uninterest in housework may have reached its logical culmination in the shacks of the women prospectors. A few kept neat, clean, and attractive homes. Ellen Nay managed to do so, both in her ranch home and during her mining days at Ellendale. All the same, several factors nudged the women prospectors in the same direction as Josie Pearl. In the first place the mobility of many prospectors' lives precluded the development of a sense of home as a place that mattered. If a prospector such as Lillian Malcolm or Louise Rupp knew she would soon be off to the next mining excitement, it made little sense to bother over the temporary quarters where she hung her hat. Those living alone in remote locales where visitors arrived rarely and unpredictably had little incentive to keep up appearances. Those who could afford it, such as Frances Williams, dispensed with housekeeping entirely by means of the widespread mining-town practice of living at a hotel and dining in restaurants. Of course, those constantly traveling in the field, such as the Wilhelms, eliminated housekeeping in a single stroke by not owning a house. Moreover, the hard physical work of prospecting and mining left these women with little energy at the end of the day for housework. Most important, the woman prospector saw mining as her profession, the all-absorbing pursuit to which she had chosen to devote herself in preference to domestic concerns. Josie Pearl was never too tired to mine, but she often declared herself too weary to dust.[39]

Because Josie lived recently enough that people who knew her can still be questioned, it is possible to gain some sense of her attitudes toward other women and theirs toward her. In the main she seems to have harbored more puritanical standards than many of the gold rush crowd, condemning prostitutes and excessive smoking and drinking. She expressed even stronger contempt for "man chasers" and "clinging vines," evidently despising their dependency. In Rueckl's words, "she was very superior. She had no use for them." Strong and self-sufficient herself, she chose other women of the same kind for her closest friends, and they entertained a similar regard for her. They included Avery Stitser, who had taken over after her husband's death as editor of the *Humboldt Star* and raised her family alone, and Dell Collins, who mined with her husband, took care of him after he was invalided in a cabin even more remote than Josie's for three years, and lived with Josie for seven years after he died. In addition to her contempt for dependency Josie rejected the shallowness she encountered in polite feminine society. Margaret Butts, an old friend, saw this plainly: "Being very sincere herself, she didn't have much patience with superficiality." Other women sometimes resented her brusque candor, and some dismissed her as a "crazy old woman."[40]

Once we catch an echo of the old prejudice that had long dogged the women prospectors. On a long and difficult journey through the snow, during which two men with a car had given Josie a ride, they stopped at a ranch, where the rancher's wife criticized Josie for "running around with a bunch of men." Josie angrily told her, "Woman, when you live miles from town, you have to get to town with man, or woman, or the devil himself! Judge not that ye be not judged!" After this blast she remained to nurse the family through the influenza.[41]

In general, however, women as well as men admired Josie for the strength and independence that enabled her to live by the work of her own hands on the fringe of the remote Black Rock through summer heat and winter blizzards. They also responded warmly to her kind heart. Like Nellie Cashman before her, she made herself a one-woman charitable institution, nursing, bringing provisions, and finally burying the old-timers who lived in the distant desert canyons as she did, and she fantasized about endowing a foundation to educate disabled children when she at last struck her long-sought bonanza.[42]

Those who knew Josie agree that although she enjoyed occasional company, she was able to live alone for most of thirty years without feeling lonely. The boys who stayed with her during the summers brought companionship as well as willing hands. She always had time to visit with any guest who stopped by, though authors seeking an interview tended to receive an initially cool reception due to Josie's apprehensions that fame might turn her into a "pet coon." The scattered old-timers who received her charities no doubt provided human contact that she valued. She saw friends on her occasional visits to town. During the evenings at Cove Canyon Josie read a great deal and listened to her battery radio. But her principal companion was the dream that never faded. Rueckl recalled, "She got up every morning believing firmly that she was going to hit the Mother Lode."[43]

In fact, Mary Grantz's life in Winnemucca during the winters may have entailed a good deal less sociability than Josie's in the desert. Mary grew still more isolated when she alienated the one person with whom she enjoyed a close relationship after her husband's death, her nephew Leon; the possessive Mary saw his marriage as an act of disloyalty, and a bitter feud commenced that was to last throughout both their lives. Fortunately for Mary, a new relationship with her dead sister Emma's daughter June relieved her isolation. Each year June came to Nevada for a vacation at the Marysville Mine in the cooler mountains where Mary spent her summers. On one of these visits June snuggled into bed, slid her hand under the pillow, and encountered a cold object—a loaded gun. Another time at the Black Diablo her feet brushed the same cold hardness at the foot of the bed, causing her to leap out in alarm.[44]

The cold objects in June's bed raise an issue inextricably linked to the lives of the women prospectors: how much did they rely on firearms and to what extent did they perceive themselves to be in danger? The only one specifically to deny any need to defend herself by force was Nellie Cashman, who depended on the universal respect accorded her. In most instances no evidence survives on whether a woman prospector kept or needed guns. Nonetheless, some cases suggest that many women prospectors relied on guns, most of them women on their own, indicating that male companions provided a sense of security that was otherwise lacking. Mollie Sawyer wore guns; Colorado prospector Ellen Jack, discoverer of the valuable Black Queen Mine, could ride a galloping horse while firing a gun in each hand and effectively defended herself in an Indian battle; Idah Strobridge, aside from her poetic musings on the desert, was an excellent shot who unfailingly felled her quarry, as was Jennie Enright; Mountain Charley, justifiably fearful of the dangers she faced, packed guns and used them successfully to defend herself against rape; those who knew Fannie Quigley uniformly praised her abilities as a superb hunter. In Colorado's San Juan country Walt Wilhelm's father told of seeing women defending their claims with shotguns. Mrs. P. J. Thomas and Nettie Hornbeck, the mother-and-daughter team of Colorado copper miners, told how they protected their mine: "The two of us have stood with shotgun loaded and guarded our claim. Each summer someone tries to get the best of us on that mine, but no one has succeeded, and there are no possibilities that they will."[45]

Guns were as ubiquitous in Josie's home as in Mary's. Ernie Pyle observed a thirty-thirty rifle beside her bed, as well as a pump gun and a double-barreled shotgun in the next room; others took note of an antiquated single-shot twenty-two. Moreover, it seems that Josie, for all her apparent fortitude, harbored many fears. Her biography is riddled with tales of close encounters with dangerous men that reveal these apprehensions (unless they represent an attempt to add excitement to the story). The more taciturn Mary, who was a crack shot like all her family and sometimes blew the head from a rattlesnake at a considerable distance, voiced no fears and told no tales of armed encounters. She simply made it clear that anyone going into the desert needed to take a gun.[46]

Mary's last years were a strange mixture of shrewdness and folly. The houses and apartments built in Winnemucca with some of her mining proceeds proved a wise investment. Yet for one who had lived and breathed mining for more than thirty years, she showed an odd gullibility about expensive mining schemes. As Devine put it, she was "easy led." Only June's warnings saved her from investing in a fraudulent oil scheme. After the Black Diablo closed, a Californian romanced Mary, gained her confidence, and convinced her that large-scale shoveling equipment could make the mine profitable again. The ore proved too low-grade to pay the freighting bills, and Mary got rid of the Californian, who sued her and won. Lawsuits had long been the hallmark of the successful mine owner—indeed, one wonders if Josie's plaints concerning lawsuits over her mines did not spring from a wish to proclaim that she had been sued just as much as Mary. Her lawsuits cost Mary dearly nonetheless. The California gold rush days, when the loser in one of these disputes would shrug his shoulders, remark "Let 'er rip," and walk off with full confidence that he would soon find an equally good claim, had long since passed.[47]

Another major folly came on the heels of the debacle at the Black Diablo. Despite more than twenty years of coming up empty-handed at the Charleston Hill, Mary retained an unreasoning faith in the mine, and another schemer convinced her that major development would open a bonanza. They purchased a great deal of expensive equipment and sank a deep shaft, but when they ran the drift back to the area where they expected to find pay ore, the Charleston Hill proved barren once again, and ten years of litigation ensued. "The Black Diablo was where she made it, and the Charleston Hill was where she lost it," observed Devine.[48]

The greater folly, however, may have been her young men, if folly it was (perhaps Ferminia Sarras would have seen it as one of the perquisites of success). Her impending marriage to one of them, a mining engineer, was aborted when the couple dined on contaminated chicken at a Winnemucca restaurant. He died; Mary, who either had the stronger constitution or had eaten less chicken, survived. She had two other romances with tall, well-built men considerably younger and poorer than she before marrying Max Magnussen, a big, fine-looking drifter twenty-five years her junior in the late 1950s. When questioned concerning Magnussen's occupation, Winnemuccans were apt to say, "All he ever done was just spend her money."[49]

Be that as it may, they seem to have been a happy and affectionate couple—and more than a little incongruous in appearance. Mary, in her last years, became too arthritic to search the hills any longer. She grew roly-poly, wore heavy makeup, dyed her hair defiantly red, and carried the jewels she did not wear (and she wore a great many at once) about with her in cigar boxes, along with four- and five-inch wads of cash that much impressed her relatives when Mary and Max made a triumphal visit to Wisconsin in the course of their travels. Max, more than the diamonds, was the primary trophy, "a real western man," in the eyes of the Wisconsin relatives, with his Stetson, his turquoise-and-silver tie, the arrow design on his suit, and his cowboy boots, standing nearly a foot taller than Mary and looking half her age. Mary lived to be ninety. Her death in the summer of 1970 was followed by a process of digging up cash buried in cans from a yard in Winnemucca and from the garage floor at the Charleston Hill, for Mary had not trusted banks. Again, we are reminded of Ferminia Sarras. Max remarried in a matter of months. With the passing of Mary's generation the curses that had formerly pelted at Mary from her Wisconsin relatives gave way to a certain pride in her as a remarkable woman. Deanna Grenz, wife of one of Mary's nephews, saw her as "the one person in the Grenz family that did something different": "Everybody else from around here did the normal things. They went out on the farm, had children, and that's it."[50] From the perspective of the Wisconsin farms, where many of the Grenzes still live, Mary had been a star.

Josie Pearl also survived to an advanced age, growing more eccentric in her last years. The blurry line between what had really happened and what Josie preferred to think had happened became more indistinct. She had always been a menace behind the wheel of her pickup truck, and her habit of driving in the middle of the road at top speed was increasingly dangerous. Whenever neighboring ranchers spotted Josie's pickup boiling down the road in a huge cloud of dust, they would say, "Uh oh, here comes Josie—head for the brush!" Unable to take care of herself any longer, she was hospitalized in Reno, where she died of heart disease in 1962.[51]

Although Josie never had a mine like the Black Diablo, in other ways she emerged ahead in the competition with Mary that lasted more than thirty years. Her biography and the articles written about her made her one of the best-known women prospectors, whereas few outside Humboldt County ever heard of Mary Grantz. More important, despite her hand-to-mouth existence, she may have been the better miner. Devine, the mining man who knew them both, pronounced his verdict: "She knew more about the mines than Mary did." During her interview in Josie's last years Murbarger was especially struck by the old woman's gaze: "The eyes that bored into mine were neither friendly nor unfriendly. They were shrewd and appraising, steady and inscrutable."[52] Such eyes have long formed an integral part of the image of the quintessential westerner. We have seen them shaded by the brim of a Stetson in numberless movies, imagined them while turning the pages of a book. But never before in the face of a woman.

# EIGHT

# "Hit Rock Bottom
# Hard Enough to Bounce":
# The Depression Years

When the Great Depression of the 1930s struck, the struggle to wrest a
lean living from the canyons and streambeds replaced the euphoric
hopes of bonanza so characteristic of turn-of-the-century prospecting.
The stock market crashed, banks failed, prices for wholesale goods and
farm products plummeted, and unemployment spread a dark pall of
desperation throughout the land. Although the number of women in
the work force actually rose by 25 percent during the depression, women
shared the pervasive hardships of the period. Two million women, a
fifth of the female labor force, could not find jobs, and it was estimated
that one in every twenty hoboes roaming the country was a woman.[1]

As the great American industrial machine sputtered and slowed,
some of the dispossessed fell back on a preindustrial way of life, swel-
ling the diminished ranks of the prospectors. In 1932 an enterprising
Coloradan announced the opening of the Opportunity School for
women prospectors, and twenty signed up, most of them unemployed
women hoping to earn a living by placering. After a morning of instruction in the theory of gold panning they assembled on the banks
of the Platte River to put theory into practice, and the *Denver Mining
Record*'s article on the stir they created among passersby might well
have been written in the 1870s, as though the last sixty years of women's
achievements in mining had never happened. The old emphasis on appearances resurfaced: "There are women in trousers, women in mother
hubbards, women in overalls, women wearing high heeled pumps and
rubber boots, young women, old women, fat ones and skinny ones."
The *Record* reported that sourdoughs "looked on in amazement" and
laughed "at the idea of teaching women to use a pan." Presumably,

these were sourdoughs of limited experience who had failed to partic-ipate in the many mining excitements at which they would have en-countered women prospectors.[2]

Elsewhere in the mining West other women turned to placering. At Mount Tenabo, in northern Nevada, where Maggie Johnson had mined so long, several women took up leases, operated small washers, and made "better than wages." Women in mining still remained uncommon enough to be newsworthy, and reports of husband-and-wife teams placering or working small mines themselves appeared in the press from time to time. Some were the new domestic partners of old-time prospectors. When novelist Rex Beach met Joe Ibach in Alaska in 1905, he admiringly described the prospector as "the nearest to a free soul of anybody I ever knew" and "venturesome, self-reliant, restless and soli-tary in his habits as a rogue elephant." At Beach's next encounter with Ibach thirty years later, the rogue elephant was not so solitary and spoke of surreptitiously mining his claims in Glacier Bay with the aid of his wife, "Muz," despite the prohibition on mining within the boundaries of the new national park.[3]

Dorothy "Dot" and Jesse Coffey were one of the few depression-era placering couples whose experience has been told in detail. In his mem-oir, *Bacon and Beans from a Gold Pan*, Jesse relates that when he lost his job in the canning industry in 1935 and despaired of finding a new one, after fruitlessly plodding from one employment agency to another and standing in long lines of jobless men at mill and factory doors only to be turned away, he and his new bride, Dot, decided to weather the hard times by working the creeks in California's Mother Lode country. The idea was Jesse's, but Dot enthusiastically endorsed it.

They erected a tent cabin on the Agua Fria and began hunting the "sweet spots" where gold flecks missed by the forty-niners and their successors, the Chinese, over eighty years of mining could still be panned. They scraped out crevices where gold accumulates in the bedrock, found a strip of gold-bearing gravel that their predecessors had missed under an agglomeration of boulders, and hunted thin lay-ers of gravel washed up by recent storms. They set up their sluice box and worked it together for about eight hours a day, shoveling gravel and periodically cleaning the accumulated gold specks and the occasional match-head-sized nugget from the riffle box. In the foundations of an old bordello that had burned they even panned the earth to extract the gold dust that had sifted down in palmier days (Dot laughingly forbade her husband to tell anyone she had made money working in a house of ill repute).[4]

To survive at the fine art of scavenging for the remaining gold specks demanded persistence and a degree of experience that not all "snipers" on the Agua Fria possessed, and many gave up in a matter of weeks. Fortunately, Jesse, the grandson of a California gold rusher, had panned gold in these hills as a boy, and Dot learned quickly. Indeed, her enthusiasm for the enterprise almost exceeded his, and she greeted their discoveries with squeals and yells. Not only did she shovel by her husband's side until her hands blistered, but soon she began exploring by herself with her own small sluice box, finding her share of sweet spots as well as the rare large nugget. Few among some forty snipers working the Agua Fria at that time had women with them, and Dot appears to have been the only woman engaged in placering.[5]

Days of long, hard work kept the Coffeys in bacon and beans. With gold then selling at thirty-five dollars an ounce, they calculated that they could feed and clothe themselves if they could make a dollar a day, because they had no rent or utilities to pay. In fact, they often exceeded that minimal goal and were eventually able to afford a pump powered by a small gasoline engine to ease their work at the sluice box. They also lived off the land as much as possible. They gathered wild mushrooms and young fiddlehead ferns. Dot tended a vegetable garden; Jesse hunted rabbits, squirrels, quail, and sometimes deer and fished for trout, although Dot confessed at one point that trout dinners had grown a little monotonous. They divided their labors along traditional lines. Dot arrived to begin her work in the river a little later than Jesse and left somewhat early in order to do household chores and cook meals. They spent one afternoon a week doing the work they enjoyed least, laundry for Dot and woodcutting for Jesse.[6]

Although the Mother Lode country presented none of the hazards of Alaska or Death Valley, it was not without peril. When the Coffeys left the rivers to mine at a mountain site, the omnipresent rattlesnakes drove them away in short order. Once an avalanche of loose rock and gravel buried Dot to the waist as she panned beside the Yuba River, where the Coffeys had moved when the pickings along the Agua Fria became too scanty. Another time on the Yuba, Dot had crawled into a crevice she discovered under a twelve-ton boulder to scoop out gold-bearing gravels and bits of broken bedrock for Jesse to pan. Their dog began to bark and tug frantically at her pants leg. Seconds after she squeezed out from the spot, the boulder dropped into the crevice with a mighty thud. Human dangers lurked as well. A pair of criminals robbed the Coffey sluice box of its painstakingly accumulated gold, as well as the sluices of many other snipers on the river, ransacked the cabin of their nearest neighbor while the old miner lay dead in his bed, and killed his dog with an ax.[7]

When World War II began Jesse took a job as a government inspector, but even the new car, the new clothes, and the visits with old friends in the city could not compensate for a strange loneliness they had never experienced in the mountains. Dot began to speak wistfully of going back where she could "smell the pine trees and see the wind blowing the grass again," and the attempt to adjust to city life lasted not much longer than it had for the Wilhelms or the Nays. Soon Jesse managed to secure an inspector's job in the Sierra foothills, where they could continue mining in their spare time, and there they remained. Dot later called the depression years when they survived by sniping on the rivers "the best and happiest days of our lives."[8]

For another prospecting wife, Lorena Trickey, the stringencies of the depression combined with scandal to propel her into the mining world. Lorena was born on 14 February 1893 and later could not remember a time when she had not ridden horseback. In a study of women rodeo riders Mary Lou LeCompte concludes that the economic hardships that ensued when Lorena and her brothers took over the family ranch drove her to compete in rodeos—yet another instance of the woman prospector's readiness to breach traditional gender barriers in several ways. Her tiny stature, only five foot two and 102 pounds, posed no obstacle she could not overcome. Lorena captured her first prize in 1919 when she was twenty-six. She went on to win the coveted McAlpin Trophy at Cheyenne Frontier Days in 1920, 1921, and 1924, as well as the bronc riding championship at Chicago in 1925 and several titles at the

Pendleton Roundup in Oregon and other competitions. Although she regarded bronc riding as her "main event," she became a noted performance artist at Roman racing, jumping, and other stunts. As a stunt rider in the movies, she once doubled for Mary Pickford. LeCompte emphasizes that like all professional athletes the rodeo cowgirls were "intensely competitive, willing to make extreme sacrifices, overcome serious injuries, and train long and hard to win and retain championships." This keen drive to compete and to cast off gender restrictions came into the open in 1924 at Pendleton when Lorena and several other professional cowgirls sought permission to contend in the same contests as the cowboys for the all-around cowboy prize. Request denied. Nevertheless, Lorena defeated men as well as women in other, less circumscribed competitions in Roman racing as well as bronc riding throughout America.[9]

Lorena's career as a top rodeo star came to a premature and sensational end in 1927 when she stabbed J. P. "Slim" Harris, her common-law husband, to death in the course of an argument. During the murder trial in Lakeview, Oregon, the prosecution saw premeditation in Lorena's purchase several days before the killing of a stockman's knife, since the dagger or stiletto she would have preferred was unavailable. They also argued that she had stabbed Slim in a jealous fury when he threatened to leave her. The defense contended that Lorena had bought the knife to defend herself against Slim's brutal batterings and used it only when her drunken lover attacked her with a steel tire wrench. The *Lake County (Oregon) Examiner* opined that the most effective defense witness was the rodeo man who told of preventing Slim from choking Lorena to death at an event in Victoria. Though she had given officers conflicting stories just after the killing, Lorena had finally settled on just one, and her account on the witness stand brought tears to the eyes of many of the friends who warmly supported her throughout the trial. When the jury returned a verdict of not guilty by reason of self-defense after just twenty minutes of deliberation, happy pandemonium erupted in the courtroom.[10]

In the course of her incarceration and trial Lorena had made two additional conquests. As she sat on the bench with bowed head, tiny, girlish, and deceptively fragile in appearance, C. H. "Oklahoma Slim"

Brad, an aspiring Prohibition agent, fell madly in love with her. Perhaps finding him one Slim too many, Lorena did not reciprocate his affection. When her friends celebrated her acquittal with a party at which beverages illegal during the Prohibition era flowed freely, Oklahoma Slim was not invited. Stung by his rejection he decided to raid the party, burst inside, and fired several shots in a futile attempt to arrest Lorena and take her away with him. Another admirer courted Lorena in more traditional fashion. He wrote her an anonymous poem, "The Story of 'Lorena': A Dramatic Poem of a Cowgirl's Love." Predating the era when sports champions involved in violent crime marketed their stories to the media for enormous sums, Lorena endeavored to raise money by selling autographed copies of the poem for fifty cents apiece.[11]

Despite her vindication, her career had been irrevocably damaged. The following year Lorena married Magnus "Pete" Peterson, a cowboy and jack-of-all-trades then running a service station, and retired from the rodeo circuit in 1929. Bad luck and hard times soon engulfed them. While running a boardinghouse in Alturas, California, they listened to the stories of an old prospector and "got bit by the mining bug," as Pete put it. Before long they were on their way to central Nevada.[12]

Under the tutelage of another elderly prospector, "Horse" Beckwith, they fruitlessly scoured the desert for a year. Then Lorena fell back on the time-honored occupation of the woman prospector since the days of Nellie Cashman and worked as a boardinghouse cook at the Longstreet Mine in the Monitor Mountains east of Tonopah, while Pete made himself useful as a handyman. After the mine closed, they tried raising chickens at ranches they rented in the area, and at every opportunity they prospected. Pete's subsequent disquisition on the finances of the prospector may well have reflected their own situation at this point: "He's in a business where he can't go broke. He's broke to start with. No one will give him credit so he can't get in debt. Being at the bottom of the economic ladder there is no place to go but up. . . . To succeed one must hit rock bottom hard enough to bounce."[13]

After Pete found work at the Tonopah Power Company, the Petersons abandoned poultry and Lorena enrolled for a two-year course at the Tonopah School of Mining and Engineering, becoming one of the few women thus far encountered who tried to approach her prospecting through formal instruction at an accredited institution of a different order than the Colorado Opportunity School. Here one glimpses the method of the professional athlete: to succeed at anything, one must train and prepare. Pete took a different view of the necessary qualifications for a prospector: "One should possess the eye of an eagle, the plodding persistence of a pack mule, the burrowing instinct of a gopher. . . . He must withstand inflation and deflation. Inflation when he finds the ore, deflation when he gets the assay returns. He should be a composite of Christopher Columbus, Thomas Edison, and Jesse James." All the same, Pete also took a course.[14]

They staked their first claim, the King Solomon, in 1934 when Lorena turned forty-one and Pete forty-five. After that date Lorena's claims clutter the record books. Despite scanty returns, they persisted, except for a brief return to Oregon during World War II. Much of the time Lorena prospected in the back country without Pete. Although they expended a good deal of effort on a quicksilver claim Lorena discovered in 1947, their best claim proved to be the Old Cowgirl, a gold discovery made by Lorena near Tybo in 1950. For a while their excitement centered on a titanium claim Lorena found in the Ellendale district in 1949. She had missed Ellie Nay, who had died two years earlier, but even if the two had met when Ellie arrived to do her annual assessment work, they might not have become friends. Like more than one woman prospector before her, Lorena associated only with men and does not seem to have been much liked by women in central Nevada. The contrast with Louise Grantham suggests that the woman prospector's willingness to socialize may have had a good deal to do with her acceptance by other women. So far as can be determined, gossip about the murder of Slim Harris did not follow Lorena to Nevada. All the same, this shaming event may have had something to do with Lorena's avoidance of the company of other women and her preference for long sojourns by herself in the desert. If so, she would not have been the first with a dark secret to take refuge in these mountains.[15]

As the years passed, Pete, who wrote a humorous newspaper column under the pen name "Malapai Mike," increasingly looked the part of the prospector, with his wide-brimmed Stetson, his bushy eyebrows and mustache, his pipe, his wispy white beard, and his faraway gaze, the result, he said, of "over indulgence in the Koyote Kid's Liquid X, a beverage that is manufactured exclusively at Hungryman's Canyon." It was said that Lorena also frequently overindulged. She had, however, lost none of the rodeo star's fondness for horses or her special ability to train them. She tamed and broke a big red mustang stallion, and as one old Tonopah resident recalled, "Any time there was a rodeo of any kind, she was there." Occasionally, the former professional athlete's urge to compete flared up again. At the first "Jim Butler Days" annual celebration in Tonopah in 1950, the drilling contest lacked entrants. Lorena came forward with an offer to find a crew of "she-males." "See that," she said, rolling up her sleeve and displaying her muscles. "It means that I can swing a mean singlejack, and I've a mind to do a little challenging myself."[16]

Death came suddenly, with no warning signs. In the autumn of 1961 Pete returned to the cabin for a forgotten lunchpail to find Lorena lying on the couch. "Pete, I'm dying," she said, and within a week, at sixty-eight, she was gone. Pete turned her red mustang stallion loose to run the range again, and in time the horse ceased coming back to look for her. Despite nearly thirty years of effort, her achievements in mining never approached her successes in the rodeo world. Intensely proud throughout her life of these victories, she would have been much pleased to know that they are now commemorated.[17]

The experiences of Dot Coffey and Lorena Peterson typify a curious circumstance concerning the women prospectors of the 1930s: in contrast to the sizable proportion of women on their own at the turn of the century, most major figures of the depression era were married women working with husbands, perhaps a reflection of the rise of companionate marriage in place of separate spheres. Other configurations such as sisters or a father-and-daughter team do not emerge in the records at all. The prospecting partnerships of Frances Patchen with two of her three husbands conformed with this pattern, but she may have been the most unlikely of women prospectors because she alone was a former socialite, existing at a farther remove from the prospector's world than the woman rodeo rider or the woman blacksmith who had already crossed the occupational Rubicon. Frances's career in mining had commenced in the Klondike, hovered in abeyance after the rush to Chisana and its tragic aftermath, and resurged with renewed intensity during the interwar years. It was a career that might not have begun at all except for a pair of pink tights.

One of eight children, Arabelle Frances Patchen was born in St. Paul on 10 August 1874. At first she was known as Belle and later, when she left her old life behind her, as Frances. In her twelfth year her family moved to Spokane, and onward to the Coeur d'Alene in 1887, her first taste of the mining world. In 1892, at just eighteen, Belle married Samuel Allen, a Spokane prosecuting attorney probably a good deal older than she, and became an ornament to Spokane society. There the story might have stalled, in a lifetime of ladies' luncheons, afternoon card parties, and balls, if the cream of society had not decided in the summer of 1895 to hold a charity circus to help pay the mortgage on the family farm for the struggling father of a boy who had broken his back on a barrel slide. Samuel Allen heartily approved the idea.[18]

That is, he approved until he saw his wife's surprise. Out in the ring rode the petite, blonde, and curvaceous Belle Frances, bareback on a white horse. She wore a pale blue costume with a fluffy skirt that ended above her knees, revealing pink tights. Samuel Allen was so shocked that he walked out of the performance immediately. The couple quarreled, and Belle left the house, never to return. The whole scandalous affair kept Spokane abuzz for months.

Belle Frances decided to become an actress. She made her debut in the spring of 1896 at Bradford, Pennsylvania, in *The Fool's Revenge*. Offstage, however, she was entangled in an unfolding saga of flight and pursuit more melodramatic than any she played behind the footlights. Not everyone had reacted as adversely as her husband to her appearance in pink tights at the charity circus. Albert Hildreth, scion of a wealthy New Orleans family, had fallen insanely in love with her on the spot. Although her mother warmly supported her throughout the circus scandal, many others undoubtedly did not, and Hildreth's admiration may have seemed a welcome change from catty gossip. It is likely that Belle Frances encouraged him at first. Samuel Allen may have had Hildreth, among others, in mind when he later accused his ex-wife of being "a siren who uses her charms to infatuate men to the point where they lavish their wealth upon her." Bitterness often sours the assessment of an ex-husband, but there could be little doubt, throughout her life, of Belle Frances's power to enchant. When the Allen wedding had started late, members of the Elks Lodge had taken a good-humored vote on who should replace the bridegroom; the results were inconclusive because every man persisted in voting for himself.[19]

Nonetheless, Belle Frances soon had good reason to wish she had never enchanted the wildly unbalanced Hildreth, who refused to cease his increasingly unwelcome attentions. The *New York Journal* described her flight from him: "She has dodged him in the mountains of Montana, in the sagebrush of Wyoming, the plains of Kansas, in the big hotels of Chicago, and now that she is in New York she hopes to keep away from him by remaining closely in her room. In the meantime, Hildreth is said to have taken an oath that he will either marry Mrs. Allen or kill her." He broke into her Chicago hotel room and rifled her trunk, purloining several letters. He attempted to beat another man who conversed with her. At last consenting to dine with him, she lightly told him that his violent threats "might spoil my appetite." Hildreth made a half-hearted lunge at her with a carving knife and only succeeded in destroying her corsage. His next, more purposeful attack with the knife was deflected by a waiter, who dropped his tray of dishes with a crash to seize Hildreth. Samuel Allen, meantime, divorced his departed wife on grounds of desertion.[20]

How a new romance could blossom for Belle Frances in the midst of repeated flights from Hildreth that had taken her twice across the continent stretches the imagination, but another suitor was about to win the prize. Thomas C. Noyes, a student at the University of Michigan who had seen her in a theatrical performance, had been instantly smitten, like so many others. Unlike the others, his affection was returned. The only man not smitten was Tom Noyes's father, a Butte mining tycoon, who angrily opposed the marriage. No doubt he had hoped for a royal alliance with another great mining family as in the marriage of his daughter Ruth to Arthur Heinze in 1899. At that wedding, dubbed in the press the "most brilliant ever celebrated in the state of Montana, if not in the West," thirty-five hundred invitations had gone forth, and the richness of the wedding gifts from the West, the East, and Europe defied the rapturous reporters' powers of description. Although the report that Tom was disinherited for his unsuitable marriage appears exaggerated, there is no doubt of the breach that split the Noyes family. "I shall conduct no training school for actresses," the elder Noyes told his son.[21] It would soon become clear that he had greatly underestimated his daughter-in-law.

Late in 1897 Frances Patchen Noyes and her new husband headed north to join the Klondike gold rush, spending the winter in a small cabin at Skagway. By 1899 they were camped with several partners by Otter Creek at the base of a glacier. Unsuccessful in their prospecting, they went on to Nome in 1900, where they stood on the beach with the rest, shoveling sand into portable rockers after each high tide. Thus far their trajectory had paralleled that of another graduate of the class of '98, Lillian Malcolm, but at the point where she departed Alaska for the deserts, they instead headed deeper into the Seward Peninsula to stake claims at Candle Creek, where they prospered. Tom became a bank president and began hatching plans for large-scale mining development. No specific detail has been preserved on the prospecting Frances did during these years, since the diaries she is believed to have kept have been destroyed. We know that she was a partner to Tom Noyes in every sense, never far from his side and fully sharing in everything he did. On a return visit to Butte, Frances and Tom, according to a newspaper, displayed nuggets "they" had gleaned in Alaska, which implied her active role. Moreover, it is likely that the skilled and committed woman prospector of later years had developed at an early stage. But her exploits on the trail have been much better documented, and they were second to none.

Already in 1908 Frances and Tom had much to recount: "perilous trips, lost trails, climbs over glacial fields, where steps had to be cut with an ax." More than once shelter in an Eskimo igloo had saved their lives. An undated fragmentary clipping tells of Frances's "wonderful courage and fortitude" on one of these dangerous journeys: she

> encouraged her husband to walk on, as to give up would have been certain death. A few feet seemed to him miles, and after they were in sight of the cabin they were both so completely exhausted that it took hours

to reach the place, and when they did the door was open and the room full of ice and snow, and again their courage was tested. . . . Two years ago they made the trip from Candle Creek to Nome in a canoe, leaving on the seventeenth of June before the ice had gone out. Their experiences on that trip were thrilling. The journey of eighteen days was fraught with danger and exposure, as at times it would be necessary for them to pull the canoe over the ice for a long distance, but as both had youth and endurance and were warmly clad in their fur parkas, the experience savored of the novel and venturesome, and one they look back on with keen delight.

Frances would always survive these perilous passages, though Tom would not fare so well.[22]

Her most famous journey made a splash in the press. In the fall of 1907 Tom traveled to New York to raise money for the expensive system of canals and piping he was constructing to develop his claims by hydraulic methods. Although he expected to be home at Candle in time for Christmas dinner with Frances, a financial panic shook the nation in October, causing banks to die like flies from coast to coast. Tom Noyes's bank in Candle also tottered on the verge of collapse. Far from raising money for his hydraulic mining operation or transferring funds to revive his ailing bank, Tom found himself so squeezed in the financial emergency that he had to pawn his watch to pay his hotel bill. Frances saved the day. She set out at once for Nome with her team of malamutes to secure the needed cash. All in all, she traveled more than four hundred miles over the snow and ice through the short days and on into the long nights. "It was a stunt few men would attempt," the *Anaconda (Montana) Standard* later observed, and at least for the time being, the bank was safe.[23]

Alongside these pioneer feats Frances retained her social polish. Even the Noyeses' first log cabin at Candle had books, pictures, and lace curtains. Hudson Stuck, an Episcopalian archdeacon they entertained at Candle, wrote Frances, "It is indeed good to a 'mushing' archdeacon to know that here and there in this vast wilderness are homes of comfort and refinement where he is made welcome, and nowhere that I have been, have I found more cordial and generous hospitality than I found with you." On return visits to Butte and Seattle after the death of Tom's

During her marriage to Tom Noyes,
Frances Patchen was both a society beauty and an
Alaska pioneer (Frances Muncaster Collection,
PCA 202-48, Alaska State Library).

father in 1902, she entertained, and was entertained by, the cream of society in the most elegant style. Clearly, the elder Noyes's disapproval of her had not been widely shared in Butte. The society pages featured her picture in a gown that heavily encrusted her ample bosom with flowers and a hat as extravagantly enormous as that of any lady of fashion. Indeed, Frances was an ornament to society on two continents. The interest Tom inherited from his father in the Rainier Grand Hotel in Seattle probably did a good deal to facilitate the glamorous life the young couple led for several years. They spent summers mining at Candle and winters visiting in the States and traveling in Europe. Frances became "the toast of New York, London, Paris, and especially Monte Carlo," in the words of one who knew her well.[24]

Nor had she lost any of her power to enchant. One of the Noyeses' partners at the Otter Creek camp later wrote Frances that he had married a woman "as like you as I could find." It seems probable that she flirted outrageously. After the winter Tom spent in New York trying to raise money while Frances remained at Candle, one lovelorn gentleman drew up a mock marriage contract with her as an April fool, in which he promised, "To be a good dog: who will come when whistled to, eat from the hand, roll over or play dead at the word of command, and mush when the time comes. The said Fannie agrees and promises to the following:—That, at any and all times, she will do as she damn pleases." In an undated poem the local doctor poetically addressed her: "Fair of Face—How can you shake me / May I not your burdens share?" Another poem written to her, by banker John Holmes, may also date from the Candle period. One stanza read,

Where is the moon? where is the sun?
Where are the forests, the flowers, the fun?
There are no wild birds, no dawn, no dew,
No life, no music, no love—without you!

No doubt she attracted many other admirers who left no written traces. Motherhood deflected their yearnings no more than did her happily married state. After several miscarriages at Candle left Tom and Frances still childless, they adopted Bonnie, a half-Eskimo girl of five, around 1905. Indeed, they seem to have enjoyed the kind of relationship with

Chisana, Alaska, where Matilda Wales and Frances Muncaster prospected
(Zacharias Collection, PCA 178-97, Alaska State Library).

the Eskimos that their obvious lack of prejudice toward their adopted daughter implies. They avidly collected Eskimo crafts, gratefully turned to the Eskimos for shelter on their journeys, and initially prospected at Candle Creek on a tip received from an Eskimo.[25]

After 1910 everything fell apart. "Tom was a first-class miner but a poor businessman," as one who later heard all the details from Frances succinctly put it. Tom's careless habit of signing checks without his official title as president of the Candle bank left him personally liable for all debts when the bank failed. He lost not only his bank but also his mining interests at Candle and his share of the Rainier Grand Hotel. In greatly reduced circumstances the former toast of London, Paris, and Monte Carlo moved to Tongass Island with her husband.[26]

When discoveries at Chisana rekindled the hopes of Alaskan prospectors, Tom hastened forth in 1913, soon joined by Frances. (One wonders if she encountered that early Chisana pioneer prospector Mabel Wales, already on the scene.) The Noyeses failed to recoup their lost fortune at Chisana, however, and the hardships took a terrible toll on

"*Hit Rock Bottom Hard Enough to Bounce*"

Tom. He struggled back to Tongass Island a "physical wreck," in the words of *Mining and Engineering World*. Unlike the adventures of earlier years, this one was not to be recalled with keen delight at soirees in Butte. With Frances always by his side, Tom was hospitalized in British Columbia in December 1915 and later moved to a St. Louis hospital. He developed pneumonia and died there on 2 February 1916, widely mourned for his "lovable disposition" and generosity. "He was just pure gold," one of his old partners on Otter Creek wrote to Frances.[27]

"You cannot stay in the North by yourself," he advised Frances in the same letter, but stay she did, although not in the wilderness. Instead, she made a living by managing the cannery store at Nakat Island, a position possibly awarded to her because the cannery owner, John Hume, was one of her admirers. Now an eligible widow, albeit past her fortieth year, Frances retained her power to enchant. Another swain, possibly John Holmes, wrote her hopeful letters until an early death from pneumonia removed him from the competition. Yet the one who eventually won her was William Muncaster, a tall, gangling young surveyor she met in the cannery. Muncaster may have been a rough diamond from humble origins with little money or education, but he was an experienced hand in the Alaskan wilderness, and his adoration for "My Own Darling Sweetheart," "Angle of Mine," "Lovie Dovie," and the one who "got hold of the reins of my life" suffuses the letters he wrote her from 1917 to 1919 (unfortunately, Frances's side of this correspondence was not preserved).

While evidently giving him some encouragement, Frances demurred over the difference in their ages: Bill Muncaster was fourteen years younger than his "little girl" or "girlie," the forms of address he constantly used, perhaps as a denial of her more advanced years as well as an allusion to her petite stature (Frances stood less than five feet tall). He responded to her concern that he would one day cease to love her with the logic of a seventeenth-century British poet, though couched in more rudimentary language: "Girlie let us try to be one and not two persons in this world if we are married that [is] what we are sopposed to be then my age will be your age and your age mine; Girlie you were born for me the other never had any wright to you And I am sure life will be full of love to us." Eventually, his unquenchable ardor carried the day, and they were married on 15 June 1919 in McCarthy, Alaska. Bill Muncaster's family saw this as a sort of Cinderella story. Once upon a time, not so many years earlier, Muncaster's mother had been the chambermaid who cleaned the room of the glamorous Mr. and Mrs. Tom Noyes when they stopped at the Rainier Grand Hotel on a trip to Europe or a round of elegant entertainments in the States.[28]

Frances and Bill, in company with her daughter Bonnie, then set off for Chisana on a honeymoon trip that took them over two glaciers to the head of the White River and downstream to Coffee Creek on the Yukon. It was not the sort of journey everyone would have considered an idyll of bliss, as several stoical entries in Frances's diary during the winter of 1919–20 show. November 21: "Broke camp at 10 A.M., just daylight. . . . Bill going ahead with ice pick some of the time. . . . Bonnie & I broke through [the ice] trying to get to the bank. Didn't get wet, froze too quick. Climbed around the cliff—pretty cold." November 24: "22 below zero this A.M. Nothing doing." December 9: "Deep snow, no bottom. Bill & I snowshoed ahead of the dogs. The sled fell through the ice." That night they put up a lean-to, made a large fire, and roasted meat on sticks. December 21: "It must be fifty below zero. The mercury has gone down into the bulb." December 30: "Broke camp at 10:45. Fierce going all day. Trail drifted over about a foot of bad snow. Camped at 4 P.M. Everybody dead tonight." At the end of January they settled in to spend the rest of the winter in a deserted cabin on Wellesley Lake, where they lived by hunting and ice fishing with a moosehide net.[29]

Despite these familiar rigors, it had been Frances who proposed the year spent in the Chisana country. Bill responded, "Go ahead and plane and what ever you decide to do I will try and go through with I have a strong body which is all for your service." His willingness to serve, along with his solid qualifications as a trail partner, had no doubt helped him win Frances. She seemed pleased with her adoring new husband. "Billy is a darling," she wrote on their wedding day. Yet memories sometimes intruded. She remembered Tom with sadness on his birthday. Stopping at a cabin on Young's Creek near the Nazina River where she had stayed with Tom on their Chisana trek, she wrote, "Everything looked different. Everything is different."[30]

After this winter spent in ice and snow Frances and Bill's honeymoon trip ended in fire the following summer. They made their way out to McCarthy through a mile of burned timber with ashes to their knees. The next day they passed over smoldering ground to camp that night in a marsh surrounded by fire. "Thus ends my year in the interior and happiness," wrote Frances in her diary. She had, however, uncovered no bonanzas in the Chisana country.[31]

This life of hardship, lived close to the bone, continued over the years to come. Bonnie married a Canadian Mountie in 1922, bore a child, and died young in 1932; Frances and Bill kept on. Years afterward Bill recalled one of their more memorable journeys in 1923: "Have seen her day after day cover 20 to 25 mile on snow shoes just took it as an ever day chore About 1923 we went from Wellsey Lake to Burwash landing about 150 mile drove a herd of horses out of the hills to good feed for the winter it was cold our thermometer went to the bulb at 56° below and stayed there for some ten day. but we had to keep going for we were out there us two 100 mile or so from nowhere but she loved it."[32]

They continued to prospect, with negligible results, as much as they could at Hootchi Lake and other locales. Frances kept in touch with the mining recorders, and they alerted her to new strikes. Only lack of money for supplies brought the Muncasters out of the wilderness. William Simonds, Bill's nephew, recalled the visits Frances and Bill made to the Muncaster family in Seattle: "My bed room was next to the one occupied by Bill & Frances and I heard her crying thousands of times wanting to go back to Alaska to prospect. . . . Bill would try to soothe her by promising to go back to Alaska as soon as he got a 'grub stake' together. . . . If there ever was a woman prospector, it was Frances. In fact, I think the reason she brought the sled dogs [three large malamutes] with her when she went 'outside' was as a sort of insurance that she must return to Alaska." The Muncasters' financial situation was worsening nonetheless. The summer of 1927 found Bill fruitlessly hunting a job and driven to conclude, "We will just have to live on love alone." He had no way of knowing that Frances had finally struck gold.[33]

When she heard rumors of Indian discoveries at a remote site in British Columbia, Bill was away hunting work, and Frances hit the trail immediately on her own, following the Indians. She is said to have been the first white prospector on the scene. Though the Indians initially resented her intrusion, she secured an appointment as mining recorder for the district, which saved them the troublesome necessity of traveling a long distance to record their claims. The convenience of having the only independent woman deputy mining recorder in British Columbia at hand improved relations considerably, as did Bill, when he later arrived and put his expertise to work surveying claims for the Indian prospectors with a thirty-foot sling rope on his pack horse. By that time Frances had already staked their own claims.[34]

William Simonds's account of his journey into Squaw Creek with Frances the following summer offers indirect testimony to her skill on the trail and the obstacles she faced when she initially went in alone. She taught Simonds how to mush dogs. They relayed their supplies by dog team, caching a haul and repeatedly going back for more. Simonds recalled being attacked by a pack of wolves, being stalked for hours by wolverines, and, after the snow began to melt, traveling by night so there would be enough crust to support the sled. When Bill joined them with pack horses, they crossed the Tatshenshini River by sliding off their horses when the animals began to swim, holding onto their tails, and hoping not to be kicked.

During the first summer hand shoveling at the sluice boxes brought an average of fifteen dollars' worth of fine gold dust a day. Frances calculated that they mined perhaps as much as thirty-five thousand dollars' worth of gold from Squaw Creek over the next twelve years. To Dot Coffey or Lorena Peterson in the depression-stricken Lower Forty-Eight, that would have sounded like a fortune, but Frances acknowledged that in the North, with its costly supplies and freight charges, their mining had yielded little more than a living. It is nonetheless evident that the absence of richer pannings had not dampened her enthusiasm a whit. In 1933 she was so eager to return to Squaw Creek that she set off, apparently alone, at the beginning of February without waiting for the ice to break up.[35]

Thenceforth the Muncasters' lives revolved around summer mining at Squaw Creek. Bringing in a bulldozer for operations on a larger scale in 1945 made little improvement in their returns. Though by then past seventy, Frances appeared as hardy on the trails as ever. Bill wrote of a blizzard that blew in from the north, drifting the snow ten feet deep in some places and delaying their departure until late November. Winters were spent in Seattle, Victoria, or Vancouver. For a while they wintered in a cabin at "thirty mile" on the Haines highway. Eventually, they passed their winters in Haines, where Bill surveyed streets and lots. As Frances's arthritis worsened and her strength ebbed, they spent less time at Squaw Creek. She died suddenly from a heart attack on 28 October 1952. Frances was seventy-eight, but her ever-adoring Bill saw her death as the untimely loss of one "still young." She herself might well have willed it that way, for she often told Bill, "If I cannot be in the hills, I would sooner be dead." In the eyes of her grief-stricken husband she had done the things that others only thought about doing.[36]

Frances's life underscored the importance of marital harmony for husbands and wives who prospected together. When a woman of powerful personality such as Josie Earp set her mind on prospecting, she could sweep a fond husband along; when a happily married couple such as the Coffeys went into the field, their mutual appreciation and their common interest in prospecting could transform poverty and hardship into a joyful time, almost a lost Eden, to which they afterward longed to return. Conversely, a discordant marriage could sour the entire experience. If Mona McCrudden had married a man like the doting Bill Muncaster, she might be mining yet. Instead, she looks back in anger on the years she wasted in "this godforsaken land."

Mona was born on 11 February 1903, the second of Joseph and Esther McCrudden's four children. She grew up in the white thatch-roofed farmhouse near Scotstown in northern Ireland where her family had lived for five generations. Despite the large numbers of Irish in western mining, she would be the first woman prospector of known Irish birth since Nellie Cashman. At age fourteen she went to work as a maid at a nearby demesne, haunted, as were all the grand old houses of Ireland. She remembers how her father put his arm around her and walked her up the stairs to the room where she was to sleep so that she would not see the devil on that first night, for the devil appears only to one alone. She was to see the apparition many times on the stairs, always wearing white with one arm upraised. Later she left Scotstown behind to work south of Belfast, except that Mona never really left anything behind. The dead reappear to her from time to time, and sorrows of long ago still wrench her heart as if they happened only yesterday.[37]

In 1923, at twenty, Mona set forth with a girlfriend to see the world. Although America was her dream, immigration restrictions obliged her to settle for Canada at first, and she also hoped to travel on to Australia and New Zealand. Her mother wept brokenly over her departure, but her father seemed to understand and told her, "The last word is yours." Around Vancouver she worked at a variety of jobs for five years until her opportunity came to go to America as a nanny for a family in Beverly Hills. Later she became a waitress in the Maryland Hotel, where she served many famous customers, including the Marx brothers ("hellions" who grabbed at her legs). No doubt she caught many eyes, for she was a lovely young woman with something of a Katharine Hepburn look, red hair worn collar or shoulder length, high cheekbones, and deep blue somewhat angular eyes. Moreover, she had a roguish wit and an abundance of Irish charm. The devil-may-care smile that won her heart, however, belonged to the hotel's husky, blond head baggageman, Gale Peer. They married around 1934 when Mona was just past thirty and Peer six years younger.

Having grown up in a mining family at Ely, Nevada, Peer had an overwhelming itch to return to mining, and Mona agreed to give up their comfortable life in southern California. Soon she found herself in the Nevada desert. A kindly old woman they met when they paused at a hot springs presented her with the gift of a baking potato and told her, "You'll love this country." Looking at the gray desolation around her, Mona thought to herself, *Like hell I will.* In fact, she liked it better than her bitterness now allows her to admit. Loelia Carl, an old friend of her mining days, recalls the characteristic enthusiasm Mona brought to everything she did: "She was always excited. She was going to get there tomorrow. The next shovelful would have been it"; she was "a joyful person to be around." So she appears in the photographs of those days, deeply tanned, slim, heavily booted, a sailor's hat sometimes perched on her shining red hair, smiling broadly as she wields the shovel, posing beside a windlass, sitting to rest with Peer on a hillside of broken scree as they prospect. Home in those early days was a small tent with just enough room for a bed and a little table. Those who knew her remember that Mona worked at their mining like a man, shoveling debris, gophering in the perilous tunnels of old mines, "cobbing," that is, breaking up a fissure of antimony in a big chunk of rock with a large, flat hammer and then scraping it out, carrying heavy rock for miles, walking the hills in search of mineral, and proud of all she could do ("There's nothing to it"). Though mining men considered Peer an excellent prospector, he disdained teaching Mona, so she learned on her own.[38]

Mona strongly exemplifies a strain present in many prospectors, the propensity to collect. The habit of keen observation, coupled with a fascination with the oddities of the natural world and the historic relics of those who have gone before, leads the prospector to pick up geodes, fossils, rusted buttonhooks, and other curiosities that have little to do with mining. Mona may have cast out the memories of some twenty years that she spent mining the deserts, but she kept the strange rocks, the old bottles, the ancient Indian beads, and all the rest she uncovered there.

News of a fresh gold strike in the Slumbering Hills north of Winnemucca initially drew the Peers into the desert. The first discoveries in the area had occurred in 1910, and woman prospector Louise Rupp had christened the new district Awakening in 1911. Modest production ensued until 1918, after which the Slumbering Hills, their smooth, treeless, rounded shapes reminiscent of sleeping forms, slumbered once again. Until 1935, that is, when new discoveries, soon to be endorsed by no less a personage than former president Herbert Hoover, created a flutter of interest in the mining world. Nonetheless, Frederick Bechdolt, who chronicled the event, rightly noted that this was no old-time mining boom like Tombstone or Goldfield, a circumstance he largely blamed on autos. The road to Jumbo, the principal mine in the district, was not dissimilar to the paths traversed by Frances Williams on the way to early Goldfield or Lillian Malcolm on her journey to Silver Peak— glaring sun on a white alkali flat, a jolting path through sagebrush, a thick cloud of dust that coated every traveler and object, and a narrow gulch climbing to a little spring and a cluster of tents. The difference was that autos enabled many to commute from Winnemucca, so the

Mona McCrudden Peer camps in the desert
(courtesy of Mona Mullins).

saloons, hotels, dance halls, and all the accoutrements of the old boomtown, where a few mined the hills and the great majority mined one
another, became superfluous. Bechdolt also took note of three women
prospecting with their husbands, and Mona recalled a couple of women
prospectors. Since Mona herself is the only one who can be named
today, this suggests that we glimpse no more than the tip of the iceberg
of women in mining.[39]

Like the artifacts Mona picked up from the ground in many places,
one tangible sign remains of her own presence, a memoir entitled "The
Bride Comes to the Desert," told by Louisa Huntington to Bechdolt and
published in the *Saturday Evening Post*. While Huntington, a young
German woman, camped at Jumbo, the threat she sensed in the desert
(like a "tiger that is sleeping") turned real in the form of a heavy cloud-
burst during her husband's absence: "The darkness grew so deep that
it was terrifying. The rain began. It was so hard that it shot right
through the heavy canvas fly and the tent roof; it was as if there were
no covering at all. The roaring of the water in the bottom of the gulch
sounded above the thunder of the flood that was pouring down from
the sky. And all at once it seemed as if the whole mountain was coming into the tent. The mud flowed through the board walls and over
the floor, six inches of mud, and I could do nothing. I could not raise
my head." Pregnant and too ill to move, Huntington simply lay helpless in the mud.[40]

Rescue came with Mona, slogging into the tent, smiling her glowing,
cheerful smile, cleaning away the pervasive mud, building a fire, and
cooking a meal that Huntington's queasy stomach could tolerate. The
collapse of the canyon wall during the flood cut Jumbo off from the
world for several days, but as soon as the track became passable, Mona
drove Huntington to the doctor in Winnemucca. To Huntington, she
seemed a savior, afterward remembered with deep gratitude. Indeed,
the quick sympathies for man and beast, the wish to feed all hungry
creatures ("the poor wee things"), the urge to take the afflicted in her
arms and say in her musical Irish brogue "I feel for ye" remain the
essence of Mona. "She took everybody under her wing," says Loelia
Carl. Yet Mona, who mothered everything around her, had no children of her own.[41]

Having found all the promising ground at Jumbo already taken, the Peers soon moved on to continue mining in the Clan Alpine Mountains, the Smoky Valley region, and Tenabo. There Mona met a woman prospector in her fifties, living in grubby squalor, who showed her a nugget of eye-popping size and swore she had a million-dollar mine under the ground. Another of the women in mining who have "gone down yonder now," as Mona says of the dead, without leaving so much as a name.

In 1939, sixteen years after her departure from Ireland, Mona returned to her parents' thatch-roofed farmhouse for a visit. She may well have discussed with her parents her increasing unhappiness with Peer, only to be told that regardless of the humiliations that wounded her, they disapproved of divorce. She learned that she no longer belonged in Ireland; her sisters and nearly everyone else had become strangers to her. So remote was the rural Irish countryside that news of the outbreak of World War II did not penetrate until two days after the event. As soon as Mona heard, she knew she must return to America immediately or risk being stranded for the duration of the war. She set off at once on a bicycle, pedaling madly for sixty miles toward the sea and the ship that would carry her back.

Together once more in the godforsaken land, Mona and Peer continued to mine with high hopes and limited success. "It seemed like everything they turned their hand to back then didn't turn out," an old friend remembers. During World War II they mined tungsten, a vital element in wartime steelmaking. Later they went broke mining antimony in the Clan Alpines on the east side of the Dixie Valley, no place for the faint of heart. Their cabin was situated more than fifty miles from the main road, and all water had to be hauled in. Others saw their antimony operation as an "outrageous job," because the slope of the "straight up and down mountain" where they hunted pods of good ore was so steep that they had to slide the rock down on pieces of tin. But the cabin they lived in most of the time more closely resembled a home than the little tent. Mona planted a garden despite the lack of water, made a pet of a mustang, and enjoyed the view from her front window of the valley below where dust devils danced across the white playa. They also attempted cinnabar and sulphur mining in the Dixie Valley area.[42]

*"Hit Rock Bottom Hard Enough to Bounce"*

At one point in their travels they lingered near Tenabo, where they found a payable prospect. It was there that Mona discovered her own turquoise mine, which she christened the "Wee Nugget," on a mountain she had seen in a dream. Peer laughed at her and called it "bull," but Mona cut and polished large, spectacular blue chunks, which she treasured until a burglar stole them from her house, and eventually she sold the mine for a small sum. She also struck amethyst and casually gave the site away to a friend. Mona's savings and occasional good returns enabled the Peers to buy a large house trailer, making Mona the first woman prospector known to have pursued an itinerant life in thoroughly modern style. Although strong winds shook the trailer like a ship in a storm at sea, it drew much admiration in the desert mining towns, where people quickly recognized it as the greatest innovation for prospectors since the car. The old tent cities were about to follow the stagecoach and the pack burro into oblivion. Soon a gathering of miners would be signaled by a convocation of trailers.[43]

The early fifties found the Peers mining south of Austin, and it was then that the final break between them came. The story that went the rounds in Fallon, where Mona fled, was that Peer had told her the hands that had prospected and cobbed ore beside him for nearly twenty years had grown too rough for his taste; now that he had made some money, he wanted a more ladylike wife. Fallon knew whose side it was on. Mona neither confirms nor denies this version; instead, she tells a story that she feels epitomizes their life together. While Peer was away trucking a load of ore, a heavy snowstorm blew in, leaving Mona marooned and alone in the desert with little food for more than a week—alone but not afraid ("I was out in the hills with God"). Her companions were her black dog, her cat, and a skunk that almost turned into a pet when she fed, named, and befriended it. Every other day Mona and her animals took a walk over the sparkling snowy expanses to a hot springs not far away. On his return Peer immediately shot the skunk. Said Mona, "When he shot me poor wee skunk, he went too far."[44]

Whatever the reasons, she left him and embarked on another life. She drove to Fallon with only five dollars in her pocket to show for all her years of hard labor in mining and stayed in the flophouse that was all she could afford. She put away the slacks that had been her daily garb for so long, never to be worn again because they were tied to the bitter memory of prospecting with Peer. She took a job as a hostess in a restaurant that thrived while Mona's Irish graciousness and warmth drew the customers in and turned into a roomful of nearly empty tables after she left. In a few year's time, after friends persuaded her with great difficulty that a man could be kind and love her devotedly, she married Bill Mullins, sheep boss of one of the large Carson Valley ranches. In the Carson Valley her sharp collector's eye became her vocation, and she opened an antique store, the "Wee Bit of Old Ireland." To Mona it was less a shop than a museum where the public could see the beautiful and interesting objects she had collected.[45]

Bill Mullins died and the Wee Bit of Old Ireland closed more than twenty years ago, but Mona still survives, in her nineties now and very much alone. Though her red hair has turned snow white and several crippling falls compel her to walk with a cane, her lively eyes are the same deep blue, and the gnarled hands that cobbed ore still have a grip of steely strength. She can still charm the birds from the trees, to say nothing of the skunks from the brush ("Dear, it does my heart good to see ye"). She still has her sense of humor: asked where she thought she was going when she accidentally jostled someone's cart in the supermarket, she waved her cane in lordly fashion and declared, "I own the place." In the garden of the small house where she lived until the final move to a rest home, ornamental rocks she had collected circled every little flowerbed and lined every winding path, silent testimony to a time she would prefer not to discuss. Above all, she retains the same fierce spirit. She refuses to "sit here in a chair all day" and rejects all offers of help that might make her life easier, saying, "I want to do my own." She can be moody and caustic. She rages and rails against the iniquities of the modern world and the husband from whom she parted more than forty years ago. No wound has ever healed; no grief has ceased to move her. She vows that she, at least, will never give up and shows a flash of the woman prospector's scorn for those less determined than she to carry on in the face of all obstacles ("What a sissy!"). Looking back on her life with the uncompromising honesty her friends admire, she repeats again and again, "I tell you, Sally, it's a rough road."[46]

NINE

# "Listen and the Mountains Will Talk to You": Happy Days and Panamint Annie

On a late fall day the dried desert plants near Tule Canyon look much like a field of flowers, glowing gold, white, and russet across the broad Lida Valley rimmed in the distance by pale blue mountains. The road drops off the edge of the plain and descends steeply between gray mountains like waves frozen as they toss, then winds for nearly fifteen miles through a sandy wash into Death Valley. The mountains beyond rise range on range, the nearest a pleated lavender escarpment, next a high blue ridge, finally sharp snow-covered peaks scooped with blue canyons. The remains of past mining are scattered throughout Tule Canyon, placer dumps, tunnels, prospect holes, and tumbled-down stone cabins, including the ruins of a Chinese hotel.

Mining has a long history here, dating back to the discovery of placer gold by Mexican miners in 1848. After 1870 a small number of placer miners, at first predominantly Mexican, then Chinese, later joined by Anglos and Shoshones, continuously worked the canyon. They mined over a million dollars in gold by 1900, but no great rush developed because the gold emerged in a gradual way, usually by the painstaking method of dry washing. After the turn of the century, when Goldfield and Tonopah kindled high hopes throughout the region, the pace quickened in Tule Canyon. The population quadrupled, and four separate towns were platted, none destined to survive and prosper. Women prospectors, perhaps unknown to one another, walked the canyon. Ferminia Sarras ran her toll road here for some years after 1885. Lillian Malcolm may well have gone this way on one of her journeys into Death Valley. Helen Cottrell and Mrs. C. A. Wright probably investigated the canyon before settling down to mine not far to the east. In

263

the postwar era the Death Valley country drew women prospectors even more strongly.[1]

One who spanned both time periods was Alice "Happy Days" Diminy. Indeed, she seemed to exist outside time, like a sort of female Baron Munchausen, but in the 1930s she comes clearly into focus. She was born in 1852 in Bavaria. After her parents died and the pleasant life of her childhood ended, she traveled to Paris, Poland, and Egypt. She spoke German, French, Polish, and English fluently. Eventually, she emigrated to New York, running a restaurant where she enjoyed dining with her customers. As a restaurateur, the time-honored occupation of the woman prospector, she found the independence her father had inculcated in her at an early age: "Alice, never work for anyone. That is slavery. Work always for yourself, no matter how hard you find it." During her next move, to Louisiana, she fell seriously ill with malaria and had to sell her silverware to pay the medical bills. After her recovery she noticed a man on the far bank of the Mississippi with a pack on his back and thought to herself how delightful it would be to travel through the West in that way. After all, she no longer had any possessions to encumber her. Not one for wistful and unfulfilled yearnings, she too started westward with a pack on her back.[2]

She had scarcely reached San Francisco when the 1906 earthquake shattered the city. At an undisclosed date she acquired a husband, but he did not accompany her when she headed for the central Nevada mining camps, sampling Tonopah and Goldfield before she hitched a ride with a freight team heading south to Rhyolite; instead, he went in the opposite direction, to Alaska. In Rhyolite she sold the boomers mulligan soup, a sandwich, and a beer for twenty-five cents, half the price of her competitors, and acquired her sobriquet. After she treated her first customer, a bum, to a free meal and gave him fifty cents, men on the street asked him how he liked the grub. Rolling his eyes in reminiscent pleasure, he answered, "Oh, happy day." The nickname suited her optimistic outlook, and it stuck. When she ran a Rhyolite saloon, she called it the Happy Days.[3]

After the Rhyolite boom slackened, Happy Days moved on with her lover, A. W. Shipway, to Lida, a small town some distance to the northwest. While running another restaurant there, she grubstaked Ship-

Happy Days Diminy with her burros on a desert journey (Nevada Historical Society).

way, who located the Tule Canyon ground. She later remembered the insidious lure of prospecting:

Did you ever suddenly find yourself a partner in a gold mine? There's a thrill. You don't know what lays ahead, but you see yourself rolling in wealth. You quit your restaurant. You move out to your piece of sagebrush land. What if you do sleep on the ground and fight rattlesnakes and feel the hot sun cook your back as you bend over with pick and shovel, lifting the dirt you hope is full of gold? Even if there is only a little gold, it's yours.

I learned to pan that sand, to shake and wash the coarse gravel over the side of a frying pan, little by little, until finally all that was left was a fine bit of metal stringing itself like a golden necklace around in the rusty pan.

But panning's slow, when there are shovels and shovels full of muck to handle. So we built a rocker, like a cradle it was, with the end out. It had slats across the bottom that held the gold as the sand washed over it. We piped the water from the spring to a tank. Maybe it is primitive, but it's made a living for me a long time.

265

When she began this life of hard labor, Happy Days Diminy was fifty-five, another of the remarkable women such as Frances Williams and Mrs. Morehouse Mallen who commenced prospecting in late middle life.[4]

The publication in a mining camp newspaper of a 1906 poem by Happy Days warmly defended the practitioners of her new profession against their detractors and offered a hint that prospectors may have been as prone to poetry as the cowboys who now congregate at annual poetry festivals. As Edward Hoagland notes, "Poetry is engendered in solitude," an element abundantly present in the prospecting life. Selections in the pages of *Miner's Magazine,* the publication of the Western Federation of Miners, attest that many miners wrote poetry; old Goldfielders remember the wonderful epic poetry written by a local prospector; and Mrs. Jean Gibbons, a sixty-five-year-old widow, wrote poetry during summer evenings in her one-room cabin on Wyoming's Sheep Mountain. Gibbons passed her winters in Laramie earning the grubstake that would enable her to mine in summer, when she spent her days chopping wood, hauling water, and working her ore deposits. Her unshakable conviction that the rich deposits in the Colorado Rockies continued when the range crossed the Wyoming state line co-existed with cultural interests; in her younger days she had studied music at the Chicago Conservatory. Jean Gibbons's versifying has been lost, however, along with that of other prospectors, and Happy Days's effort remains a rare example from what may once have been a flourishing genre. She concluded her ode to the prospector,

> Yes! Laugh, but remember while laughing
> The West owes all to such men,
> Our country, our history, our grandeur
> Is made by them now and then.
> So give them a good word while passing,
> Please don't consider them scamps,
> And don't for a moment consider
> That all "Prospectors" are "Tramps."[5]

Happy Days next appeared in the news in the spring of 1909 as a witness in a trial. Her lover, Shipway, had accused another man of stealing his gun, and Happy Days appeared in court to identify the weapon. The opposing attorney attempted to discredit her by forcing her to admit on the witness stand that she was living with a man not her husband. Instead of burying her face in shame, Happy Days defiantly pronounced herself a "good woman." When the attorney inquired what she meant (one almost feels the sarcasm sifting like fog over the question), he got an earful. The witness explained that a good woman, in her opinion, was one who "did no wrong to her acquaintances," "treated everyone in distress as a brother," fed the hungry, and looked after the sick. "Her living with Shipway was just for the heart to say. If she loved him and was true to him, that was all that was necessary." In mining towns, consensual unions abounded, but no one publicly asserted with flags flying that free love was a moral act. Not in 1909. The tongue-clucking headline in the *Goldfield News* read,

Says Affinities Are Quite Proper.[6]

Meanwhile, her mining in Tule Canyon continued. She did the heavy labor in her diggings herself, with only occasional help from a young man named H. L. Smith. Shipway had "dropped out," as she put it, and an anticipated reunion with her husband on his return from Alaska evidently did not result in the elusive and long-gone Mr. Diminy's taking up residence in Tule Canyon. The nuggets and coarse gold she displayed in Goldfield in the summer of 1912 aroused some interest, at least enough for San Francisco investors to sample her ground—but not to buy. She found her richest pannings in a spot where a dream had directed her. The Goldfield press, which more than once had reported a mining discovery as a result of a dream, did not scorn extrasensory methods as unscientific. Instead, the *Tribune* admiringly called her "a woman prospector and miner, one who is no delicate, publicity-seeking, effeminate imitation but the genuine article."[7]

Along with her prophetic dreams and her poetry Happy Days had another side. As Roberta Childers, who once interviewed her, observes, she was an educated woman who "also had been educated in being a little rough and tough when she needed to be." Happy Days christened the cabin she built herself using timber she had hauled from the mountains the "Isle of Peace," but at times the "Den of Brawls" might have been a more accurate description. Take the spring of 1913 when a dispute between Happy Days and her hired hand, Smith, turned physical. The *Tonopah Bonanza* called it a "rough and tumble scrap." Although the sixty-one-year-old woman held her own, a third party eventually intervened to put the finishing touches on her adversary. One wonders if Happy Days, who sometimes used rough language when provoked, cursed the hapless Smith in French, German, Polish, and English, perhaps peppered with an Arabic epithet or two. Smith, suffering from numerous cuts and abrasions and a broken arm, was taken to the hospital "for repairs"; Happy Days disdained hospitalization, despite comparable injuries. Placed under bonds to keep the peace, she returned to Tule Canyon.[8]

Over the years her tall, slender figure, always clad in boots, Levis, Stetson, and a red-and-white checked shirt, became familiar to Goldfielders. She might be absent for long periods, such as the winter when she remained snowbound at her desert outpost for four months, but she always reappeared. She would start out from her cabin at midnight walking with her two burros and reach Goldfield the following midnight; although she probably shortened the sixty-five-mile distance over present roads by taking a more direct path, it remains a considerable walk by any route for a woman in her later years. She always brought little vials of gold flakes to sell. Although Goldfielders believed she barely made enough from her mining to "feed a jackrabbit," she enjoyed a high professional reputation among Death Valley miners and she saw the life she led as idyllic. "This desert is a free country," she told Childers. "No one need be a pauper here. Don't stay chained to a job. Get out and see the world. It's a beautiful world. And then find yourself a place on the desert, where you can be free. Rock your living from the sand, as I have done since 1907."[9]

In September 1921 she took a new husband, Herbert Jester, a small, worn old man with the slightly bent posture of the prospector who has spent many years walking with his eyes fixed on the ground. Despite his white beard and elderly appearance, Jester was considerably younger than his sixty-nine-year-old bride. He owned the Tule Canyon mining claims adjacent to hers, a situation with great potential for disagreement, but it seemed that Happy Days had decided to love him rather than fight him. Later it became clear that the Jesters did a good deal of both. Happy Days's trips to town with her burros ceased when the Jesters acquired an old Model T Ford, over which they fought. They also mined together, hunting the ledge from which the gold flakes panned on Happy Days's claim had chipped: "We dig holes in the gravel, sometimes going down a dozen feet before we strike hardpan. Of course we quit then and begin another. We've got an old windlass and bucket to hoist the muck. Many's the time my back ached all night, but I always met the morning eager. Sometimes we have good days." Other times they did not, and the ledge, like the holy grail, remained forever out of reach.[10]

After more than thirty years of fruitless search Happy Days began to entertain a heresy: perhaps Tule Canyon contained no ledge, and the gold she panned had been carried there eons ago by an ancient stream from a faraway source. She had made one last effort to nail down a major sale after she located the Mariposa group of claims. In 1935 she rode the rails to call on investors back East, where she cut an exotic figure in her boots and red-checked shirt. Dressing the part sometimes figured in a prospector's sales effort. Harry Stimler, half Shoshone and one of the original locators of Goldfield, though well known in Nevada and California for elegant suits and expensive cars, used to garb himself as a simple Indian prospector when courting eastern investors. Whatever they thought of the "genuine article," the investors were unimpressed by Happy Days's mining properties, and Happy Days was equally unimpressed by New York. She visited briefly with relatives, who urged her to remain. "I couldn't be cooped," she declared and returned to Tule Canyon.[11]

During the thirties the sobriquet that had once fit her sunny disposition turned into a misnomer as Happy Days grew increasingly cantankerous, a condition far from exceptional among prospectors in the western hinterlands during the interwar years. Prospector Carl Lewis recalls that virtually every ghost town had a resident prospector, often a disabled or shell-shocked veteran of World War I (conceivably a tradition for the veteran unable to readjust to civilian life that stretches back to the Civil War). Sometimes their eccentricities bordered on insanity and turned dangerous. One of them was "Bicycle Chain" John Peeler, who lived on top of Mount Hamilton near Ely, Nevada, and could be approached only by old acquaintances who called out his name for half a mile to announce their arrival and avoid being shot; even with them Bicycle Chain kept his rifle handy at all times.[12]

Happy Days herself admitted that she had turned to guns and rocks in her disputes with claim jumpers and cattlemen who trespassed on her territory, and complaints against her multiplied at the county courthouse in Goldfield. Childers, however, suspected that her opponents had resorted to arson on the day Happy Days's cabin mysteriously burned down. The loss of some of her mining claims to men who took advantage of her imperfect understanding of changes in the mining laws did little to sweeten her opinion on the law and its enforcers. Perhaps her anger over injustices real and imagined had been simmering for some time in 1938 when she assaulted the Esmeralda County district attorney. The immediate cause was District Attorney John Houlahan's refusal to arrest Herbert Jester for taking the old Ford. Useless to explain to a woman in a hysterical fury that the Model T was community property belonging to her husband as well as to her. It was a battle of the octogenarians: Houlahan was then eighty-nine; Happy Days, eighty-six. She smashed his shining bald pate with her cane, inflicting severe injuries. The sheriff briefly clapped her in a cell. No charges were filed, but when Houlahan died less than a month later, some believed Happy Days's cane had been a contributing cause.

Before his death Houlahan attempted to have Happy Days committed to the state mental hospital as a person "dangerous to be at large." Childers took a seat in the courtroom at the commitment hearing:

> In all my life I have never seen equaled the sheer drama of the moment that the doctors declared her not only sane, but remarkably clear-minded for her age. The court room was packed on that gray winter day with the old timers of the desert. More than a claim or a human life was at stake. All of the honor, the square-deal reputation of the west was on trial, too. The judge, before he read the doctor's verdict, with mild eyes, sweeping the tense faces there, asked there be no demonstration, but as his quiet voice told them Mrs. Jester would be afforded the protection of the law to re-establish her right to the claims, and then read the doctor's verdict, the room rose in a body and cheered.

Albert Bradshaw, great-grandson of Ferminia Sarras, thought the turning point in the proceedings arrived when the judge put a question to Happy Days and she responded in an affronted and highly refined manner, "For a man of your ability and position, don't you think that's a very improper way to put a question to a person like me?" Fifty years later Bradshaw remembered the moment vividly. It was evident that despite the attack on the district attorney, many still admired Happy Days for her spirit. Goldfielder Frances Carlson recalls, "She had a lot of fire in her. She wanted her way, and she would fight for it too."[13]

In 1942 Happy Days sued her husband for divorce. At the age of ninety, after more than twenty years of marriage, a good many would have turned aside from so drastic a change, but not Happy Days. She charged Herbert Jester with extreme cruelty and testified that he had beaten her, to say nothing of being lazy and unwilling to work. "He spoiled my happiness when he came into my home," she told the judge. Goldfielders who saw Happy Days as the "ruling hand" in the marriage found the beating hard to believe, although they knew the Jesters had fought a great deal. Since Herbert made no appearance in court, his side of the story remained unheard. Happy Days received her divorce and half the mining claims on which the couple had labored so hard together.[14]

Roberta Childers, who drove out to Tule Canyon to interview Happy Days, provides a glimpse of the old woman as she neared her ninetieth year. Her dark brown hair had turned snow white, a striking contrast with her deeply tanned olive skin, but her lively dark eyes were still sharp enough to read a newspaper without glasses. Although rheumatism had crippled her so badly that she could no longer carry out the hard labor of earlier times, she continued to pan a little gold. And she could still sing. When Childers requested the "old songs," presumably those learned long ago in her European girlhood, Happy Days rose to sing them, with arms outflung, in a voice as clear and beautiful as ever. One imagines that voice ringing out over the high peaks of Tule Canyon and wonders if Herbert Jester had endured her violent temper for twenty years because he liked her singing.

Although Happy Days declared herself perfectly content with her life at the Isle of Peace, she soon embarked on another drastic change.

Perhaps, as her health worsened, the prospect of a snowbound winter alone in Tule Canyon looked more formidable than she admitted. Her strength may have failed, but she could still turn to the mystical side that had led her to her richest ground by way of a dream. With the coming of winter she left for San Francisco to tell fortunes, planning to return in the spring. After her return, illness, and possibly a loss of heart, hospitalized her for a while in the spring of 1943 after another suspicious fire in Tule Canyon. She resumed fortune-telling.[15]

And that is the last anyone heard of her. She had told Childers that she wished to be buried in a cave in the peak overlooking the Isle of Peace, and for years it was thought that perhaps her wish had been fulfilled. After all, unusual burials enjoyed a certain precedent in Tule Canyon. In the winter of 1889–90 the Mexican miner Marijilda, remembered for his discovery of an amazing nine-hundred-dollar nugget, had been found frozen to death in a crouched position beside the road with the jug of whiskey he had traveled to Lida to buy cradled between his knees; they buried him the way they found him, complete with jug. The dredges recently working Tule Canyon have already chucked up skulls from a forgotten burial place. Perhaps one day they would rip open a cave where the skeleton of an old woman sits in a rocking chair with a bunch of faded flowers in her hand.

But Happy Days did not receive the death she had wanted. What Nevadans in the deserts around Tule Canyon could tolerate as cantankerousness, and even admire as fiery spirit, San Franciscans considered madness. California mortality records show that in 1946 Happy Days was committed to the mental hospital at Stockton. She died there two years later.[16]

So far as we know, Happy Days had no children. Yet the saga of the women prospectors had not yet ended, and a kind of rebirth and continuity can be traced in other lives. When Happy Days, in her remarkable old age, entered her last decade of mining in Tule Canyon, the career of Panamint Annie, another woman prospector in the Death Valley country, was just beginning. We do not know if Happy Days and Panamint Annie ever met face to face, but they surely knew each other by reputation. Born in the twentieth century, Annie did not start prospecting until the thirties, and although many women prospectors had been ahead of their times, she carried modernity even farther. In contrast to Klondike Helen Seifert's inability to deal with cars or Louise Grantham's reversion to burros, Annie's mechanical skills made her well suited to the motor age. Her experiment with an alternative living arrangement took her far from a conventional home. Her vociferous opinions need no interpretation to be recognized as feminism. Though she did not attain the venerable age of Happy Days, she lived on into the late twentieth century.

The future Panamint Annie was born Mary Elizabeth White on 22 June 1910 in Washington DC, the daughter of an army surgeon and a full-blooded Iroquois woman. Young Mary Elizabeth had smooth black hair and brown eyes: "You could see the Indian in her," in the words of her daughter, Doris Bryant Riemersma. A touch of the devil and a reckless disregard for conventions on proper behavior also appeared early. When she was twelve her father grounded her for roaring around the army base on a motorcycle. The punishment prevented her from joining her mother and sister on an airplane trip—and also saved her from the plane crash that killed them both. The lesson Mary Elizabeth drew from this tragedy was that she had survived because she was "a stinker." In her teens her father wanted her to enter the medical field, and she announced that she would become a doctor. Told by her father that women could not be doctors and she should instead train for nursing, she refused. Again, the future Panamint Annie can be glimpsed. No compromise. No bending by so much as an inch. She will do things her own way or not at all.[17]

By her early twenties Mary Elizabeth had crammed a variety of experiences into her short life. Her first marriage, at age fifteen in Boston, came and went quickly, and her husband kept her second child, a son (her firstborn had died in infancy). She turned to driving trucks of bootleg liquor from Canada to Chicago and throughout her life remained skillful at repairing cars, a knack that adapted her to auto prospecting. She then headed west, sampling Texas and New Mexico and lingering longer in Colorado, where she cooked at dude ranches. At this point in her brief and intense existence it appeared that she had little time left to live. She had contracted tuberculosis in her late teens, and her condition was worsening. When her doctors, holding out little hope for her recovery, prescribed a dry climate, Mary Elizabeth chose the driest of the dry—Death Valley.[18]

After her arrival in 1931 when she was twenty-one Mary Elizabeth White realized that she could not earn her living by cooking at dude ranches where none existed, so she took up prospecting. She spent as much time as possible soaking in the hot springs at Shoshone and drinking in the healing warmth and stillness of the desert. Soon the bleeding lesions in her lungs had healed, and she had regained her beauty: strong clean features, straight black hair cut short to cause no trouble, and skin with the bronze flush of her Iroquois mother. In the years to come she would climb mountains all day in her search for mineral, arm wrestle any man who thought he could play with her, and muck out the ore in her mines as though she had never been ill. When her cure was complete, she briefly returned to Colorado in 1936 and married a cowboy named Bryant, who died when she was seven months pregnant with their child. Panamint Annie returned to the desert, where her daughter Doris was born in 1938. Over her lifetime Annie gave birth to eight children, only four of whom survived.[19]

Soon the name Mary Elizabeth White became a mere technicality; other prospectors had started calling her Panamint Annie, because she reminded them of the original Panamint Annie. The story of this prototypical Death Valley prospector has unfortunately been lost with the memories of these old men, but they used to say that Mary Elizabeth reminded them of the original in several ways: she came from "back East," she prospected, she was a "rough gal," and she sent her daughter away to school.[20]

Although Doris stayed with her paternal aunt in San Bernardino during several school terms, her recollections provide a fascinating glimpse of the life Panamint Annie lived in the 1940s and probably during the depression years before Doris's birth. Home was a 1929 Model A truck, later an old army ambulance. Annie was apparently the first woman prospector to outfit the flatbed of a truck with beds and a tent, turning it into living quarters much like the wagons that had served many prospectors of an earlier age. High in the Panamints, where Annie had claims, winter nights sometimes turned cold enough to freeze the hot-water bottle they used to keep warm. When Doris fretted about where their next meal was coming from, her mother would tell her, "Don't worry about it. Between me and God, we'll take care of it." And a meal always appeared. Sometimes it was a stew from a snake or rabbit Annie had shot. Sometimes the cuisine was not very haut, as when the rabbit was diseased (a food most prospectors would scorn). On those nights Annie would tell Doris if a grub could survive cooking, it had to be "a better being than we are." Once in a while Annie herself went to bed without eating but never hungry enough to sell her keepsake, the first vial of gold she had ever mined.[21]

A good deal of the time Panamint Annie and Doris teamed up with other prospectors. Death Valley ranger and historian Kari Coughlin estimates that at least two hundred people prospected and mined in the mountains of the Death Valley country during these years. Special legislation permitted continued mining after the creation of Death Valley National Monument in 1933, and the west side of the Panamint Mountains lay outside monument boundaries. Although Doris recalls twelve or fourteen women prospectors, mostly working with husbands, Annie was the only woman to join a prospector "family," an informal group of eight or ten, on a comradely basis with no romantic involvements. The family camped in the mountains, sending someone into town for supplies every two to four weeks if they could scrape together the money. Despite limited physical contact with the outside world, radio had greatly reduced the prospector's isolation. On their odyssey across the desert in the summer of 1914 Josephine and George Scott did not learn of the outbreak of World War I until a passing traveler told them; during World War II Annie's Death Valley family gathered each evening around a radio to listen to the news and move the thumbtacks representing the positions of the opposing armies around on a map.[22]

In the division of domestic tasks among family members, even this tough and unconventional woman accepted a fairly traditional role as laundress, baker, and healer. Everyone shared the cooking over a communal campfire. Annie made special treats, baking cinnamon rolls and, most memorably, frying potato chips on the occasion when an intrepid vendor sold the family a fifty-pound sack of potatoes. She also did the laundry, probably out of consideration for her companions, having observed that "men hate to wash." In return they gave her extra water and food. When first aid was necessary, she administered it with firm yet gentle hands fully capable of healing fingers slashed to the bone in an accident, setting broken bones, or delivering a baby, as she had done more than once, a hint of the doctor she might have become.

Doris was treated like a little treasure by eight strict but kindly uncles called Old Man Black, One-Eyed Jack, and so forth. No one ever swore in her presence, including her mother, who was known for "language that would blister the ears of a drill sergeant." The uncles insisted that Doris have her sponge bath each evening, even when they ran so low on the water they brought up in large galvanized tanks from the spring at the base of the hill that they had to go without the prime necessity of a miner's existence—his coffee.[23]

The main business of the family, of course, was prospecting. Each pursued this on his own and so intensively that sometimes it continued into the night by lantern light. When someone made a strike, he would "come dancing in." After the family heard the news, absolute discretion was the rule. No loose talk at the assayer's shop. No spreading the word through the bars on a drunken spree of celebration. Mining claims belonging to anyone in the family were never discussed with outsiders, no matter how drunk one became. Living as they did, far beyond the reach of the law, where a deputy sheriff might be glimpsed once a year or so, the family guarded against claim jumpers on their many unrecorded claims by patrolling for one another and "watching our own backs."[24]

Although the older family members saw the thirties and forties as safer than the days when desperadoes had been known to rob a prospector of his gold, his claim, and his life, the desert itself remained as deadly as in the time of Lillian Malcolm and Mrs. Riggs. Nonetheless, Panamint Annie had no tales to tell of perils narrowly survived, because she avoided dangerous situations and scrupulously followed her own rules for desert survival. Whenever Doris returned from another term at school, her mother would rehearse her in the catechism: "Anything that looks like a rope coiled, stay away. Never put your hand on a rock without looking. So many people get disoriented. Fix your stationary block wherever you're going. Whether it's this mountain or this rock, always remember that if you pass it more than twice you're going the wrong way. Never leave a vehicle, because the distance is so vast that you can't comprehend it." Annie's invariable summer uniform consisted of jeans, T-shirt, light shirt, and high miner's boots to guard against snakebite. (Only Klondike Helen Seifert coexisted comfortably with snakes; she said it pleased her to encounter anything alive in the desert and always allowed snakes to slither on their way in peace.) Annie, by contrast, carried a gun solely for the purpose of shooting rabbits for dinner and snakes. Aside from rattlers, only one thing alarmed her: when she lost her teeth in old age, she refused to wear dentures for fear she might swallow them.[25]

Annie's prospecting methods were a combination of instinct and looking for the colors according to the mystical rule the old-timers had taught her: "Listen and the mountains will talk to you. They'll tell you where the gold is if you listen." Annie listened and tirelessly hunted a wide variety of minerals from gold to uranium. Always excited by the unlimited possibilities awaiting her, she would be out before daylight, with her hammer on her belt, a holed-up shovel, and her pick in hand, not returning until after dark. Doris tagged along at her heels. When her mother said, "I think that mountain has something in it," and commenced to walk back and forth over the ground before zeroing in on the spot where she would take samples, Doris settled down to play with lizards and horned toads. When Annie developed a mine, she did the timbering, blasting, and mucking herself and made her own candles for underground work in order to save money on kerosene.[26]

Occasionally, she made a good strike worth as much as ten thousand dollars, but, as Doris recalls, "she blew it as fast as she made it." Supporting her children had top priority, next came debts to be paid, a stake for her next prospecting trip, necessities long postponed such as new tires for the truck, and quiet charities such as shoes and food for Indian friends. Then came the binge drinking and, above all, the gambling. Annie never touched liquor until she turned forty-five, after which her three-day benders became part of Death Valley folklore. One time she broke her back in a fall and started driving to Las Vegas for medical attention; the trip took her three days because she painfully dragged herself into every bar along the way. Her back healed with no ill effects beyond an inability to raise her arm above her head, but on another occasion, her drinking lost her the best gold strike she ever made. When she came into town for supplies, she went on a prolonged binge with a group of men. After the alcoholic fog cleared from her mind, the place where she found gold had vanished from memory. "I know it's up there," she would say. "I'll find it. You wait." But she never did. Perhaps even a bonanza would scarcely have altered her way of life, because she would have gambled away the proceeds at blackjack or keno. Doris, who grew up with a longing for certainties, saw her mother's gambling as an intrinsic part of the prospector's mindset. Prospecting itself was a gamble. Waking each morning, as Annie did, with an unreasoning belief that this would be the day she would finally "hit it" in the mountains seemed to Doris the very essence of gambling.[27]

Panamint Annie may have lied about her mines, like many a prospector before and since, though she would insist that she merely "exaggerated," but she always repaid her grubstakers with scrupulous fairness. Indeed, she was one of the few women prospectors known to work on grubstakes and to receive some of them from another woman. Annie split her ten-thousand-dollar strike with this woman, the owner of a grocery store near Death Valley Junction. When her prospecting yielded nothing, Annie endeavored to repay her grubstaker all the same by repairing the transmission on the woman's car. Annie also had a woman partner for some years, Mrs. Frederica Hessler, a Georgia schoolteacher who had inherited the entire town of Rhyolite from her brother, after the booming mining camp of the early twentieth century had turned into a ghost town where wind moaned through the ruins of massive gray stone walls. On a nearby mountain Panamint Annie and Frederica worked together at their gold mine, a site that today is being extensively mined for great profit.[28]

As these working partnerships suggest, Annie's relationships with other women were based on friendship and cooperation rather than competition. She knew and liked Louise Grantham. Although she bristled whenever she saw a woman standing helplessly by the road unable to change a tire, Annie harbored no scorn for women who had led conventional lives and lacked her ability to survive in the wilderness. In Doris's words, "Mom always had a philosophy that each individual has their own capabilities, whether you use your mind or your body, your strength, or God-given talent. She never looked down at anybody." Nor did conventional women hold their skirts aside from her as they did from Lillian Malcolm. Her encounters with visitors to Death Valley demonstrate this. When Annie appeared on one occasion in her last years, unwashed, bizarrely clothed, giving full vent to her opinions in sulphurous language, and preceded by her reputation as one who would "bum around with anyone who had the price of a bottle and didn't much care what was in it," a middle-class woman sightseer warmed to her at once. Somehow the sheer force of Annie's charismatic personality swept all before it. One fervent admirer saw Annie and John Wayne as the last immortals in the West.[29]

Panamint Annie usually dealt with problems by denying they existed, and child care was no exception. She strapped her baby girl Mary Ann onto her back and took her down into the mines much as her Iroquois forebears would have done and as she herself had probably done with Doris when the child was too small to remember. At other times Annie neutralized the perennial incompatibility of prospecting and child care by having Doris watch the younger children. All the same, when her youngest son, Bill, born the year she turned thirty-seven in 1947, reached school age and she could not arrange to send him away, she felt obliged to move down from the mountains into a makeshift cabin in Beatty, a small settlement across the hills from Rhyolite, where he could attend school. During this period she mined nearby with Frederica Hessler and prospected intensively throughout the area.

The passing parade of Annie's husbands and live-ins showed one common characteristic: all shared her passion for mining. "Some of them would live, sleep, and die mining," commented Doris. On the whole, these liaisons appeared neither long-lasting nor deeply felt. "Some of them treated her nice. Some of them didn't. There was nothing unusual about them," was Doris's dry assessment. And all had to fit in with Annie's freewheeling way of life, which was "I do whatever I want to do when the mood is on me." Perhaps mining engineer Bill Skogli, with whom Annie worked a mine near Shoshone and went on long prospecting sojourns in the hills, stood out a little

Panamint Annie with her daughters, Doris (*standing*)
and Mary Ann (courtesy of Doris Riemersma).

from the rest. At least, when he left to mine in Arizona and neither wrote nor returned, Annie took sufficient notice to make a false report that he had stolen her car in order to find out what became of him. When she learned that Skogli had died from a heart attack, she said in her usual stoic way, "I really cared for him but he just goes off and dies on me."[30]

Annie would not have classified that false report as a lie, nor would anyone else in Death Valley, where she was known for her raw honesty and a kind of emotional absolutism. She never mentioned people she disliked: they simply did not exist. She buried pain deep within herself. When little Mary Ann fell and died from a concussion at age two, Annie was so grief-stricken that she forebade anyone to mention Mary Ann's name again. Only once did Doris ever see her mother cry, and that was at Mary Ann's funeral. After that day Annie's sorrow stayed inside, breaking out only when her little son Bill struck his head in a fall and she went temporarily berserk with fear that it could happen all over again. (Bill suffered no ill effects). Usually, she brushed difficulties aside with the maxim "Tomorrow will take care of itself." More than twenty years after her death it was her unashamed and undiluted candor, her way of stripping things down to the stark essentials the way she had stripped her life, that people remembered most: "She wasn't afraid to tell you what it was, no matter how bad it hurt."

Although she never acknowledged pain, hunger, grief, or obstacles, Annie voiced strong opinions on a wide variety of subjects, sometimes telephoning the Nevada governor with unsolicited advice. Equality for women was a strong theme of hers, and none could doubt that she had lived what she believed, ever since she took her fateful motorcycle ride. She thought, and often said, a woman could do any job a man could do, the only difference being that a woman could not lift quite so heavy a load. She strongly favored equal pay for equal work and as strongly opposed female dependency ("Don't wait for a man to do something for you, or you'll be waiting for an eternity"). She raised Doris to be what she believed all women should become—independent. Like many women prospectors before her, she saw the wilderness as a proving ground for independence. When Doris once burst into tears and said she hated the desert, Annie laughed long and hard and told her,

"Doris, if you only knew—and you will someday. When you're in a city, everyone does things for you. You got people taking care of running water, electricity, picking up trash for you. When you're out on your own by yourself, there's no one to do it for you. You have to learn to do it yourself." Annie's belief in woman's equality also encompassed sexual behavior and justified her many lovers: "It's no big deal. Men do it all the time." She was, in many ways, a thoroughly modern woman in an archaic way of life.[31]

Deep pleasure in the wilderness remained a powerful element in prospecting from the beginning, but Annie, more than any woman except perhaps Fannie Quigley, exemplified the prospector as naturalist. Although she acknowledged that the desert was "the worst thing in the world on humans," she knew the land and all the living things on it as no one else did and treasured them, from the young buck glimpsed on a mountain ledge ("Now you show me a more beautiful sight than that!") to the swift-moving roadrunner and the nesting eagle. When Doris once picked a bunch of wildflowers, her mother cautioned her to take only two or three, because the flowers are "God's decoration for the desert." It was said that she knew every bird's nest from Death Valley to Tonopah, and Death Valley rangers and naturalists had a high regard for her knowledge of the flora and fauna. As the *Los Angeles Times* put it, "she probably knows more about the National Monument than any person alive." Annie herself was modest: "I haven't seen it all, but I'm gaining on it." In her last years, when the strength that had formerly moved boulders failed her, she still went up Titus Canyon, where she had often mined, to see the view and hear the mountains talk. "The desert is the sea," she used to say. "It moves just like waves in the ocean."[32]

Toward the end, crippled by arthritis, ravaged by cancer until she lost nearly half her normal weight, and unable to mine, she scraped a living by selling homemade jewelry and other souvenirs from her station wagon. But she still spoke of prospecting: "As soon as I get a stake, I'm going out in the hills and make another strike." There was another dream she talked about from time to time: "There's places in this world no man has ever been, and I'm going to find it." Born earlier, she would no doubt have become the mountain woman and explorer on new frontiers that she was so well suited to be. She died in September 1979 and was buried in the little cemetery at Rhyolite. When the shaggy Joshua palm over her grave bloomed the following spring for the first time in living memory, Doris saw the shining white blossom as a kind of benediction.[33]

# TEN

# Anna Rechel:
# The Last Prospector
# in Rawhide

As Goldfield began sliding into decline, Tex Rickard sold his share in the once prosperous Northern Saloon and tacked a sign over the door of an abandoned church:

> This Church Is Closed. God Has Gone to Rawhide.

If that was so, the Almighty neither stayed long nor exerted His influence strongly, for Rawhide became chiefly known for two things, the brevity of its boom and the chicanery of its stock promotions. Initial gold discoveries in 1906 northeast of Walker Lake in Nevada led to the organization of a mining district the following year and a boom that brought perhaps seven thousand hopefuls flocking into the arid hills by the summer of 1908. An instant city with every modern convenience sprang up, only to be partially destroyed by a fire in September of that year. Although much was rebuilt, it became increasingly evident that Rawhide's ore deposits had yielded little to support the fantastic promises of its promoters. Extensive development efforts had produced less than a million and a half dollars' worth of gold. A ghost town rapidly replaced the instant city. By 1910 only a few more than five hundred people of the teeming thousands once crowding the streets remained; ten years later the number had dwindled to fifty.[1]

As usual, women prospectors had joined the Rawhide boomers. Mrs. Lillian Hall, a former Klondiker, her husband apparently divorced or dead, made locations in the area in the winter of 1907–8 and remained long enough to construct a large, two-story house. Newspaperwoman Belle Dormer, another former Klondiker, secured claims in the area and wrote poetry in the newspaper. Irish-born Nora Boyle deserted Goldfield for Rawhide, where she prospected and thought of herself as a "lucky girl." As the exodus gathered momentum, however, even the lucky girl decided she would have no luck in Rawhide, and these women departed with the rest. By the time the woman who was to be the last living resident of Rawhide arrived on the scene, no memory remained of the women prospectors who had gone before her.[2]

Anna Frances Elleser was no native of the mining frontier. Born the youngest of seven children on 1 January 1884 to prosperous German immigrant parents in Pearl River, New Jersey, she grew up in Tappan, New York, in a gracious, two-story suburban mansion with a veranda overhung by vines and a glassed-in sunroom overlooking green, wooded hills. Though she learned no more than a few words of German from her family, her cooking reflected her German background, and her sauerbraten is still remembered with pleasure. She became a beauty; a picture of her at twenty shows auburn hair worn in a smoothly bouffant upsweep, a dimpled chin, a slightly wide mouth, and an expression of calm sweetness. Her parents died in 1905–6, and Anna operated an ice cream parlor with the man who was to be her close companion and friend wherever she went for most of her life, her older brother Walter. She also married and bore a son, who died soon after his birth. Nothing is known of the marriage except that it was unhappy and that Anna refused to tolerate her situation. As her daughter-in-law later said of her, "She was probably about five foot two or three. But when she was strong-minded, you'd have thought she was six feet tall." A divorce was still an unusual and daring step for a young woman in the East. Nonetheless, Anna obtained one, and when she learned that a technicality might invalidate her second marriage in 1911 to George Rechel, the dark, dashing, clean-shaven man she had fallen in love with, the Rechels set off in 1912 for Nevada, already a mecca for easy divorce. There Anna divorced her first husband anew and remarried George.[3]

The old saying that the West was "fine for men and dogs but hell on women and horses" has been thought to apply with particular force to the deserts, and indeed women themselves not infrequently testified to this effect. Women who traveled the overland trails often saw the desert as an ordeal to be put behind them as quickly as possible; the wife of a Portuguese miner in Golconda wrote a poem concluding, "And women

Anna Rechel around 1904 (courtesy of Rees Mortensen).

can never tell / How the desert makes of our life a hell"; journalist Frederick Bechdolt observed of a woman reluctantly compelled to spend her life in a desert outpost she disliked, "The desert had defeated her as it had defeated many another woman." Anna turned out to be the antithesis of this widespread female antipathy to the arid wastelands of the West. According to her daughter Rees, she "fell in love" with the desert as soon as she saw it, and during more than half a century of hardship and privation, it never defeated her.[4]

Accompanied by Anna's faithful brother Walter, the Rechels homesteaded a ranch south of Fernley, Nevada. Over the next nine years Anna gave birth to six children in the ranch house bedroom. Four survived: Rees, born in 1914; Fern, 1915; George, 1919; and Walter, nicknamed "Pal," in 1921. In the crevices between the hard work of a ranch wife and the birthing and raising of children, an obsession started to take root. A prospector named Bill Stewart began stopping by the ranch with his wagon and horses on his journeys to and from Fernley. The scene is a familiar one in the lives of mining women. Idah Strobridge wrote of the prospector's tale that carries "conviction to the heart" in a way that surpasses the written word: "For you will believe. Ay! you will believe it is true; you will believe that there is a marvel of gold there for the lucky one who is to find it. . . . Strange thoughts will be yours, of things that—in that strange land—in your heart, you feel might very well be. And the truth of what you may hear, you will not question." Thus did Helen Cottrell listen to the story of the lost mine; so too did the Petersons fall under the spell of the prospector who drew them into the desert. As the big wood stove warmed the Rechel ranch house kitchen with its checked curtains and the Coleman lamp with the globular shade burned late into the night, Stewart spoke and Anna listened with rapt attention to his tales of fortunes narrowly missed, lost mines, and bonanzas waiting in the hills. It was the moment of enchantment.[5]

Anna absorbed herself in every book and journal on mining that she could find and began studying rock kits. The books became so worn from constant perusal that she had to re-cover them. Soon the family began heading into the hills in the hay wagon to prospect for the day or the weekend. The thought of finding a bonanza excited Anna's husband, but he strolled around the hills rather casually and dismissed every rock he encountered as "malachite." Anna, by contrast, prospected intensively, pounding every likely-looking specimen and eagerly examining it with her glass. Nonetheless, many years would pass before even an enthusiast such as she struck a prospect worth developing. No matter. For Anna there was another dimension. "She was in love with the hills," says Rees. Prospecting gave her the way to enter the world she glimpsed on the horizon.[6]

Despite a great deal of hard work, the homestead failed to prosper. The Rechels tried raising rabbits for the San Francisco market in addition to their hay crop; they tried leasing part of their land to a sheep rancher while George and Walter took jobs in town and Anna did the remaining ranch work. As economic conditions for the small rancher worsened with the approaching depression, nothing they tried helped much. They decided to abandon the homestead, and after a brief sojourn in Fallon they embarked on a different life. Around 1931 they moved into the ghost town of Rawhide, where they could live cheaply and Anna could prospect full-time; George worked for the highway department as an inspector and visited his family on weekends.[7]

In those days the absence of trees, the piles of white and cream-colored tailings, the rounded hills, and the farther mountains, broken as though trampled and collapsed, gave the old ghost town the look of an abandoned sandbox. The venerable stone jail still stood, with the metal cage used as a cell inside; so did the stone cellar, but the trench beside it that used to give customers in Tex Rickard's Northern Saloon quick access to the prostitutes working in Stingaree Gulch led into empty space, like most of the roads that webbed the hills and crisscrossed the flats. The Rechels moved into one of the larger and better surviving structures, the two-bedroom frame cabin that had belonged to Tex Rickard. Saloon owners had always looked to their comforts, and Anna's soft quilts, antiques, and other touches made the old house a still more comfortable home.

Nonetheless, even in the best of cabins Rawhide offered few amenities. It had "no telephones, no gas stations, no water, no groceries, no nothing," said Jim Mortensen, one of Anna's sons-in-law, adding somewhat incongruously, "It was a great town." Rawhiders caught as much water as possible in rain barrels and hauled in the rest nine miles or more from Dead Horse Wells or the hot springs; the mineralized hot spring water turned so yellow within a few days that fastidious visitors refused to drink it. Later it turned black from repeated reuse. With no refrigeration or fresh meat, canned salmon was a staple of Rawhide cuisine. The most critical item, however, was "get away gas," the five-gallon can that every Rawhider kept at hand for getting out of town if necessary.[8] It was a very different world from the gracious suburban mansion where Anna had grown up, but she preferred it to any other.

Jim Mortensen estimates that about a hundred people lived and worked within a ten-mile radius of Rawhide at the time of the Rechels' arrival. In the cities, he remembers, "you'd starve to death" because there was "no work at all" during the depression; in Rawhide you could simply pick out a deserted cabin, move in for nothing, and make enough to feed yourself by mining, the sole occupation of the Rawhiders. In more abundant places, such as the Arctic village where Nellie Cashman spent her last years, people made "side money" and supplied their own needs in a variety of ways, by hunting, trapping, fishing, berrying, woodcutting, and so forth. The gray sage desert at Rawhide offered no such opportunities. People lived by working the tailings left by the old mines of the boom days. They ran the dirt through a dry washer, agitating it up and down so that the heavy gold bits lingered on the riffle board; then they panned down the gold-bearing material and drew it out with quicksilver. On the next trip to town Rawhide miners sold what they had accumulated to the gold buyer in Fallon, who paid sixteen dollars an ounce, half the normal price, because Rawhide gold was low grade and came in small quantities. Rawhiders had lower expectations than the Coffeys on the Agua Fria in the same period. If a Rawhider made a dollar a day, he saw it as "pretty big money." Despite the melancholy message implicit in the old prospect holes that peppered the ground at every turn, the undying hope of uncovering the glory hole that others had overlooked leavened the harshness of this existence, for Anna no less than the rest. Said Rees, "She just knew that she was going to find it. It kept her going." Among all those working the Rawhide region Anna was the only woman prospector.[9]

When the Rechels moved to Rawhide, their sons George and Pal were only twelve and ten, and Anna faced the perennial problem of the woman prospector: how to educate her children in a remote place. The solution was a unique one. The boys attended a one-room school taught by their sister Rees until 1934, when the dwindling population of Rawhide could no longer supply the required minimum of five pupils and the school closed. The boys then boarded at Schurz, a village on the Indian reservation some distance away while they attended school. Later Anna's brother Walter returned from New York, where he had taken a job for some years after the homestead failed, and lived in Fallon to maintain a home for Pal during school terms. Anna may have payed a price for this separation in the rocky relationship that developed with her son Pal.[10]

Difficulties with her younger son were eclipsed, however, by the tragedies that struck Anna in the late 1930s. A stroke left her husband partially paralyzed and able to walk only haltingly with a cane. While boarding at Schurz to attend school, her son George suffered a burst appendix. Despite emergency surgery, he made a poor recovery, and in July 1937 he died at seventeen from peritonitis. The following January, soon after her fifty-fourth birthday, Anna's husband died as well. Her daughters had married and moved away. Thus, of the family of seven once clustered around the kitchen table, there remained only her younger son Pal and her brother Walter. The disappearance of his entire savings in a depression-era bank failure had left Walter dispirited and almost childlike in his emotional dependence on Anna. His faith in her strength was not misplaced. Anna had lost a great deal but never her delight in the desert or her effervescent hopes. She stayed on in Rawhide.

Over the decades that followed, changes in the world outside reverberated in remote Rawhide. World War II came. Pal married and joined the army. Although he had never taken an interest in mining, Anna henceforth staked claims in his name to provide a legacy in the event of her death. With Walter assisting her, she poured all her energies into mining tungsten for the war effort. Wearing a hardhat and jeans, Anna would climb a twenty-five-foot ladder down the mine shaft they had dug, set the dynamite fuses, then hasten up the ladder before the blast. After the dust settled she descended to shovel rock fragments into a bucket attached to a pulley and Walter cranked up the windlass by hand. If that struck some as remarkably hard labor for a small and slender woman, it would not have occurred to Walter that there was something his sister could not do, and he usually left anything that came up in her capable hands. On one occasion a flat tire needed patching and repair. Anna left it for quite some time, hoping that it might dawn on Walter that he should fix it. Nothing happened, so Anna finally hauled out the tire and took it off the rim. Walter made no move to help, but he and several men standing about with him did offer comments and advice (Panamint Annie would not have been surprised).[11]

The shadow of greater loss fell over Anna when word came that Pal was missing in action. But on a memorable midnight his bride, LaRae, arrived in Rawhide, driven by a friend who knew the road, with news that Pal had been taken prisoner by the Germans and might yet be alive. When daylight came LaRae saw the old ghost town for the first time and thought to herself that Anna must be "a little off her rocker" to live in such a desolate place. LaRae had been raised in green, lush farming country near the Snake River in Idaho: "I thought, 'Where's my mountains? Where's my pine trees? Where's my green grass? Where's all the greens?' She taught me to see the beautiful colors in the mountains here. . . . She taught me to love the desert." And instead of regarding Anna as slightly mad, LaRae began to understand her mother-in-law: "I got to know her, and know what she was, and what she stood for, and her reasons for what she was doing. I got to admire her more all the time because I thought, 'This lady does what she wants to do. She goes ahead and does it. She doesn't listen to what other people tell her you ought to do.'" That admiration only increased in the years after Pal came home and settled down with LaRae in Fallon.[12]

The 1950s arrived, bringing the uranium boom that electrified the mining world, its women prospectors along with the rest. Anna walked the hills with a Geiger counter, Panamint Annie declared she had found uranium, and Josie Pearl fantasized about making a million with some "elegant" uranium claims. The craze that produced more than three hundred thousand mining claims in four Utah counties undoubtedly included other women who embarked on their mining careers too late to fall within the confines of this book. The main exceptions, precursors to this midcentury surge of amateurs with clicking machines and scant acquaintance with mining, were two Wyoming women, Mrs. S. F. Gillespie, an experienced prospector who found radium in 1929, and the somewhat better known Minnie Belle McCormick. While she was still a small child, Minnie Belle's father abandoned the Kansas farm where she was born around 1880 to go prospecting in the Rockies. She grew up in Leadville and Cripple Creek, Colorado. Before she turned ten she began waiting on tables, the commencement of a life of hard work as a cook similar to Josie Pearl's. She also resembled Josie in a passion for prospecting that dated from girlhood. In 1903 she married William McCormick, a man who shared her interests; the press described him as "a rancher by trade, but a prospector at heart." The couple moved to Wamsutter, Wyoming, with their three children in 1916, and Minnie Belle continued to work as a cook and to prospect. Her first notable find, carbon and alum deposits south of Wamsutter, came in 1925, but she failed to attract investment capital to develop them.[13]

Minnie Belle's next discovery came in 1936 after her usual seasonal work cooking at a sheep shearing camp. One of the sheepherders had told her of seeing gold nuggets in the Lost Creek area, so when the McCormicks set off for a family picnic, Minnie Belle suggested Lost Creek. After her initial investigation yielded no treasures, her little grandson lost interest and slid down the steep bank to wade in the creek. And there they were—yellow stones gleaming in the furrows cut in the red earth by his heels. What they might be proved a difficult question, however. As Minnie Belle collected samples, she quickly realized that their weight was too light and their color too greenish to be gold. She considered sulphur, but the taste seemed wrong. Back in her little house in Wamsutter she pored over her mineralogy books without finding any answers. Numerous analysts to whom she sent samples declared themselves equally puzzled. A year afterward a Harvard scientist confirmed her theory that the mystery rocks were carnotite, a complex mineral compound often containing uranium. Later the substance was positively identified as uranium.

For several years nothing happened. Until World War II and the advent of the atomic bomb the American market for uranium remained small. When the national atomic energy program began after the war, government geologists tested the Lost Creek claims and Minnie Belle received one of the limited number of licenses granted by the government for mining uranium. Asked what she planned to do with the great wealth that now seemed within reach, Minnie Belle voiced no grandiose plans. She felt disinclined to leave her little house, papered with calendars and magazine covers, for anything more luxurious, but at nearly seventy she confessed to feeling "old and tired" after a lifetime of hard work. She would have liked to hang up her apron and quit cooking. Unfortunately, like most uranium prospectors, she found no buyer for her claim. Overshadowed by other discoveries, the Lost Creek deposits remained undeveloped, and at the time of her death in 1951, Minnie Belle still had not achieved her one modest ambition.[14]

Anna Rechel also had her share of big mine sales that failed to materialize. She corresponded with a number of investors, and some actually came to Rawhide to examine her claims. Others never quite arrived. The promoter Bill Brettner announced five or six times that he was bringing in a serious investor eager to develop Anna's properties and make millions for everyone concerned. Sometime later Brettner would glibly explain that his investor had suffered a heart attack at the airport or some other last-minute calamity. Despite the fact that she never sold a claim, Anna continued to believe that Rawhide mining would yield bountiful returns when, and only when, a large company brought in sufficient capital to develop the mines. Time would show how right she was.

Brettner's charades failed to dent Anna's enthusiasm for prospecting. After her titanium mining ceased with the end of the war, she worked with an exceptionally competent Rawhide miner named Smedley, who prospected with her and taught her a great deal. Every morning at an early hour—for Anna believed and often quoted the old German saying that "the morning hours have gold in their teeth"—she would walk a half-mile down the trail to meet Smedley, and they would spend the day side by side dry-washing placer gold. After Smedley pulled up stakes, she prospected alone once more. She rediscovered an old Spanish turquoise mine not far from Rawhide and polished and sold the greenish, heavily veined turquoise herself. Dreams and intuition played no part in her prospecting. She relied on her pick and on various mechanical aids: her metal detector, her Geiger counter, and her black light, a battery-operated device about the size of a large camera that was supposed to reveal metals by showing different colored lights. Like Panamint Annie and her Death Valley family, Anna often continued her prospecting into the night. She would bed down on a mattress she kept in the back of her truck and enjoy the beauty of the desert by moonlight. She spoke to her family of the pleasure she took in watching a pack of wild dogs race yelping over the hills. Perhaps in spirit she ran with them.[15]

The pickup truck in which Anna slept was an old rattletrap that barely ran and continually tried her patience. If those rich investors who repeatedly vaporized at the airport with Brettner had ever presented her with real cold cash, the one fantasy she would have indulged in was as modest as Minnie Belle McCormick's desire to quit cooking: she would have liked to buy a new truck. Since she visualized it as an unstoppable powerhouse roaring straight up the mountains, her family was slightly relieved that she never realized her wish. It was through the vagaries of her old truck that Anna's last romance began. Her prospecting had taken her far out in the hills when the battery in her truck died. Fortunately, Alvin Nelson, an old miner from Gabbs, happened to be prospecting not far away, and he presented her with his spare battery.

Soon Nelson began stopping by to visit Anna in Rawhide. He saw that this slim, still beautiful woman was the mistress of a comfortable home and so fine a cook that people used to say, "I'd rather have Anna's leftovers than anyone else's banquet" (unlike the customer in Nellie Cashman's restaurant, no one had to be forced at gunpoint to eat Anna's cooking). It did not take Nelson long to figure the way to Anna's heart: he promised that if she married him they would buy a new four-wheel-drive vehicle and prospect together far and wide over the hills. And Nelson was a talker. He held forth for hours, painting a picture in glowing detail of the exciting life that lay ahead of them. Anna listened. The death in 1954 of her brother Walter, the lifetime companion who had outlasted husbands and children, may have left her a little lonely. At seventy-two, she thought a companionable marriage to someone who shared her interest in prospecting made a good deal of sense. Besides, there was the lure of that new truck. When Anna and Alvin Nelson went to the courthouse for a marriage license, county officials, who had never seen such elderly applicants before, laughingly gave them the document free of charge.

A rude awakening ensued. Nelson did not buy the new truck. In fact, Anna soon realized that her bridegroom was too elderly and infirm to do any of the things he had so vividly described. He had really wanted not a prospecting partner but a nurse who would stay home, take care of him, cook delicious meals, and wash his socks. Anna declined to be anyone's nurse. Her life's work lay out in the desert, and as Rees put it, "She wasn't about to be tied down." In short order, Anna divorced Nelson. Her admiring daughter-in-law LaRae saw this refusal to allow the husband who had promised Anna a full and active partnership in mining to turn her into a housewife as an integral part of her strength of character and modern sense of women's rights, "about fifty years ahead of her time."[16]

Although this brief marriage late in life was now behind her and all her family had died or departed, Anna never lacked company. Because of her gracious, hospitable ways and her gift for making every visitor feel warmly welcome, Anna's kitchen became the gathering place for the remaining residents of Rawhide, and a good deal of socializing was characteristic of old mining camps. Anna herself remarked, "As for seeing people, I probably see more than I would in Fallon. In towns everybody is just too busy to visit." In times of crisis, as on pleasant evenings and during convivial winter lunches that lasted well into the afternoon, Anna's kitchen was the gathering place. When the Atomic Energy Commission embarked in 1962 on the Plowshare Project, an experiment in using atomic power to dig harbors, canals, and other excavations, an atomic blast was detonated not far from Rawhide. Barbara and Dorothy Powell, who then lived "just a whoop and a holler" from Anna's home, remembered, "Now what we decided to do—this was a human need—was to get together. And the place you would naturally get together was at Annie Rechels' kitchen. . . . Nobody thought about going anywhere else." They found Anna's calm fatalism very soothing: "She was so relaxed about it. Her way of looking at it was if the government blew us up, they just simply would blow us up."[17]

Anna may have viewed the possibility of being blown to bits by atomic bomb testing with equanimity, but many of her political ideas were forward looking, deeply held, vigorously expressed, and far from passive. As Rees says, "she was always reforming the world." In the presidential campaign of 1924 she passionately favored the third-party candidacy of the midwestern Progressive Robert La Follette. She leveled many a withering blast at the railroad monopolies. She believed in an equality of opportunity that would allow people to choose the work that interested them. She saw an oppressed working class, its members compelled to work at jobs they disliked for subsistence wages in order to live. In a rightly ordered society, she often said, women would not be compelled to work for such low wages that they could barely support their families, or to depend on men for their support. The government should provide free day care for children, women should receive equal pay, and above all, society's attitude toward the working woman needed to change. Instead of being tied to the roles of mother and housewife, women should be free to pursue the careers that interested them. This included prospecting, which she considered essential, because the American economy depended on the prospector's discoveries. And none could doubt that Anna had lived what she believed. In Rees's words, "she was a women's libber from the beginning."[18]

Overall, the available sources do not support the theory that women prospectors were too removed from normal society and too absorbed in their wilderness adventures for political involvement. Even before the days of woman suffrage Nellie Cashman had exerted her political influence and raised funds for the Irish cause; Josie Pearl had been a Republican activist and had lobbied the Nevada legislature to revise the teachers' pension law; Lydia Adams-Williams, a descendant of the famous New England family and the first woman locator at Dutch Creek, Nevada, in 1906, ran unsuccessfully for the U.S. Senate in the 1922 Nevada primary; and Panamint Annie, who had emphatic opinions on every subject from speed limits to women's rights, treated the Nevada governor to her unsolicited advice. The main exception was the Coloradan Mrs. Atwood, who proclaimed disinterest in politics and only once exercised her right to vote.[19] Possibly, the thread of activism among the women prospectors originated because staking out a position far beyond traditional boundaries obliged them to define and defend it. Women who had crashed through the occupational barriers would scarcely turn back from political participation as an unsuitable activity for females. Nor would these almost uniformly strong-minded, self-confident, and independent women suddenly mutate into hesitant, deferential creatures when they entered the political realm.

Anna's political ideas, like her conclusions on most subjects, emerged as the result of deep and searching thought. More than any other woman in a century of prospecting the mining frontier, she typified the intellectual side of the prospector, and there is some evidence to suggest that the prospector's common image as an illiterate primitive missed the mark. Among the prospectors at South Pass, Wyoming, journalist James Chisholm met "some grave and temperate men of sedate habits and superior intelligence with whom it is a pleasure to converse; who love to talk on history, politics, science and literature; who are well versed in geological theories. . . . They take broad and liberal views. They are thinkers, for their experience is obtained at first hand and they have to shape their information into thought for themselves." Author Robert Marshall administered intelligence tests to the gold miners in the Koyukuk and found four times more in the superior range than in a group of typical Americans. Anna would surely have ranked equally high. For pleasure, a stimulating discussion of ideas, especially controversial ones, was second only to a conversation on mining. Although her education had not advanced beyond the eighth grade, she could do algebra and played chess whenever she could find a partner. Day in and day out, she read voraciously. Despite her preference for mining books and journals, she was intensely interested and well informed on a plethora of subjects.[20]

As the years passed and the last hangers-on in Rawhide died or "skinned out," it became harder to find a chess partner. Anna stayed on. In the earlier years she had dashed off with the rest when new mining excitements erupted at Talapoosa, Rabbithole, and other sites. "She couldn't wait to get up there," said Rees. "It was a dream and a story. . . . When they'd hear about it, they'd have to go look at it. It was just in their blood." But she had always returned to Rawhide, drawn back to the hills of cream-colored sand, speckled with tiny dots of gray sagebrush and topped with squared gray crests of exposed rock, back to the familiar lavender-gray shape of Pilot Cone, like a volcano with a rounded tip, and to the rose-banded mesas in the far distance. Anna came to see herself as the guardian of Rawhide. She would not allow even members of her own family to take so much as a board from the deserted buildings with their fine wooden desks and other furnishings undisturbed inside since the day their owners had departed. Occasionally, tourists curious to see a ghost town peered inside the windows. Often they were invited to have a cup of tea by a gracious old lady whose refinement amid the crude ruins took them by surprise. Some visitors were so charmed that they returned each year, less to see the stone jail and the other old buildings than to see Anna. Like Panamint Annie, she lived long enough to become something of a tourist attraction in her own right—but never what Josie Pearl would have called a "pet coon."[21]

Finally, the time came in the 1960s when no one remained in Rawhide but Anna and a big, rugged old miner named Bill McGrath who had lived there as long as she, more than thirty years. McGrath, quiet, clean-shaven, and always gentlemanly, came over each evening to have dinner with Anna, and one night he died there, sitting in his usual rocking chair. Anna had him buried in the Rechel family plot because in the deepest sense he was family.[22] Now Anna was alone.

Although worsening arthritis curtailed her ability to prospect for the same long hours as in her younger days, she still walked the hills with the same spirit. An observer visiting in the Sierra found that working for years at claims yielding scant returns usually altered the miner's personality: "Disappointments have often changed his whole nature. . . . His energy has about died out; he is content to work in the primitive way of mining, living from hand to mouth. . . . Solitude has soured his temper, and made him morose in the society of his fellow men." Anna, by contrast, belonged among the few the traveler encountered with hearts "still fresh." More than thirty years of scraping a lean living from the Rawhide hills had not altered her conviction that she would strike a bonanza at any moment. "Oh, this is going to be good someday!" she would enthusiastically exclaim over each promising streak of ore. It was characteristic of Anna to christen the last claim she staked, in the spring of 1960, the Hope.[23]

If the spirit still soared, the flesh was failing. Sometimes even Anna was obliged to acknowledge it: "I don't think I'm any older than eighteen—it's just my body that's too old." One day, struggling to start her antique truck, she decided to push it down a hill and jump on the running board as it began to roll. The truck knocked her down, leaving her bruised but not otherwise harmed. She waited for quite some time before telling Rees about this incident, because her children, worried about the hazards that could befall an old woman in so remote a place, had started pressing her to move into Fallon. Nor did she hasten to inform them about the huge rattlesnake that entered the living room and slithered slowly over her feet as she, with remarkable sangfroid, sat still as a statue in her rocking chair. Anna had shot that snake, but dangers brushed aside in past years began to loom larger.

Newer anxieties started to surface as well. Disturbing incidents of vandalism erupted in Rawhide. People broke the windows of the deserted buildings and blasted away with guns at the purple bottles of desert glass that Anna picked up and placed on her roof to turn a deeper shade before she sold them. One night two strange, long-haired men came to Anna's house asking for a drink of water. With the sixth sense that develops in people who live in solitude Anna sensed danger from them, and for the first time in her life, she felt afraid. She told them she had no water, and the strangers went away. Yet her instincts may not have lied. Not much time would pass before Charles Manson wrote his name on the wall of the Belmont Courthouse and unsolved murders occurred in the Death Valley country. Nor were Manson and his followers the only dangerous ones roaming the deserts in the sixties.

Finally, Anna's children insisted on moving her into Fallon. "It is breaking her heart to pack up and move from the town she loves," observed the newspaper reporter who visited her. "One wonders if it might not be kinder to let her live out her days where she is so happy." Anna would not accept the move and at first kept running away to Rawhide. Idah Strobridge, knowing the prospectors as she did, would have understood: "All the years of his life the Old Prospector gives to the Desert his best and his all—gives hope, and joy, and love, even as he gave youth. He gives his very soul; then, finally, he commits his body to the Desert's keeping—to sleep there in its everlasting silence. . . . In death the body rests where the heart found its joy in life. What lover could ask more?"[24]

If that was the death Anna would have preferred, it was not the one she received. In the middle of the night LaRae and Pal received a phone call from Anna's little house in Fallon asking them to come over because her heart hurt. When they arrived they realized at once that Anna had suffered a heart attack. LaRae wanted to call an ambulance, but she was overruled because neither Anna nor her son would concede that she might be incapable of walking into the hospital. "Strong-minded" Anna remained, to the very end. By the time morning came on 21 August 1967, she was dead.

Rawhide did not long survive her, nor had Anna believed it would when she was no longer there to keep watch. One night, it is said, young vandals put Rawhide to the torch and drank beer while they watched the town burn. Only the old stone jail and cellar and the hills remained.

Rawhide mining followed exactly the course Anna had foreseen. When new technology and high gold prices made working low-grade deposits highly profitable in the 1980s, a large company with development capital came in to work the pock-marked ground that Rawhide miners had dry-washed for their daily bread during the Great Depression. Because of legal technicalities, the family received nothing for the Rawhide properties on which Anna had paid taxes throughout her lifetime, taxes her family continued to pay, as a memorial to her, after her death.[25] The woman who had delivered such eloquent diatribes against the railroad monopolies and the oppression of the working class might have made a few remarks about that.

Today Rawhide is a large hole in the ground with a fence around it.

# Epilogue: A Century of
# Women Prospectors

In the century that elapsed between the California gold rush and the days when Panamint Annie walked the mountains of Death Valley with pick in hand, the woman prospector's world had changed more than the woman prospector. It was still possible to be very much alone in the vast spaces of the West, but the frontier had passed, and by the mid–twentieth century Panamint Annie could only fantasize about finding a place where no one else had ever been. At the same time, a hundred years of intensive prospecting had greatly diminished the chances of uncovering an overlooked bonanza, although no one could convince Anna Rechel of this, and mining grew ever more capital intensive. In the not-too-distant future microgold could be profitably mined at old sites with expensive equipment on a Brobdingnagian scale, but not by a woman with a strong back and a handcranked windlass or a riffle box.

The old boomtowns had gone forever, and with them a principal ingredient of the prospecting life, the thrill of the stampede. No more races across wild terrain to be one of the "first on the ground," no more jostling with the excited crowds on the fresh board sidewalks of a brand-new town where life surged at "full tide." The hope that had spread like a contagious fever throughout the nation stimulated prospecting enormously and probably does much to explain the heavy concentration of women prospectors in the era surrounding the Klondike and Goldfield booms. Of the seventy-seven women whose activities can be dated with reasonable certainty, 47 percent either began prospecting or are first mentioned in the exceptional twelve-year period from 1898 to 1910.

This turn-of-the-century explosion may have gained impetus from slow but nonetheless real changes in attitudes toward women. The period after 1870 saw the rise of the "New Woman," college-educated, em-

301

*Epilogue*

ployed, and often unmarried. In the workplace women laid claim to new job categories such as secretary and found more positions in fields from academia to dentistry. Perhaps the synergy between this new spirit of independence and capability and the bonanza dreams of the Klondike-Goldfield period produced the surge of women prospectors around the turn of the century. The golden age of the New Woman was succeeded by what author Caroll Smith-Rosenberg has called a "retreat from professional prominence and economic autonomy," a period when women turned away from many of the gains they had made and the number of professional women shrank. Since women prospectors on their own such as Lillian Malcolm often saw themselves as career women, their pattern may have paralleled that of the women doctors and lawyers.[1]

The number of prospectors of both sexes sharply diminished after World War I, but in the 1930s the economic hardships of the Great Depression brought a new wave of subsistence miners. These desperate times had driven the Coffeys to live by working the gravels of the Agua Fria and had certainly affected the Rechels' move to Rawhide after the loss of their homestead. It seems likely that other women followed the same course, but their stories are lost because newspapermen found nothing romantic and colorful about women scratching out a bare existence while living like hermit crabs in ghost town shacks or camping in tents and truckbeds. Moreover, after the disappearance of the lively boomtown newspapers, the primary source of information on women prospectors at the turn of the century, reporters from the surviving big-city newspapers and the abbreviated small-town weeklies encountered the woman prospector less often and stories about her exploits appeared infrequently. The actual number of depression-era women prospectors was likely two or three times greater than those now remembered. All the same, the woman prospector remained the unusual figure she had always been. Dot Coffey was the only woman sniping on the Agua Fria, and Anna Rechel was the only woman prospector when perhaps a hundred miners worked the Rawhide region.

With the arrival of New Deal social programs and the better economic times accompanying World War II, necessity no longer drove women to subsistence mining, and some no doubt dropped away.

Nonetheless, Panamint Annie, Anna Rechel, and Josie Pearl, deeply committed prospectors all, continued to live just as they had during the starving thirties. Perhaps the contrast between the relative scarcity of prospectors during the depression and the surge at the turn of the century means that hope made a more powerful incentive than necessity. At the same time, the advancing dominance of the mining engineers reduced the stature and credibility of all prospectors without professional training. This trend would be only briefly reversed when the uranium boom of the early 1950s sent a new horde of amateurs with outsized hopes swarming over the Colorado Plateau. "No Talk under $1,000,000," ordered the signs over the humblest lunch counters and everywhere else.[2]

Although the feminist revolution still lay ahead and the strong, independent woman as a heroine had not yet replaced patient Griseldas and cookie bakers in popular esteem, other women had finally accepted the woman prospector, with a mixture of curiosity and astonishment. But battles loomed over lingering male prejudices against women in mining. Even in the nineteenth century men admired the pluck of the woman prospector, but they never tolerated women in the underground work force. Although sociologists have observed that men attempt to exclude women from work that is traditionally the male domain, the barrier in mining has generally been ascribed to the superstition, especially strong among the West's many Cornish miners, that the appearance of a woman underground would result in a terrible accident. (It is notable, however, that Mrs. Jennings, Helen Cottrell, and others who frequently went underground to supervise in their own mines evidently had no difficulty finding miners willing to work for them, suggesting that the prohibition had more to do with eliminating potential rivals for jobs than with Cornish superstition.) Some states codified the old prejudice in laws such as Colorado's Dangerous Occupations Act forbidding the employment of women in underground mining in the guise of protecting them. As historian Alice Kessler-Harris observes, protective labor legislation "tended to reflect the prevailing sense of women's proper roles." Three years after two women mining engineers challenged the law in 1968, it was finally amended. Since the period of challenge fortunately coincided with a hirsute phase in men's hairstyles and the employment of long-haired hippies, rumblings over the unsuitability of women for dangerous work because of their long hair could not be taken seriously. Nonetheless, it took an antidiscrimination class-action suit by rock mechanic Janet Bonema in 1972 to gain admission underground. Shouts of "Get those women out of here!" greeted the appearance of Bonema with a *Denver Post* reporter, and sixty men walked off the job.[3]

Despite this display of antique prejudice, times had changed. Although prospectors were passing into history at the very moment the feminist revolution had brought legal remedies for unequal treatment, women mining engineers appeared in larger numbers, women became especially valued in certain mining jobs such as hoist operator, and Union Carbide and other companies actively sought female employees. Similar changes appear to have been under way beyond the borders of the United States. The Australian National Library has no sources on women prospectors before 1950, but in 1991 fledgling Australian mining engineer Jeanette Kuoni told a newspaper reporter that the number of women geology students at her university had expanded to half the class and that people had ceased to regard the profession of mining engineer as a "male domain." Using modern scientific methods, Kuoni pursued the search that had occupied women prospectors for years. She spoke of the distant places in the outback that she would not otherwise have seen as one of the attractions of her "fantastic job," a hint of the old lure of the great beyond, even if Kuoni's training directed her to other methods than listening to the mountains speak.[4]

Much as the woman prospector preferred to live apart from society, cultural forces unavoidably affected her. One sign of this may be the paucity of women prospectors in Utah after the days when Mrs. Reid and Mrs. Burlingame gave their own water to the mules on the trek across the sandy plain. When I drew a sizable sample of womens' names during the period 1902–7 from the mining location records of Uintah County and pursued them through reminiscences and other sources in the exceptionally well organized Regional History Collections at the Uintah County Library, I found many tales of pioneer valor but no signs of women prospectors unknown and unsung, suggesting that other prospectors had simply staked claims under the names of female

*Epilogue*

friends and relatives. This theory is corroborated by the work of other researchers, who found mining women almost nonexistent in Utah until the turn of the century; after that date they were rare and invariably non-Mormon. Mormonism seems to be the significant factor, for mining women abounded in the neighboring states of Nevada and Colorado. Although Brigham Young supported a limited number of carefully controlled mining ventures, he saw farming, not mining, as the foundation of the Mormon community. He expressed pity for brethren who dashed off to the mining excitements; that women might do the same would no doubt have seemed an abomination. Under the powerful influence of Mormon culture, woman's domestic role as wife, mother, and homemaker was prescribed in absolute terms. Her mission was childbirth and service to the Lord, and any deviation in the direction of the woman prospector would doubtless have been subject to social control by the community and sanctions by the elders of the church. It is surely no accident that Utah's most notable women prospectors were non-Mormons.[5]

The domestic ideals of Mormonism would have cut off an incipient woman prospector "just behind the ears," as Brigham Young liked to say, but the free and tolerant mining camps provided a climate where she could flourish. Especially in the early stages of a mining boom weak social controls, an absence of clearly defined roles, mobile populations, and a wide-open atmosphere gave mining camp women freedoms they did not enjoy elsewhere. Moreover, the scarcity of women and the admiration accorded to those daring enough to join a rush gave women more options. This could mean choosing among many suitors (women "get too independent with so many desert millionaires fawning at their feet," declared the *Goldfield Chronicle*), and some joined mining booms for the express purpose of marrying well. But expanded choices also had a career component. If a woman who had joined a rush with no grander design than opening a profitable restaurant caught mining fever, nothing prevented her from pursuing her dream. Several women prospectors—Helen Cottrell, Nellie Cashman, Ellen Jack, and Happy Days Diminy—were bitten by the bug while working at other occupations in mining camps, and lack of detailed information probably obscures many other instances.[6]

*Epilogue*

Although the number of women prospectors is too small to produce statistics satisfying to an actuary or a quantitative sociologist, it far exceeds the handful of anomalies previously presumed to exist. Over the entire period from 1850 to 1950 seventy-seven women indisputably prospected, an additional nineteen who were physically engaged in mining may well have done so, and no doubt the names of many others are now lost to us. Though incomplete records often reduce the size of the group that can be considered for any given characteristic, collectively the numbers confirm the impressions suggested by a look at their lives.

Of those women prospectors whose birthplaces are known, roughly a quarter were foreign-born; others, such as Anna Rechel, were only a generation removed from the old country. Compared with some cosmopolitan mining town populations, this proportion of foreign-born does not amount to much. The largest group of women prospectors born in the United States and Canada came from the West and Alaska, followed by the Midwest and the South. Only two were born in the Northeast. They showed little racial diversity, although if Indian women such as Jim Richardson's slave girls had been more fully described, the number of Indians would surely expand. Women prospected in nine western states and territories, and a few extended their range to Canada, Mexico, and even South Africa. Some, such as Mrs. Morehouse Mallen, ensconced for twenty-two years among the craggy peaks of the Colorado Rockies, stayed in a limited area throughout their careers; Nellie Cashman and others stampeded to several states and even nations. Lillian Malcolm's route from the Klondike to Nome to the central Nevada mining boom was not uncommon.[7]

What did these women do for a living before "beautiful fascination" set in and they took to the wilds? Suprisingly, in an era when keeping house was the commonest female occupation and three-quarters or more of the women in mining towns fell into this category, former housewives did not loom large among the women prospectors. Indeed, more had held the jobs that cropped up repeatedly since the days when a customer had to be forced at gunpoint to eat Nellie Cashman's beans. Working as a restaurant or boardinghouse cook or waitress brought women in frequent contact with prospectors, with many opportunities to hear the stories that fired the imagination. In some measure this

306

was also true of an only slightly smaller group of women with backgrounds in entertainment—running saloons, working in dance halls, or acting on the stage. Nearly as many were professionals who turned to prospecting, a group consisting of two teachers, a doctor, a stockbroker, and a newspaper editor.

In contrast to their late-twentieth-century counterparts, training relevant to the mining field was practically nonexistent, and few women prospectors had any higher education. Only Dorothy "Dolly" O'Neil and Gertrude Sober, the "Queen of the Arbuckles," graduated from college; for Sober, college was the coda to a career then largely behind her, but O'Neil went on to many years of mining in Alaska and Nevada. Of course, such signs as Happy Days Diminy's mastery of several languages and Anna Rechel's intellectual interests indicate the presence of some fine minds among the women prospectors, with or without formal education.

Another cluster of women moved directly from ranching or farming to prospecting, as did Sober when she abandoned the failing effort to raise kafir corn and began riding into the Arbuckles with a hammer on her saddlehorn. A number of others, Ellie Nay, Mary Grantz, and Lorena Peterson among them, had been raised on farms and ranches. What Mark Twain had characterized as the "promiseless toil" of prospecting Josie Pearl saw as easier and much more interesting than the farm work of her girlhood.

A scattering of other occupations turn up: one hairstylist (Mary Grantz), one nurse (Louise Grantham), and so forth. Sometimes a woman passed through so many occupations that her main line cannot be readily unscrambled. Jennie Enright, cattle rancher, craftswoman, cashier, bakery and boardinghouse operator, and real estate agent, is a case in point and a display of the flexibility typical of the frontier. What is absent from the occupational spectrum is almost as significant as what is present: no domestics, aside from Mona Peer's early employment as a nanny, and no factory workers, although the greater part of the female labor force worked in these fields during most of the period. Perhaps the independence so characteristic of the woman prospector spelled instant antipathy to the regimentation of a factory worker and the subordination of a servant.[8]

Once a woman took up prospecting, she rarely left it. Like Josie Pearl, she woke up every morning "believing firmly that she was going to hit the Mother Lode." Old age and ill health or a promising discovery might dictate a shift from wandering to development of a single site, but many had very long careers, despite the large proportion of late starts in middle age. Some spent many years in the field before even a modest strike (nearly thirty years elapsed between the Klondike rush and Frances Muncaster's locations at Squaw Creek), and there were several who never found much. Of those women whose careers can be dated from start to finish, twenty, thirty, and often more than forty years in mining were not uncommon. Setting aside those who began in girlhood, Frances Muncaster remained the longest (fifty-four years). Only six women entirely abandoned prospecting; most of the time only failing health or death could end their careers. It had taken a fatal heart attack to stop Anna Rechel from running away to Rawhide.[9]

At what age did the hairstylist, the boardinghouse cook, the rancher–craftswoman–cashier–boardinghouse operator–real estate agent, and all the rest turn to prospecting? For thirty-seven women, the age when they began is stated or the date they are first mentioned in the press can be used as a benchmark. Of these, a few began prospecting in girl-hood. A larger group (45 percent) started as young women between ages twenty and thirty-nine. The greater part of the women who started prospecting with a husband fell into this category. The most striking finding is that an almost equal number of women prospectors were forty or older, and more than half these were at least fifty. In her age the woman prospector markedly differed from the typically youthful male gold rusher. A 1900 census study of Alaskan gold rush communities found 68 percent of men aged twenty to thirty-nine and only 10 percent over fifty; a similar examination of an Idaho mining county in 1870 and 1880 showed an even younger population, with 90 percent of the men between twenty and forty-four.

Several reasons might be advanced for the substantial presence of older women in a calling where youth predominated among men. Some may have been widows like Idah Strobridge, drawn to an occupation that would bring them solace through the beauty and solitude of the wilderness. For others, the midlife stage when children were grown and husbands dead or departed may have brought an absence of family responsibility that allowed them to engage in a risky endeavor they could not previously indulge. Midlife may also have brought an awareness that only a limited number of years remained in which a pursuit demanding great physical vigor could be undertaken.[10] Until what age, after all, could one expect to leap from one ice cake to another in the Alaskan rivers on a snowshoe journey to Nome?

Despite the often perilous rigors of prospecting, the women prospectors themselves saw it as a healthy, outdoor life and took pardonable pride in their exploits. Lillian Malcolm called prospecting the "grandest and healthiest life known," and she may not have been far wrong. A study of mortality records in Goldfield during the boom days showed that prospectors were the most long-lived occupational group in the camp. In addition to the rigorous physical conditioning their work provided, the solitude in which they spent much of their time may have saved them from exposure to the infectious diseases, primarily tuberculosis and influenza/pneumonia, that were the leading causes of death for much of the period. Moreover, if researchers are correct in suggesting that a sense of helplessness and hopelessness affects mortality, the obvious resilience and resourcefulness of the women prospectors may have contributed to their longevity. Certainly they lived to ripe old ages compared with most women of their era. Happy Days Diminy, who died at ninety-six, was the oldest, and others survived past seventy. Of those whose ages at death are known, none died young. The youngest was the one-time swaggering, cigar-smoking Mollie Sawyer at fifty-seven, and when she died in 1902 in the insane asylum where she had been confined for many years, she had already long surpassed normal life expectancy for women in her time—less than forty-five.[11]

Although we may suspect that physical stress and lack of medical care in remote places contributed to some miscarriages, no woman prospector died or suffered long-term damage from her experiences in the field, and Frances Muncaster survived the Chisana ordeal that eventually killed her husband. The one who brushed closest to death was Mrs. Helen C. Quigley, a prospector from Utah who ventured into Death Valley alone with a horse and a pack mule in 1907. Six weeks later miners entered a cave in the Funeral Mountains to find Quigley, her hair whitened by alkali and sun, without food or water, feverish, and barely alive. Her narrow escape deterred Quigley not at all. As soon as her rescuers had nursed her back to health, through weeks of delirium, she set off into the desert to return to the ledge she had discovered.[12]

A final tally lays to rest, six feet deep at least, the presumption that women who prospected merely helped their husbands. In fact, women on their own, single, widowed, or divorced, more than doubled the number of married women (fifty to twenty-two). In this they showed closer resemblance to male gold rushers than to other frontier women. In several Alaskan gold rush communities in 1900 two-thirds to three-quarters of the women were married, compared with less than a third of the men. Similarly, a study of four Idaho mining communities in 1870 and 1880 uncovered large proportions of adults living alone without relatives. Admittedly, marital status is a slippery subject, partly because some women prospected as both single and married women, and married women continued as widows. The fact that women are often referred to as Mrs. Such-and-such, with no husband present, further complicates the issue.

To deal with these murky matters, I classified women as married or unmarried depending on their marital status when they began prospecting or were first mentioned in newspaper stories, and the Mrs. Such-and-suches were assumed to be widowed or divorced if no husband appeared. It should also be recalled that not all married women prospected with their husbands. Take, for instance, Mrs. Robert English and Mrs. James George, living with miner husbands but preferring to prospect with each other. Similarly, Mrs. Reid and Mrs. Burlingame left their husbands at home and teamed up with each other. If we consider only the married women who prospected with their husbands, the number dwindles even further, to 21 percent working with husbands; the overwhelming majority were on their own or with other partners. Omitting couples such as the Earps and the Nays, who prospected on the wife's initiative, leaves only a small number of women who might have been assistants to their husbands.[13]

One of the fascinating aspects of the marital lives of the women prospectors is their predilection for much younger husbands and lovers, from the time Ferminia Sarras celebrated the sale of a mine with a binge and another young man right down to the days when Mary Grantz paraded her new husband before her Wisconsin relatives. In twenty-eight marriages in which the ages of husbands and wives could be contrasted, the husband was five to thirty years younger than the wife in 29 percent. These marriages included women who married two or three times, and most unions ended in widowhood rather than divorce. Why this startling difference from the usual pattern of American marriages, in which a much younger husband is a rarity? From the husband's point of view the bride's wealth may sometimes have been a factor. Mary Grantz's relatives assumed that this was the reason an impecunious drifter married the successful owner of the Black Diablo. But obviously, money could not account for all these marriages. When Frances Noyes at last succumbed to the ardent wooing of Bill Muncaster, the Noyes fortune had evaporated. Financial circumstances aside, the scarcity of women on the mining frontier may have greatly diminished the importance of age differences. Also, the ability and willingness of a woman prospector to live in the wilderness may have enhanced her allure to a mining man regardless of her age. Yet one suspects the presence of a more important factor: not a few of the women prospectors seem to have possessed charismatic charm that might have overshadowed the usual considerations.[14]

Why did so large a proportion of women prospectors fly in the face of prevailing custom? Let us bear in mind that if the woman who married more than once had a young husband, he was her last spouse in all instances but one. When an elderly tycoon takes a bride half his age, speculation about his reasons does not even arise, because the lure of young flesh is presumed to be self-evident. Ferminia Sarras may not have been immune to that lure, and Mary Grantz flaunted a trophy husband in the same way successful older men parade pretty, young brides. Needless to say, the woman prospector, unconventional by definition, would hardly be deterred by the gossip such behavior was likely to arouse when undertaken by a woman. Yet to dismiss the young husbands as trophies and sex objects probably omits a key element of their appeal: they made better trail partners than many of the men as old or older than the woman prospector herself. Take Anna

Rechel's divorce from Alvin Nelson, whose poor health in old age led him to insist that she stay home and care for him. One also suspects that young Bill Muncaster's qualifications as a trail partner helped him prevail over Frances's other suitors.

Young husbands were a surprising presence, but children remained a notable absence throughout the period. Twenty-four women prospectors had none; for a somewhat larger number, no children are mentioned (probably they had none or their children were grown). Of the eleven women with young children, six left their children behind when prospecting, and only three attempted to bring them along even part of the time. The two postwar mothers, Panamint Annie and Anna Rechel, appear more conscientious about schooling their children than Dora Wilhelm or Ellie Nay (perhaps a reflection of the new sense of parental responsibilities that developed after 1920), but the advent of the automobile age failed to erase the distance between school and mine. Although Panamint Annie and Rechel never temporarily placed their children in orphanages as Ferminia Sarras and Mountain Charley had done, they otherwise relied on much the same mix of methods as women in the days of the single-blanket jackass prospector. They took their children along where they mined, placed them with relatives, or boarded them near schools. When all else failed, Panamint Annie made the supreme sacrifice and moved into town so her son could attend school. That it was a supreme sacrifice for a woman prospector is obliquely suggested by the fact that motherhood remained so uncommon. For women who attempted to combine mining and motherhood, the usually valid distinction sociology draws between the working woman who shapes her work around her family and the husband who shapes his family life around his work fit poorly.[15]

The dearth of children undoubtedly contributed to the disappearance of women prospectors from western history. For other pioneer women, devoted sons and daughters often recognized and preserved the memories of their remarkable mothers, donating letters and diaries to historical institutions and writing memoirs. Children of women prospectors showed the same devotion (Walt Wilhelm wrote an article on his mother's mining and a book detailing the family adventures, and Leafy King left an oral history on her mother, Ellie Nay). But the scarcity of children reduced the pool of possible preservers of the past to a puddle, and many women prospectors died without issue.

In the final analysis a few women prospectors made important discoveries: Belle Butler, Helen Cottrell, and Louise Grantham. Others, such as Mary Grantz, found little through their own prospecting but profitably developed claims they had acquired by purchase or inheritance. Despite the common image of the prospector as a ragged creature cadging grubstakes and living a hand-to-mouth existence, the women prospectors proved surprisingly successful on the whole. We should, of course, bear in mind that large sales and profitable production were more newsworthy than disappointing results. Of those women about whom some financial information exists, nearly a quarter can be termed very successful and an additional 40 percent moderately or modestly so (almost two-thirds of the total). This sharply differentiates them from the general run of nineteenth-century women on the mining frontier, where few females even owned property; for instance, a census of several Idaho mining camps in 1870 revealed a grand total of one female property owner. Twenty-six percent of the women prospectors made small discoveries or mined on a subsistence level—by no means an unimportant alternative to starvation. Only five women were complete failures, and all of them would certainly have disputed that assertion with indignation and true prospector hyperbole.[16]

How did the women prospectors, both the affluent and those sustained by great expectations, plan to spend their money? When questioned, several mentioned charitable undertakings. Lillian Malcolm wanted to create an organization to assist temporarily destitute women on their own; Josie Pearl spoke of the Pearl Foundation to educate disabled children; Josie Bishop, for twenty-five years a California prospector in the Mojave Desert, hoped to establish a home for disabled prospectors. Though charities provided a more praiseworthy answer for reporters than diamond bracelets or trophy husbands, the many beneficent acts of the women prospectors suggest a genuine impulse, perhaps sharpened by years of firsthand experience with poverty. By the time of her death the philanthropy of Belle Butler had grown to such bountiful dimensions that she was known as the "Mother of

Nevada"; Nellie Cashman's assistance to the poor and needy has been widely chronicled; Ferminia Sarras aided the destitute on a generous scale; Josie Pearl, although only a subsistence miner herself, wholeheartedly shared the little she had with the less fortunate.[17]

Becoming a lady bountiful was not, however, the whole story of the woman prospector and her money. By and large she conformed to the patterns of the mining camp culture to which she belonged. One of its elements was the hallowed prospector tradition of spending on a royal spree as Ferminia Sarras did or gambling in the style of Marie Pantalon and Panamint Annie. The fondness for expensive personal display among mining camp women that had shocked thriftier folk from the Comstock to Goldfield may not have been wholly absent, but like many male mining tycoons, the women prospectors seem to have taken more pleasure in investing their money in the mining business than in spending it. Although Mary Grantz may have had her diamonds and her trophy husband, she poured much of her fortune into the attempt to turn the Charleston Hill into a profitable mine. As her niece has said, "mining was her life." Similarly, Frances Williams lived without ostentation and spent the money raked in from the Frances Mohawk lease in developing other mines. Two women, Ellie Nay with her ranch and Marie Pantalon with her vineyard, used money acquired in mining to establish themselves in more stable agricultural enterprises, although Ellie never entirely abandoned prospecting.[18]

How the women prospectors did *not* spend their money reveals as much about them as how they did. Social ambition is conspicuously absent: no woman prospector built a pretentious seaside mansion with gold doorknobs. Perhaps the lesson on "how little one really needs, to live" articulated by Idah Strobridge could never be wholly undone. With the exception of Frances Muncaster, whose social activities may have been largely an obligation arising from the position of her second husband's family, women prospectors took no European tours, held no society-page entertainments, and made no attempts to launch themselves in society. In this they resembled their counterparts among the male mining magnates, some of whom were afflicted with social climbers as wives when they clearly would have preferred to live in a simpler style and attend to their business interests. For the women prospectors, pleasure lay in achievement, not in leisure, as Ellie and Joe Nay found during their brief retirement to southern California, when they learned that their idea of the good life was really very different.[19]

Where did the woman prospector acquire her immunity to the social ambitions so evident among newly rich mining wives such as Eilley Bowers, Louise Mackay, and the "unsinkable" Molly Brown? A large part of it may have sprung from the woman prospector's rejection of conventional values. Acceptance in society entailed displaying one's wealth in almost ritualistic ways to other rich people and winning their favor. For much of the period, social acceptability also involved conformity to the code of behavior dictated by the doctrine of separate spheres, anathema to the fiercely unconventional women prospector. Must fundamentally, the woman prospector who had worked hard and succeeded "on her own hook" probably developed a surer sense of self than the social-climbing wife. Indeed, many, such as Nellie Cashman and Lillian Malcolm, appear supremely self-confident. The subtext of much social climbing is insecurity, a need to be validated through the eyes of others. Perhaps the women prospectors lacked the compulsion to seek this sort of approval because they had a solid sense of their own worth based on accomplishment.[20]

To succeed is to find what one seeks, and dollar returns were only one strand in the odyssey of the woman prospector. More important, she was engaged in what Carl Wikstrom called painting her name on the mountain, a fundamentally modern form of self-expression. The women prospectors voiced advanced ideas on such specifics as woman's role, child care, and equal pay, but their essential modernity showed above all in the primacy they gave self-fulfillment, which has been called the major theme of the twentieth century. And this was true from beginning to end. Nellie Cashman might not have befriended Panamint Annie or Anna Rechel, but she would have been obliged to recognize them as kindred spirits—strong-minded women and ahead of their time. If they now seem distant, exotic, and difficult to comprehend, the reason may lie in their solitary nature. The current mode of coping with loss and aging is a group approach focusing on a symptom, not withdrawal into the wilds. In our time these eccentric loners would quickly be labeled "dysfunctional," advised how to live with the rest of society in twelve easy steps, and told to join a self-help group.

That was not the way of the woman prospector, to whom the wilderness was a dream, a mirage of treasure, an addiction, a challenge, an adventure, and a quasi-religious experience. Only two women prospectors had much to do with organized religion, Nellie Cashman, with her Catholicism and her fund raising for the church, and Josephine Scott, a devout Christian Scientist. Josephine believed Christian Science had cured her of bad lungs, heart disease, and an internal abscess and helped her to stop using morphine and strychnine. The Scotts "prayed continuously, declaring the truth" over their rattlesnake-bitten dog, attempted to convert an Indian they encountered, and regularly held services wherever they happened to be on their desert journey.[21]

In this practice they were exceptional, for the other women prospectors who made their views known were religious but rejected affiliation with organized churches, a widespread practice in the mining camps from an early date and a clearcut deviation from the much-proclaimed civilizing mission of women on the frontier. As Carl Lewis said of the prospectors he had known, they often made up their own religion. Catherine Rueckl believed Josie Pearl's code of conduct on "how life should be lived and how other people should be treated" amounted to a personal religion. Anna Rechel read and discussed the Bible, but she interpreted it in her own way. To these women God seemed closest in the wilderness, and their belief in Him often fused with a mystical sense of the land. "You tell me where it says in the Bible that I have to go to church," said Panamint Annie. "I go to church every single day in God's country." Mona Peer spoke of being "out in the hills with God," and Josie Earp voiced similar feelings: "The peaceful, yet awesome desert nights never failed to move me to informal prayer directed to my German mother's 'Lieber Gott.' I talked over my thoughts with Him, my hopes, anxieties, fears."[22]

When lesser motives were stripped away, this fusion with the wilderness was the heart of the matter. Prospecting provided a reason for venturing inside it and a means for remaining there. From Nellie Cashman, waxing lyrical on the beauty of the Arctic, to Anna Rechel, teaching her daughter-in-law to see the beauty of the desert, love of the

*Epilogue*

far country suffuses the lives of the women prospectors. It was a place of healing for the stricken, where one could feel the "pulse-beat of the universe" and the nearness of God, a place where the young woman could seek adventure and the older woman could find the peace to undertake what Germaine Greer has called "the journey inwards towards wisdom and serenity."[23] It was a world that few of them would ever leave. When the vigor to mine had finally ebbed and the dreams of bonanza had faded, the love of the land remained. Thus, near the end of her life Panamint Annie made her way up Titus Canyon to see the desert rippled below her in waves like the sea. Frances Muncaster said it plain: when she lost the strength to go out in the wilderness, she would prefer to die.

317

# Notes

INTRODUCTION

1. Frank Lewis, interview with author, Reno, Nevada, 31 Aug. 1991; Boyer, *I Married Wyatt Earp*, 214–15; Catherine Rueckl, interview with author, Reno, Nevada, 7 May 1992 ("Mother Lode" quotation).

2. Strobridge, *Sagebrush Trilogy*, 42.

3. Burford, *North to Danger*, 249 (Quigley); Schulmerich, *Josie Pearl*, 94, 111, 190–94; Doris Riemersma, telephone and personal interviews with author, Beatty, Nevada, 29 Apr. 1994–5 Feb. 1995 (Panamint Annie).

4. Olephia King, interview with author, Fallon, Nevada, 20 Aug. 1982.

5. Young, *Western Mining*, 6–21, 27–28; Spence, *Mining Engineers and the American West*, 6–7.

6. Riemersma interviews (Panamint Annie). Also see Young, *Western Mining*, 20–21, 26–27.

7. Twain, *Roughing It*, 163; Young, *Western Mining*, 27–28.

8. Young, *Western Mining*, 30–31; Shamberger, *Goldfield*, 14; Zanjani, *Goldfield*, 83. Nevada law specified an excavation four feet wide by six feet long by ten feet deep to satisfy the requirements of location work.

9. John Koontz, interview with author, Carson City, Nevada, 8 Apr. 1988.

10. Carl Wikstrom, interview with author, Reno, Nevada, 30 Sept. 1991; Stickney, "Colorado Women Successful" (McCarthy).

11. Wikstrom and Riemersma interviews.

12. Degler, *At Odds*, 26–28, 377, 382–86, 409. Also see Wertheimer, *We Were There*, 195, 210; Jeffrey, *Frontier Women*, 9; and, on women's purported physical limitations, Rothman, *Woman's Proper Place*, 23–26.

13. *Goldfield (Nevada) Chronicle*, 26 Apr. 1908. On gender-divergent goals, see Scharff, "Gender and Western History," 65.

14. Barbara Powell, interview with author, Winnemucca, Nevada, 8 May 1992.

15. Lewis interview; Wilhelm, *Last Rig*, 94 (quotation); Dempsey and Fell, *Mining the Summit*, 19, 23 (Grannis).

16. *Goldfield Chronicle*, 26 Sept. 1907.

17. Young, *Western Mining*, 5; Paul, *California Gold*, 339–40.

319

1. ELLEN CASHMAN

1. Lecompte, "Independent Women," 20–21. Woyski, "Women and Mining," 38. On women in the early gold rush camps, see Downie, *Hunting for Gold*, 72.

2. Joyaux, "De Cotton's *A Travers le Dominion*," 58–59; *Territorial Enterprise* (Virginia City, Nevada), 21 Apr. 1871. City directories for Virginia City, 1873–79, at the Nevada Historical Society list Suize as a wine and liquor dealer. See also U.S. manuscript census, 1880; Ransch and Hoover, *Historic Spots in California*, 2:21; and Goldman, *Gold Diggers and Silver Miners*, 120–21.

3. Bentz, "Frontier Angel," 6 (Clum quotation). Also see Rochlin, "Good Woman," 281; Seagraves, *Women of the West*, 125; Lake, "Irish Nellie," 19.

4. Mayer, *Klondike Women*, 193.

5. Chaput, *Nellie Cashman* 1–5. Also see *Arizona Star* (Tucson), 11 Jan. 1925; *Bisbee (Arizona) Review*, 1 Apr. 1948; Schrier, *Ireland and the American Emigration*, 3–4; Niethammer, "Lure of Gold," 73; Anderson, "They Called Her Angel," 11. On domestic service, see Duff, *Irish in the United States*, 18; and Rothman, *Woman's Proper Place*, 92.

6. The Cashmans do not appear in city directories or the surviving Virginia City records, but tax records were burned in the fire of 1875, and the Cashmans may not have been involved in any of the legal and financial transactions that would appear in the records (Storey County Courthouse, Virginia City; and Nevada Historical Society, Reno). Chaput doubts that the Cashmans were there; see *Nellie Cashman*, 7. Also see Bentz, "Frontier Angel," 6; Rochlin, "Good Woman," 283; U.S. manuscript census, 1870.

7. Ralph Mann found that half the women in Grass Valley, California, in 1850 took in boarders or ran hotels with their husbands; see *After the Gold Rush*, 44. Also see Bentz, "Frontier Angel," 6; Myres, *Westering Women*, 244–45; and the account by Sarah Royce in *Frontier Lady*, 83.

8. Paher, *Nevada Ghost Towns*, 291, 296. Also see Abbott, "Pioche," 178; Edwards, *Two Hundred Years in Nevada*, 182; Niethammer, "Lure of Gold," 73.

9. Hulse, *Nevada Adventure*, 145. Also see Paher, *Nevada Ghost Towns*, 291; and Edwards, *Two Hundred Years in Nevada*, 181–82.

10. Abbott, "Pioche," 178; Clum, "Nellie Cashman," 2; Downie, *Hunting for Gold*, 109, 137; O'Connor, *High Jinks*, 89.

11. Ledbetter, *Nellie Cashman*, 4; tax records, Lincoln County Courthouse, Pioche, Nevada, 1874, list Fannie Cashman. See also the *Anchorage Weekly Times*, 24 Jan. 1925.

12. *Anchorage Weekly Times*, 24 Jan. 1925; Chaput, *Nellie Cashman*, 14, 19–20;

Rochlin, "Good Woman," 292; Niethammer, "Lure of Gold," 83 (quotation); Brophy, "God and Nellie," 2; J. P. Gray manuscript, Arizona Historical Society, Tucson.

13. Niethammer, "Lure of Gold," 73; Rochlin, "Good Woman," 284. On the Stikine region see Berton, *Klondike Fever,* 225–31.

14. Niethammer, "Lure of Gold," 71–72; Chaput, *Nellie Cashman,* 22–23.

15. O'Connor, *High Jinks,* 85 (Morgan quotation); Seagraves, *Women of the West,* 131.

16. Bentz, "Frontier Angel," 7–8 (quotations); Niethammer, "Lure of Gold," 72.

17. Rochlin, "Good Woman," 284; Niethammer, "Lure of Gold," 72. On scurvy see Groh, *Gold Fever,* 118–19, 236–39.

18. Service, "The Spell of the Yukon," in *Best Tales,* 120.

19. Clum, "Nellie Cashman," 2; Bentz, "Frontier Angel," 8, 60.

20. Clum, "Nellie Cashman," 2.

21. "Women in Mining Camps," *Denver Times,* 15 Jan. 1898, Denver Public Library (DPL), "Women as Miners" file. On Tombstone see Faulk, *Tombstone,* 8, 29–30, 67.

22. Nellie's business moves in this period are difficult to unscramble, and no two authors agree on all details. It is possible that the sale of her Tombstone interests had less to do with Tom Cunningham's death than with the abortive move to Bisbee. See Niethammer, "Lure of Gold," 74–75; Bentz, "Frontier Angel," 8; Rochlin, "Good Woman," 283, 286–87; Chaput, *Nellie Cashman,* 47.

23. Burns, *Tombstone,* 36–37. Also see Faulk, *Tombstone,* 127; Niethammer, "Lure of Gold," 75–76; and on frontier foodways, Conlin, *Bacon, Beans, and Galantines,* esp. 111–32.

24. Faulk, *Tombstone,* 95, 106; Niethammer, "Lure of Gold," 74; Bentz, "Frontier Angel," 60; Chaput, *Nellie Cashman,* 43–44.

25. Niethammer, "Lure of Gold," 75. Also see Faulk, *Tombstone,* 112; Bentz, "Frontier Angel," 60.

26. J. P. Gray MS. Also see Bentz, "Frontier Angel," 60.

27. Mayer, *Klondike Women,* 224; also see Bentz, "Frontier Angel," 8.

28. Clum, "Nellie Cashman," n.p.; Niethammer, "Lure of Gold," 77; Rochlin, "Good Woman," 283 (quotation). On frontier mortality, see Zanjani, "To Die in Goldfield," esp. 49.

29. Faulk, *Tombstone,* 97–98; Niethammer, "Lure of Gold," 77; Mayer, *Klondike Women,* 223.

30. For one of the most intriguing Mexican messenger stories, see Dobie,

*Apache Gold and Yaqui Silver,* 197–99. On Nellie's activities, see "Women in Mining Camps," 15 Jan. 1898, DPL, "Women as Miners" file.

31. Bentz, "Frontier Angel," 60; on mining in Baja, see Chaput, Mason, and Loperena, *Modest Fortunes.*

32. Bentz, "Frontier Angel," 60. Also see Rochlin, "Good Woman," 289–91.

33. Bentz, "Frontier Angel," 60. Presumably, this story referred to the chapel still in use, since the Santa Gertrudis mission has been abandoned since 1822.

34. Niethammer, "Lure of Gold," 78. Another version relates that a Mexican storekeeper, alerted by Mexican travelers, sent the water that saved Nellie's party; see Chaput, *Nellie Cashman,* 61–62.

35. Niethammer, "Lure of Gold," 78. Also see Rochlin, "Good Woman," 291. On prospecting in Baja in this period, see *Mining and Scientific Press* 46 (16 June 1883): 401; (23 June 1883): 417, 424; and (30 June 1883): 447. Chaput concludes that Nellie's party turned back without reaching the placers; see *Nellie Cashman,* 62.

36. Niethammer, "Lure of Gold," 78; Chaput, *Nellie Cashman,* 55–56. On Doc Holliday, see O'Neal, *Encyclopedia of Western Gun–Fighters,* 144–45; on tuberculosis on the frontier, see Shikes, *Rocky Mountain Medicine,* 156–63.

37. Mayer, *Klondike Women,* 224. On professional women, see Evans, *Born for Liberty,* 147.

38. Brophy, *Arizona Sketch Book,* 174.

39. Anderson, "They Called Her Angel," 11–12.

40. Martin, *Tombstone's Epitaph,* 226–31.

41. Martin, *Tombstone's Epitaph,* 226–31; Brophy, *Arizona Sketch Book,* 173–74; Chaput, *Nellie Cashman,* 65–70. Skeptics may find it curious that no trace of the grandstand incident appears in the press accounts reproduced by Martin in *Tombstone's Epitaph.* On executions in American history, see Friedman, *Crime and Punishment,* 168–70.

42. Brophy, *Arizona Sketch Book,* 175; Bentz, "Frontier Angel," 60.

43. Brown, *Irish-American Nationalism,* 101–15; Anderson, "They Called Her Angel," 13; Bentz, "Frontier Angel," 60; Rochlin, "Good Woman," 283; Ledbetter, *Nellie Cashman,* 43–44; J. P. Gray MS.

44. Faulk, *Tombstone,* 160–72. On Kingston, see Fergusson, *New Mexico,* 307.

45. Wheat, *Shirley Letters,* 131; Blanche Crabtree, telephone interviews with author, 9 Sept. 1991 and 2 Dec. 1995.

46. On Mountain Charley, see Guerin, *Mountain Charley,* 20–21, 67–68. Fred M. Mazzulla and William Kostka, authors of the introduction, suggest that Mountain Charley may have been a composite of "several interesting

young ladies," xii; the book includes another version of her life in which she had no living children during these adventures.

47. Anderson, "They Called Her Angel," 12; Niethammer, "Lure of Gold," 80; Brophy, *Arizona Sketch Book,* 179; Lake, "Irish Nellie," 43.

48. Stanley, "Kingston Story," 13–14; Rochlin, "Good Woman," 291. Chaput convincingly argues that no evidence supports the legend that Ed Doheny, of Teapot Dome infamy, was Nellie's dishwasher in Kingston; see *Nellie Cashman,* 76–77.

49. Bentz, "Frontier Angel," 60; Niethammer, "Lure of Gold," 81; Ledbetter, *Nellie Cashman,* 42–43; *Bisbee Review,* 1 Apr. 1948. Chaput has uncovered a newspaper report of a planned Cashman marriage to Mike Sullivan, a successful Irish miner in 1889 when Nellie was nearly forty-four. Although the report proved false, it may reveal an actual romance; see Chaput, *Nellie Cashman,* 79–80.

50. Niethammer, "Lure of Gold," 80–81.

51. Service, "The Prospector," in *Best Tales,* 94–95.

52. Rochlin, "Good Woman," 292–94; Niethammer, "Lure of Gold," 81–82; *Bisbee Review,* 1 Apr. 1948; Chaput, *Nellie Cashman,* 87, 92–95. It is unclear whether Tom Cunningham, who had planned to join her, ever arrived, and the Arizona miners she expected may also have dropped out.

53. Niethammer, "Lure of Gold," 81–82 (*Colonist* quote); Mayer, *Klondike Women,* 222. On the Dyea Trail, see Berton, *Klondike Fever,* esp. 247–53.

54. Morgan, *God's Loaded Dice,* 63–64.

55. Morgan, *God's Loaded Dice,* 64–66; *Anchorage Weekly Times,* 24 Jan. 1925; Berton, *Klondike Fever,* 417. Nellie's own remarks on the journey, drawn from an interview in her last years with a journalist who may have misquoted her, differ from Morgan's recollections on two principal points. Nellie mentions the Dyea Trail, whereas Morgan seems to indicate that she came over the White Pass Trail, as he did. They did not meet, however, until Lake Laberge, well beyond the point where the two trails converge. The major discrepancy lies in Nellie's mention of running White Horse Rapids in a boat, but Morgan makes it clear that those rapids were still frozen at the date both travelers passed them. Perhaps Nellie alluded to other rapids later in the journey. Since her recollections have not invariably proved accurate, Morgan's account appears the more reliable.

56. Mayer, *Klondike Women,* 221–23, 250 (quotation); Berton, *Klondike Fever,* 300–301; Chaput, *Nellie Cashman,* 103–5. Nellie herself recalled naming her restaurant the Delmonico; see the *Anchorage Weekly Times,* 24 Jan. 1925.

57. O'Connor, *High Jinks*, 89; Mayer, *Klondike Women*, 221–22.

58. Mayer, *Klondike Women*, 221–23. On McDonald, see Berton, *Klondike Fever*, 83–86, 190–91, 401–2.

59. *San Francisco Call*, 13 Jan. 1899, 1; *San Jose Evening News*, 14 Jan. 1899, 8.

60. Mayer, *Klondike Women*, 223 (quotation); Lake, "Irish Nellie," 43.

61. *Arizona Daily Star*, 24 Oct. 1895.

62. Mayer, *Klondike Women*, 226.

63. O'Connor, *High Jinks*, 89–90; on the appearance of the gold rushers, see Berton, *Klondike Fever*, 257.

64. Marshall, *Arctic Village*, 9, 37–44.

65. Niethammer, "Lure of Gold," 83; Clum, "Nellie Cashman," n.p. (first quotation); Rochlin, "Good Woman," 282 (second quotation).

66. Niethammer, "Lure of Gold," 83–84; Mayer, *Klondike Women*, 224–26 (quotations).

67. Niethammer, "Lure of Gold," 84 (first quotation); Brophy, *Arizona Sketch Book*, 180–81 (second quotation). The number of prostitutes prior to her arrival recorded by Marshall suggests that Nellie was by no means the first white woman in the Koyukuk; see *Arctic Village*, 37–38.

68. Mayer, *Klondike Women*, 224.

69. Brophy, *Arizona Sketch Book*, 180; Rochlin, "Good Woman," 282 (quotation). On St. Patrick, see O'Connor, *The Irish*, 116–17.

70. Niethammer, "Lure of Gold," 84–85; Mayer, *Klondike Women*, 226–27; Lake, "Irish Nellie," 44; *Bisbee Review*, 1 Apr. 1948.

## 2. FERMINIA SARRAS

1. The bells are displayed in the Mineral County Museum, Hawthorne, Nevada. Information about them was provided by Georgeanna Main, museum director; interview with author, 11 Sept. 1991. For one version of the map story, see Chalfant, *Tales of the Pioneers*, 121. On fantasizing a Spanish heritage, see Gutiérrez, "Significant to Whom?" 523–24. On Tule Canyon, see Vanderburg, *Placer Mining*, 79–80.

2. Esmeralda County, tax rolls, 1881, Esmeralda County Courthouse, Goldfield, Nevada. I was fortunate to view and photograph the Sarras portrait when it was in the possession of Harlow Kiblinger in 1988; its present whereabouts are unknown.

3. U.S. manuscript censuses, 1880, 1900, 1910. The censuses are inconsistent on Ferminia's marriages and her immigration date, given as 1876 in the 1910 census and 1867 in 1900. A case can be made for either date, but in the

absence of clear evidence, 1876 better comports with her daughter Jennie's birth in Nicaragua in 1868. Genealogical research on the family was done by the late Helen Mariscans; Jack Mariscans, telephone interview with the author, 14 Aug. 1989. On the Contreras family, see Stone, *Heritage of the Conquistadores,* 50, 54–55, 178–84.

4. *True Fissure* (Candelaria, Nevada), 27 Nov. and 4 Dec. 1880; other women's names among the early locators were Mary A. Benedict and Elizabeth Sutcliffe. Also see Shamberger, *Candelaria,* 1; Nevada state census, 1875; U.S. manuscript census, 1880; Marie Thomason, letter to author, 13 Jan. 1989; *Territorial Enterprise,* 11 Feb. 1881.

5. Shamberger, *Candelaria,* 30–33, 39; U.S. manuscript census, 1880. On John Marshall, also see Esmeralda County, Index to Mining Locations, bk. B, Esmeralda County Courthouse, Goldfield, Nevada; and the *Walker Lake (Nevada) Bulletin,* 4 Aug. 1905; on Antone Marshall, also see Esmeralda County, tax rolls, 1884.

6. U.S. manuscript census, 1880. *True Fissure,* 11 Dec. 1880; also see the slightly different account in the *Esmeralda Herald* (Aurora, Nevada) of the same date and Spears, *Sketches of Death Valley,* 157–58. On the social context of lynching, see Brown, *Strain of Violence,* 4–5.

7. On the Hispanic view of love, see the interview with Gabriel García Márquez, *New York Times,* 22 Aug. 1991, B1.

8. Meadows, *Sagebrush Heritage,* 74 (first quotation); Drury, *Editor on the Comstock Lode,* 239–41; William H. Shockley to his mother, 14 Jan. and 30 July 1884, 29 Mar. 1888, Central Nevada Museum, Tonopah (third quotation); Murbarger, *Ghosts,* 111 (fourth quotation); Paher, *Nevada Ghost Towns,* 444–45; *True Fissure,* 25 Dec. 1880.

9. On production figures, see Shamberger, *Candelaria,* 96–97. Other details are from Paher, *Nevada Ghost Towns,* 444–52; Murbarger, *Ghosts,* 109, 116; Leonard K. Ralston to Lorena E. Meadows, 12 Jan. 1965, Meadows letter file, Central Nevada Museum; *True Fissure,* 7 and 28 Apr. and 12 May 1883; *Esmeralda Herald,* 18 Dec. 1880.

10. Shamberger, *Candelaria,* 169 (Drury); *True Fissure,* 27 Nov. 1880; *Esmeralda Herald,* 18 Dec. 1880. Population figures are from Paher, *Nevada Ghost Towns,* 444–52; other sources set the population somewhat lower.

11. *Esmeralda Herald,* 18 Dec. 1880; *True Fissure,* 5 Feb. 1881; Murbarger, *Ghosts,* 113.

12. Esmeralda County, tax rolls, 1881–85, and Index to Mining Locations, bk. B. Details on the weather are from the April 1883 issues of *True Fissure.*

13. Esmeralda County, tax rolls, 1885; U.S. manuscript censuses, 1880 and 1910; Official Register of Luning Precinct, Mineral County, 1914, Nevada State Division of Archives and Records, Carson City; Marie Thomason, letter to author, 2 Feb. 1989. Ferminia's toll road may have been all or part of the Piper toll road, constructed in the 1870s to connect Palmetto, Gold Mountain, and Tule Canyon; see Murbarger, *Ghosts,* 95.

14. Esmeralda County, tax rolls, 1885–1905, and Index to Mining Locations, bk. B; U.S. manuscript census, 1910; *Los Angeles Times,* 1 June 1914. Informal unions on the mining frontier have been widely noted; see esp. Johnson, "Sharing Bed and Board"; Boyer, *I Married Wyatt Earp,* 20, 25; and on Latin American traditions, Lavrin, introduction to *Sexuality and Marriage,* 2.

15. Esmeralda County, Index to Mining Locations, bk. B; Albert Bradshaw, interviews with author, Tonopah, Nevada, 5 Nov. 1988, 20 Feb. 1989, and by telephone 11 Aug. 1989. On testing for copper, see Young, *Western Mining,* 28–29.

16. Bradshaw interviews; Homsher, *South Pass,* 121. On wolves, see Leonard K. Ralston to Lorena E. Meadows, 11 Apr. 1968, Meadows letter file; on the prospector's outfit, see *Goldfield (Nevada) News,* 17 Aug. 1907.

17. *Goldfield News,* 6 Aug. 1909.

18. Wheat, *Shirley Letters,* 83–84.

19. Smith, *Daughters of the Promised Land,* 276–77.

20. *True Fissure,* 5 Feb. 1881.

21. *Reno Evening Gazette,* 6 Sept. 1905; Esmeralda County tax rolls, 1895–98; *Western Nevada Miner* (Mina), 6 Feb. 1915. While laundry work cannot be entirely ruled out, none of Ferminia's properties are listed as "wash houses" on the tax rolls, and in Belleville and Candelaria there would have been severe competition from the Chinese laundries. On mining camp laundries, see James, Adkins, and Hartigan, "Competition and Coexistence," 164–84.

22. *Reno Evening Gazette,* 6 Sept. 1905.

23. Esmeralda County, Index to Mining Locations, bk. B; U.S. manuscript censuses, 1900 and 1910; Harlow Kiblinger, interview with author, Hawthorne, Nevada, 4 Nov. 1988; Thomason letters.

24. Esmeralda County, Index to Mining Locations, bk. B; Mineral County, Deeds, bk. I, 193, Mineral County Courthouse, Hawthorne, Nevada.

25. Bradshaw interviews; for claim sales, see *Walker Lake Bulletin,* 20 June 1902.

26. On the Hispanic way of life, see Schurz, *Latin America,* 301–3.

27. Other versions on the naming of Mina have appeared; see Carlson, *Nevada*

*Place Names,* 168; and Shamberger, *Goldfield,* 52–53. A newspaper item written when the town was established confirms that it was named for Ferminia; see the *Walker Lake Bulletin,* 18 Aug. 1905. On McCormack, see the *Goldfield (Nevada) Review,* 3 Aug. 1905; on values, see Stone, *Conquistadores,* 56.

28. *Reno Evening Gazette,* 6 Sept. 1905; Bradshaw interviews.

29. *Reno Evening Gazette,* 6 and 14 Sept. 1905 (quotation from 6 Sept.); U.S. manuscript censuses, 1900 and 1910. On communicating with Hispanics, see Wheat, *Shirley Letters,* 121–23.

30. *Goldfield News,* 13 Oct. 1905; *Reno Evening Gazette,* 14 Sept. 1905.

31. *Goldfield Review,* 20 July 1907.

32. The *Los Angeles Times* story (1 June 1914) recounted the death of McCormack eight years earlier, and he does not appear in the 1910 census, but he may have lived longer, because Ferminia did not begin claiming a widow's exemption until 1913 (Esmeralda County tax rolls) and she stated in the 1910 U.S. manuscript census that her present marriage was of fifteen years' duration. Also see the 1905–6 tax rolls; Kiblinger interview; Louisa McDonald (great-granddaughter), interview with the author, Las Vegas, Nevada, 19 Feb. 1989; and the 1910 U.S. manuscript census entry for Jennie Williamson, Jennie's new married name. Another uncertainty remains: Kiblinger believed Joe Marshall had a brother; Ferminia stated that she had only five children, however, all of whom can be accounted for. I have not been able to uncover any evidence of a sixth child.

33. U.S. manuscript census, 1910. On the importance of Spanish blood in Central America, see Stone, *Conquistadores,* 63–71.

34. Mineral County, Deeds, bk. I; when Esmeralda County was divided to create Mineral County in 1911, the Santa Fe district became part of the the new county. Also see Hill, *Mines,* 158, 163–64, 168–69; Lincoln, *Mining Districts,* 153; Elliott, *Mining Booms;* 301; *Western Nevada Miner,* 14 Dec. 1912; *Engineering and Mining Journal* 84 (14 Dec. 1907): 1127–28.

35. *Los Angeles Times,* 1 June 1914; the principal source for the story, in addition to Ferminia and her attorney, appears to have been Dr. F. A. Plymire, a Luning businessman then visiting Los Angeles.

36. *Western Nevada Miner,* 6 Feb. 1915. Fermina Sarrias will and probate file, Mineral County Courthouse, Hawthorne, Nevada; U.S. manuscript census, 1910. I am much indebted to Helene Weatherfield for her invaluable assistance in locating a copy of the will.

37. Ferminia had written her will under the surname she had used in one vari-

ant or another for thirty-five years, Sarrias; her name, however, appears in the probate records as Fermina Sarrias Arrioga. Sarrias will and probate file; U.S. manuscript census, 1910; Bradshaw, McDonald, and Kiblinger interviews.

38. Bradshaw, McDonald, and Kiblinger interviews.

39. Bradshaw, McDonald, and Kiblinger interviews; *Western Nevada Miner,* 6 Feb. 1915.

### 3. "HUSTLERS OF NO MEAN ABILITY"

1. Lingenfelter, *Death Valley,* 1, 113.

2. *Territorial Enterprise,* 21 Apr. 1871. On feminine fashions, see Gernsheim, *Victorian and Edwardian Fashion,* 63, 67. Although Pantalon cited the need to dress efficiently while working as her reason for preferring male attire, sociologist Marion S. Goldman suspects lesbianism; see *Gold Diggers and Silver Miners,* 120–21.

3. Hedrick, "Newest Manhattan," 261; *Territorial Enterprise,* 21 Apr. 1871 (Pantalon). On the dime novel heroine, see Smith, *Virgin Land,* 116–19.

4. Guerin, *Mountain Charley,* 19, 21, 80.

5. *Goldfield News,* 13 Oct. 1905 (reprint from the *Bullfrog [Nevada] Miner);* Earl, "Petticoat Prospector," 2E.

6. Earl, "Petticoat Prospector"; U.S. manuscript census, 1900; another account places Malcolm's entry into prospecting a little earlier in 1896; see the *Rhyolite (Nevada) Herald,* 29 Sept. 1905.

7. Black, *My Ninety Years,* 72.

8. On the rise of the single woman and figures on marriage, see Degler, *At Odds,* 160; May, *Great Expectations,* 115–17; and U.S. Census Bureau, *Abstract of the Twelfth Census, 1900,* 23. On social trends in Dawson, see Alberts, "Petticoats and Pickaxes," 158.

9. *Goldfield News,* 13 Oct. 1905.

10. Caldwell, "Woman's Experience at Cape Nome," 258–62.

11. Caldwell, "Woman's Experience at Cape Nome," 259; Earl, "Petticoat Prospector"; U.S. manuscript census, 1900.

12. Earl, "Petticoat Prospector."

13. *Tonopah (Nevada) Bonanza,* 15 Nov. 1902, 20 Feb. 1904, and 2 Nov. 1907; *Goldfield News,* 13 Oct. 1905; Earl, "Petticoat Prospector"; *Rhyolite Herald,* 29 Sept. 1905; Paher, *Nevada Ghost Towns,* 424; Nye County, Index to Mining Locators, 1864–1903, and bks. B–L, Nye County Courthouse, Tonopah, Nevada; Esmeralda County, Index to Mining Locations, bks. B–H.

14. Harris, "Chasing Rainbows," 229; Steele, "Southwest from Bullfrog," 215.

15. *Goldfield News*, 3 Nov. 1905.

16. *Goldfield News*, 3 Nov. 1905.

17. *Goldfield News*, 3 Nov. 1905.

18. *Goldfield News*, 3 Nov. 1905; *Colonist* (Victoria, British Columbia), 11 Jan. 1925; Spears, *Sketches of Death Valley*, 66.

19. Guerin, *Mountain Charley*, xi, 80–83.

20. Guerin, *Mountain Charley*, 80–83.

21. *Humboldt Star* (Winnemucca, Nevada), 26 July 1911; *Goldfield News*, 29 Dec. 1905; Lingenfelter, *Death Valley*, 284–86.

22. Lingenfelter, *Death Valley*, 242.

23. Lingenfelter, *Death Valley*, 242, 249, 260–67. According to the *Goldfield News* account, Key was half Choctaw; see 29 Dec. 1905.

24. Lingenfelter, *Death Valley*, 258–59, 264, 267–69, 286–87, 308; *Goldfield News*, 29 Dec. 1905; *Bullfrog Miner*, 20 Apr. 1906; *San Bernardino (California) Sun*, 11–12 Apr. 1906.

25. Lingenfelter, *Death Valley*, 267–69; *San Bernardino Sun*, 15 Apr. 1906.

26. *Tonopah Bonanza*, 2 Nov. 1907. On the Pittsburgh Silver Peak mining operation and on Rhyolite, see Paher, *Nevada Ghost Towns*, 317, 424; on the stock crash in Goldfield, see Zanjani, *Goldfield*, 61–62.

27. *Reno Evening Gazette*, 14 June 1910, and *Rhyolite Herald*, 29 Sept. 1905.

28. *Reno Evening Gazette*, 14 June 1910. On the need for female friendship, see Riley, *Female Frontier*, 73.

29. *Eureka (Nevada) Sentinel*, 6 July 1911; *Tonopah Bonanza*, 28 July 1911.

30. *Tonopah Bonanza*, 25 Sept. 1911. On Scott, see Lingenfelter, *Death Valley*, 273; on Awakening, see Paher, *Nevada Ghost Towns*, 148.

31. *Tonopah Bonanza*, 25 Sept. 1911. On Jarbidge, see Paher, *Nevada Ghost Towns*, 206–10.

32. *Reno Evening Gazette*, 14 June 1910; Downie, *Hunting for Gold*, 132.

33. *National (Nevada) Miner*, 24 Nov. 1911. On prejudice against the woman miner, see the *Denver Post*, 10 Nov. 1972, DPL, "Women as Miners" file.

34. Stickney, "Colorado Women Successful."

35. Stickney, "Colorado Women Successful."

36. Mouat, "Flotation Process," 2–3, 10; "Carrie J. Everson and Flotation"; Macdonald, *Feminine Ingenuity*, 150–57.

37. Mouat, "Flotation Process," 17–18, 24 n. 13 (quotation). For patronizing sarcasm on Everson, see Young, *Western Mining*, 132; and "Everson Myth."

38. "Women as Miners—They Never Fail," DPL, "Women as Miners" file (the

Tracy sisters); *Tuscarora (Nevada) Times Review,* 13 Jan. 1883 (the Ely sisters).

39. Clipping dated 29 Oct. 1899, DPL, "Women as Miners" file.
40. *Goldfield News,* 16 June 1906.
41. *Reno Evening Gazette,* 29 Apr. 1907.
42. *Mining Age,* Dec. 1901, p. 8, DPL, "Women as Miners" file.
43. Clipping entitled "Women in Mining Camps," 15 Jan. 1898, DPL, "Women as Miners" file.
44. Clipping dated 14 Jan. 1912, DPL, "Women as Miners" file.
45. Clipping dated 14 Jan. 1912, DPL, "Women as Miners" file.
46. *Goldfield Chronicle,* 24 Oct. 1907; *Goldfield (Nevada) Sun,* 21 July 1906. Nevada had three camps or mining districts named Central or Central City; Helen Cottrell probably ran her boardinghouse at the one located near Manhattan; see Paher, *Nevada Ghost Towns,* 367, 485.
47. *Goldfield Chronicle,* 14 Oct. 1907; *Goldlfield Sun,* 21 July 1906.
48. *Goldfield Chronicle,* 24 Oct. 1907; *Goldfield (Nevada) Tribune,* 19 Feb. 1909; *Reno Evening Gazette,* 22 May 1909. Helen Cottrell's name was evidently misspelled "A. Cotterell" when she filed four claims in the Antelope district on 1 July 1907; Nye County, Index to Mining Locators, bk. I, 1907; in 1909 Helen recorded placer claims at Manhattan, listed in bk. J, 1907–9.
49. On the subsequent development of the Orleans, see Lingenfelter, *Death Valley,* 414; the discrepancy between production figures for promotional purposes (often exaggerated) and tax reports (often understated to avoid taxes) makes the true figures hard to determine. A Goldfield mining property, Orleans Silver, a name suggesting Helen Cottrell's involvement, produced moderately well in the 1921–24 period; see Couch and Carpenter, *Mineral Production,* 64.
50. Fay, "Southwest Davis Zinc Field."
51. Clipping marked *Times,* 8 July 1901, DPL, "Women as Miners" file.
52. Marie Jensen Peterson, "History of Peterson Mine, 1922," and introduction, both in John G. Peterson Family Papers, 1861–1961, Alaska Historical Library, Juneau; also see Redman, "Juneau Gold Belt," 181–84.
53. Riley, *Female Frontier,* 73, 99.
54. Strobridge, *Sagebrush Trilogy,* 42.
55. Strobridge, *Sagebrush Trilogy,* 55; introduction and foreword by Richard A. Dwyer and Richard E. Lingenfelter, 1–11. On the recent rediscovery of "ecopsychology," see Goleman, "World Beyond the Self," E6.
56. Clipping marked *Times,* 24 Mar. 1902, p. 10, DPL, "Women as Miners" file.

57. Faragher, *Overland Trail*, esp. 143, 174; also see Jeffrey, *Frontier Women*, 73–78.
58. Waite, *Adventures in the Far West*, 132–36 (Burlingame journal).
59. Waite, *Adventures in the Far West*, 132–36.
60. Waite, *Adventures in the Far West*, 132–36; Madsen, *Glory Hunter*, 106–8. The many references on early Utah mining, all of which accept the picnic version, include Sloane and Sloane, *American Mining*, 204; Arrington, "Abundance from the Earth," 192–219; and Stenhouse, *Rocky Mountain Saints*, 713.
61. *Goldfield Review*, 20 Apr. 1907; Albert, *Desert Prospector*, 43. Two Goldfield prospectors, Mrs. Kate McLisle, a veteran of the rush to Nome, and Mrs. Kate Gabber, provided an additional instance of female partnership; *Goldfield Sun*, 3 Sept. 1906. On the 1907 women prospector's association, see *Nevada State Journal* (Reno), 15 Sept. 1907.
62. Interview with David Mackenzie, *New York Evening Post*, 2 Dec. 1924, in the privately held Carol E. Hines Family Papers; Stickney, "Colorado Women Successful"; clipping dated 14 Jan. 1912, DPL, "Women as Miners" file.

#### 4. THE STEAM ENGINE AND THE LOST BREYFOGLE

1. *Tonopah Bonanza*, 9 May 1908. The *Bonanza* apparently harbored unspecified doubts on the Verrault story, which was reprinted from the *Los Angeles Examiner*.
2. *Goldfield Sun*, 21 Aug. 1906; Vanderburg, *Placer Mining*, 29–30.
3. Ellis, *Ordinary Woman*, 253; *Goldfield Tribune*, 11 Mar. 1907.
4. *Goldfield Tribune*, 5, 6, and 11 Mar. 1907 (quotation from 5 Mar.).
5. Ellis, *Ordinary Woman*, 253.
6. *Goldfield News*, 28 July 1906; *Lyon County (Nevada) Times*, 11 Aug. 1906 (this newspaper is dated 1916, but other news items on the same page indicate that it is mislabeled and the actual date should be 1906). Nye County, Index to Mining Locators, bks. F–G, 1905–6. On Enright, see *Goldfield Tribune*, 5, 6, 8, 9, and 11 Mar. 1907 and 12 Dec. 1910; U.S. manuscript census, 1910; *Goldfield Sun*, 21 Aug. 1906; and Ellis, *Ordinary Woman*, 253.
7. Nevada Historical Society, "First Woman in Goldfield" (based on a story in the *Pueblo [Colorado] Chieftain*); *Goldfield News*, 27 Mar. 1909. Though consistent on most points, these sources diverge in some respects. In those instances I have placed greater reliance on the obituary in the *Goldfield News* because it was written in the community where Frances Williams had lived for six years and was well known. Some elements, though unusual,

are not implausible: for instance, giving birth to sixteen children with only one or two surviving until adulthood is consistent with Rh incompatibility, a condition not yet understood in Frances's time; there are, of course, other possibilities.

8. *Goldfield Tribune*, 27 Mar. 1909 (Colburn); *Tonopah (Nevada) Sun* and *Goldfield Tribune*, 25 Mar. 1909; Zanjani, *Goldfield*, 24–25; Nye County, Index to Mining Locators, bks. G, 1905–7, and J, 1907–9; Esmeralda County, Index to Mining Locations, bks. B–E, 1899–1906. For a harsh critique of Williams's credentials as a Goldfield pioneer from a local resident, see Ruth ? to Hugh Shamberger, 28 Nov. 1977, Nevada Historical Society, Reno.

9. Nevada Historical Society, "First Woman in Goldfield"; *Tonopah (Nevada) Miner*, 16 July 1904. On Coaldale, also see Carlson, *Nevada Place Names*, 80.

10. *Tonopah Miner*, 27 Aug. and 3 Sept. 1904. On the Coaldale townsite, also see Paher, *Nevada Ghost Towns*, 426.

11. Koontz interview; see also Ruth ? to Shamberger and *Silver State* (Winnemucca, Nevada), 5 Aug. 1907. Interest in the Coaldale coal revived sporadically over the years, and during World War II when a fuel shortage loomed, the U.S. Bureau of Mines conducted new tests; see the *Reno Evening Gazette*, 24 July 1943.

12. *Tonopah Bonanza*, 27 Aug. 1904; Zanjani, *Goldfield*, 53–55, 61–62; De Armond, *"Stroller" White*, 114–15; Glasscock, *Gold in Them Hills*, 66–67. One story of a petty scam involving a woman prospector emerges in the memoirs of Josie Earp: at Rampart, Alaska, in 1898–99, a Mrs. Morse, who had prospected unsuccessfully, "used her gilt paint to transform small, heavy pebbles into nuggets" and was arrested; it is not clear, however, how long and seriously Mrs. Morse had prospected; see Boyer, *I Married Wyatt Earp*, 178.

13. *Tonopah Bonanza*, 27 Aug. 1904; Miles, "Recollections of Goldfield."

14. *Tonopah Miner*, 27 Aug. 1904 and 7 Jan. 1905; *Walker Lake Bulletin*, 6 Jan., 1905. Also see Fraser, *Warrior Queens*, 127.

15. *Tonopah Miner*, 27 Mar. 1909; *Goldfield Tribune*, 25 Mar. 1909; *Goldfield News*, 10 Apr. 1909 and 16 June 1906. Both Frances and her husband were buried in Los Angeles. This fact, combined with her absence from the the San Francisco City Directory in 1900, the U.S. manuscript census of the same year, and San Francisco newspaper indexes, raises some doubt regarding her place of residence in California; a reference in her own 1908 letter to closing her medical practice in San Francisco, however, remains the strongest piece of evidence on the subject; see Williams to Jeanne E. Weir, 4 Nov. 1908, Nevada Historical Society, Reno.

16. Zanjani, *Goldfield,* 43–45, 171; Shamberger, *Goldfield,* 184; Rice, *My Adventures,* 100–101; Glasscock, *Gold in Them Hills,* 176–77; *Goldfield News,* 27 Mar. 1909, and the 1906–7 annual issue, 44.

17. The descriptions are from the *Goldfield News,* 10 and 17 Apr. 1909.

18. *Hornsilver (Nevada) Herald,* 16 May and 13 June 1908. On Mrs. C. A. Wright, see the *Goldfield Review,* 26 Oct., 1905.

19. *Goldfield Chronicle,* 18 July 1908; "Report on the Royal Flush Mine at Gold Mountain, Nevada," 2; and "Early History of the Mine," Royal Flush Mine Papers, Nevada Historical Society, Reno. A newspaper story stated that Frances had staked the Gold Mountain claims herself, but mining records suggest that she had probably purchased them; see the *Goldfield Chronicle,* 18 July 1908. One report on the Royal Flush discovery indicated that Miss M. T. Marquise and Mrs. S. W. Smith, an attorney's wife, sought involvement; when Frances organized the Frances Gold Mountain Mining Company, however, S. W. Smith appears among the officers and directors, but these women do not; see the *Goldfield Chronicle,* 18 July 1908, and the Royal Flush Mine Papers.

20. *Goldfield Chronicle,* 18 July 1908; *Goldfield Review,* 5 Jan. 1907; "Report on the Royal Flush Mine" and "Early History of the Mine," Royal Flush Mine Papers.

21. Addison N. Clark to Jeanne E. Weir, 15 Dec. 1946, Royal Flush Mine Papers; *Rhyolite (Nevada) Bulletin,* 17 Nov. 1908; *Goldfield News,* 10 Apr. 1909. For an outstanding history of Breyfogle and the lost lode, see Lingenfelter, *Death Valley,* 73–79.

22. Frances E. Williams to Weir, 4 Nov. 1908, Nevada Historical Society, Reno; *Goldfield News,* 10 Apr. 1909.

23. "Report on the Royal Flush Mine," Royal Flush Mine Papers; *Goldfield News,* 10 Apr. 1909. The State Bank and Trust, which failed, was the exclusive fiscal agent for Affiliated Corporations; see the *Tonopah Miner,* 17 Sept. 1904. On Mackenzie's further career, see a clipping from the *New York Evening Post,* 2 Dec. 1924, in Hines Family Papers. On the suit against the Frances-Mohawk, see Zanjani, *Goldfield,* 70; and *Goldfield Mohawk Mining Company v. Frances-Mohawk Mining and Leasing Company, Nevada Reports* 33 (1910): 491–508.

24. *Goldfield Tribune,* 25 Mar. 1909; *Goldfield News,* 27 Mar. 1909; Clark to Weir, 15 Dec. 1946; and "Report on the Royal Flush Mine," Royal Flush Mine Papers. The sources reveal nothing on the extent of Frances Williams's involvement in the Frances-Mohawk when the trial commenced.

There is a suggestion in the Royal Flush Mine Papers that Goldfielders attributed the sudden death of the vigorous and energetic Frances to a bank failure, but no institutions at which Frances had known deposits failed at the time of her death; the timing of the lawsuit fits exactly and also conforms with the theory of stress caused by a serious financial reversal.

## 5. ELLEN NAY

1. *Goldfield News*, 14 June 1909.
2. Joseph Clifford, interviews with author, Stone Cabin Ranch, Aug. 1980 and 1981. On accidental discoveries, see *Goldfield Review*, 28 Sept. 1905. Young places little credence in such stories; see *Western Mining*, 21.
3. *Tonopah Sun*, 21 June 1909; *Goldfield News*, 14 June 1909.
4. U.S. manuscript censuses, 1880, 1900, 1910; Nye County, tax records, 1883, Nye County Courthouse, Tonopah, Nevada; *Tonopah Bonanza*, 15 Apr. 1916; *Tonopah Sun*, 19 June 1909; on Barcelona and Tybo, see Paher, *Nevada Ghost Towns*, 348, 361.
5. Clifford interviews. On the isolation of central Nevada in this period, also see Ludwig, "Belmont Memories," 12.
6. King, "Dust and Desire," 2.
7. King, "Dust and Desire," 2.
8. King, "Dust and Desire," 1; Nay, oral history tape.
9. Nay, oral history tape; Wanda McNair, interview with author, Fallon, Nevada, 17 July 1991, and by telephone 8 Oct. 1991; *Tonopah Bonanza*, 3 Apr. 1938.
10. *Belmont (Nevada) Courier*, 25 Nov. and 12 Dec. 1899.
11. Keeler, "Nye County," 966–67; King, "Dust and Desire," 11, 13; *Tonopah Bonanza*, 11 Jan. 1902 and 15 Apr. 1916; *Tonopah Sun*, 5 June 1909.
12. King, "Dust and Desire," 12–13; Carpenter, Elliott, and Sawyer, *Mining at Tonopah*, 8.
13. Zanjani, *Jack Longstreet*, 80–95, 128.
14. King, "Dust and Desire," 9–11; Scrugham, *Nevada*, 3:60.
15. Zanjani, *Goldfield*, chap. 2.
16. Aston, "Esmeralda County," 867; Aston unfortunately does not specify Ed Clifford senior or junior, but joining the rush to Goldfield would have been consistent with the senior Clifford's past and future activities.
17. Nay tape; *Tonopah Bonanza*, 19 Mar. 1904; King, "Dust and Desire," 14; King, letter to author, 18 Oct. 1986.

18. *Goldfield News,* 29 Dec. 1905; Paher, *Nevada Ghost Towns,* 332; Zanjani, *Jack Longstreet,* 98; King, "Dust and Desire," 14; Nye County, Index to Mining Locators, bks. C–D, 1905–6.
19. *Goldfield Sun,* 3 Sept. 1906.
20. King interview.
21. King interview; King, "Dust and Desire," 15.
22. King interview; King, "Dust and Desire," 14–15; *Tonopah Bonanza,* 15 Apr. 1916.
23. *Goldfield News,* 14 June 1909.
24. *Goldfield News,* 14 June 1909.
25. *Goldfield News,* 14 June 1909; *Tonopah Sun,* 5 June 1909.
26. *Tonopah Sun,* 5 June 1909; Will C. Russell, public letter dated 10 June 1909, in the *Tonopah Miner,* 12 June 1909.
27. *Tonopah Sun,* 5 June 1909; Glasscock, *Gold in Them Hills,* 77–80. Nye County, Index to Mining Locators, bks. J–K, 1907–12.
28. *Tonopah Miner,* 12 and 26 June 1909; *Goldfield News,* 10 and 14 June 1909.
29. *Tonopah Sun,* 12 June 1909; McNair interviews; King, undated letter to author.
30. *Ellendale (Nevada) Star,* 19 June 1909; *Tonopah Sun,* 5 June 1909. Actually, the record books show that Ellie included the names of both her parents on her claims. Since the two earliest dates, 19 May and 10 June, show four claims under Joe's name and four under Ellie's and neither one recorded the name of the other, the whole matter sounds like a sexist quibble; see Nye County, Index to Mining Locators, bk. J, 1907–9.
31. Russell letter; *Ellendale Star,* 12 June 1909; *Goldfield News,* 14 June 1909; *Tonopah Miner,* 19 and 26 June 1909; *Tonopah Sun,* 12 May, 11–12, 19, 26, and 28 June 1909.
32. *Ellendale Star,* 19 and 26 June, 3, 17, 24, and 31 July 1909; *Tonopah Sun,* 5, 19, and 26 June 1909; *Tonopah Miner,* 12 and 19 June 1909.
33. *Goldfield News,* 14 June 1909; ironically, the *News* reporter, though skeptical of the Ellendale strike, was the only newsman on the scene who paid any attention to Ellie Nay.
34. Myres, *Westering Women,* 269; *Nevada State Journal,* 15 Sept. 1907; *Black Hills Times* (Deadwood City, Dakota Territory), 21 Apr. 1879; *Goldfield Tribune,* 8 Apr. 1907.
35. *Ellendale Star,* 10 July 1909.
36. *Ellendale Star,* 17 July 1909; *Tonopah Miner,* 10, 17, and 24 July 1909; Lingenfelter and Gash, *Newspapers of Nevada,* 69–70.

37. King, "Dust and Desire," 16–17, and undated letter to author.
38. Couch and Carpenter, *Mineral Production*, 50, 112–13; Murbarger, *Ghosts*, 259.
39. King, "Dust and Desire," 9; Coolidge, *Death Valley Prospectors*, 81–86 (Lemoigne).
40. Zanjani, *Unspiked Rail*, 86 (desert poet); Peterson, *Bonanza Rich*, 63 (Brown); Lilliard, *Desert Challenge*, 212 (Bowers); Ruskin, "Letters to Lizzie," 123 (chaff).
41. King, "Dust and Desire," 9, 18–19, 39–40; King interview; Jim Wolf, interview with author, Barley Creek ranch, 8 Nov. 1992; I am indebted to Mr. Wolf for kindly showing me the features of the ranch, which he now owns. On women blacksmiths, see Wertheimer, *We Were There*, 12, 40–41; and U.S. Census Bureau, *Occupations at the Twelfth Census*, cxxxiv.
42. King interview; King, "Dust and Desire," 6–7.
43. King and McNair interviews.
44. *Tonopah (Nevada) Times-Bonanza*, 4 Apr. 1939 and 4 and 11 Apr. 1947.

6. "HERS WERE THE ONLY HANDS TO ASSIST ME"

1. Riley, *Female Frontier*, 2–3, 199–201; Degler, *At Odds*, 116–19; Agnes Reddenbaugh to Sonia De Hart, undated 1992 or 1993 letter, author's collection.
2. Clipping marked "Times," 26 Nov. 1902, DPL, "Women as Miners" file.
3. *Arizona Daily Star*, 3 Mar. 1928; *Jessen's Weekly* (Alaska), 17 Mar. 1955, 13.
4. Clipping marked "Times," 15 Jan. 1898, DPL, "Women as Miners" file. On Harqua Hala, also see Arline, "Harqua Hala"; and Ransom, "Harquahala Bonanza," 15–19.
5. *Goldfield Chronicle*, 3 Mar. 1908.
6. Hunt, *Golden Places*, 234–35; Robert L. Spude, letter to author, 23 Aug. 1993.
7. *San Francisco Mail*, 27 May 1877; *Arizona Daily Gazette* (Phoenix), 28 Apr. 1895; *Arizona Journal Miner* (Prescott), 30 Dec. 1897; all in the George Monroe file, Arizona Historical Society, Tucson.
8. *Arizona Miner* (Prescott), 11 May 1877; *Arizona Republican* (Phoenix), 30 Apr. 1895; *Prescott (Arizona) Courier*, 27 Nov. 1902; all in Monroe file; Johnson, "Sharing Bed and Board," 85–86.
9. *Phoenix Herald*, 26 Apr. 1895, Monroe file (Sawyer); *Tonopah Miner*, 20 July 1907 (Miller).
10. *Goldfield News*, 4 May (early visitor) and 23 Mar. 1906; Hedrick, "Newest Manhattan," 261; Nye County, Index to Mining Locators, bks. D–F, 1905–6.

11. Downie, *Hunting for Gold,* 173 (forty-niner); Zanjani, "Indian Prospectors," 53–55; Zanjani, *Jack Longstreet,* 114–15 (Scott); Caruthers, *Death Valley Trails,* 84, 90–91.

12. *Goldfield Sun,* 12 Feb. 1906; according to this account, the name of Edward Clifford senior appeared on the location notices he assisted in staking.

13. *Goldfield Sun,* 12 Feb. 1906. On the town of Clifford/Helena, see Paher, *Nevada Ghost Towns,* 345; on mining production, see Couch and Carpenter, *Mineral Production,* 108–21; on the embezzlement, see *Tonopah Sun,* 15 May 1909.

14. U.S. manuscript census, 1880. I am much indebted to Walter Wilson for providing me with sources and insights on the Butlers and Donohue from his forthcoming history of Tonopah; interviews 6 Aug. 1991 and 4 Mar. 1992, Reno, Nevada.

15. Wilson interviews. Also see Myles, "Jim Butler," 60–63.

16. Myles, "Jim Butler," esp. 62 n. 2; Mary McCann Sharp, undated oral history tape, Nevada Historical Society, Reno; *Eureka Sentinel,* 22 Sept. 1888; *Reno Evening Gazette,* 21 Sept. 1888; *Belmont Courier,* 29 Sept. 1888.

17. Myles, "Jim Butler," 63; Curtis Littlebeaver, interview with author, Tonopah, Nevada, 26 May 1990; Zanjani, "Indian Prospectors," 53–55.

18. William A. Douglass and Robert A. Nylen have rightly pointed out that Oddie showed no undue excitement in his letter to his mother following the assay of the Butler ore, but the account by Glasscock on the Indian runner appears to have originated with Oddie himself; see Douglass and Nylen, *Correspondence of Tasker L. Oddie,* 225, 365 n. 175; and Glasscock, *Gold in Them Hills,* 23–25, 27.

19. Glasscock, *Gold in Them Hills,* 23. The Butler claims, subsequently recorded in November, appear in Nye County, Index of Locators, 1864–1903. See also Reddenbaugh letter.

20. Glasscock, *Gold in Them Hills,* 27; *White Pine (Nevada) News,* 4 Aug. 1911; *Tonopah Bonanza,* 23 June 1922.

21. Scrugham, *Nevada,* 3:59; *Tonopah Bonanza,* 23 June 1922; *Tonopah Miner,* 17 Feb. 1906.

22. Homsher, *South Pass,* 94, 104; Todd Guenther, curator, South Pass City State Historic Site, Wyoming, letter to author, 13 Jan. 1993. On Mrs. Brennan, see Pfaff, *Atlantic City Nuggets,* 116; on rockers, see Young, *Western Mining,* 113.

23. Clipping marked "Post," 23 Aug. 1936, DPL, "Women as Miners" file.

24. *Angels and Altaville (California)*, 21 Nov. 1896. The name of one of these claims, the Amelia, suggests that Amelin may have been a misprint.

25. Burford, *North to Danger*, 254.

26. Joraleman, *Adventure Beacons*, 308; Patty, *North Country Challenge*, 76, 80; Bundtzen, "Kantishna Hills," 152, 154, 161 n. 13.

27. Patty, *North Country Challenge*, 79; Burford, *North to Danger*, 244; Davis, *We Are Alaskans*, 198.

28. Joraleman, *Adventure Beacons*, 310–11; Bundtzen, "Kantishna Hills," 157; Brown, *Denali–Mount McKinley Region*, 1:112, 117; Burford, *North to Danger*, 243–44, 258. I am deeply indebted to Jane Haigh for sharing information with me from her forthcoming biography of Fannie Quigley.

29. Glasscock, *Gold in Them Hills*, 255–58.

30. Glasscock, *Gold in Them Hills*, 255–58.

31. Glasscock, *Gold in Them Hills*, 255–58.

32. Glasscock, *Gold in Them Hills*, 255–58; Scott, "Thousand Miles," 2:209. Dates given by Glasscock for the discovery of the Riggs Mine are not entirely consistent, nor does the date of Mrs. Riggs's death tally with the Scott account. The Scotts do not name the Riggses, but the location of the mine they describe is fully consistent with the Riggs Mine.

33. Boyer, *I Married Wyatt Earp*, 37–38, 59 n. 18, 113, 118–19 n. 2, 122, 154, 161, 200, 206–7; Kintop and Rocha, *Earps' Last Frontier*, 21–27, 44–52. The prospecting phase of the Earps' lives marked the resumption of a less focused period of desert travel that they had undertaken before the Klondike gold rush changed their plans, but this time the initiative was Josie's.

34. Boyer, *I Married Wyatt Earp*, 206–9, 214 (quotation); Kintop and Rocha, *Earps' Last Frontier*, 29–30.

35. Boyer, *I Married Wyatt Earp*, 214–15; Kintop and Rocha, *Earps' Last Frontier*, 31–32.

36. Boyer, *I Married Wyatt Earp*, 218–22, 226–27, 233–36, 237 nn. 9, 10.

37. Boyer, *I Married Wyatt Earp*, 207–8, 229–30.

38. Scott, "Thousand Miles," 1:31, 95; 2:240–41; 3:275, 298, 374.

39. Scott, "Thousand Miles," 1:39, 74.

40. Scott, "Thousand Miles," 1:70, 127; 3:282, 286, 316, 363. On burros, also see Wilhelm, *Last Rig*, 147–48.

41. Scott, "Thousand Miles," 2:166; 3:265, 319, 361.

42. Scott, "Thousand Miles," 2:245, 247, 249, 251–52, 259; 3:286, 316.

43. Scott, "Thousand Miles," 2:244, 254; 3:346.

44. Scott, "Thousand Miles," 2:234, poem facing p. 142; 3:320, 328–29.

45. Scott, "Thousand Miles," 1:66, 88–89; 2:178–79, 182, 187; 3:271, 275, 322.
46. Etulain, "Wallace Stegner," 8.
47. Wilhelm, *Last Rig*, 3–5, 15–20; Homsher, *South Pass*, 63.
48. Wilhelm, *Last Rig*, 24, 68.
49. Wilhelm, *Last Rig*, 69.
50. Wilhelm, *Last Rig*, 68, 91, 102–8, 130.
51. Wilhelm, *Last Rig*, 23, 109.
52. Wilhelm, *Last Rig*, 276–82; Wikstrom interview.
53. Wilhelm, *Last Rig*, 286–88.
54. Wilhelm, *Last Rig*, 289, 294–95, 307–8; Wilhelm, "Dora's Diggin's," 15–16. On southern California as the new retirement mecca, see White, *Your Misfortune*, 425.
55. Guerin, *Mountain Charley*, 54.
56. Alberts, "Petticoats and Pickaxes," 155; Downie, *Hunting for Gold*, 96–97.
57. Alberts, "Petticoats and Pickaxes"; Degler, *At Odds*, 46–49. Burlingame and Reid apparently did not take their husbands along on their prospecting expeditions either, but their trips were shorter than those of Jennings and Williams. Riley uncovered more mixed results on female initiative: some women suggested the move to the Plains; see Riley, *Female Frontier*, 96; Faragher, *Overland Trail*, 111, 163.
58. On Chisana, see Hunt, *Golden Places*, 231–32, 238–39.
59. On the married woman's loss of identity in newspaper stories, see Cloud, "Images of Women," 202.
60. Stickney, "Colorado Women Successful."

7. QUEEN MARY AND THE TUGBOAT ANNIE OF THE DESERT

1. Chalfant, *Tales of the Pioneers*, 115–16.
2. Albert, *Desert Prospector*, 10; *Elko (Nevada) Independent*, 24 Jan. 1907 (Dyer). On early auto prospecting, see Zanjani, *Goldfield*, 87–89; on the rapid acceptance of autos in the West, see Pomeroy, "Computers in the Desert," 8–11; on women's increasingly liberal attitudes toward their less conventional peers, see Riley, *Female Frontier*, 134.
3. Harris, "Chasing Rainbows," 241; *Reno Evening Gazette*, 14 May 1938.
4. *Lovelock (Nevada) Review-Miner*, 19 Sept. 1930; also see Glasscock, *Gold in Them Hills*, 319.
5. *Reno Evening Gazette*, 14 Apr. 1907.
6. Fielder, *Silver Is the Fortune*, 97–105.
7. *Eureka Sentinel*, 9 Aug. 1924.

8. Census reports are discrepant on Maggie's birthdate and the number of her children: the 1900 U.S. manuscript census lists her birthdate as 1855 and records that she had one child, who was still living; the 1910 census states that her birthdate was 1857 and she was the mother of five children, all dead. Also see *Eureka Sentinel,* 9 Aug. 1924; *Battle Mountain (Nevada) Scout,* 24 July 1920. On black women in the West, see Myres, *Westering Women,* 85–86; on Mill Canyon and Cortez, see Paher, *Nevada Ghost Towns,* 165. Johnson's Louisiana origin and the date of her arrival in Nevada raise the speculation that she might have been an "exoduster" driven by the oppressive conditions of Reconstruction to migrate to Kansas in 1879; some from this movement later dispersed to other western states; see Painter, *Exodusters.*

9. Spears, *Sketches of Death Valley,* 70; Celeste Lowe, telephone interview with author, 24 May 1993. Other Death Valley mining women of the period included Myra Benson, reputedly the discoverer of a claim near Salsbury Pass that she and her husband occasionally mined (Lowe interview; Caruthers, *Death Valley Trails,* 133–35), and Mrs. Orpha Hart and Mrs. Mary Ann Thompson, a formidable pair of sisters who wielded guns and lawsuits to hold some ninety claims in the Panamints against armed rivals (*Nevada Mining Record and Reporter,* 2 Aug. 1930; Lingenfelter, *Death Valley,* 414; Ralph Lisle, telephone interview with author, 1 Feb. 1994).

10. Lowe interview; Caruthers, *Death Valley Trails,* 66, 70; Lowe, "Lady Prospectors," 8; Lisle interview.

11. Lowe, "Lady Prospectors," 8.

12. Lowe, "Lady Prospectors," 8; Lowe interview; Caruthers, *Death Valley Trails,* 68, 158; Greene, *History of Mining,* 1:133.

13. Lowe, "Lady Prospectors," 8; Russell, "Ledge of Gold!" 15–17, 34–35; Lowe interview.

14. Lowe, "Lady Prospectors," 8; Caruthers, *Death Valley Trails,* 139–40 (quotation), 190; Greene, *History of Mining,* 263–65; Lowe interview.

15. Greene, *History of Mining,* 263, 269; Lowe, "Lady Prospectors," 8; Russell, "Ledge of Gold!" 15, 34. On uses of talc, see Evans, Taylor, and Rapp, "Mines and Mineral Deposits," 527.

16. Greene, *History of Mining,* 266, 288–90; Lowe, "Lady Prospectors," 8; Evans et al., "Mines and Mineral Deposits," 527.

17. Earl, "Woman Prospector," 4; Schulmerich, *Josie Pearl,* 35–63 (quotation, 63). Some discrepancies exist on Josie's place and date of birth: the 1910 U.S. manuscript census gives a birthdate of 1875, which would make Josie

two years younger than the other sources, and lists Tennessee as her birthplace.

18. Schulmerich, *Josie Pearl,* 65–70, 87, 116–17 (quotation, 117). An eleven-year discrepancy exists between the marriage date (1892) given by Schulmerich for the Pearls and the one in the 1910 U.S. manuscript census. In the absence of any documentation by Schulmerich I consider the census date given when Josie was young and her memory was better to be more plausible, with the caveat that the censuses sometimes contain errors.

19. *Nevada State Journal,* 22 July 1970; June Anderson, telephone interviews with author, 1 Nov. 1992 and 7 Feb. 1993. I am much indebted to Mrs. Anderson for providing me with photographs of her aunt, Mary Grantz. By 1919 Mary had altered the spelling of her surname to Grantz, possibly because it sounded less Germanic during the wartime wave of anti-German feeling.

20. Schulmerich, *Josie Pearl,* 117–23, 150–53; Pyle, *Home Country,* 210. On the Palm Grill, see Zanjani, *Goldfield,* 150. Josie did not mention the Pearl Restaurant to her biographer, but the name is suggestive; see the *Goldfield Tribune,* 25 Mar. 1907.

21. Schulmerich, *Josie Pearl,* 153–56.

22. Schulmerich, *Josie Pearl,* 134–35, 143–44, 166.

23. Schulmerich, *Josie Pearl,* 166–83; Edna Simmons, telephone interview with author, 3 Feb. 1994; Arthur and Janet Thomas, telephone interview with author, 3 Nov. 1994; Pyle, *Home Country,* 210; Wilhelm, *Last Rig,* 18–19 (quotation); Robert D. Stitser, telephone interview with author, 5 May 1992; Humboldt County, Index to Notices, bks. 6–7, Humboldt County Courthouse, Winnemucca, Nevada. On the Betty O'Neal mine, see Paher, *Nevada Ghost Towns,* 163; on the Taylor ranch, see Georgetta, *Golden Fleece,* 367–78. Some discrepancies exist on the sequence of events: Schulmerich places Josie at the Taylor ranch, then Bodie, followed by the Betty O'Neal (see *Josie Pearl,* 170–87); Arthur Thomas, however, clearly recalls her in Bodie in 1928 and Edna Simmons places her at the Taylor ranch in 1931–32, which suggests that the sequence was Bodie, followed by the Betty O'Neal, then the Taylor ranch. On Josie's first husband, the 1910 U.S. manuscript census on the Pearls and others nearby contains an unusual set of notations in the marital status column, "M1," "M2," etc., evidently recording the number of marriages. Josie's notation is "M2," indicating another husband before Lane Pearl.

24. Schulmerich, *Josie Pearl,* 7, 190–92; Wikstrom interview.

25. Schulmerich, *Josie Pearl,* 190–95; Pyle, *Home Country,* 209; Stitser interview.

26. Anderson interviews; Edith Patri, telephone interview with author, 19 Oct. 1992; Alice Singstock, telephone interview with author, 18 Nov. 1992; Walter Grenz, telephone interview with author, 6 Nov. 1992.

27. Patri and Anderson interviews; Vanderburg, "Mining Districts in Humboldt County," 39; Humboldt County, Deeds, bk. 52, Humboldt County Courthouse, Winnemucca, Nevada. It is, of course, also possible that Mary met Clough in Florida or in northern Nevada.

28. Anderson and Grenz interviews; Laura Stanley, telephone interview with author, 3 Sept. 1991; Humboldt County, Index to Notices, bk. 5. On mining camp mores, see Zanjani, *Goldfield*, 110, 179.

29. Anderson and Stanley interviews.

30. Anderson and Stitser interviews; Duane Devine, interview with author, Winnemucca, Nevada, 9 May 1992, and by telephone, 15 Aug. 1991.

31. Stitser, Devine, Simmons, Rueckl, and Anderson interviews; Albert Montero, telephone interview with author, 11 May 1992; Pyle, *Home Country,* 209.

32. Stitser, Rueckl, Anderson, and Devine interviews; *Lovelock Review-Miner,* 31 Dec. 1937.

33. Devine interviews.

34. Devine interviews; also see the Stanley and Anderson interviews and Nevada Inspector of Mines, Reports. The Black Diablo closed for about two years after the war until the stockpiled manganese had been depleted.

35. Devine interviews; Humboldt County, Index to Notices, bk. 7; Deanna Grenz, telephone interview with author, 7 July 1992.

36. Humboldt County, Index to Notices, bk. 7; and Deed Indexes; Rueckl and Stitser interviews; Schulmerich, *Josie Pearl,* 217–18. It is unclear whether the opals Rueckl saw sold on the streets were the same as the tourmalines Stitser helped Josie mine, or whether Josie possessed mines that yielded both gems.

37. Pyle, *Home Country,* 209–10; Rueckl and Stitser interviews; Murbarger, "Josie Pearl," 177.

38. Murbarger, "Josie Pearl," 177; Rueckl interview.

39. Smith, *Daughters of the Promised Land,* 205; Boydston, *Home and Work,* 112; Mathews, *Ten Years in Nevada,* 131–32; Schulmerich, *Josie Pearl,* 195. On alternate living arrangements, see Cowan, *More Work for Mother,* 101–50.

40. Rueckl interview; Margaret Butts, interview with author, Winnemucca, Nevada, 8 May 1992; Schulmerich, *Josie Pearl,* 182–83, 245.

41. Schulmerich, *Josie Pearl,* 225–27.

42. Schulmerich, *Josie Pearl,* 243–47, 266–67.

43. Stitser and Rueckl interviews; Murbarger, "Josie Pearl"; Schulmerich, *Josie Pearl,* 264.

44. Anderson, Stanley, and Singstock interviews.

45. Mayer, *Klondike Women,* 226; Dwyer and Lingenfelter, introduction to Strobridge, *Sagebrush Trilogy,* 5; Wilhelm, *Last Rig,* 21; "Mother and Daughter Who Work in Their Own Mine," DPL, "Women as Miners" file (Thomas and Hornbeck); *Rocky Mountain News,* 5 Nov. 1995, 71A.

46. Stitser and Anderson interviews; Pyle, *Home Country,* 210.

47. Devine and Anderson interviews; Ada Magnussen, 10 July 1992, telephone interview with author. On gold rush lawsuits, see Downie, *Hunting for Gold,* 101.

48. Devine interviews.

49. Devine and Anderson interviews.

50. Anderson, Magnussen, and Deanna Grenz interviews; *Nevada State Journal,* 22 July 1970.

51. *Humboldt Star,* 3 Jan. 1963; Earl, "Woman Prospector," 4; Simmons interview.

52. Devine interview; Murbarger, "Josie Pearl."

8. "HIT ROCK BOTTOM HARD ENOUGH TO BOUNCE"

1. Degler, *At Odds,* 415–16; Ware, *Holding Their Own,* 33–34.

2. *Denver Mining Record,* reprinted in *Nevada State Journal,* 6 June 1932.

3. *Goldfield News and Weekly Tribune,* 5 Aug. 1938 (Tenabo); Hunt, *Golden Places,* 324 (Ibach).

4. Coffey and Hoeper, *Bacon and Beans,* 1–5, 13–14, 36–38, 42–44.

5. Coffey and Hoeper, *Bacon and Beans,* 5, 8, 12–13, 45, 62, 104, 112.

6. Coffey and Hoeper, *Bacon and Beans,* 13, 17–18, 60–62, 102.

7. Coffey and Hoeper, *Bacon and Beans,* 93–94, 113–15, 132–35, 161–64.

8. Coffey and Hoeper, *Bacon and Beans,* 173–79.

9. *Tonopah Times-Bonanza,* 17 Nov. 1961; LeCompte, *Cowgirls of the Rodeo,* 77–78, 88; Farnsworth, "Cowgirl Prospector," 16.

10. *Lake County (Oregon) Examiner,* 15 Sept., 10 and 17 Nov. 1927.

11. *Lake County Examiner,* 15 Sept., 17 and 24 Nov. 1927.

12. LeCompte, *Cowgirls of the Rodeo,* 91; *Tonopah Times-Bonanza,* 9 Feb. 1968.

13. Farnsworth, "Cowgirl Prospector," 17; *Tonopah Times-Bonanza,* 9 Feb. 1968; Peterson, "Reel History."

14. Farnsworth, "Cowgirl Prospector," 17; *Tonopah Times-Bonanza,* 9 Feb. 1968; Peterson, "Reel History"; LeCompte, *Cowgirls of the Rodeo,* 91.

15. Alice Lorigan, telephone interview with author, 12 Nov. 1992; Nye County, Index to Mining Locators, bks. S–V; Farnsworth, "Cowgirl Prospector," 18; *Tonopah Times-Bonanza,* 9 Feb. 1968. On another central Nevada mountain dweller with a shadowy past, see Zanjani, *Jack Longstreet.*

16. Peterson, "Reel History"; Lorigan interview; Earl, "Tonopah's Anniversary"; *Tonopah Times-Bonanza,* 17 Nov. 1961.

17. Farnsworth, "Cowgirl Prospector," 50.

18. Louetta Ward, "Introduction," 2–3; undated and incomplete letter to Frances from her mother, Emma L. Patchen, both in Frances Noyes Muncaster Papers, 1850–1952, and Photographs (henceforth Papers), Alaska Historical Library, Juneau. On companionate marriage, see Evans, *Born for Liberty,* 178–79.

19. Ward, "Introduction," 2–3; Patchen letter; *New York Journal,* 5 Sept. 1897; clipping tentatively dated 21 Sept. 1892; all in Papers.

20. *New York Journal,* 5 Sept. 1897 and undated clipping; undated clipping from *Chicago Chronicle; Allen v. Allen,* Superior Court for Spokane County, 19 July 1897; all in Papers.

21. Ward, "Introduction," 3; clipping tentatively dated 15 June 1899, Papers.

22. Ward, "Introduction," 3.

23. Ward, "Introduction," 3; *Anaconda (Montana) Standard,* 13 Dec. 1908 and undated clipping; a different version in the *Seattle Times,* 14 June 1908, states that Frances brought cash from Candle to the bank in Nome; all in Papers.

24. *Anaconda Standard,* 13 Feb. 1910; *Butte (Montana) Evening News,* 20 Feb. 1910; *Seattle Times,* undated clipping; Ward, "Introduction," 4; Hudson Stuck to Mrs. Noyes, 11 Mar. 1906; William A. Simonds to Ward, 1 Feb. 1985; all in Papers.

25. Capt. William K——? to Frances, 25 Dec. [1916?]; poems to Mrs. T. C. Noyes by the Candle doctor; poem to Mrs. T. C. Noyes by John Holmes; "April foolimony contract" between Mrs. T. C. Noyes and P. H. Watt; Ward, "Introduction," 5 and inventory; Simonds letter; all in Papers.

26. Simonds letter.

27. *Mining and Engineering World,* 12 Feb. 1916; Capt. William K——? to Frances, 28 May 1916; Ward, "Introduction," 6; all in Papers. These sources do not indicate whether Bonnie accompanied her parents to Chisana.

28. William Muncaster to Frances, esp. 10 Apr. 1918, 16 Feb. 1919, and 26 Mar. 1919; Simonds letter; Jack to Frances, 25 Apr. and 27 June 1917; undated clip-

ping on John Holmes's death; John S. Hume to Mrs. Noyes, 17 Dec. 1917; all in Papers.

29. Muncaster to *Alaska Empire,* 29 Oct. 1952; Frances Muncaster diary, 1919–20; Ward, "Introduction," 7; all in Papers.

30. Muncaster to Frances, 28 Mar. 1919; diary entries, 15–16 June 1919; both in Papers.

31. Ward, "Introduction," 7.

32. Ward, "Introduction," 8; Muncaster to Jack Daum, editor of *Alaska Empire,* 11 Nov. 1952, Papers.

33. Simonds letter; Muncaster to Frances, 17 and 20 June and 23 Aug. 1927, Papers.

34. Muncaster to *Alaska Empire,* 29 Oct. 1952; 1940 clipping; clipping marked "West, Jan. 14, 1928"; all in Papers. Frances had herself designated an "independent" mining recorder to circumvent the legal provision that forebade a recorder to stake claims.

35. Simonds letter; *Vancouver Sun,* 3 Feb. 1933; 1940 clipping; all in Papers.

36. Muncaster to Honorable Minister of Mines, 14 Dec. 1945; Muncaster to *Alaska Empire,* 29 Oct. 1952; Muncaster to Daum, 11 Nov. 1952; Ward, "Introduction," 8; all in Papers.

37. Mona Mullins, interviews with author, Minden, Nevada, at irregular intervals from 14 May 1991 to 23 Sept. 1992. My research was much assisted by the access Mona graciously gave me to her photograph album and collection of clippings.

38. Mullins interviews and album; Loelia Carl, interview with author, Fallon, Nevada, 4 Dec. 1991, and telephone interview on 7 Dec.; Tharon Turley, interview with author, Fernley, Nevada, 4 Dec. 1991.

39. *Reno Gazette-Journal,* 9 Aug. 1987, 1D, 3D; Mullins interviews. On the Jumbo excitement, see Paher, *Nevada Ghost Towns,* 148; *Eureka Sentinel,* 6 July 1911; Bechdolt, "Stampede," 14–15, 53–56; *Time,* 31 Aug. 1936, 43–44; and Austin, "Depression Mining Venture," 178–79. Paher dates the Awakening district from 1910, but the *Eureka Sentinel* places the initial strike in 1911.

40. Huntington, "Bride," 92.

41. Huntington, "Bride," 92; Mullins and Carl interviews.

42. Mullins interviews and album; *Reno Gazette-Journal,* 9 Aug. 1987; Turley interview. The Peers' prospecting was temporarily interrupted when Gale entered the armed forces for military service that had been deferred during the war when he was engaged in tungsten production.

43. Mullins interviews and album.

44. Mullins and Carl interviews; Mary Corkill, letter to author, 28 Jan. 1991.

45. Mullins and Carl interviews.

46. Mullins interviews.

## 9. "LISTEN AND THE MOUNTAINS WILL TALK TO YOU"

1. Paher, *Nevada Ghost Towns*, 409–10; Lingenfelter, *Death Valley*, 111, 344–45; Murbarger, *Ghosts*, 92–99.

2. Childers, "Happy Days"; The birthdate I have used is based on Happy Days's death certificate and is consistent with information in the Childers article; Phillip Earl, however, considers 1861 a more likely date; see "Happy Days Diminy," 2E.

3. Childers, "Happy Days"; *Goldfield News*, 29 Mar. 1909; *Goldfield Tribune*, 7 Aug. 1912. The reports of the Nevada State License and Bullion Tax Agent do not list a Happy Days Saloon among the Rhyolite licensees; perhaps the name was an informal one or the establishment preceded the first report in 1908; see *Appendix to the Journals of the Senate and Assembly*, 1909–11.

4. Childers, "Happy Days." Childers gives Shipway's name as Shipler.

5. Earl, "Happy Days Diminy"; *Wyoming Eagle* (Cheyenne), 22 Mar. 1949 (Gibbons); Zanjani, *Goldfield*, 233 (Goldfield prospector poet); Hoagland, "Buckaroo Poets," 3, 17.

6. *Goldfield News*, 29 Mar. 1909.

7. *Goldfield Tribune*, 7 Aug. and 25 Nov. 1912 (quotation from 7 Aug.). Other instances of mining discoveries resulting from dreams were reported in the *Goldfield Review*, 25 Jan. 1906, and the *Tonopah Miner*, 11 June 1904.

8. Roberta Childers, interview with author, Fallon, Nevada, 9 May 1988; *Tonopah Bonanza*, 17 May 1913.

9. Childers, "Happy Days"; Koontz interview; Riemersma interviews.

10. *Jester v. Jester*, 17 June 1942, No. 1041, Fifth Judicial District Court, Esmeralda County Courthouse records, Goldfield, Nevada; Earl, "Happy Days Diminy"; Childers, "Happy Days" (quotation).

11. Childers, "Happy Days" (quotation); Zanjani, *Goldfield*, 247 (Stimler).

12. Lewis interview.

13. Childers, "Happy Days"; Francis Carlson, interview with author, Tonopah, Nevada, 5 Nov. 1988; *Reno Evening Gazette*, 11 Aug. 1938; *Goldfield News*, 2 Sept. 1938; Koontz interview; Bradshaw interview; [Alice Jester], Complaint and Commitment for Insanity, 15 Aug. 1938, Esmeralda County Courthouse records.

14. *Jester v. Jester;* Carlson interview.
15. Childers, "Happy Days"; *Reno Evening Gazette,* 22 May 1943. Childers apparently interviewed Happy Days in the summer of 1941 but did not publish her article for nearly a year.
16. Childers, "Happy Days"; Murbarger, *Ghosts,* 96–97 (Marijilda); certificate of death of Alice Diming, 15 Feb. 1948, California Department of Health Services, Vital Statistics Branch, Sacramento. On her death certificate Happy Days was listed as a widow, presumably a reference to Diminy, whose name she had assumed again; Herbert Jester had died two years earlier but would no longer have been viewed as a spouse after the divorce.
17. Riemersma interviews, scrapbook, and family papers; Kari Coughlin interview with Riemersma, Beatty, Nevada, Mar 1991, Kari Coughlin collection; *Las Vegas Sun,* 27 Sept. 1979, Coughlin collection. I am much indebted to Kari Coughlin, National Park Service historian, for providing me with materials on Panamint Annie.
18. Riemersma interviews; typescript of a Sept. 1980 article by Clare Keefner in Sept. 1980 *Ruralite,* Coughlin collection.
19. Riemersma interviews. Some sources indicate a later date, 1935 or 1936, for Annie's arrival in Death Valley. According to Riemersma, the infants who did not survive included twins stillborn when Annie was forty-eight and a late miscarriage brought on by changing a tire.
20. Riemersma interviews.
21. Riemersma interviews.
22. Riemersma interviews; Kari Coughlin, telephone interview with author, 27 Apr. 1994. On Death Valley mining regulations, see Lingenfelter, *Death Valley,* 466. In view of the woman prospector's tenuous connection to domesticity, Annie's experiment with an alternate living arrangement comes as no surprise; see Cowan, *More Work for Mother,* 111–19, 145–50.
23. Riemersma interviews; Lew Orrell, interview with author, Georgetown, Colorado, 7 June 1994; Coughlin interview with Riemersma.
24. Riemersma interviews.
25. Riemersma interviews; Coughlin interview with Riemersma.
26. Riemersma interviews; Coughlin interview with Riemersma.
27. Riemersma interviews; Coughlin interview with Riemersma.
28. Riemersma interviews; on Frederica Hessler, see *Reno Gazette–Journal,* 4 Dec. 1977, 8A.
29. Riemersma and Orrell interviews. On the reactions of tourists and others

to Annie, especially see Kari Coughlin, telephone interview with Mrs. Dwight Warren, 26 Apr. 1991, Coughlin collection.

30. Riemersma interviews; Keefner typescript.

31. Riemersma interviews; Keefner typescript; *Las Vegas Sun*, 27 Sept. 1979.

32. Coughlin interview with Riemersma; undated clipping from *Los Angeles Times*, Coughlin collection; Warren interview.

33. Keefner typescript; Riemersma and Orrell interviews; *Las Vegas Sun*, 27 Sept. 1979. Annie's use of the sea as a metaphor for the western landscape was a common reaction among early travelers on the plains; see Webb, *Great Plains*, 487–89.

10. ANNA RECHEL

1. Lilliard, *Desert Challenge*, 267; Paher, *Nevada Ghost Towns*, 456; Shamberger, *Rawhide*, 21; U.S. Census Bureau, *Statistics for Nevada*, 1910.

2. For Boyle, see *Churchill County (Nevada) Eagle*, 14 Aug. 1909; for Dormer, see Shamberger, *Rawhide*, 4; and *Tonopah Bonanza*, 2 May 1908. I have assumed that the Mrs. James Hall described in the *Nevada State Journal*, 21 Mar. 1908, as an early Rawhide prospector, the Mrs. Hall referred to by Shamberger (p. 10), and the Lillian Hall who appears in Esmeralda County, Index to Mining Locations, 1907–8, bk. H, are all the same person.

3. Rees and James Mortensen, interviews with author, Reno, Nevada, intermittently from 13 July 1992 through 4 Nov. 1994; LaRae Rechel, interview with author, Fallon, Nevada, 28 Sept. 1992, and by telephone, 8 Dec. 1993. I deeply appreciate the access granted to me by the Mortensens to their family photographs and the genealogical research on Anna provided by LaRae Rechel. On the continuing stigma of divorce in the East twenty years later, see Zanjani, *Unspiked Rail*, 333–36.

4. Mortensen interviews. Also see Bechdolt, "Stampede, 1936 Model," 53; and Warrin, "Portuguese Pioneers in Nevada," 44.

5. Mortensen interviews; Rechel genealogical records; Strobridge, *Sagebrush Trilogy*, 25–26.

6. Mortensen interviews.

7. Mortensen interviews.

8. Mortensen interviews. Also see Shamberger, *Rawhide*, 38–39, 42.

9. Mortensen and Rechel interviews. Also see Marshall, *Arctic Village*, 101–2.

10. Mortensen and Rechel interviews.

11. Mortensen and Rechel interviews; Mineral County, Index to Mining Locations, bks. 2–4, Mineral County Courthouse, Hawthorne, Nevada.

12. Rechel interviews.

13. Mortensen and Riemersma interviews; Schulmerich, *Josie Pearl*, 265–66; Malone and Etulain, *American West*, 249 (Utah uranium prospecting); *Pinedale (Wyoming) Roundup*, 5 Dec. 1929 (Gillespie). On McCormick, see Gipson, "Minnie's Yellow Treasure"; and *Rawlins (Wyoming) Daily Times*, 11 Mar. 1948.

14. Gipson, "Minnie's Yellow Treasure"; *Rawlins Daily Times*, 16 Aug. 1951. Gipson's account that Madame Curie identified the samples as uranium appears unlikely, because Marie Curie died in 1934, two years before McCormick's discovery; perhaps the ore was tested at the Curie Institute. On uranium mining, also see Gomez, *Golden Circle*, 10, 18; Taylor and Taylor, *Uranium Fever*, 79, 101.

15. Mortensen and Rechel interviews; Mineral County, Deed Indexes, bks. 2–3.

16. Mortensen and Rechel interviews.

17. Mortensen interviews; "A Woman's Viewpoint," undated clippings from the *Mason Valley (Nevada) News*, in the privately held Mortensen Family Papers. On the Plowshare Project, see Elliott, *History of Nevada*, 341; on mining camp socializing, see Marshall, *Arctic Village*, 8–9.

18. Mortensen and Rechel interviews.

19. Schulmerich, *Josie Pearl*, 152, 165; *Reno Evening Gazette*, 8 Mar. 1921, and *Nevada State Journal*, 7 Sept. 1922 (Adams-Williams); Stickney, "Colorado Women Successful," DPL, "Women as Miners" file (Atwood).

20. Homsher, *South Pass*, 111; Marshall, *Arctic Village*, 53; Mortensen and Rechel interviews.

21. Mortensen, Powell, and Rechel interviews. On Talapoosa and Rabbithole, see Paher, *Nevada Ghost Towns*, 77, 123.

22. Mortensen interviews.

23. Downie, *Hunting for Gold*, 140–41; Mineral County, Index to Mining Locations, bk. 5, 1960–65; Mortensen interviews.

24. Strobridge, *Sagebrush Trilogy*, 116; "A Woman's Viewpoint"; Mortensen and Rechel interviews.

25. Mortensen and Rechel interviews.

EPILOGUE

1. Kessler-Harris, *Out to Work*, 119; Smith-Rosenberg, *Disorderly Conduct*, 281; Evans, *Born for Liberty*, 147; similarly, Richard O'Connor writes on the new independence and assertiveness of women in the Klondike rush; see *High Jinks*, 70–71, 188. Among 77 women who indisputably prospected at fairly

definite dates, 21 began or were first mentioned between 1850 and 1897; 36 between 1898 and 1910; and 20 after these dates. Most of them appear in the narrative by name.

2. Taylor and Taylor, *Uranium Fever*, 5. On mining engineers, see Spence, *Mining Engineers and the American West*, 77.

3. *Rocky Mountain News*, 1 Dec. 1968; *Denver Post*, 10 Nov. 1972, 24, and 16 Nov. 1972, 51; all in "Women as Miners" file, DPL. See also Kessler-Harris, *Out to Work*, 181; on Utah mining laws, see James and Taylor, "Strong Minded Women," 137; on superstitions, see Earl, "Mules and Rats Revered," 3E.

4. *Sydney Morning Herald*, 24 Oct. 1991, 15.

5. James and Taylor, "Strong Minded Women," 137; Arrington, "Abundance from the Earth," 194, 201; Madsen, *Glory Hunter*, 105. I am especially indebted to Joy Horton, Regional History Collections clerk at the Uintah County Library, Vernal, Utah, for her assistance in this endeavor.

6. Zanjani, *Goldfield*, 109–10.

7. Of 35 women whose origins can be determined with reasonable certainty, 8 were foreign-born and 27 were from the United States and Canada. Of the Americans, 11 were from the West and Alaska (6 from Nevada and California), 8 from the Midwest, 5 from the South, and 2 from the Northeast. The relatively small proportion of the foreign-born contrasts with the high figures for general mining town populations in 1870 and 1880 found by Elliott West in "Five Idaho Mining Towns," 111, and by Ronald M. James (for 1880) in "Women of the Mining West," 160. The 77 prospected in various locales: 35 in Nevada; 10 in California; 4 in Alaska; 3 each in Arizona, Colorado, and Wyoming; 2 each in Idaho and Utah; 1 in Oklahoma; and 14 in several states and in some cases, nations, including Canada.

8. In a total group of 35 whose previous pursuits are fairly clear, 8 kept house; 9 worked as restaurant or boardinghouse cooks (sometimes combined with a proprietary role) or waitresses; 6 worked in the entertainment field as saloon proprietors, dance hall girls, or actresses; 5 were professionals; 4 had farmed or ranched; and others pursued a variety of jobs. Some women, such as Jennie Enright, had worked in several different fields, in which case the last one previous to prospecting was designated. In addition to the absence of former domestics and factory workers, ex-prostitutes are notably missing. This is a subject on which information is likely to be scanty, although scandalous rumors might survive, and some of those in the entertainment field might have dipped into prostitution. It is interesting to speculate, however, that if aversion to submissive and subordinate

roles kept the women prospectors away from domestic service, the same attitudes may have applied to prostitution. On Dolly O'Neil, see *Reno Evening Gazette*, 15 Jan. 1938, 15. On the large proportion of mining town women keeping house and working as domestics, references include West, "Five Idaho Mining Towns," 111; James, "Women of the Mining West," 158, 165; Smith, "San Juaner," 148; and Ducker, "Gold Rushers North," 88.

9. In a total group of 26, 4 women began prospecting in girlhood and continued through life, 6 abandoned prospecting, 15 continued from the time they began until death or ill health forced them to stop, and 1 left mining for reasons unknown after many years. At least 11 had careers exceeding 40 years, and 6 spent 20 to 35 years. Some, like Ellie Nay, who continued prospecting on an occasional basis for life but became primarily a rancher, are difficult to classify; some points remain cloudy, such as the starting dates for Belle Butler, Ellen Jack, and Dorothy O'Neil, and Louise Grantham's reasons for leaving mining.

10. In a total group of 38, 17 women were ages 20–39 when they started prospecting or were first mentioned, 5 started as girls, and 16 were 40 or older (10 of them past 50). Of the 8 who started prospecting with a husband, 5 were 20–39. On new directions after age 50, also see Greer, *The Change*, 49.

11. Zanjani, "To Die in Goldfield," 59; Sagan, *Health of Nations*, 111–88.

12. *Reno Evening Gazette*, 3 June 1907.

13. Marital status here refers to the time a woman began prospecting or was first mentioned. In a total group of 72, 22 were married; 24 were single (including 2 who prospected with lovers); and 26 were widowed or divorced, or presumably so, if no husband was on the scene with Mrs. Such-and-such. The marital status of several women was too uncertain for them to be included in the group. See also Ducker, "Gold Rushers North," 83; West, "Five Idaho Mining Towns," 113; Smith, "San Juaner," 148; and James, "Women of the Mining West," 158.

14. This group did not include Myra Benson, one year older than her husband, because the age difference was insignificant. Josie Pearl's last and much younger husband was included, although his existence rests solely on the Simmons interview.

15. In a total group of 68: 24 had no children; 4 had grown or teenaged children; for an additional 29, no children were mentioned (probably they had none or their children were grown); 11 had young children, and of these, 6 left their children behind all or part of the time when prospecting, 3 took

their children along, and the child care arrangements of 2 are not known. Ducker found a similar pattern in 1900 in the new Alaskan camps, where a large percentage of couples had no children or did not bring them; see "Gold Rushers North," 84. On shaping work around the family, see Degler, *At Odds*, 434.

16. The total group numbered 51. Information on finances, of course, rests on limited sources. See also Blackburn and Ricards, "Unequal Opportunity," 36; and Mann, *After the Gold Rush*, 109.

17. Schulmerich, *Josie Pearl*, 243–47, 266–67. On Bishop, see *Reno Evening Gazette*, 13 July 1951.

18. On the Comstock, see Mathews, *Ten Years in Nevada*, 130–32; on Goldfield, see Zanjani, *Goldfield*, 110; on male mining tycoons, see Peterson, *Bonanza Rich*, esp. 142–43.

19. Strobridge, *Sagebrush Trilogy*, 52; also see Peterson, *Bonanza Rich*, esp. 134.

20. Although no woman prospector gained as much wealth as John Mackay, some had returns more than sufficient to spend in the style of Eilley Bowers if they had wished to do so. See Earl, "Woman of Fortune," 20–22.

21. Scott, "Thousand Miles," 1:86, 2:209–10. On twentieth-century self-expression, see Friedman, *Crime and Punishment*, esp. 203, 435–49.

22. Lewis, Rueckl, Rechel, Coughlin-Riemersma, and Mullins interviews; Boyer, *I Married Wyatt Earp*, 218. For an example of the absence of organized religion in an early mining camp, see Marryat, *Mountains and Molehills*, 272–75.

23. Greer, *The Change*, 12.

# Bibliography

Abbott, James W. "Pioche, Nevada." *Mining and Scientific Press* 95 (10 Aug. 1907): 176–79.

Albert, Herman W. *Odyssey of a Desert Prospector.* Norman: University of Oklahoma Press, 1967.

Alberts, Laurie. "Petticoats and Pickaxes." *Alaska Journal* 7 (summer 1977): 146–59.

Anderson, Mary W. "They Called Her Angel." *Tombstone Epitaph* 17 (Nov. 1990): 1, 11–13, 20.

Arline, Kenneth. "Harqua Hala for Ghosts Only." *Phoenix Gazette,* 20 Apr. 1973.

Arrington, Leonard J. "Abundance from the Earth: The Beginnings of Commercial Mining in Utah." *Utah Historical Quarterly* 31 (summer 1963): 192–219.

Aston, M. B. "Esmeralda County." In *The History of Nevada,* edited by Sam P. Davis. Vol. 2. Los Angeles: Elms, 1913.

Austin, Gregory G. "Depression Mining Venture." In *Nevada: Official Bicentennial Book,* edited by Stanley W. Paher. Las Vegas: Nevada Publications, 1976.

Bechdolt, Frederick R. "Stampede, 1936 Model." *Saturday Evening Post* 209 (14 Nov. 1936): 14–15, 53–54, 56.

Bentz, Donald N. "Frontier Angel." *The West,* July 1972, 6–8, 60–61.

Berton, Pierre. *The Klondike Fever.* New York: Carroll and Graf, 1958.

Black, Martha Louise. *My Ninety Years.* Anchorage: Alaska Northwest, 1976.

Blackburn, George M., and Sherman L. Ricards. "Unequal Opportunity on a Mining Frontier: The Role of Gender, Race, and Birthplace." *Pacific Historical Review* 62 (Feb. 1993): 19–38.

Boydston, Jeanne. *Home and Work: Housework, Wages, and the Ideology of Labor in the Early Republic.* New York: Oxford University Press, 1990.

Boyer, Glenn G., ed. *I Married Wyatt Earp: The Recollections of Josephine Sarah Marcus Earp.* Tucson: University of Arizona Press, 1976.

Brophy, Frank C. *Arizona Sketch Book.* Phoenix: AMPCO, 1952.

———. "God and Nellie." *Alive,* Oct. 1973, 2–3, 28.

# Bibliography

Brown, Richard M. *Strain of Violence*. New York: Oxford University Press, 1975.

Brown, Thomas N. *Irish-American Nationalism, 1870–1890*. Westport CT: Greenwood Press, 1966.

Brown, William E. *A History of the Denali–Mount McKinley Region, Alaska.* Vol. 1, *Historical Narrative*. Santa Fe: National Park Service, 1991.

Bundtzen, Thomas K. "A History of Mining in the Kantishna Hills." *Alaska Journal* 8 (spring 1978): 151–61.

Burford, Virgil. *North to Danger*. Caldwell ID: Caxton, 1969.

Burns, Walter Noble. *Tombstone*. New York: Grosset and Dunlap, 1929.

Caldwell, Eleanor B. "A Woman's Experience at Cape Nome." In *Tales of Alaska and the Yukon*, edited by Frank Oppel. Secaucus NJ: Castle, 1986.

Carlson, Helen S. *Nevada Place Names: A Geographical Dictionary*. Reno: University of Nevada Press, 1974.

Carpenter, Jay A., Russell R. Elliott, and Byrd Sawyer. *The History of Fifty Years of Mining at Tonopah, 1900–1950*. University of Nevada Geology and Mining Series, no. 51. Reno: Nevada Bureau of Mines, 1953.

"Carrie J. Everson and Flotation." *Mining and Scientific Press* 112 (15 Jan. 1916): 82.

Caruthers, William. *Loafing along Death Valley Trails*. Palm Desert CA: Desert Magazine Press, 1951.

Chalfant, Willie A. *Tales of the Pioneers*. Stanford: Stanford University Press, 1942.

Chaput, Don. *Nellie Cashman*. Tucson: Westernlore Press, 1995.

Chaput, Donald, William M. Mason, and David Zarate Loperena. *Modest Fortunes: Mining in Northern Baja California*. Los Angeles: Natural History Museum of Los Angeles County, 1992.

Childers, Roberta. "'Happy Days,' Now Ninety Years of Age, Retains Youthful Spirit at Home in Desert." *Nevada State Journal*, 14 June 1942, 8.

Cloud, Barbara. "Images of Women in the Mining-Camp Press." *Nevada Historical Society Quarterly* 36 (fall 1993): 194–207.

Clum, John P. "Nellie Cashman." *Arizona Historical Review* 3 (Oct. 1931): 1–27.

Coffey, Jesse, and George Hoeper. *Bacon and Beans from a Gold Pan*. New York: Ballantine Books, 1972.

Conlin, Joseph R. *Bacon, Beans, and Galantines: Food and Foodways on the Western Mining Frontier*. Reno: University of Nevada Press, 1986.

Coolidge, Dane. *Death Valley Prospectors*. Morongo Valley CA: Sagebrush Press, 1985.

# Bibliography

Couch, Bertrand F., and Jay A. Carpenter. *Nevada's Metal and Mineral Production.* University of Nevada Bulletin 38. Reno: Nevada State Bureau of Mines, 1943.

Coughlin, Kari. Collected materials on Death Valley pioneer women. Death Valley CA.

Cowan, Ruth Schwartz. *More Work for Mother.* New York: Basic Books, 1983.

Davis, Mary Lee. *We Are Alaskans.* Boston: W. A. Wilde, 1931.

De Armond, R. N., ed. *"Stroller" White: Tales of a Klondike Newsman.* Vancouver: Mitchell Press, 1969.

Degler, Carl N. *At Odds: Women and the Family in America from the Revolution to the Present.* New York: Oxford University Press, 1980.

Dempsey, Stanley, and James E. Fell, Jr. *Mining the Summit: Colorado's Ten Mile District, 1860–1960.* Norman: University of Oklahoma Press, 1986.

Dobie, J. Frank. *Apache Gold and Yaqui Silver.* Boston: Little, Brown, 1928.

Douglass, William A., and Robert A. Nylen, eds. *Letters from the Nevada Frontier: Correspondence of Tasker L. Oddie, 1898–1902.* Norman: University of Oklahoma Press, 1992.

Downie, William. *Hunting for Gold.* 1893. Reprint, Palo Alto CA: American West, 1971.

Drury, Wells. *An Editor on the Comstock Lode.* 2d ed. Palo Alto CA: Pacific Books, 1948.

Ducker, James H. "Gold Rushers North: A Census Study of the Yukon and Alaskan Gold Rushes, 1896–1900." *Pacific Northwest Quarterly* 85 (July 1994): 82–92.

Duff, John B. *The Irish in the United States.* Belmont CA: Wadsworth, 1971.

Earl, Phillip I. "Celebrating Tonopah's Anniversary." Undated newspaper clipping, Central Nevada Museum, Tonopah.

———. "'Happy Days' Diminy Was an Eccentric Dreamer." *Reno Gazette-Journal,* 27 Mar. 1988, 2E.

———. "Mules and Rats Revered, but Women Shunned in Mining Superstitions." *Reno Gazette-Journal,* 24 June 1984, 3E.

———. "Petticoat Prospector Staked Claim for Woman Miners." *Reno Gazette-Journal,* 20 Mar. 1988, 2E.

———. "A Woman of Fortune." *Nevada* 54 (Mar./Apr. 1994): 20–22.

———. "Woman Prospector Settled Down in Black Rock Desert." *Reno Gazette-Journal,* 22 and 28 Nov. 1993, 4.

Edwards, Elbert B. *Two Hundred Years in Nevada.* Salt Lake City: Publishers Press, 1978.

# Bibliography

Elliott, Russell R. *History of Nevada*. Lincoln: University of Nebraska Press, 1973.

———. *Nevada's Twentieth-Century Mining Booms: Tonopah, Goldfield, Ely*. Reno: University of Nevada Press, 1966.

Ellis, Anne. *The Life of an Ordinary Woman*. 1929. Reprint, Lincoln: University of Nebraska Press, 1980.

Etulain, Richard W. "A Conversation with Wallace Stegner." *Montana: The Magazine of Western History* 40 (summer 1990): 2–13.

Evans, James R., Gary C. Taylor, and John S. Rapp. "Mines and Mineral Deposits in Death Valley National Monument, California." In *Geology and Mineral Wealth of the California Desert*, edited by Donald L. Fife and Arthur R. Brown. Santa Ana CA: South Coast Geological Society, 1980.

Evans, Sara M. *Born for Liberty: A History of Women in America*. New York: Free Press, 1989.

"The Everson Myth." *Mining and Scientific Press* 112 (15 Jan. 1916): 78.

Faragher, John Mack. *Women and Men on the Overland Trail*. New Haven: Yale University Press, 1979.

Farnsworth, Harriet. "The Cowgirl Prospector." *True West*, Oct. 1967, 16–18, 50.

Faulk, Odie B. *Tombstone: Myth and Reality*. New York: Oxford University Press, 1972.

Fay, Robert O. "The Southwest Davis Zinc Field." National Mining Hall of Fame collection, Leadville CO.

Fergusson, Erna. *New Mexico: A Pageant of Three Peoples*. New York: Alfred A. Knopf, 1951.

Fielder, Mildred. *Silver Is the Fortune*. Aberdeen SD: North Plains Press, 1978.

Fraser, Antonia. *The Warrior Queens: The Legends and the Lives of Women Who Have Led Their Nations in War*. New York: Vintage Books, 1988.

Friedman, Lawrence M. *Crime and Punishment in American History*. New York: Basic Books, 1993.

Georgetta, Clel. *Golden Fleece in Nevada*. Reno: Venture, 1972.

Gernsheim, Alison. *Victorian and Edwardian Fashion: A Photographic Survey*. New York: Dover, 1981.

Gipson, Fred. "Minnie's Yellow Treasure." *Rocky Mountain Empire Magazine*, 14 Nov. 1948, 2–3.

Glasscock, Carl B. *Gold in Them Hills*. New York: Grosset and Dunlap, 1932.

Goldman, Marion S. *Gold Diggers and Silver Miners: Prostitution and Social Life on the Comstock Lode*. Ann Arbor: University of Michigan Press, 1981.

# Bibliography

Goleman, Daniel. "Psychology's New Interest in the World beyond the Self." *New York Times,* 29 Aug. 1993, E6.

Gomez, Arthur R. *Quest for the Golden Circle: The Four Corners and the Metropolitan West, 1945–1979.* Albuquerque: University of New Mexico Press, 1994.

Gray, J. P. Manuscript. Arizona Historical Society, Tucson.

Greene, Linda W. *A History of Mining in Death Valley National Monument.* Vol. 1. Denver: National Park Service, 1981.

Greer, Germaine. *The Change: Women, Aging, and the Menopause.* New York: Ballantine Books, 1991.

Groh, George W. *Gold Fever.* New York: William Morrow, 1966.

Guerin, Mrs. E. J. *Mountain Charley.* 1861. Reprint, New York: Ballantine Books, 1968.

Gutiérrez, David G. "Significant to Whom? Mexican Americans and the History of the American West." *Western Historical Quarterly* 24 (Nov. 1993): 519–39.

Harris, Frank "Shorty." "Chasing Rainbows." In *Death Valley Lore: Classic Tales of Fantasy, Adventure, and Mystery,* edited by Richard E. Lingenfelter and Richard A. Dwyer. Reno: University of Nevada Press, 1988.

Hedrick, Harry. "The Newest Manhattan." *Sunset* 17 (Sept. 1906): 258–62.

Hill, James M. *Mines of Battle Mountain, Reese River, Aurora, and Other Western Nevada Districts.* U.S. Geological Survey Bulletin 594. 1915. Reprint, Las Vegas: Nevada Publications, 1983.

Hoagland, Edward. "Buckaroo Poets: Whoop-ee-ti-yi-yo, Get along Little Doggerel." *New York Times Book Review,* 8 Jan. 1989, 3, 17.

Homsher, Lola M., ed. *South Pass, 1868: James Chisholm's Journal of the Wyoming Gold Rush.* Lincoln: University of Nebraska Press, 1960.

Hulse, James W. *The Nevada Adventure: A History.* Reno: University of Nevada Press, 1966.

Hunt, William R. *Golden Places: The History of Alaska-Yukon Mining.* Anchorage: National Park Service, n.d.

Huntington, Louisa, told to Frederick R. Bechdolt. "The Bride Comes to the Desert." *Saturday Evening Post* 209 (10 Apr. 1937): 30–31, 88, 90, 92.

James, Laurence P., and Sandra C. Taylor. "'Strong Minded Women': Desdemona Stott Beeson and Other Hard Rock Mining Entrepreneurs." *Utah Historical Quarterly* 46 (spring 1978): 136–50.

James, Ronald M. "Women of the Mining West: Virginia City Revisited." *Nevada Historical Society Quarterly* 36 (fall 1993): 153–77.

# Bibliography

James, Ronald M., Richard D. Adkins, and Rachel J. Hartigan. "Competition and Coexistence in the Laundry: A View of the Comstock." *Western Historical Quarterly* 25 (summer 1994): 164–84.

Jeffrey, Julie Roy. *Frontier Women: The Trans-Mississippi West, 1840–1880*. New York: Hill and Wang, 1979.

Johnson, Susan L. "Sharing Bed and Board: Cohabitation and Cultural Difference in Central Arizona Mining Towns, 1863–1873." In *The Women's West*, edited by Susan Armitage and Elizabeth Jameson. Norman: University of Oklahoma Press, 1987.

Joraleman, Ira B. *Adventure Beacons*. New York: Society of Mining Engineers of AIME for the Mining and Metallurgical Society of America, 1976.

Joyaux, Georges J. "An Excerpt from Louis de Cotton's *A Travers le Dominion et la Californie*." *Nevada Historical Society Quarterly* 32 (spring 1989): 53–70.

Keeler, P. E. "Nye County." In *The History of Nevada*, edited by Sam P. Davis. Vol. 2. Los Angeles: Elms, 1913.

Kessler-Harris, Alice. *Out to Work: A History of Wage-Earning Women in the United States*. New York: Oxford University Press, 1982.

King, Olephia. "Dust and Desire, Laughter and Tears: Recollections of a Nevada Pioneer Cowgirl and Poet." Oral history, University of Nevada–Reno, 1978–80.

Kintop, Jeffrey M., and Guy Louis Rocha. *The Earps' Last Frontier: Wyatt and Virgil Earp in the Nevada Mining Camps, 1902–1905*. Reno: Great Basin Press, 1989.

Lake, Ivan C. "Irish Nellie, Angel of the Cassiar." *Alaska Sportsman* 14 (Oct. 1963): 19, 42–45.

Lavrin, Asunción. "Introduction: The Scenario, the Actors, and the Issues." In *Sexuality and Marriage in Colonial Latin America*. Lincoln: University of Nebraska Press, 1989.

Lecompte, Janet. "The Independent Women of Hispanic New Mexico, 1821–1846." *Western Historical Quarterly* 12 (Jan. 1981): 17–35.

LeCompte, Mary Lou. *Cowgirls of the Rodeo: Pioneer Professional Athletes*. Urbana: University of Illinois Press, 1993.

Ledbetter, Suzann. *Nellie Cashman: Prospector and Trail Blazer*. El Paso: Texas Western Press, 1993.

Lilliard, Richard G. *Desert Challenge: An Interpretation of Nevada*. Lincoln: University of Nebraska Press, 1942.

Lincoln, Francis Church. *Mining Districts and Mineral Resources of Nevada*. 1923. Reprint, Las Vegas: Nevada Publications, 1982.

# Bibliography

Lingenfelter, Richard E. *Death Valley and the Amargosa: A Land of Illusion.* Berkeley: University of California Press, 1986.

Lingenfelter, Richard E., and Karen Rix Gash. *The Newspapers of Nevada: A History and Bibliography, 1854–1979.* Reno: University of Nevada Press, 1984.

Lowe, Deke. "Death Valley's Lady Prospectors." *Death Valley Gateway Gazette,* 10 Jan. 1992, 8.

Ludwig, Lydia. "Belmont Memories, 1873–1875." *Central Nevada's Glorious Past* 15 (May 1992): 11–13.

Macdonald, Anne L. *Feminine Ingenuity: Women and Invention in America.* New York: Ballantine Books, 1992.

Madsen, Brigham D. *Glory Hunter: A Biography of Patrick Edward Connor.* Salt Lake City: University of Utah Press, 1990.

Malone, Michael P., and Richard W. Etulain. *The American West: A Twentieth-Century History.* Lincoln: University of Nebraska Press, 1989.

Mann, Ralph. *After the Gold Rush: Society in Grass Valley and Nevada City, California, 1849–1870.* Stanford: Stanford University Press, 1982.

Marryat, Frank. *Mountains and Molehills.* London: Longman, Brown, Green, and Longmans, 1855.

Marshall, Robert. *Arctic Village.* New York: Literary Guild, 1933.

Martin, Douglas D. *Tombstone's Epitaph.* Albuquerque: University of New Mexico Press, 1951.

Mathews, Mary McNair. *Ten Years in Nevada or Life on the Pacific Coast.* 1880. Reprint, Lincoln: University of Nebraska Press, 1985.

May, Elaine T. *Great Expectations: Marriage and Divorce in Post-Victorian America.* Chicago: University of Chicago Press, 1980.

Mayer, Melanie J. *Klondike Women: True Tales of the 1897–1898 Gold Rush.* Athens: Swallow Press/Ohio University Press, 1989.

Meadows, Lorena E. *A Sagebrush Heritage.* San Jose CA: Harlan-Young Press, 1972.

Miles, Henry W. "Recollections of Goldfield, Nevada." Manuscript. Nevada Historical Society, Reno, 1948.

Morgan, Edward E. P., with Henry F. Woods. *God's Loaded Dice: Alaska, 1897–1930.* Caldwell ID: Caxton, 1948.

Monroe, George. File, Arizona Historical Society, Tucson.

Mouat, Jeremy. "The Development of the Flotation Process: Technological Change and the Genesis of Modern Mining, 1898–1914." Paper presented to the Third International Mining History Conference, Golden CO, June 1994.

Muncaster, Frances Noyes. Papers, 1850–1952, and photographs. Alaska Historical Library, Juneau.

Bibliography

Murbarger, Nell. *Ghosts of the Glory Trail.* Palm Desert CA: Desert Magazine Press, 1956.

———. "Josie Pearl, Queen of Black Rock." In *Nevada: Official Bicentennial Book,* edited by Stanley W. Paher. Las Vegas: Nevada Publications, 1976.

Myles, Myra T. "Jim Butler: Nevada's Improbable Tycoon." *Montana: The Magazine of Western History* 26 (Jan. 1976): 60–69.

Myres, Sandra L. *Westering Women and the Frontier Experience, 1800–1915.* Albuquerque: University of New Mexico Press, 1982.

Nay, Charlotte Stimler. Oral history tape. Nevada Historical Society, Reno, n.d.

Nevada Historical Society. "First Woman in Goldfield." *Apple Tree,* 13 Nov. 1977, n.p.

Nevada Inspector of Mines. Reports. In *Appendix to the Journals of the Senate and Assembly,* 1939–55. Carson City.

Nevada State License and Bullion Tax Agent. Reports. In *Appendix to the Journals of the Senate and Assembly,* 1909–11. Carson City.

Niethammer, Carolyn. "The Lure of Gold." In *The Women Who Made the West,* edited by the Western Writers of America. New York: Doubleday, 1980.

O'Connor, Richard. *High Jinks on the Klondike.* New York: Bobbs-Merrill, 1954.

———. *The Irish: Portrait of a People.* New York: G. P. Putnam's Sons, 1971.

O'Neal, Bill. *Encyclopedia of Western Gunfighters.* Norman: University of Oklahoma Press, 1979.

Paher, Stanley W. *Nevada Ghost Towns and Mining Camps.* Berkeley: Howell North Books, 1970.

Painter, Nell I. *Exodusters: Black Migration to Kansas after Reconstruction.* New York: Alfred A. Knopf, 1977.

Patty, Ernest N. *North Country Challenge.* New York: David McKay, 1969.

Paul, Rodman W. *California Gold: The Beginning of Mining in the Far West.* Lincoln: University of Nebraska Press, 1947.

Peterson, John G. Family papers, 1861–1961. Alaska Historical Library, Juneau.

Peterson, Magnus F. "Malapai Mike." "Reel History and Hysterical Events of Nevada." Tonopah NV: *Tonopah Times-Bonanza,* [1967].

Peterson, Richard H. *Bonanza Rich: Lifestyles of the Western Mining Entrepreneurs.* Moscow ID: University of Idaho Press, 1991.

Pfaff, Betty C. *Atlantic City Nuggets.* By the author, 1978.

Pomeroy, Earl. "Computers in the Desert: Transforming the Simple Life." *Western Historical Quarterly* 25 (spring 1994); 7–19.

Pyle, Ernie. *Home Country.* New York: William Sloan Associates, 1947.

# Bibliography

Ralston, Leonard K. Letters to Lorena E. Meadows, 12 Jan. 1965 and 11 Apr. 1968. Meadows letter file, Central Nevada Museum, Tonopah.

Ransch, Hero E., and Mildred B. Hoover. *Historic Spots in California: Valley and Sierra Countries.* Stanford: Stanford University Press, 1933.

Ransom, Jay E. "Harquahala Bonanza." *Desert Magazine* 16 (May 1953): 15–19.

Redman, Earl. "History of the Mines in the Juneau Goldbelt." Manuscript. Alaska Historical Library, Juneau, 1987.

Rice, George Graham. *My Adventures with Your Money.* 1911. Reprint, New York: Bookfinger, 1974.

Riley, Glenda. *The Female Frontier: A Comparative View of Women on the Prairie and the Plains.* Lawrence: University Press of Kansas, 1988.

Rochlin, Harriet. "The Amazing Adventures of a Good Woman." *Journal of the West* 12 (April 1973); 281–95.

Rothman, Sheila M. *Woman's Proper Place.* New York: Basic Books, 1978.

Royal Flush Mine Papers. Nevada Historical Society, Reno.

Royce, Sarah. *A Frontier Lady: Recollections of the Gold Rush and Early California.* 1932. Reprint, edited by Ralph H. Gabriel, Lincoln: University of Nebraska Press, 1977.

Ruskin, Evey. "Letters to Lizzie: A Koyukuk Gold Seeker Writes Home." *Alaska Journal* 16 (1986): 120–26.

Russell, Asa M. "We Lost a Ledge of Gold!" *Desert* 31 (Nov. 1968): 14–17, 34–35.

Russell, Will C. Public letter dated 10 June 1909. *Tonopah Miner*, 12 June 1909.

Ruth ? to Hugh Shamberger. Letter, 28 Nov. 1977. Nevada Historical Society, Reno.

Sagan, Leonard A. *The Health of Nations: True Causes of Sickness and Well-Being.* New York: Basic Books, 1987.

Scharff, Virginia. "Gender and Western History: Is Anybody Home on the Range?" *Montana: The Magazine of Western History* 41 (spring 1991): 62–65.

Schrier, Arnold. *Ireland and the American Emigration, 1850–1900.* Minneapolis: University of Minnesota Press, 1958.

Schulmerich, Alma. *Josie Pearl.* Salt Lake City: Desert, 1963.

Schurz, William L. *Latin America.* New York: E. P. Dutton, 1941.

Scott, Josephine Hanson. "A Thousand Miles of Desert and Mountains: A Prospecting Trip across Nevada and over the Sierras." 1914. Diary, 3 vols. Special Collections, University of Nevada–Reno Libraries.

Scrugham, James G. *Nevada.* 3 vols. Chicago: American Historical Society, 1935.

Seagraves, Anne. *High-Spirited Women of the West.* Lakeport CA: Wesanne Publications, 1992.

# Bibliography

Service, Robert W. *Best Tales of the Yukon*. Reprint, Philadelphia: Running Press, 1983.

Shamberger, Hugh A. *Candelaria and Its Neighbors*. Carson City: Nevada Historical Press, 1978.

———. *Goldfield*. Carson City: Nevada Historical Press, 1982.

———. *Rawhide*. Carson City: Nevada Historical Press, 1970.

Sharp, Mary McCann. Oral history tape. Nevada Historical Society, Reno, n.d.

Shikes, Robert H. *Rocky Mountain Medicine: Doctors, Drugs, and Disease in Early Colorado*. Boulder CO: Johnson Books, 1986.

Shockley, William H. Letters to his mother, 14 Jan. and 30 July 1884, 29 Mar. 1888. Central Nevada Museum, Tonopah.

Sloane, Howard N., and Lucille L. Sloane. *A Pictorial History of American Mining*. New York: Crown, 1970.

Smith, Duane A. "The San Juaner: A Computerized Portrait." *Colorado Magazine* 52 (1975): 137–52.

Smith, Henry N. *Virgin Land: The American West as Symbol and Myth*. Cambridge: Harvard University Press, 1950.

Smith, Page. *Daughters of the Promised Land*. Boston: Little, Brown, 1970.

Smith-Rosenberg, Carroll. *Disorderly Conduct: Visions of Gender in Victorian America*. New York: Alfred A. Knopf, 1985.

Spears, John R. *Illustrated Sketches of Death Valley and Other Borax Deserts of the Pacific Coast*. 1892. Reprint, Morongo Valley CA: Sagebrush Press, 1977.

Spence, Clark C. *Mining Engineers and the American West: The Lace-Boot Brigade, 1849–1933*. 1970. Reprint Moscow: University of Idaho Press, 1993.

Stanley, F. (Stanley Crocchiola). "The Kingston, New Mexico Story." Pantex TX: n.p., 1961.

Steele, Rufus Milas. "Southwest from Bullfrog." In *Death Valley Lore: Classic Tales of Fantasy, Adventure, and Mystery*, edited by Richard E. Lingenfelter and Richard A. Dwyer. Reno: University of Nevada Press, 1988.

Stenhouse, Thomas B. H. *The Rocky Mountain Saints*. New York: D. Appleton, 1873.

Stickney, Mary E. "Colorado Women Successful in Managing Mining Business." *Denver Times*, 19 Jan. 1902. Denver Public Library, "Women as Miners" file.

Stone, Samuel Z. *The Heritage of the Conquistadores: Ruling Classes in Central America from the Conquest to the Sandinistas*. Lincoln: University of Nebraska Press, 1990.

## Bibliography

Strobridge, Idah Meacham. *Sagebrush Trilogy: Idah Meacham Strobridge and Her Works.* Reno: University of Nevada Press, 1990.

Taylor, Raymond W., and Samuel W. Taylor. *Uranium Fever.* New York: Macmillan, 1970.

Twain, Mark. *Roughing It.* 1871. Reprint, New York: Signet, 1962.

Uintah County Regional History Collections. Uintah County Library, Vernal UT.

U.S. Census Bureau. *Abstract of the Twelfth Census of the United States, 1900.* Washington DC: Government Printing Office, 1902.

———. Manuscript censuses, 1870, 1880, 1900, 1910. Microfilm, Nevada Historical Society, Reno.

———. *Occupations at the Twelfth Census.* Washington DC: Government Printing Office, 1904.

———. *Statistics for Nevada, 1910.* Washington DC: Government Printing Office, 1913.

Vanderburg, William O. *Placer Mining in Nevada.* University of Nevada Bulletin. Reno: University of Nevada, 1936.

———. "Reconnaissance of Mining Districts in Humboldt County, Nevada." Bureau of Mines Report U.S. Department of the Interior. Washington DC: Government Printing Office, Feb. 1938.

Waite, Catharine V. *Adventures in the Far West and Life among the Mormons.* Chicago: C.V. Waite, 1882.

Ware, Susan. *Holding Their Own: American Women in the 1930s.* Boston: Twayne, 1982.

Warrin, Donald. "Portuguese Pioneers in Nevada." *Nevada Historical Society Quarterly* 35 (spring 1992): 40–57.

Webb, Walter Prescott. *The Great Plains.* Boston: Ginn, 1931.

Wertheimer, Barbara Mayer. *We Were There: The Story of Working Women in America.* New York: Pantheon Books, 1977.

West, Elliott. "Five Idaho Mining Towns: A Computer Profile." *Pacific Northwest Quarterly* 73 (July 1982): 108–20.

Wheat, Carl I., ed. *The Shirley Letters from the California Mines, 1851–1852.* New York: Alfred A. Knopf, 1970.

White, Richard E. *It's Your Misfortune and None of My Own: A New History of the American West.* Norman: University of Oklahoma Press, 1991.

Wilhelm, Walt. "Dora's Diggin's." *Desert Magazine* 2 (July 1939): 15–16.

———. *Last Rig to Battle Mountain.* New York: William Morrow, 1970.

Williams, Frances. Letter to Jeanne E. Weir, 4 Nov. 1908. Nevada Historical Society, Reno.

# Bibliography

"Women as Miners" file. Denver Public Library, Denver CO.

Woyski, Margaret S. "Women and Mining in the Old West." *Journal of the West* 20 (Apr. 1981): 38–47.

Young, Otis E., Jr. *Western Mining*. Norman: University of Oklahoma Press, 1970.

Zanjani, Sally. *Goldfield: The Last Gold Rush on the Western Frontier*. Athens: Swallow Press/Ohio University Press, 1992.

———. "Indian Prospectors." *Nevada* 28 (Nov.–Dec. 1986): 53–55.

———. *Jack Longstreet: Last of the Desert Frontiersmen*. Athens: Swallow Press/ Ohio University Press, 1988.

———. "To Die in Goldfield: Mortality in the Last Boomtown on the Mining Frontier." *Western Historical Quarterly* 21 (Feb. 1990): 47–69.

———. *The Unspiked Rail: Memoir of a Nevada Rebel*. Reno: University of Nevada Press, 1981.

# Index

# Index

# Index

# Index

Hart, Orpha, 340 n.9
Hayes, George, 133–34
Helena NV (previously Clifford), 151–52, 173
Hessler, Frederica, 278, 279
Hildreth, Albert, 244, 245
Hilton, Jennie, 168–69, 202
Hispanics, 25, 60, 63, 68, 263. *See also* Sarras, Ferminia
Hoagland, Edward, 266
Hogan, Bill, 42
Holliday, Doc (John Henry), 44
Holmes, John, 249
homicide, 30, 175, 177, 240
Hoover, Herbert, 257
Hoover, Theodore, 105
Hope, Dr. R. C. "Dad," 112
Hornbeck, Nettie, 12, 107, 120, 201; motivation for prospecting of, 108–9, 112
Hot Steam (prospector), 119
Houlahan, John, 270
Huhn, Ernest. *See* Siberian Red
Hume, John, 251
Huntington, Louisa, 259
Hurtado, Maria, 63

Ibach, Joe and "Muz," 237
Indian Mining and Development Company, 112
Indians, 25, 46, 131, 149, 155, 173–74, 177, 249–50. *See also* Panamint Annie
insanity, 72, 171, 269–72
Ireland, 47–48

Jack, Ellen, 232, 305, 351 n.9
James, William, 170, 199
Jarbidge NV, 102
Jennings, Mrs. John J., 12–13, 108, 197, 339 n.57; clothing worn by, 107, 121; mining by, 107, 303
Jester, Herbert, 268–69, 270, 271, 347 n.16
Johnson, Charles, 166
Johnson, Maggie, 209–10, 237, 340 n.8
Johnson, Rose Long, 168–69

Johnson, Susan L., 171
Joyce, Milt E., 42
Jumbo NV, 257, 259–60

Kent, Mary, 104
Kessler-Harris, Alice, 303
Ketchum, Dorothy, 211–14, 215
Key, Bill, 97, 98–99, 329 n.23
Kiblinger, Harlow, 83–84, 324 n.2
King, Leafy (Olephia) Nay, 148, 151, 161, 163; on Ellie Nay, 160, 162, 312–13; prospecting remembered by, 152–53, 155
Kingman AZ, 112–13
Kingston NM, 48, 50, 323 n.48
Klondike, 52–54, 301
Klondike Helen. *See* Seifert, Klondike Helen
Koontz, John, 130
Koontz, Louis K., 130
Kostka, William, 322 n.46
Koyukuk district (Alaska), 57, 297
Kuoni, Jeanette, 304

La Follette, Robert, 296
*Last Rig to Battle Mountain* (Wilhelm), 193–94
Las Vegas NV, 188
lawsuits, 55, 92, 138–39, 174, 233–34
Lecompte, Janet, 25
LeCompte, Mary Lou, 239, 240
Lee, Leander, 95
Lemoigne, John, 161
Lewis, Carl, 269, 316
Lewis, Dio, 72
Lewis, Mrs. George, 122, 123–24, 126
Lichau, Mrs. Amelin, 181–82, 338 n.24
Lind, Henry, 133
Lingenfelter, Richard, 85, 97
Longstreet, Jack (Andrew Jackson), 145, 148, 149
Lost Breyfogle ledge, 137–39, 140, 154
Lowe, Charles, 91
Lowe, Deke, 213

369

# Index

Mackay, John, 352 n.20
Mackay, Louise, 315
Mackenzie, David, 120, 134, 136, 138–39
Madsen, Brigham M., 118
Magnussen, Mary. *See* Grantz, Mary
Magnussen, Max, 234, 235
Malcolm, Lillian, 88; clothing worn by,
    85, 87, 89; contemporary views of, 89,
    90, 96, 100, 102, 200; in Death Valley,
    93, 94, 96–97, 211; early life of, 89;
    housekeeping by, 230; mentioned, 5,
    107, 158, 185, 199, 207, 257, 263, 276, 302,
    306, 309, 315; in Nome, 91–92, 205, 246;
    philanthropy by, 313; promotional
    skills of, 5–6, 99–100, 123, 132, 169;
    prospecting by, 89–90, 91–93, 94, 97,
    98, 101–2, 151; prospectors viewed by,
    95; and the queen bee syndrome, 119,
    120; relationships with men, 90, 99,
    110, 116, 170; storytelling by, 90, 92,
    102; traits of, 12, 166; viewed by other
    women, 8, 206, 279; women viewed
    by, 90, 94–95, 100–101, 103
Mallen, Mrs. Morehouse, 116, 127, 196,
    266, 306
manganese mining, 227, 228
Mann, Ralph, 320 n.7
Manson, Charles, 299
Marijilda, 272
marriage: and prospectors, 197, 326 n.14;
    and women, 90; and women prospec-
    tors, 44–45, 197–99, 201–2, 310–12, 339
    n.57, 351 n.13
Marsh, William, 149, 154–55
Marshall, Antone, 64, 66
Marshall, Charley, 64–65.
Marshall, John, 64, 66
Marshall, Joseph A.: father of, 63–64, 66,
    70; mentioned, 67, 68, 75, 78, 83, 327
    n.32; prospecting by, 74, 79, 82
Marshall, Robert, 57, 297, 324 n.67
Mathews, Mary McNair, 230
Mau, Anna, 107, 122
Mazzulla, Fred M., 322 n.46

McCabe, Tom, 89, 94
McCann, Jack, 65
McCarthy, Delia, 6
McCarthy, Mrs., 11
McCauley, Anthony, 89, 94
McCormack, Archie, 70, 74, 75, 77; death
    of, 79, 327 n.32
McCormick, Minnie Belle, 292–93, 294,
    349 n.14
McCormick, William, 292
McCrudden, Joseph and Esther, 255
McDonald, Big Alex, 55
McDonald, Louisa Enright, 82
McGrath, Bill, 298
McKenzie, Angus, 182
McLean, Mrs., 117
McLisle, Kate, 331 n.61
McNamee, Jim, 55
Mexican: in mining lore, 41–42, 109
Miller, Anna, 123, 126
Miller, Bessie, 122–24, 126, 151, 158
Miller, Emma Grenz, 217, 222, 223
Miller, Ernest, 223
Miller, Mr. and Mrs. James, 172
Miller, June, 223, 224, 225, 232, 233
Mina NV, 76, 77, 83
mining: legal requirements for, 5; and the
    lore of the Mexican, 41–42, 109; mid-
    twentieth-century changes in, 301;
    women involved in, 103–6, 303–5
Mizpah Mine, 178, *179*, 180, 185
Monnette, M. B., 133–34
Monroe, George, 170–71
Monroe, Mollie. *See* Sawyer, Mary E.
    "Mollie"
Morgan, Edward, 34, 53, 323 n.55
Mormonism, 305
Morse, Mrs., 332 n.12
mortality, 49, 309–10
Mortensen, Jim, 288–89
Mortensen, Rees Rechel, 290, 299; on
    Anna Rechel, 287, 288, 289, 295, 296,
    297
Mouat, Jeremy, 105

# Index

299–300; prospecting by, 287–88, 289, 290–91, 293–94, 298, 303, 308; views of, 10, 295–96, 297, 300, 316–17

Rechel, Fern, 287

Rechel, George (father), 285, 288, 289, 290

Rechel, George (son), 287, 289–90

Rechel, LaRae, 291, 295, 300

Rechel, "Pal" Walter, 287, 289–90, 291, 300

Rechel, Rees. *See* Mortensen, Rees Rechel

Reddenbaugh, Agnes, 165, 178

Redpath, James, 48

Reid, Mrs. Robert K., 117–18, 221, 304, 310, 339 n.57

religion, 316

Rhyolite NV, 85, 93–94, 100, 264, 278–79, 283

Rice, George Graham (Jacob Herzig), 132, 134

Rice, M. A., 166, 202

Richardson, Jim, 173, 306

Rickard, Tex, 284, 288

Ricketts, Mrs. C. T., 106, 132

Riemersma, Doris Bryant, *280;* Panamint Annie remembered by, 273, 274–75, 276, 277, 278–79, 281–82, 283

Riggs, Mrs. Frank, 183–85, 338 n.32; and Death Valley, 183, 199, 200, 211; mentioned, 197, 202, 276

Riley, Glenda, 113, 339 n.57

Rope, Helen, 72

Round Mountain NV, 106–7, 172

Royal Flush Mine, 136, 139, 140, 333 n.24

Rueckl, Catherine: on Josie Pearl, 228, 229, 230, 232, 316, 342 n.36

Rupp, Louise, 23, 101–2, 120, 257

Russell, Asa, 213

Salsbury Wash (Nevada), 152, 153

Sarras, Ferminia: claims sold by, 77–78, 80; contemporary descriptions of, 60, 73–74, 75, 76, 78–79, 81–82, 327 n.35; enterprises undertaken by, 69, 73, 74, 263, 326 n.13 n.21; and family life, 49–50, 61, 63–64, 69, 79, 312, 327 n.32;

fortune made by, 83–84; lineage of, 60, 61, 79–80, 84, 324 n.3; men in life of, 61, 63, 64–66, 70, 75, 79, 80–81, 82, 234, 311; mentioned, 6, 10, 13, 123, 186, 235, 271, 314; Mina named for, 76, 77, 83, 326 n.27; portrait of, 60–61, 62, 324 n.2; prejudice against, 67–69; prospecting by, 63, 64, 70–71, 74–75, 76–77, 80, 82, 84; will made by, 81, 327–28 n.37

Sawyer, Mary E. "Mollie," 170–71; mentioned, 197, 198–99, 200, 232

Schieffelin, Ed, 37

Schulmerich, Alma, 216, 220

Scott, Josephine and George, 188–91, *192,* 192–93; mentioned, 199, 206, 221, 275, 316

Scott, Mary, 173

Scott, Walter (Death Valley Scotty), 97–99, 102

Seabright, Orlean R., 110

Seifert, Klondike Helen, 207–8, 273, 277

Service, Robert, 36, 51–52

Seybolt, Fred, 159

Sharp, Mary McCann, 175, 177

Sheddon, Jack, 48

Shipway, A. W., 264, 265, 266–67

Shoshone, 131, 149, 173–74, 177

Shoshone CA, 211–15, 274

Siberian Red, 213–14

Siegel, Joseph, 74

silver mining. *See specific sites*

Silver Peak NV, 73–74, 186

Silverton CO, 104, 107

Simonds, William, 253, 254

Skogli, Bill, 279, 280

Smedley (miner), 293

Smith, H. L, 267, 268

Smith, Mark, 42

Smith-Rosenberg, Caroll, 302

Sober, Gertrude Selma, 111–12, 307

South Pass WY, 180–81, 297

Spears, John, 95, 211

Springmeyer, George, 125

373